AF776766

APPLICATIONS FROM ENGINEERING WITH MATLAB CONCEPTS

Edited by **Jan Valdman**

Applications from Engineering with MATLAB Concepts
http://dx.doi.org/10.5772/61386
Edited by Jan Valdman

Contributors

Mahmut Sinecen, Tolga Yuksel, Eduardo Corral, Jesús Meneses, Juan Carlos García-Prada, Jan Urban, Raul Campos-Rodriguez, Mildreth Alcaraz-Mejia, Uriel Alejandro Sanchez-Ramirez, Claudio Urrea Oñate, Ricolindo L Carino, Mark F. Horsetemeyer, Arsen Arakelyan, Lilit Nersisyan, Anna Hakobyan, Oliver Baars, David H. Perlman, Abdurrahman Sahin, Alemdar Bayraktar, Niculescu Titu, Marcu Marius, Niculescu Vlad

Published by InTech

Janeza Trdine 9, 51000 Rijeka, Croatia

© The Editor(s) and the Author(s) 2016

The moral rights of the editor(s) and the author(s) have been asserted.
All rights to the book as a whole are reserved by InTech. The book as a whole (compilation) cannot be reproduced, distributed or used for commercial or non-commercial purposes without InTech's written permission. Enquiries concerning the use of the book should be directed to InTech's rights and permissions department (permissions@intechopen.com).
Violations are liable to prosecution under the governing Copyright Law.

Individual chapters of this publication are distributed under the terms of the Creative Commons Attribution 3.0 Unported License which permits commercial use, distribution and reproduction of the individual chapters, provided the original author(s) and source publication are appropriately acknowledged. More details and guidelines concerning content reuse and adaptation can be found at http://www.intechopen.com/copyright-policy.html.

Notice

Statements and opinions expressed in the chapters are these of the individual contributors and not necessarily those of the editors or publisher. No responsibility is accepted for the accuracy of information contained in the published chapters. The publisher assumes no responsibility for any damage or injury to persons or property arising out of the use of any materials, instructions, methods or ideas contained in the book.

Publishing Process Manager Ana Simcic

Technical Editor SPi Global

Cover InTech Design team

First published July, 2016

Printed in Croatia

Additional hard copies can be obtained from orders@intechopen.com

Applications from Engineering with MATLAB Concepts, Edited by Jan Valdman

p. cm.

Print ISBN 978-953-51-2459-7
Online ISBN 978-953-51-2460-3

We are IntechOpen, the world's leading publisher of Open Access books

Built by scientists, for scientists

3,800+
Open access books available

116,000+
International authors and editors

120M+
Downloads

151
Countries delivered to

Our authors are among the
Top 1%
most cited scientists

12.2%
Contributors from top 500 universities

WEB OF SCIENCE™

Selection of our books indexed in the Book Citation Index
in Web of Science™ Core Collection (BKCI)

Interested in publishing with us?
Contact book.department@intechopen.com

Numbers displayed above are based on latest data collected.
For more information visit www.intechopen.com

For EU product safety concerns:
IN TECH d.o.o., Prolaz Marije Krucifikse Kozulić 3, 51000 Rijeka, Croatia,
info@intechopen.com or visit our website at intechopen.com.

Meet the editor

Dr. Jan Valdman is an associate professor of applied mathematics at the University of South Bohemia (České Budějovice, Czech Republic) and a researcher at the Institute of Information Theory and Automation (Prague, Czech Republic). He obtained MSc degrees from Mathematical Research Institute (Utrecht, the Netherlands) and University of West Bohemia (Pilsen, Czech Republic) in 1998. He graduated from University of Kiel (Germany) for his PhD thesis on modeling of elastoplasticity in 2002. After spending many years at several foreign institutions (Linz, Bergen, Reykjavik, and Leipzig), he returned back to Czech Republic. He defended his habilitation in applied mathematics at Technical University Ostrava in 2011. His areas of interests include computational nonlinear mechanics of solids and a posteriori error estimates. He published several vectorized codes for finite elements computations in MATLAB.

Contents

Preface

More than 30 years have passed since MATLAB was introduced by Cleve Moler in 1984. With its initial idea to provide numerical linear algebra packages to students without demanding the knowledge of FORTRAN language, MATLAB became very popular with engineers and scientists from many fields. Having been an undergraduate student of applied mathematics and engineering, I can still remember building a Simulink model and solving underlying nonlinear ordinary differential equation numerically more than 20 years ago. Every time since I have used MATLAB in my computations and also in teaching of numerical analysis and linear algebra, I was also involved in projects where the core part of the code was written in C/C++ to get some time speedup. At the final stage of every project I ended up at writing all my codes again in MATLAB. Recently, I became fascinated with the vectorization of MATLAB codes for the numerical solution of partial differential equations by the finite element method.

The work on this book started in 2015, when I was asked by InTech, the open access publisher, to act as an editor of a book on MATLAB. Currently, there are many books on MATLAB, ranging from introductory courses for beginners up to advanced books on various accelerations techniques including parallel computing. The aim of this book is to present selected scientific problems of contributors and demonstrate their solutions in MATLAB. Chapters include image and signal processing, mechanics and dynamics, models and data identification in biology, fuzzy logic, discrete event systems, and data acquisition systems. Instead of giving exhausting amount of technical details, authors were advised to explain relations of their problems to actual MATLAB concepts. During the selection process, many contributions with no relation to MATLAB were received and had to be rejected. In the presented version of this book, most chapters contain links to functioning MATLAB codes that can be tested. I believe that the availability of the codes increases the readability of chapters.

I am thankful to each author for the technical effort presented in each book chapter and the patience when working on revisions. My biggest thanks goes to Ms. Ana Simčić, Publishing Process Manager from INTECH, who instructed me through many stages of the editorial process. Together, we did our best to ensure the book quality.

I hope our book entitled "Applications from Engineering with MATLAB Concepts" will serve as a useful reference to students, scientists, or engineers and will motivate them to use MATLAB more intensely.

Dr. Jan Valdman
Institute of Mathematics and Biomathematics, University of South Bohemia
České Budějovice, Czech Republic
Institute of Information Theory and Automation of the ASCR
Prague, Czech Republic

Chapter 1

Digital Image Processing with MATLAB

Mahmut Sinecen

Additional information is available at the end of the chapter

http://dx.doi.org/10.5772/63028

Abstract

The chapter relates to the Image Processing Toolbox in MATLAB. We learn about its general information and some examples will be solved using it. After finishing this chapter, you can use MATLAB Image Processing Toolbox and write script for processing of images.

Keywords: MATLAB, digital, image, processing, Fundamental

1. Digital image processing

The image may be defined as a two-dimensional visual information that are stored and displayed. An image is created by photosensitive devices which capture the reflection light from two-dimensional surface of object in the three-dimensional real world (**Figure 1**). Each image has intensity or gray value in x – y coordinate plane. If it is finite and discrete quantities, image is called digital image. In **Figure 2**, some digital images are shown.

Digital image processing (DIP) has the different techniques for processing of digital images. DIP has been applying many fields with technological advances, such as Medicine, Geographical Information Technologies, Space Sciences, Military Applications, Security, Industrial Applications.

1.1. Pixel

Pixels, which are called pel or picture elements, may be defined as the smallest addressable element in the digital image. Pixels of a color image have Red, Green, and Blue gray values (**Figure 3**).

INTECH
open science | open minds

© 2016 The Author(s). Licensee InTech. This chapter is distributed under the terms of the Creative Commons Attribution License (http://creativecommons.org/licenses/by/3.0), which permits unrestricted use, distribution, and reproduction in any medium, provided the original work is properly cited.

Figure 1. Image.

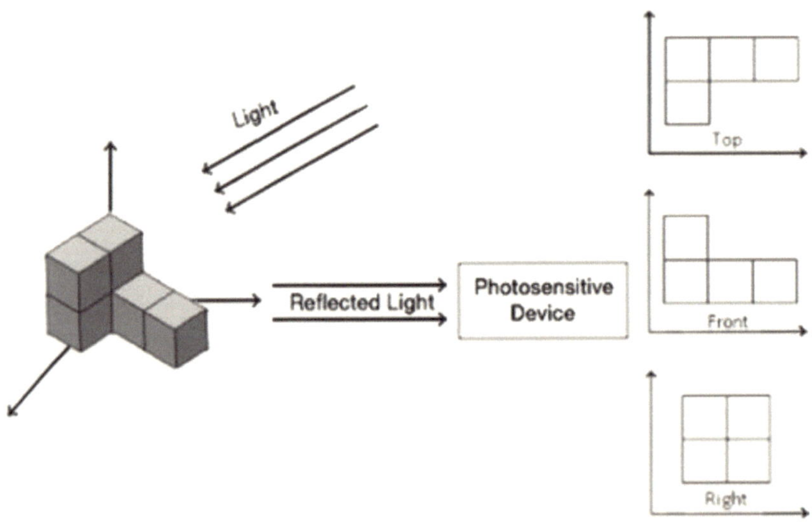

Figure 2. Digital images.

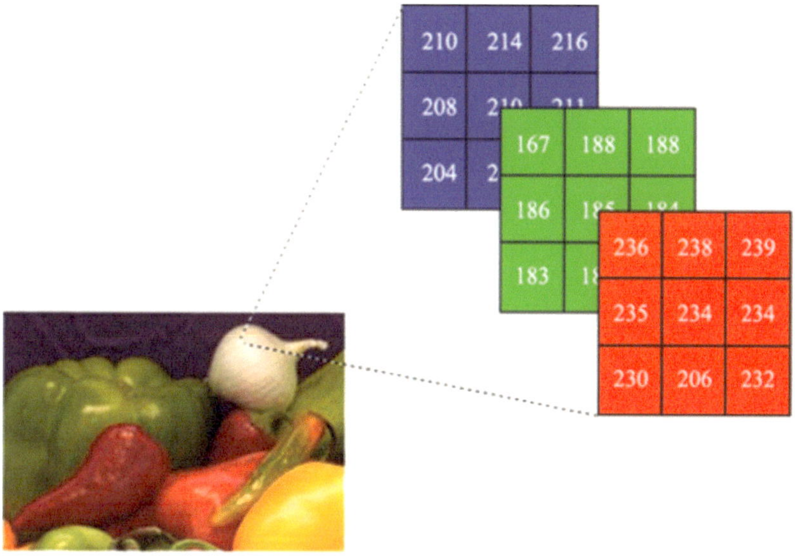

Figure 3. Pixels of a color image.

1.1.1. Pixels relationships

1.1.1.1. Neighbors of a pixel

A pixel has three different neighbor types that are 4, 8, and diagonal. As shown in **Table 1**, neighbor of a pixel (p) in the x, y point of image (f) is defined in that 4-neighbors;

f(x - 1, y - 1)	f(x - 1, y)	f(x - 1, y + 1)
f(x, y - 1)	p	f(x, y + 1)
f(x + 1, y - 1)	f(x + 1, y)	f(x + 1, y + 1)

Table 1. Neighbor of a pixel.

$N_4(p)$ is shown as 4-neighbor of p pixel. Any pixel p in the image has two vertical and horizontal neighbors, and each of them is a unit distance of p, given by

$$N_4(p) = \{f(x, y - 1), f(x - 1, y), f(x, y + 1), f(x + 1, y)\}$$

Diagonal neighbors;

Although diagonal neighbors are the same of 4-neighbor, neighbor pixels are the corner of pixels (p) and each of them is at Euclidean distance of p, given by

$$N_D(p) = \{f(x-1, y-1), f(x-1, y+1), f(x+1, y+1), f(x+1, y-1)\}$$

8-neighbors;

8-neighbors is a combination of $N_4(p)$ and $N_D(p)$ and shown as $N_8(p)$.

$$N_8(p) = \begin{Bmatrix} f(x-1, y-1), f(x-1, y+1), f(x+1, y+1), f(x+1, y-1), \\ f(x, y-1), f(x-1, y), f(x, y+1), f(x+1, y) \end{Bmatrix}$$

1.1.1.2. Adjacency

If two pixels are neighbors and their gray level values satisfy some specified criterion, then they are connected. A set of intensity values (V) is used to define adjacency and connectivity. There are three types of adjacency (**Figure 4**).

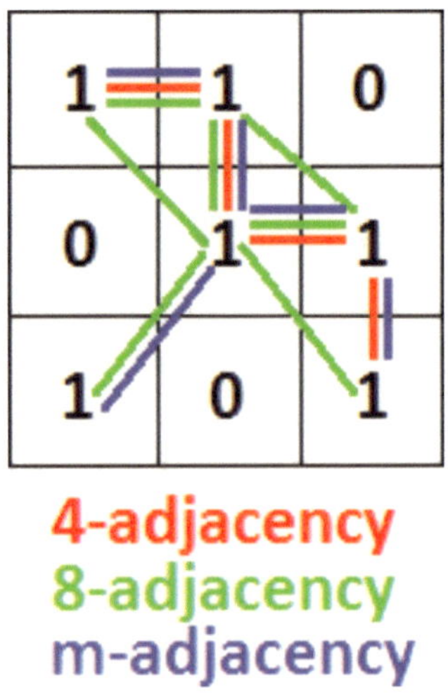

Figure 4. Pixel adjacency.

4-adjacency

p and q pixels are 4-adjacency if they are $N_4(p)$ with values from V.

8-adjacency

p and q pixels are 8-adjacency if they are $N_8(p)$ with values from V.

m-adjacency (mixed)

p and q pixels are m-adjacency if;

- q is in $N_4(p)$ or,

http://dx.doi.org/10.5772/63028

- q is in $N_D(p)$ and,
- $N_4(p) \cap N_4(q) = \emptyset$ with values from V.

1.1.1.3. Path

A path from pixel p with coordinate (x, y) to pixel q with coordinate (s, t) with values from V is defined as 4- ,8- , or m-paths depending on the type of adjacency specified.

According to V = {2,3,5}, If we want to find p and q pixels 4-, 8- and m-path, (**Figure 5**)

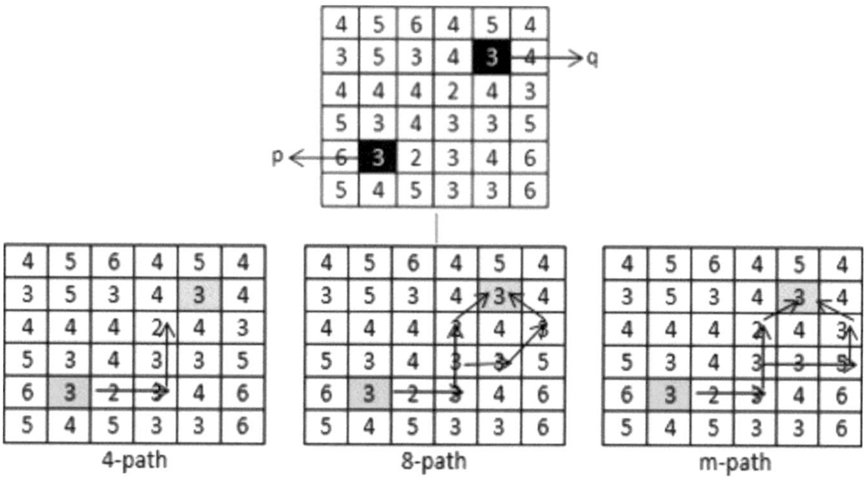

Figure 5. Finding 4-, 8-, m-path between p and q pixels.

1.1.1.4. Distance measures of pixels

- Euclidean Distance (D_e)

$$D_e(p,q) = \sqrt{(x-s)^2 + (y-t)^2}$$

- City-block Distance (D_4)

$$D_4(p,q) = |x-s| + |y-t|$$

- Chessboard Distance (D_8)

$$D_8(p,q) = \max(|x-s|,|y-t|)$$

- D_m Distance; it is defined as the shortest m-path.

According to V = {2,3,5}, if we want to find D_m distance from p pixel to q pixel (**Figures 6**, **7**, **8**);

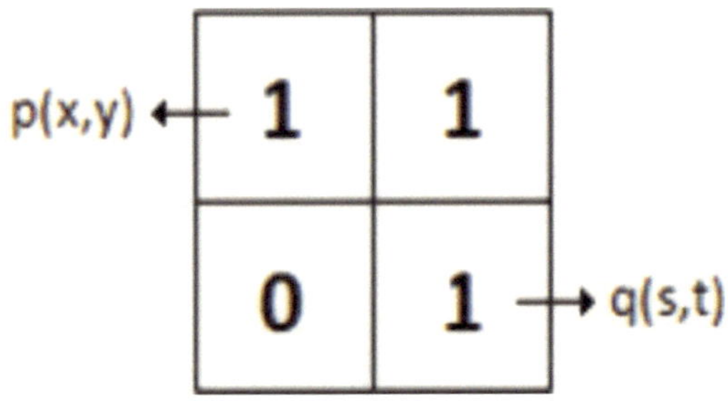

Figure 6. Distance between p and q pixels.

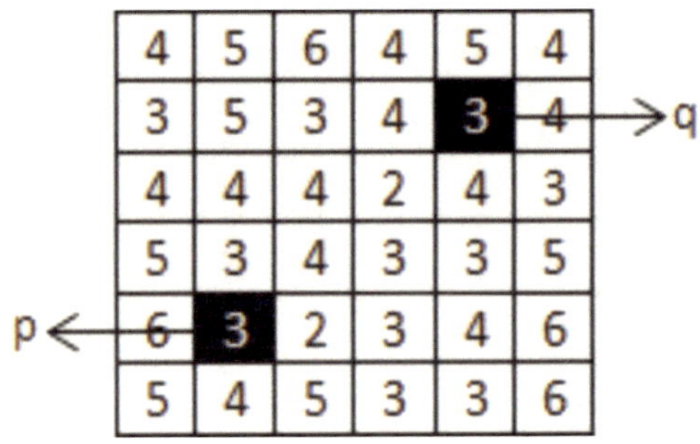

Figure 7. Example about the shortest m-path.

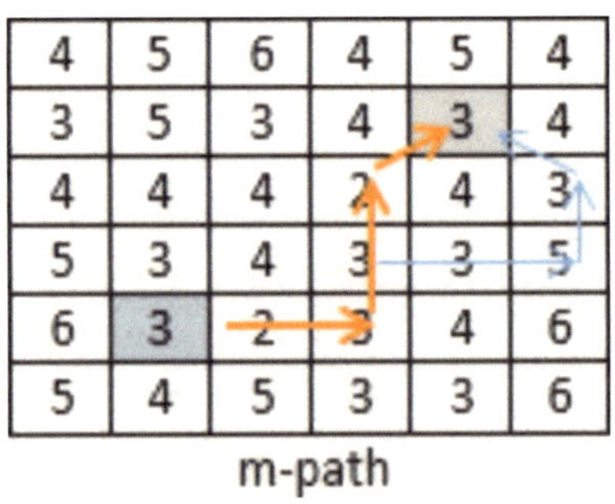

Figure 8. Solving example in the Figure 7.

D_m is 5 because orange path is shorter than blue path.

http://dx.doi.org/10.5772/63028

```
bw = zeros(200,200);
bw(50,50) = 1;
bw(50,150) = 1;
bw(150,100) = 1;

D1 = bwdist(bw,'euclidean');
D2 = bwdist(bw,'cityblock');
D3 = bwdist(bw,'chessboard');
D4 = bwdist(bw,'quasi-euclidean');

figure
subplot(2,2,1);
subimage(mat2gray(D1));hold on, imcontour(D1);title('Euclidean');
subplot(2,2,2);
subimage(mat2gray(D2));hold on, imcontour(D2);title('City Block');
subplot(2,2,3);
subimage(mat2gray(D3));hold on, imcontour(D3);title('Chessboard');
subplot(2,2,4);
subimage(mat2gray(D4));hold on, imcontour(D4);title('Quasi-Euclidean');
```

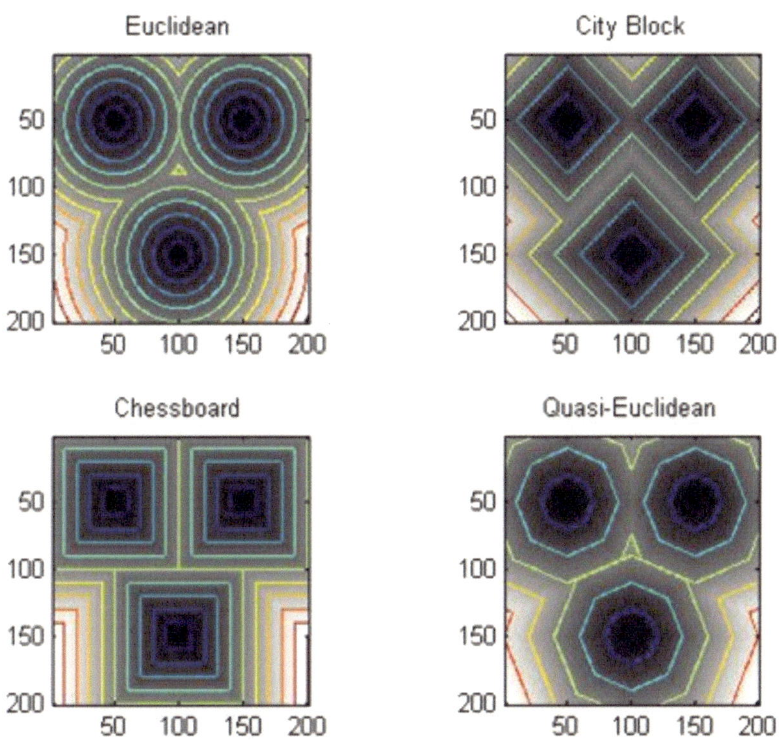

Figure 9. Distance measuring types.

1.2. Spatial resolution

Spatial resolution can be defined as the number of pixels per inch. Different spatial resolutions of same image are shown in the **Figure 10**. Spatial resolution has different measuring methods for different devices.

Figure 10 .Different spatial resolutions of same image.

1.2.1. Dots per inch (DPI)

DPI is generally used in monitors. Sometimes it is called PPI (Pixels Per Inch). But the two expressions have a difference. DPI is also used for measuring spatial resolution of printers. It means DPI defines how many dots of ink on printed image per inch.

1.2.2. Pixels per inch (PPI)

PPI is generally used in tablets, mobile phones, etc. If a and b are height and width resolutions of image, we can calculate ppi value of any device using Equation 1.

$$PPI = \frac{\sqrt{a^2 + b^2}}{Diagonal\ Size\ of\ Devices} \tag{1}$$

For example; 1080 × 1920 pixels, 5.5 inch Iphone 6s Plus PPI value;

$$PPI = \frac{\sqrt{1080^2 + 1920^2}}{5.5} \cong 401 \ (it\ is\ shown\ in\ apple\ web\ site)$$

http://dx.doi.org/10.5772/63028

$$PPI = \frac{\sqrt{1080^2 + 1920^2}}{5.5} \cong 401 \; (\textit{it is shown in apple web site})$$

1.2.3. Lines per inch (LPI)

LPI is referred lines of dots per inch of printers. Printer has different LPI values as shown in **Tables 2**.

Printer	LPI value
Screen printing	45–65 LPI
Laser printing (300 dpi)	65 LPI
Laser printing (600 dpi)	85–105 LPI

Table 2. LPI Value of Printer.

1.3. Image file formats

Image file formats are important for printing, scanning, using on the Internet, etc. The different formats are used in the world. The most common formats are jpg, tif, png, and gif (**Figures 11**). In this section, the most common file formats (JPG, TIF, PNG, and GIF) are explained.

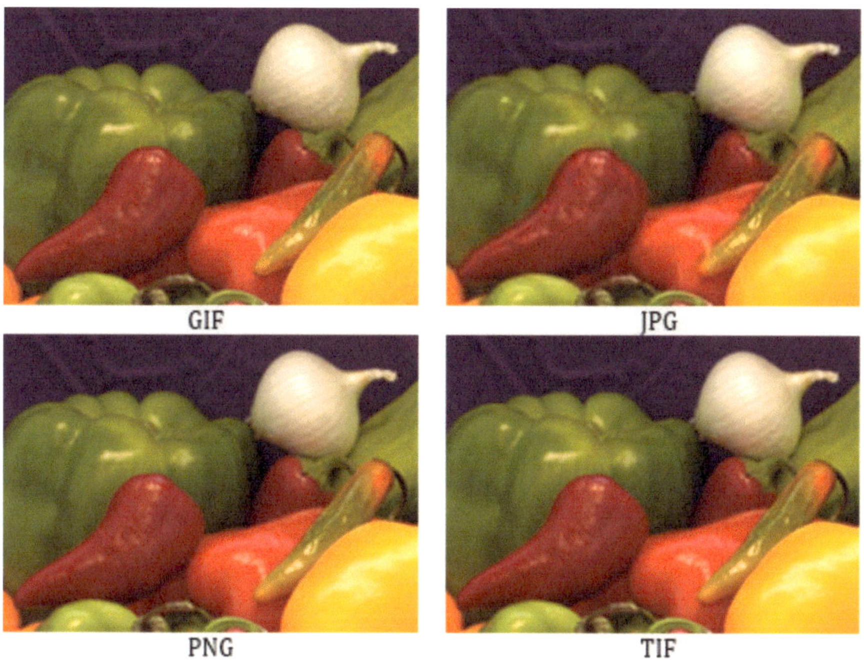

Figure 11. Image formats.

1.3.1. JPG (Joint Photographic Expert Group)

JPEG or JPG is the most common standard for compressing digital image. It is used in web pages, document, email, etc. Because digital images have smaller size than other file formats. However, JPEG images have very low resolution.

1.3.2. TIF (Tagged Image File Format)

TIFF or TIF has the best resolution for using commercial works. Although it is very high quality, the files have very big size.

1.3.3. GIF (Graphics Interchange Format)

GIF, which was used 8-bit video for the people connecting to internet using dial-up modem, was designed by CompuServe.

1.3.4. PNG (Portable Network Graphics)

PNG file format has smaller size than TIF and more resolution than GIF and JPG. Nowadays, it is used in the web pages because of having transparency property.

2. Basic image processing with MATLAB

MATLAB is a very simple software for coding. All data variable in MATLAB are thought a matrix and matrix operations are used for analyzing them. MATLAB has the different toolboxes according to application areas. In this section, MATLAB Image Processing Toolbox is presented and the use of its basic functions for digital image is explained.

2.1. Read, write, and show image

imread() function is used for reading image. If we run this function with requiring data, image is converted to a two-dimensional matrix (gray image is two-dimensional, but, color image is three-dimensional) with rows and columns including gray value in the each cell.

I = imread('path/filename.fileextension');

imread() function only needs an image file. If the result of imread() function is equal to a variable, a matrix variable (I) is created. File name, extension, and directory path that contains image must be written between two single quotes. If script and image file are in the same folder, path is not necessary.

The matrix variable of image is showed using imshow() function. If many images show with sequence on the different figure windows, we use "figure" function for opening new window.

http://dx.doi.org/10.5772/63028

imwrite() function is used to create an image. This function only requires a new image file name with extension. If the new image is saved to a specific directory, the path of directory is necessary.

```
% Clear all workspace
clear
% Close All Open Images
close all
% Clear Command Windows
clc
% Read Image
I = imread('onion.png');
% Show Image
imshow(I);
% Create New Image that has different format
imwrite(I,'onion.jpg');
% Create New Image that has different format and save specific directory
imwrite(I,'C:\NewImageDirectory\onion.jpg');
```

2.2. Image reverse

Image reserve technique, each all elements of the matrix is replaced to be the top row elements to bottom row and the bottom row elements to top row. In the other words, the image rotates on the vertical axis.

MATLAB Image Processing Toolbox does not have function for it. Either the script is written or flipdim function can be used (**Figure 12**).

```
I = imread('onion.png');            % Original Image
I_mirror  = flipdim(I,2);           % Mirror Image
I_reverse = flipdim(I,1);           % Reverse Image
I_mirrev  = flipdim(I_reverse,2);   % Reverse + Mirror Image

figure,
subplot(2,2,1), imshow(I);title('Original Image');
subplot(2,2,2), imshow(I_mirror);title('Mirror Image');
subplot(2,2,3), imshow(I_reverse);title('Reverse Image');
subplot(2,2,4), imshow(I_mirrev);title('Reverse + Mirror Image');
```

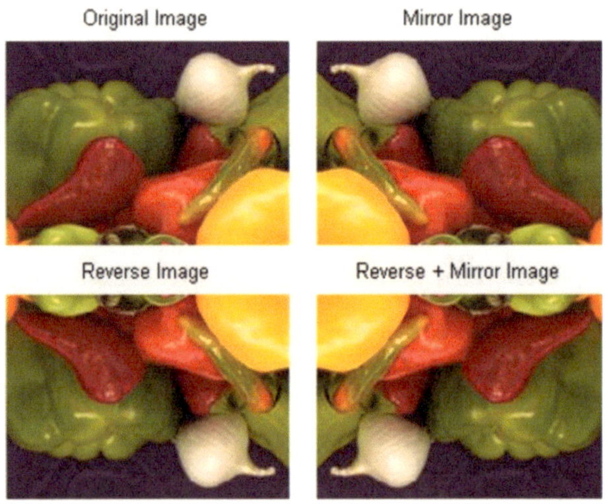

Figure 12. Vertical and horizontal reverse.

2.3. Image mirroring

Mirroring technique is the rotating of reversed image on the horizontal axis. In MATLAB Image Processing Toolbox has imrotate() function for rotating image. This function needs three properties which are image matrix variable, rotating angle, and interpolation method (**Figure 13**).

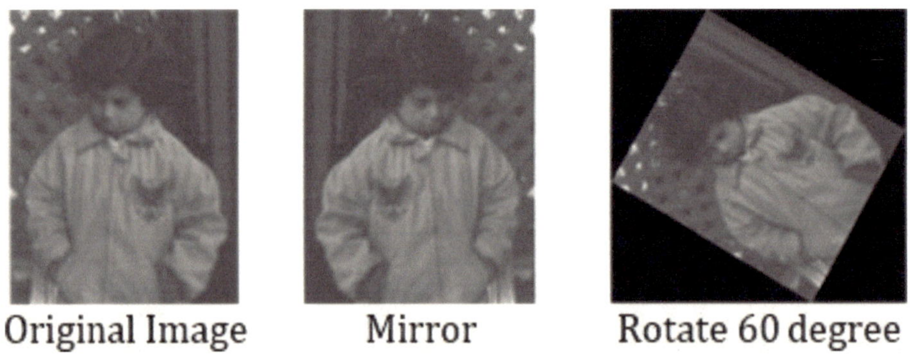

Figure 13. Image rotate.

I_rotate = imrotate(Image Matrix Variable, Angle, Interpolation Method)

Interpolation method

- 'nearest': Nearest-Neighbor Interpolation

http://dx.doi.org/10.5772/63028

- 'bilinear': Bilinear Interpolation
- 'bicubic': Bicubic Interpolation

Example

```
I = imread('pout.tif');
imshow(I);
I_mirror = flipdim(I,2);
figure, imshow(I_mirror);
I_rotate = imrotate(I,60,'bilinear');
figure, imshow(I_rotate);
```

2.4. Image shift

Sometimes, an image can be wanted to shift up to certain pixel value on the horizontal and vertical axis. imtranslate() function is used to shift of an image. In the **Figure 14** the image shifts 15 px right and 25 px bottom.

```
I = imread('pout.tif');
imshow(I);
I_shift = imtranslate(I,[15, 25]);
figure, imshow(I_shift);
```

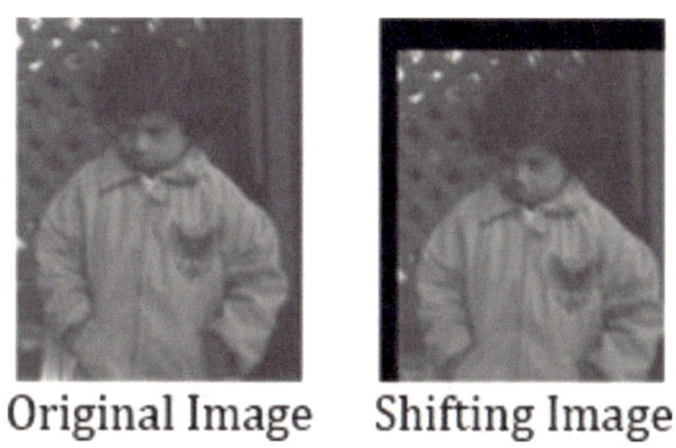

Figure 14. Image shift.

2.5. Image resize

If an image is displayed big or small size for showing details or general view, its resolution must be changed. These situations are called zoom-in and zoom-out. Digital cameras or photosensitive devices use optic lenses for zoom-in and zoom-out. But, interpolation methods are only used for digital images. Most common problem of interpolation methods is the changing quality of image (**Figures 15, 16**).

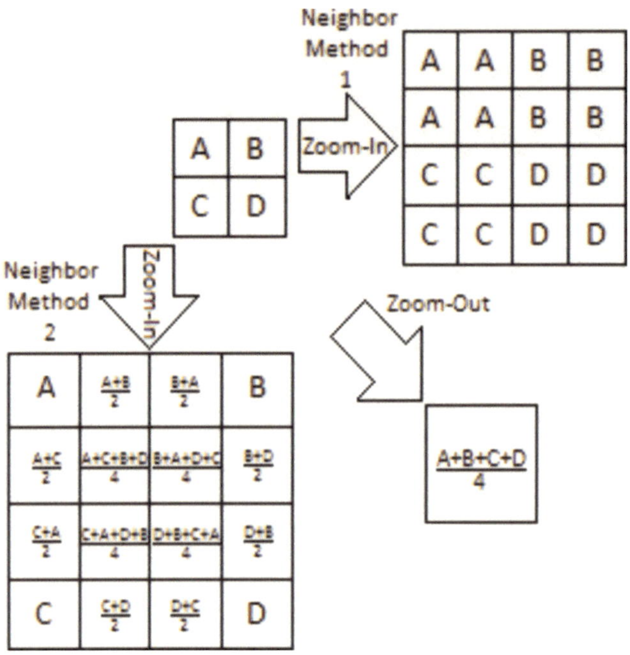

Figure 15. Zoom-in and zoom-out.

I_resize = imresize(I, Resize Rate, Interpolation Method)

I is image variable, if Resize Rate is bigger than 1, it means zoom-in, otherwise zoom-out.

```
I = imread('pout.tif');
imshow(I);
% 50% Increase Image Size (Zoom-In)
I_resize_big = imresize(I, 1.5, 'nearest');
figure, imshow(I_resize_big);
% 50% Decrease Image Size (Zoom-Out)
I_resize_small = imresize(I, 0.5, 'nearest');
figure, imshow(I_resize_small);
```

Figure 16. Image resize.

3. Image enhancement

In some cases, an image has useless or insufficient information for extracting objects because of different defects. So that, the image must be processed using different digital image processing techniques for removing the defects or artifacts. In this section, some principal methods are explained for increasing the visibility and decreasing defects.

3.1. Brightness

Brightness of an image is adjusted with adding or subtracting a certain value to gray level of each pixel.

$$G(i,j) = F(i,j) + b \quad \begin{matrix} b > 0 \, Brightness\ incerease \\ b < 0 \, Brightness\ decrease \end{matrix}$$

I_adjust = imadjust(I, [low_in; hig_in], [low_out;high_out])

New image (I_adjust) intensity values are between low_out and high_out gray values (**Figure 17**).

```
I = imread('pout.tif');
figure, imshow(I);
I_adjust = imadjust(I);
figure, imshow(I_adjust);
I_adjust = imadjust(I, [0.2; 0.3], [0.5; 0.7]);
figure, imshow(I_adjust);
```

Figure 17. Changing brightness of the image.

```
I = imread('onion.png');
imshow(I);
% [low_in(R) low_in(G) low_in(B); high_in(R) high_in(G) high_in(B)] map to
% [low_out(R) low_out(G) low_out(B); high_out (R) high_out (G) high_out(B)]
I_adjust = imadjust(I, [0.2 0.3 0.4; 0.3 0.5 0.5], [0.3 0.5 0.6; 0.7 0.6
0.8]);
figure, imshow(I_adjust);
```

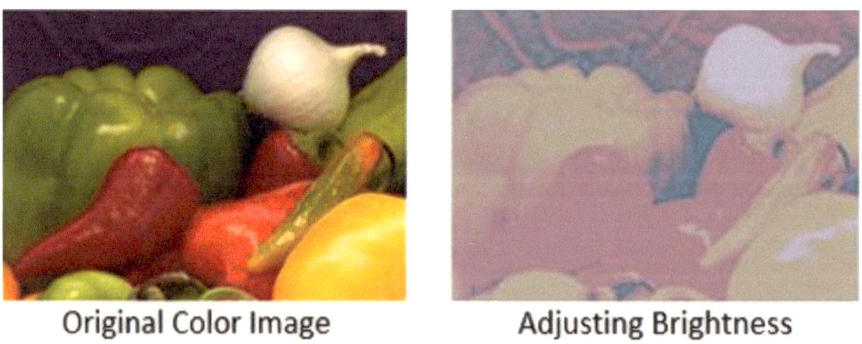

Figure 18. Adjusting Brightness of Color Image.

The MATLAB script above is used for gray image, but we want to change brightness of color image, so, we must change all intensity values of R (red), G (green) and B (blue) channel of the image (**Figure 18**).

3.2. Contrast

Contrast of an image can be changed by multiplying all pixel gray value by a certain value.

http://dx.doi.org/10.5772/63028

$$G(i,j) = c * F(i,j) \begin{matrix} c > 0 \, contrast\, increase \\ c < 0 \, contrast\, decrease \end{matrix}$$

MATLAB Image Processing Toolbox has the Contrast Adjust tool to change contrast of an image. As shown in **Figure 19**, GUI allows the user for changing contrast using handling.

```
I = imread('pout.tif');
imshow(I);
% Open Contrast Tool
imcontrast();
```

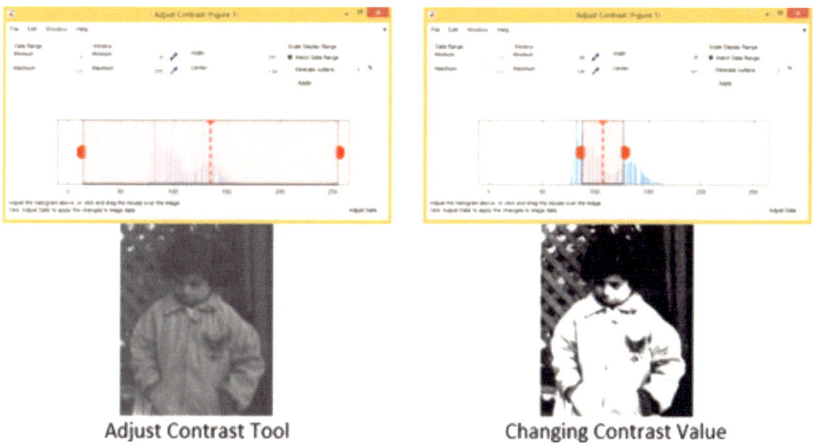

Figure 19. Adjust contrast tool.

3.3. Negative

Intensity values of image are reversed as linear for negative image (**Figure 20**).

```
I = imread('pout.tif');
% Negative Image
I_neg = imcomplement(I);
subplot(1,2,1);imshow(I);title('Original Image');
subplot(1,2,2);imshow(I_neg);title('Negative Image');
```

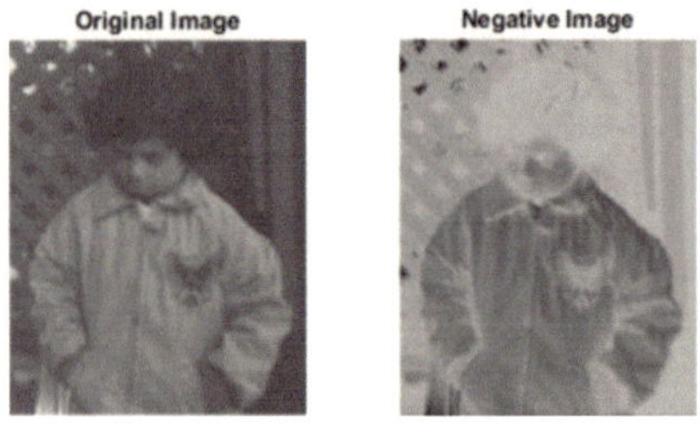

Figure 20. Negative Image.

```
I = imread('pout.tif');
% Calculate Histogram of Image
I_hist = imhist(I);
% Calculating threshold value
T = graythresh(I);
% Applying threshold value to image and convert binary image
I_thresh = im2bw(I,T);
% Add brigtness value
b = 50;
I_new = I + b;
figure, imshow(I_new);
figure,
subplot(2,2,1);imshow(I);title('Original Image');
subplot(2,2,2);imhist(I);title('Histogram of Original Image');
subplot(2,2,3);imhist(I);title('Histogram of Image');
subplot(2,2,4);imshow(I_thresh);title('New Binary Image');
```

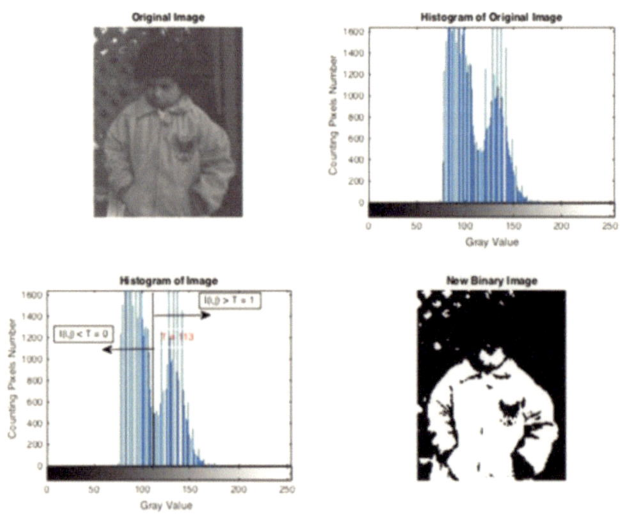

Figure 21. Thresholding.

http://dx.doi.org/10.5772/63028

3.4. Thresholding

Thresholding is generally used for converting image to binary image (0 and 1 gray value). The algorithm of thresholding is defined in Equation 2.

$$G(x,y)=\begin{cases} I(x,y)\geq T & 1 \\ I(x,y)<T & 0 \end{cases} \tag{2}$$

I is original image, x and y are row and column number, T is threshold value, G is new image fter applying threshold (**Figure 21**).

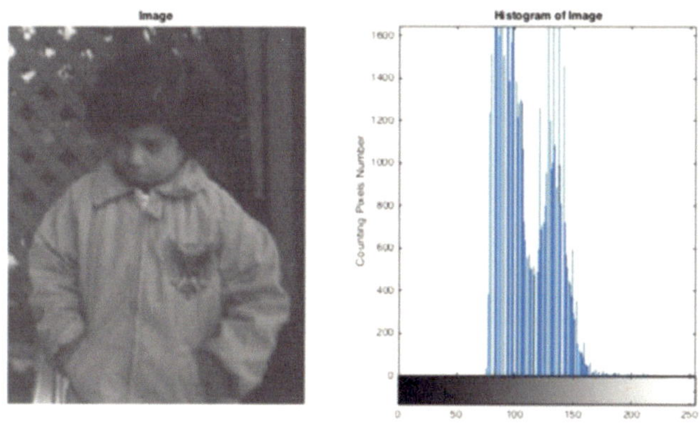

Figure 22. Histogram of the image.

Gray value	Counting of pixel number
75	2
76	38
77	0
78	389
79	1245
80	0
81	1518

Table 3. Histogram of Specific Gray Values.

3.5. Histogram

Histogram counts the number of gray value of pixels in the images. Each pixel in the image has gray value between 0 and 255. As shown in **Table 3**, counting pixels give us information about image or objects in the image. The histogram of image is shown in **Figure 22**.

The histogram of image is calculated using imhist(image) function in the MATLAB.

```
I = imread('pout.tif');
I_hist = imhist(I);
subplot(1,2,1);imshow(I);title('Image');
subplot(1,2,2);imhist(I);title('Histogram of Image');
```

3.6. Histogram equalization

Histogram equalization is defined a technique for adjusting contrast of an image using all gray values to equalize as much as possible. Some situations work fine and image are shown very well; sometimes, it is not good and new image is darker than original image (**Figure 24**).

1	1	1	1	1
3	3	0	0	2
3	3	2	2	2
6	4	4	2	6
6	7	7	5	5

Table 4. An Image Pixel Gray Values.

We explain histogram equalization with an exam. You think about an image, and, its intensity mapping is shown below. There are eight possible gray levels from 0 to 7. If we apply histogram equalization to the image pixel gray values that are shown in **Table 4**, how new image histogram will be?

Step 1: Find histogram of the image (**Table 5**)

I	0	1	2	3	4	5	6	7
f(I)	2	5	5	4	2	2	3	2

Table 5. Histogram.

Step 2: Calculate Cumulative Frequency Distribution (CFD)

I	0 1	2	3	4	5	6	7
f(I)	2 5	5	4	2	2	3	2
CFD	2 2+5=7	7+5=12	12+4=16	16+2=18	18+2=20	20+3=23	23+2=25

Table 6. Calculate Cumulative Frequency Distrubiton (CFD).

Step 3: Calculate new pixel gray value using **Equation 3**

$$h(v) = floor\left(\frac{CFD(v) - CFD_{min}}{(MxN) - CFD_{min}} x(L-1)\right) \tag{3}$$

h is new gray value, v is pixel number, MxN is image row and column value, L is gray level (in our image L is 8)

If we calculate the 4 number pixel;

$$h(4) = floor((16-2)/((5x5)-2)x(8-1)) \cong floor(4,26) \cong 4$$

1	1	1	1	1
3	3	0	0	2
3	3	2	2	2
6	4	4	2	6
6	7	7	5	5

Original Image

1	1	1	1	1
4	4	0	0	3
4	4	3	3	3
6	4	4	3	6
6	7	7	5	5

New Image

Figure 23. Original and new image gray values.

After all pixel gray values are calculated using Equation 3 the results of new gray values will be like in **Table 7**.

I	0	1	2	3	4	5	6	7
f(I)	2	5	5	4	2	2	3	2
CFD	2	7	12	16	18	20	23	25
h	0	1	3	4	4	5	6	7

Table 7. New Gray Values.

After histogram equalization is applied to the image, new gray values are shown in the **Figure 23**.

```
I = imread('pout.tif');
I_histeq = histeq(I);
subplot(2,2,1);imshow(I);title('Original Image');
subplot(2,2,2);imhist(I); title('Histogram of Original Image');
subplot(2,2,3);imshow(I_histeq);title('New Image');
subplot(2,2,4);imhist(I_histeq);title('Histogram of New Image');
```

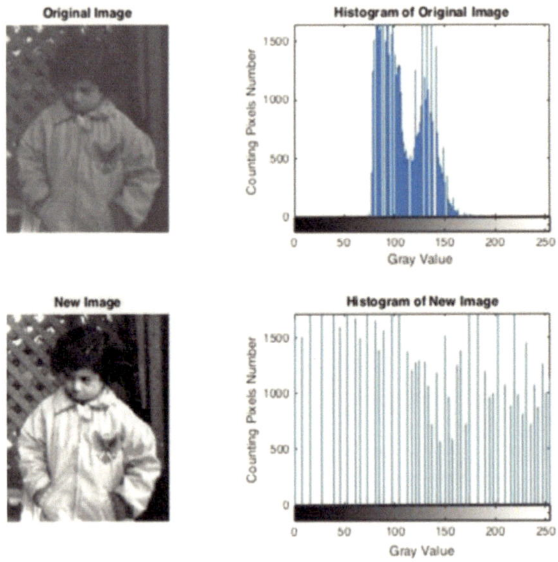

Figure 24. Histogram equalization.

Matlab Image Processing Toolbox has the different filter types as shown in **Table 8**.

4. Color

Humans have very good photosensitive devices that are called eyes. Newton discovered that the light has different color spectrum passing through the glass prism. We think human eye is a glass prism that is called the lens. The lens focuses light to the retina of eyes. So that, humans see visible color spectrum of light reflected from the objects. Color spectrum is shown in the **Figure 25**. Human senses wavelength of light between 400 and 700 nm.

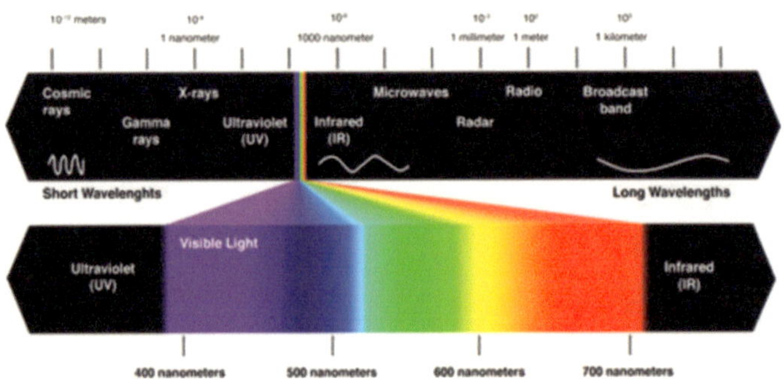

Figure 25. Color spectrum.

http://dx.doi.org/10.5772/63028

Eyes see colors as combining of primary that are Red (R), Green (G), and Blue (B). So that, all visible colors are produced from primary colors. Secondary colors, which are produced with adding of primary colors, are Yellow (Red + Green), Magenta (Red + Blue), and Cyan (Green + Blue) as shown in **Figure 26**.

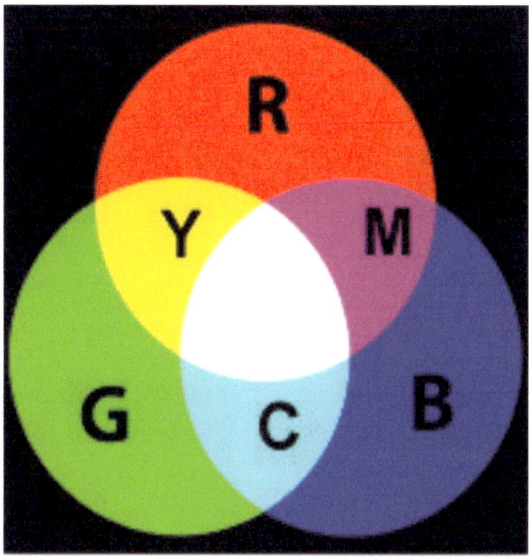

Figure 26. Primary and secondary colors.

In the MATLAB Image Processing Toolbox, a color image has three-dimensional uint8 (8-bit unsigned integer) data. Each dimension corresponds to a color channel that is Red, Green, or Blue channel. If we want, we can process each color channel. As shown in **Figure 27**, each color channel splits from image.

Workspace

Name	Value	Min	Max
B	<135x198 uint8>	0	233
G	<135x198 uint8>	2	248
I	<135x198x3 uint8>	0	255
R	<135x198 uint8>	16	255

Figure 27. R, G, B channel values in the MATLAB workspace.

```
I = imread('onion.png');
imshow(I);
% Red Channel
R = I(:,:,1);
% Green Channel
G = I(:,:,2);
% Blue Channel
B = I(:,:,3);
subplot(2,2,1);imshow(I);title('Original Image');
subplot(2,2,2);imshow(R);title('R');
subplot(2,2,3);imshow(G);title('G');
subplot(2,2,4);imshow(B);title('B');
```

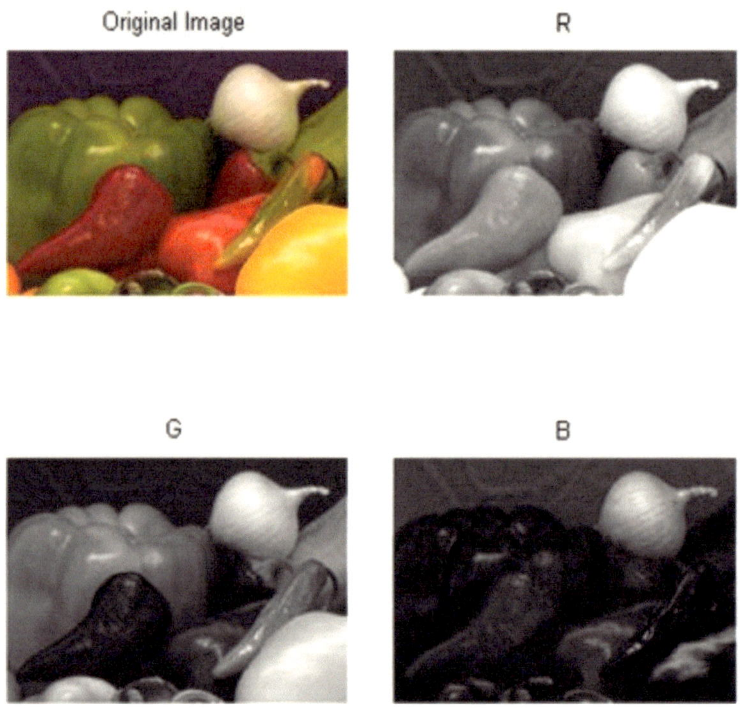

Figure 28. R, G, B channel.

4.1. HSI

As shown in **Figure 29** each color represents three components as H (Hue), S (Saturation), I (Intensity). The Hue, which can be defined rate of pure color, is an angle form between 0° and 360°. Red, Green, Blue are 0°, 120°, and 360°, and Yellow, Cyan, and Magenta are 60°, 180°,

http://dx.doi.org/10.5772/63028

300°. The Saturation, which shows how the color to be pure, takes value between [0, 1]. The intensity is the dimensions of lightness or darkness. The range of intensity is between 0 (black) and 1 (white).

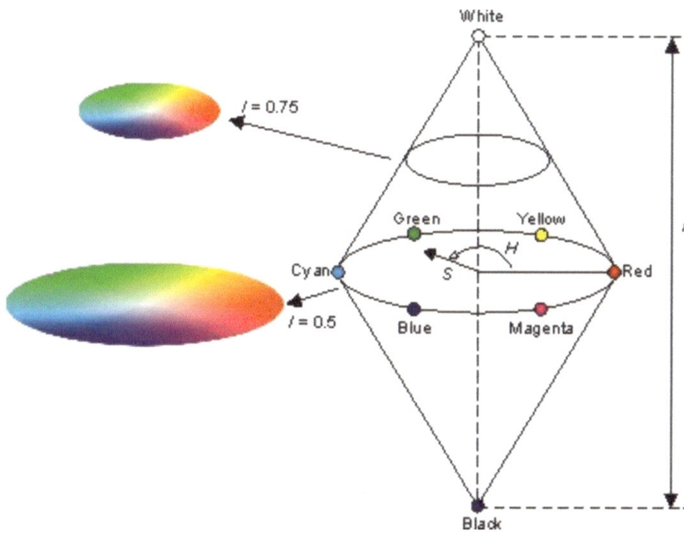

Figure 29. HSI components.

```
% HSI Converting
HSI = rgb2hsv(I);
subplot(2,2,1);imshow(I);title('Original Image');
subplot(2,2,2);imshow(HSI(:,:,1));title('H');
subplot(2,2,3);imshow(HSI(:,:,2));title('S');
subplot(2,2,4);imshow(HSI(:,:,3));title('I');
% Converting from HSI to RGB
RGB = hsv2rgb(HSI);figure, imshow(I);
```

MATLAB use rgb2hsv(image) or write script using **Eqs. (4)–(6)** for converting the color image to HSI components. If we want to convert from HSI image to RGB image, we use hsv2rgb(hsi image).

$$H = \begin{cases} \theta & if\ B \le G \\ 360 - \theta & if\ B > G \end{cases} with\ \theta = cos^{-1} \left\{ \frac{\frac{1}{2}\left[(R-G)+(R-B)\right]}{\left[(R-G)^2+(R-B)(G-B)\right]^{1/2}} \right\} \tag{4}$$

$$S = 1 - \frac{3}{(R+G+B)}\left[min(R,G,B)\right] \tag{5}$$

$$I = \frac{1}{3}\left[R+G+B\right] \tag{6}$$

Figure 30. HIS of the image.

4.2. YIQ

YIQ, which is defined by the National Television System Committee (NTSC), produces the luminance and the chrominance. We use Equation 7 for producing of YIQ components from RGB image (**Figure 31**), and Equation 8 is used for converting from YIQ to RGB.

$$\begin{bmatrix} Y \\ I \\ Q \end{bmatrix} = \begin{bmatrix} 0.299 & 0.587 & 0.114 \\ 0.596 & -.0274 & -0.322 \\ 0.211 & -0.523 & 0.311 \end{bmatrix} \begin{bmatrix} R \\ G \\ B \end{bmatrix} \tag{7}$$

$$\begin{bmatrix} R \\ G \\ B \end{bmatrix} = \begin{bmatrix} 1 & 0.986 & 0.621 \\ 1 & -.0272 & -0.649 \\ 1 & -1.106 & 1.703 \end{bmatrix} \begin{bmatrix} Y \\ I \\ Q \end{bmatrix} \tag{8}$$

http://dx.doi.org/10.5772/63028

```
RGB = imread('onion.png');
R = RGB(:,:,1);
G = RGB(:,:,2);
B = RGB(:,:,3);
Y =  0.299   * R + 0.587   * G + 0.114   * B;
I = -0.14713 * R - 0.28886 * G + 0.436   * B;
Q =  0.615   * R - 0.51499 * G - 0.10001 * B;
YIQ = cat(3,Y,I,Q);
```

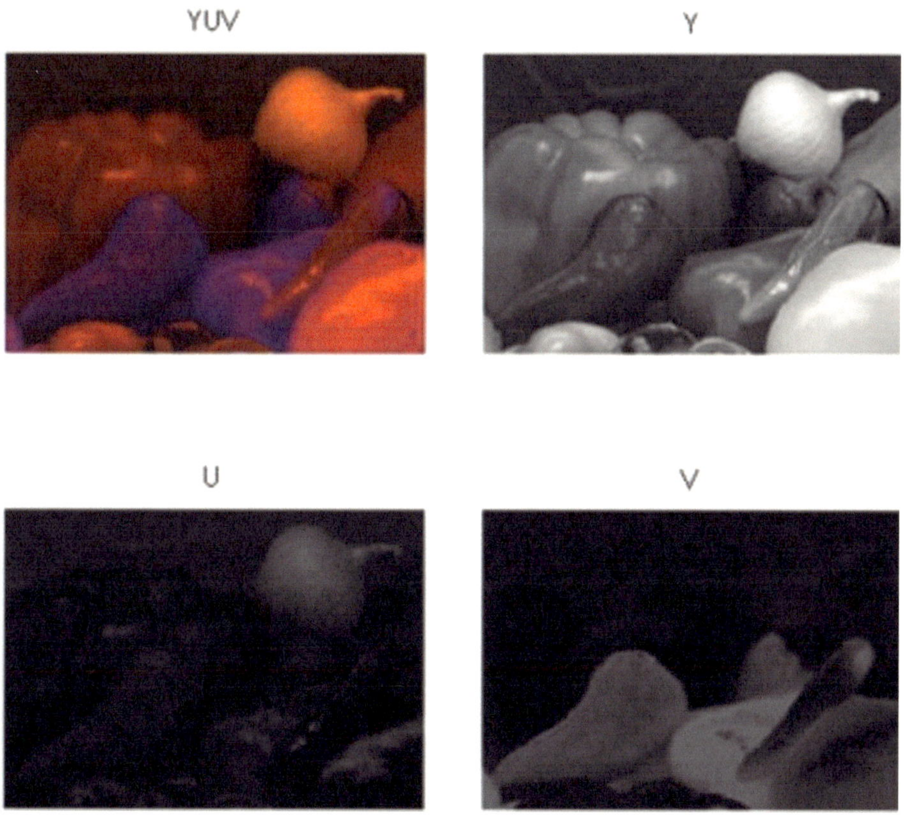

Figure 31. YIQ of the Image.

4.3. Gray image

Gray image is produced using Equation 9 by NTSC standards. However, we can calculate different methods, but MATLAB uses NTSC standards and it has rgb2gray(RGB image) function (**Figure 32**).

$$GI = 0.299R + 0.587G + 0.114B \tag{9}$$

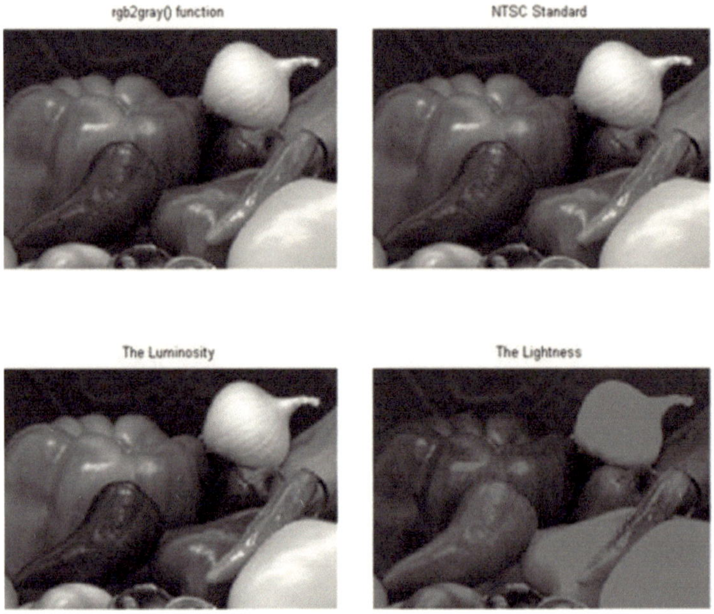

Figure 32. Gray image.

Other methods;

- The average; $GI = 0.33R + 0.33G + 0.33B$
- The lightness; $GI = (max(R,G,B) + (min(R,G,B))/2$
- The luminosity; $GI = 0.21R + 0.72G + 0.07B$

```
RGB = imread('onion.png');
R = RGB(:,:,1);
G = RGB(:,:,2);
B = RGB(:,:,3);
RGBgraymet1 = rgb2gray(RGB);
RGBgraymet2 = 0.299.*R + 0.587.*G + 0.114.*B;
RGBgraymet3 = 0.21.*R + 0.72.*G + 0.07.*B;
RGBgraymet4 = (max(RGB, [], 3)+min(RGB, [], 3))/2;
subplot(2,2,1);imshow(RGBgraymet1);title('rgb2gray() function');
subplot(2,2,2);imshow(RGBgraymet2);title('NTSC Standard');
subplot(2,2,3);imshow(RGBgraymet3);title('The Luminosity');
subplot(2,2,4);imshow(RGBgraymet4);title('The Lightness');
```

http://dx.doi.org/10.5772/63028

5. Morphologic operations

MATLAB Image Processing Toolbox only use binary image for morphologic operations such as opening, closing, etc.

5.1. Structuring element

Structuring element (SE) is a shape that has different sizes (3 × 3, 4 × 4, 5 × 5, etc.) and shapes (**Figure 33**). SE is applied to an image for drawing results on how the objects change in the image (**Figure 34**). SE is generally used for dilation, erosion, opening, closing operations.

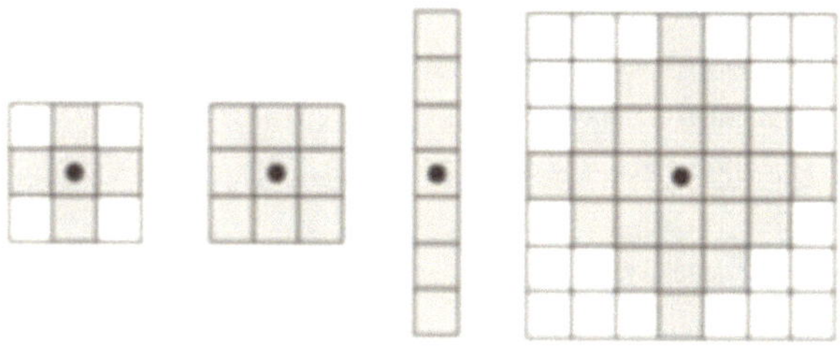

Figure 33. Different structuring elements.

5.2. Dilation

Dilation is a morphologic processing for growing an object in the binary image. It is shown with ⊕ image (**Figure 35**).

$$C = A \oplus B$$

C is the new image, A is the original image, and B is the structuring element.

```
se = strel('square', 3);
dilationsq = imdilate(binary, se);
se = strel('diamond', 3);
dilationdm = imdilate(binary, se);
se = strel('line', 9, 0);
dilationbl = imdilate(binary, se);
figure,
subplot(2,2,1);imshow(binary);title('Original Binary Image');
subplot(2,2,2);imshow(dilationsq);title('Dilation Image (3x3) Square SE');
subplot(2,2,3);imshow(dilationdm);title('Dilation Image (3x3) Diamond SE');
subplot(2,2,4);imshow(dilationbl);title('Dilation Image Line SE');
```

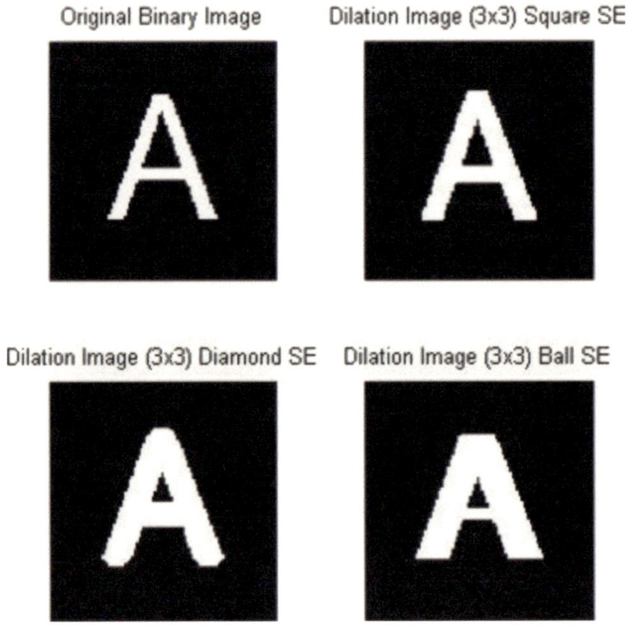

Figure 34. Dilation.

5.3. Erosion

Erosion is the other morphologic operator of a binary image for using eroding the pixels of objects in the image. It is shown as ⊖ symbol.

$$C = A \ominus B$$

```
se = strel('square', 3);
dilationsq = imerode(binary, se);
se = strel('diamond', 3);
dilationdm = imerode(binary, se);
se = strel('line', 9, 0);
dilationbl = imerode(binary, se);
subplot(2,2,1);imshow(binary);title('Original Binary Image');
subplot(2,2,2);imshow(dilationsq);title('Erosion Image (3x3) Square SE');
subplot(2,2,3);imshow(dilationdm);title('Erosion Image (3x3) Diamond SE');
subplot(2,2,4);imshow(dilationbl);title('Erosion Image Line SE');
```

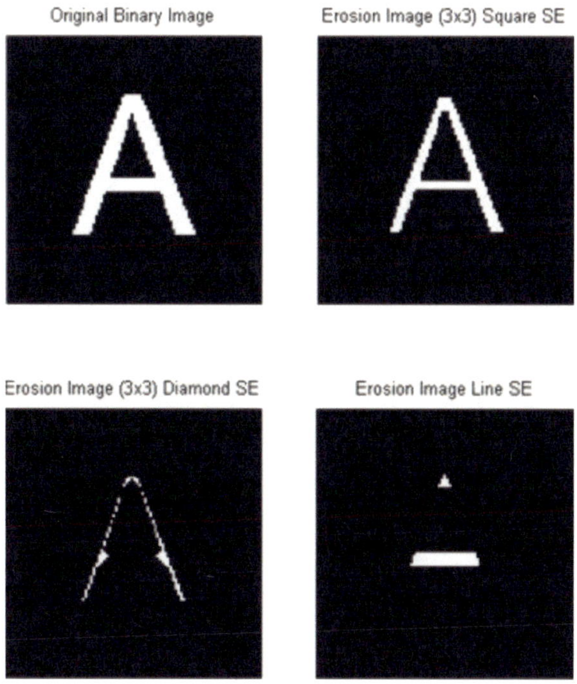

Figure 35. Erosion.

5.4. Opening and closing

As shown in (**Figure 36**), opening and closing are the combination of erosion and dilation operators as shown in Equations 10 and 11.

$$C = (A \ominus B) \oplus B \tag{10}$$

$$C = (A \oplus B) \ominus B \tag{11}$$

```
se = strel('ball', 10,10);
open = imopen(binary, se);
close = imclose(binary, se);
closeopen = imopen(imclose(binary,se), se);
subplot(2,2,1);imshow(binary);title('Original Binary Image');
subplot(2,2,2);imshow(open);title('Opening');
subplot(2,2,3);imshow(close);title('Closing');
subplot(2,2,4);imshow(closeopen);title('Closing + Opening');
```

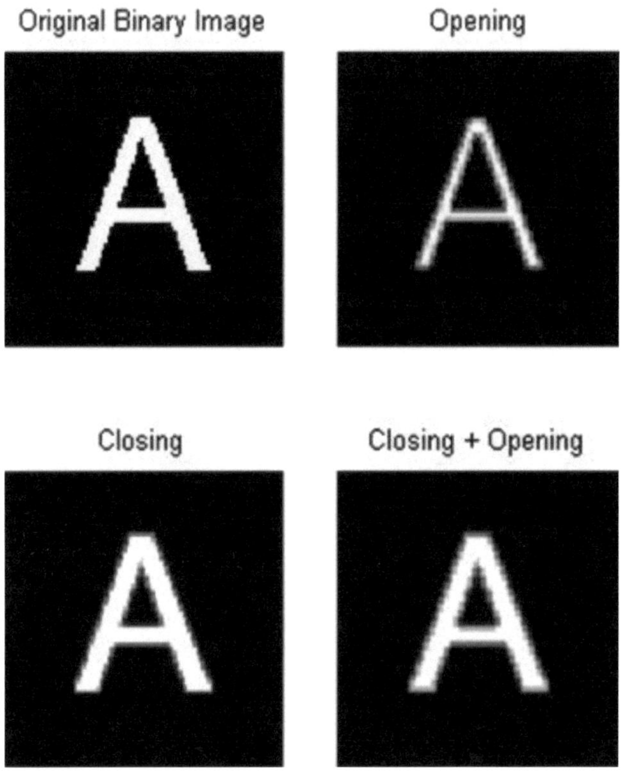

Figure 36. Opening and closing.

5.5. Convolution

Convolution is generally used for modifying the spatial characteristic of an image (**Figure 38**). In the convolution, a new pixel gray value is found by the weighted average pixels that are neighbor of it. Neighbor pixels gray value is weighted by a matrix coefficient that is called convolution kernel. According to the applications, kernel matrix has different sizes such as 3 × 3, 5 × 5, 7 × 7 (**Figure 37**).

Mathematical definition of convolution is shown in Equation 12;

$$G(x,y)=\sum_{n}^{j=-n}\sum_{m}^{i=-m}k(i,j)F(x-i,y-j)=k*F \tag{12}$$

k: convolution kernel matrix

F: processing image

if w and h are row and column of image ⇒(m = (w - 1)/2) | (n = (h - 1)/2)

http://dx.doi.org/10.5772/63028

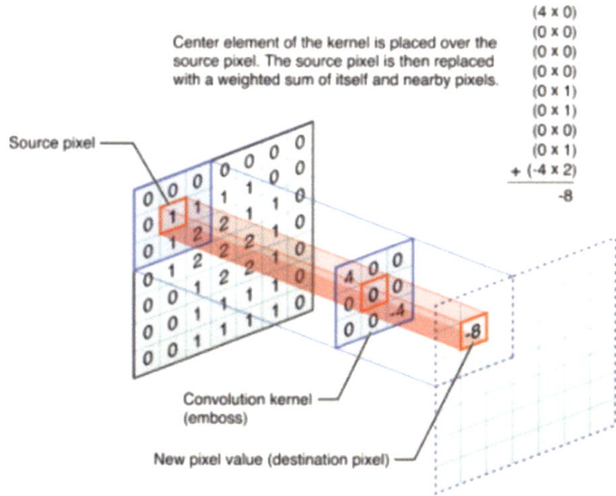

Figure 37. Kernel matrices.

```
I = imread('onion.png');
H = fspecial('disk',10);
blurred = imfilter(I,H,'replicate');
H = fspecial('motion',20,45);
MotionBlur = imfilter(I,H,'replicate');
H = fspecial('sobel');
sobel = imfilter(I,H,'replicate');
subplot(2,2,1);imshow(I);title('Original Image');
subplot(2,2,2);imshow(blurred);title('Blur Kernel');
subplot(2,2,3);imshow(MotionBlur);title('Motion Blur Kernel');
subplot(2,2,4);imshow(sobel);title('Sobel Kernel');
```

Matlab Image Processing Toolbox has the different filter types as shown in **Table 8**.

Value	Description
average	Averaging filter
disk	Circular averaging filter (pillbox)
gaussian	Gaussian low-pass filter
laplacian	Approximates the two-dimensional Laplacian operator
log	Laplacian of Gaussian filter
motion	Approximates the linear motion of a camera
prewitt	Prewitt horizontal edge-emphasizing filter
sobel	Sobel horizontal edge-emphasizing filter

Table 8. Matlab Image Processing Toolbox Filter Types.

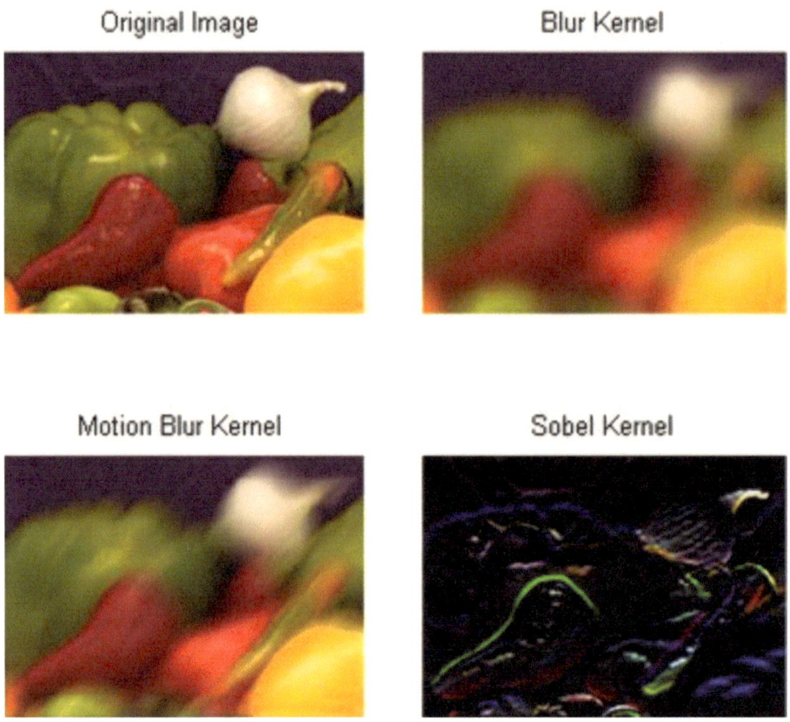

Figure 38. Applying different filters.

5.6. Edge detection

Edge detection is used for finding the border of objects in the image (**Figure 39**). Common edge detection algorithms are Sobel, Canny, Prewitt, Roberts, etc.

```
I = imread('pout.tif');
Iprewitt = edge(I,'prewitt');
Icanny = edge(I,'canny');
Isobel = edge(I,'sobel');
subplot(2,2,1);imshow(I);title('Original Image');
subplot(2,2,2);imshow(Iprewitt);title('Prewitt');
subplot(2,2,3);imshow(Icanny);title('Canny');
subplot(2,2,4);imshow(Isobel);title('Sobel');
```

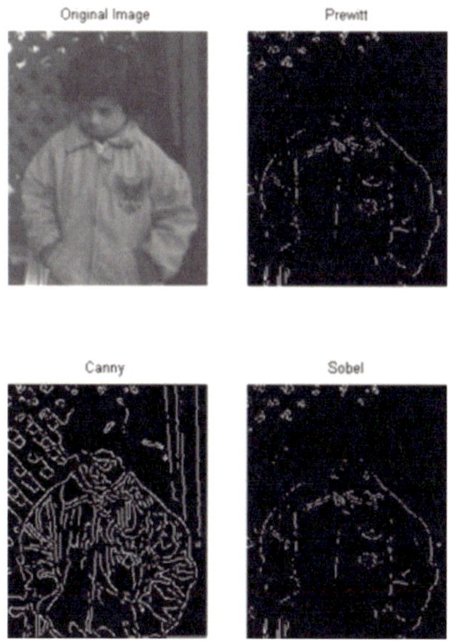

Figure 39. Edge detection.

5.7. Labeling

Pixels are assigned different labels because of belonging to different regions (or components or objects). In **Figure 40**, the objects in the image have the different label values and show different colors in the MATLAB.

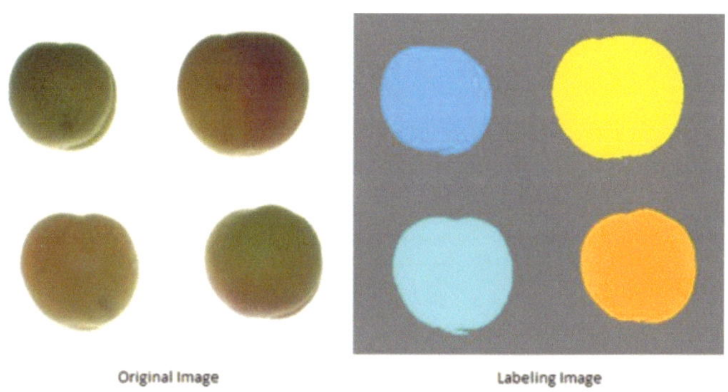

Figure 40. Labeling.

[Boundary,Labels] = bwboundaries(binary image, 'noholes') function uses for labeling. Firstly, the image must be binary image, if it is not, you must convert to binary image. Secondly, all objects must be white (1) and background must be black (0) for using 'noholes' method. We use this function with two variables. One of them is address of boundary pixels, and other one is label numbers and their addresses.

6. Sample application

The last section in this chapter is a sample application that is about extraction of some morphological features of multiple apricots in a digital image. Firstly, original and background digital images are read (**Figures 41, 42**). After that, cropped original image is subtracted from background image. Cropping process is used for extracting specific area from original image (**Figure 42**). Subtracted image (**Figure 44**) converts to gray image as shown in **Figure 45**. Thresholding process is applied to gray image for converting binary image (**Figure 46**). Sometimes, some artifacts can occurred in binary images. Before labelling, connecting pixel groups which are smaller than specific value (smaller than 50 px in this application) are removed (**Figure 47**). After labelling (**Figure 48**), we can find all objects morphological features as shown in **Figure 49**.

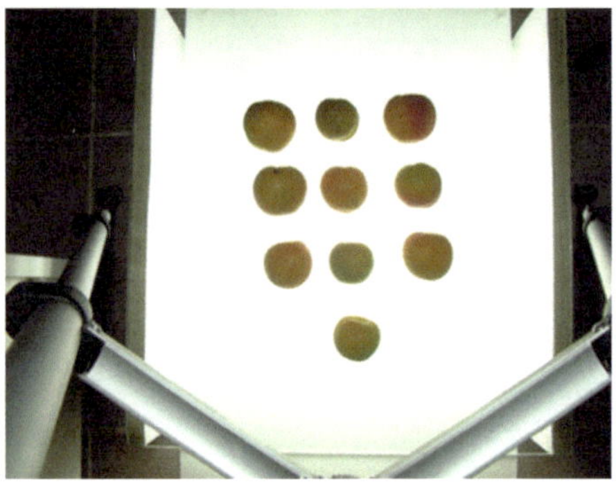

Figure 41. Original digital image.

Figure 42. Background image.

http://dx.doi.org/10.5772/63028

Figure 43. Background image.

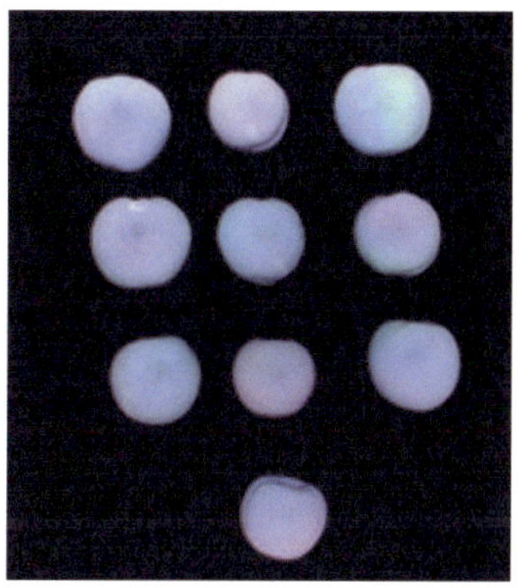

Figure 44. Subtracting from background to cropped image.

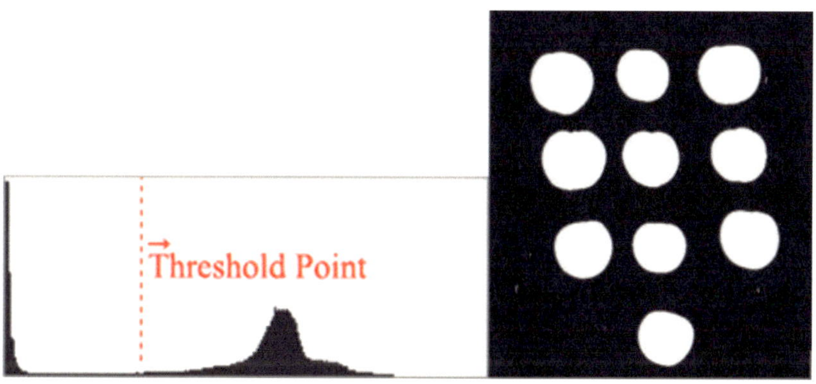

Figure 45. Converting gray image.

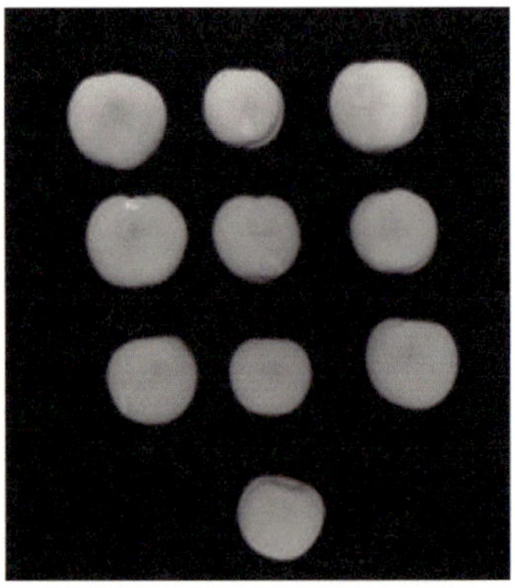

Figure 46. Thresholding.

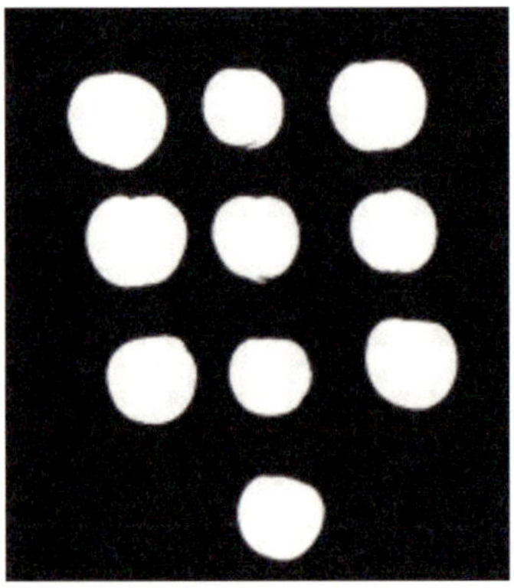

Figure 47. Remove artifacts.

Figure 48. Labelling.

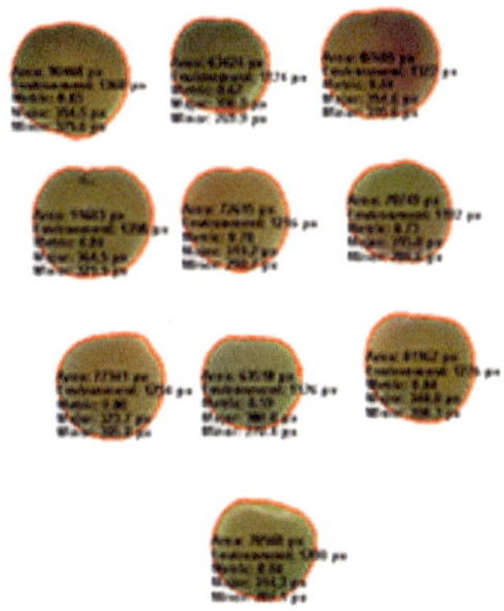

Figure 49. Show morphological features.

```
clear       % Clear Workspace
close all   % Close all opened figures
clc         % Clear Command Window

% Read Image
RGB = imread('image.JPG');
figure,imshow(RGB);

% Read Backgroung Image
RGBback = imread('back.jpg');
figure,imshow(RGBback)

% Cropping Area Coordinate Value
% [StartPoint(x),Startpoint(y),
% Distance(s = x1(StopPoint) - x(StartPoint)),
% Distance(t = y1(StopPoint) - y(StartPoint))]
% x = 1380 and y = 390, x1 = 3180 and y1 = 2340
% s = x1 - x = 3180 - 1380 = 1800px
% t = y1 - y = 2340 - 390 = 1950px
CropCoordinate = [1380,390,1800,1950];
RGBcrop = imcrop(RGB,CropCoordinate);
figure,imshow(RGBcrop);

% Substracting Cropping Image and Background Image
I_sub = imsubtract(RGBback,RGBcrop);
figure,imshow(I_sub);

% RGB Image convert to Gray Image
I_gray = rgb2gray(I_sub);
figure,imshow(I_gray);


% Finding threshold value of Gray Image
threshold = graythresh(I_gray);

% Applying threshold value to Gray Image for converting Binary Image
```

```
bw = im2bw(I_gray,threshold);
figure,imshow(bw);

% If count of connecting pixel groups is smaller than 500,they are removed
bw = bwareaopen(bw,500);
figure,imshow(bw)

% If objects in the image have not holes, they are labeling.
% B is boundary coordinate values, L is labeling values.
[B,L] = bwboundaries(bw,'noholes');

% Show labeling objects in different colors.
figure,imshow(label2rgb(L, @jet, [.5 .5 .5]))

figure,imshow(RGBcrop);
% Open the last figure (Cropping Image)
hold on

% Plot the boundary of objects in the image
for n = 1:length(B)
  boundary = B{n};
  plot(boundary(:,2), boundary(:,1), 'r', 'LineWidth', 2)
end

% Finding specific morphological values
stats = regionprops(L,bw,'Area','Centroid','BoundingBox',...
    'MaxIntensity','MinIntensity','MeanIntensity','ConvexArea',...
    'ConvexHull','ConvexImage','Eccentricity','MajorAxisLength',...
    'MinorAxisLength','Solidity','EquivDiameter','Extent');

% Each object has the different morphological values, so that, finding
% all values and saving to a variable.

% How many objects in the image are calculated length(B).
for o = 1:length(B)

  boundary = B{o};
  % Calculating Area and Metric
  delta_sq = diff(boundary).^2;
  perimeter = sum(sqrt(sum(delta_sq,2)));
  area = stats(o).Area;
  metric = 4*pi*area/perimeter^2;
```

```
    % Area and Environment of Minimum Bounding Box
    axiss = stats(o).BoundingBox;
    environment = 2*(axiss(:,3)+axiss(:,4));
    areabounding = axiss(:,3)*axiss(:,4);

    % Mean, Max, Min Intensity Values
    maxInt = stats(o).MaxIntensity;
    minInt = stats(o).MinIntensity;
    meanInt = stats(o).MeanIntensity;

    % Convex Calculation
    conArea = stats(o).ConvexArea;
    conHull = stats(o).ConvexHull;
    conImage = stats(o).ConvexImage;

    % Major and Minor Axis Length
    major = stats(o).MajorAxisLength;
    minor = stats(o).MinorAxisLength;

    % Centroid
    center = round(stats(o).Centroid);

    x_axis = center(:,1) - 75;
    y_axis = center(:,2) - 75;

    box = [x_axis,y_axis,150,150];

    P = [area,double(metric),environment,areabounding,...
              double(maxInt),double(minInt),double(meanInt),...
              conArea,...
              major,minor];

  px',minor),'FontWeight','bold');
  end
```

Author details

Mahmut Sinecen

Address all correspondence to: mahmut@adu.edu.tr

Adnan Menderes University, Computer Engineering Department, Aydin, Turkey

References

[1] Rafael C. Gonzalez, Richard E. Woods. Digital image processing. 3rd ed. United States of America: Pearson; 2008. 943 p.

[2] John C. Russ. The image processing handbook. 5th ed. United States of America: CRC Press; 2007. 795 p.

[3] Henri Maitre. Image processing. 1st ed. Great Britain: Wiley-ISTE; 2008. 359 p.

[4] Maria Petrou; Costas Petrou. Image processing the fundamentals. 2nd ed. Singapore: Wiley; 2010. 781 p.

[5] John D. Cook. Three algorithms for converting color to grayscale [Internet]. 24.08.2009. http://www.johndcook.com/blog/2009/08/24/algorithms-convert-color-grayscale/. Accessed 02.01.2016

[6] Shindong Kang. http://www.slideshare.net/uspace/ujavaorg-deep-learning-with-convolutional-neural-network [Internet]. 26.05.2015 . http://www.slideshare.net/uspace/ujavaorg-deep-learning-with-convolutional-neural-network. Accessed 29.12.2015

[7] Sung Kim. Applications of Convolution in Image Processing with MATLAB [Internet]. 20.08.2013. http://www.math.washington.edu/~wcasper/math326/projects/sung_kim.pdf. Accessed 12.12.2016

Chapter 2

Information Entropy

Jan Urban

Additional information is available at the end of the chapter

http://dx.doi.org/10.5772/63401

Abstract

"The chapter begins with the short description about the concept of entropy, formula, and matlab code. Within the main chapter body, three different approaches how to use the information entropy in dataset analysis: (i) for data segmentation into two groups; (ii) for filtration of the noise in the dataset; (iii) for enhancement of the entropy contribution via point information gain. Finally, the conclusion is briefly about extended analysis using more generalized entropy, and the usability of described algorithms: advantages and disadvantages."

Keywords: information, entropy, Shannon, segmentation, thresholding, filtration, point information gain

1. Introduction

MATLAB environment enables advanced data processing and analysis, especially using its toolboxes like signal processing, image processing, and statistics.[1] The real signals have to be evaluated with numerous methods for filtration, transformation, alignment, comparison, and so on to extract the hidden knowledge. These methods are belonging to the large group of data processing and analysis. Their origin is different from statistics, physics, artificial intelligence, or systems theory. Recently, Katajama [1] pronounced a clear distinction between the processing and analysis (**Figures 1** and **2**).

Processing

[1] MATLAB and its toolboxes are trademarks or registered trademarks of The MathWorks, Inc.

INTECH
open science | open minds

© 2016 The Author(s). Licensee InTech. This chapter is distributed under the terms of the Creative Commons Attribution License (http://creativecommons.org/licenses/by/3.0), which permits unrestricted use, distribution, and reproduction in any medium, provided the original work is properly cited. (cc) BY

- is the necessary step before the analysis.
- transforms the raw data into more transparent format for the analysis.
- includes tasks as calibration, filtering, feature detection, alignment, normalization, modeling, and so on.

Analysis

- is the interpretation of the processed data.
- consists of comparison, classification, clustering, decomposition, pattern recognition, identification, and so on.

One of the most useful plots in the signal or image analysis is the signal histogram, an expression of signal abundance, first introduced by Pearson [2]. The estimation of proper histogram, as a representation of the probability distribution function, suffers with the question of the proper binning. However, in the digital era, we are live with the datasets, which are discrete representation of discrete events of the real signal. Thus, the amount of bins is usually given by the amount of quantization levels during the sampling process (**Figures 3** and **4**).

In this chapter, the question of image processing is discussed. The lecture opens the intensity histogram function, and the induction continues through the statistical parameters, like central moments, to the information entropy. Three different methods for using the entropy in image processing are introduced, entropy filtration, entropy segmentation, and point information gain. The description is completed by mathematical equations as well as by commented MATLAB commands. The results of the commands are the plots and figures presented within the text. This chapter aims to serve as guiding overview for the entropy consideration as a processing method. The simple examples show the methods steps and additional features (**Figure 5**).

2. Histogram function

In digital image representation, intensity histogram $H(p)$ of a grayscale image is an intensity function shows count of pixel $\Phi(i,j)$ with the intensity equals d independently on the position (i,j):

$$
\begin{aligned}
H(d) &= \sum_{i,j} h(i,j,d); \\
h(i,j,d) &= 1, if\ \Phi(i,j) = d; \\
&= 0, if\ \Phi(i,j) \neq d;
\end{aligned}
\tag{1}
$$

Figure 1. Image of circuit.

In MATLAB, the grayscale image *circuit*[2] could be loaded by the following commands:

Im = imread('circuit.tif'); %load the image;

Im = double (Im) / 255; %convert to double, range 0-1;

figure, imshow (Im); %show the image;

title ('Image of circuit'); %add caption to the image;

Do not forget the ';' symbol at the end of each command, otherwise MATLAB will write all the pixels values!

The image is loaded into the variable *Im*. Its intensity levels are between zero and 255 (8-bit coding) with single precision. The second command coverts the image *Im* into double precision and rescale the intensity values for the range from zero to one. The size of the image is *MxN*, which is also the amount of the pixels in the image.

$$\begin{aligned} &i \in < 0; M >; \\ &j \in < 0; N >; \\ &\sum_{i,j} = \sum_{0,0}^{M,N}; \\ &d \in < 0,1 >; \end{aligned} \tag{2}$$

To compute the histogram:

[H,d] = imhist (Im); %compute histogram of the image;

figure, plot (d, H); %show the histogram function;

xlabel ('d'); %add caption to the x-axis;

ylabel ('H'); %add caption to the y-axis;

[2] MathWorks builtin demo image pre-packaged into MATLAB.

title ('Histogram of circuit'); %add caption to the plot;

where the variable H is the histogram function, and variable d are the d values (intensity levels). The H is a function of d.

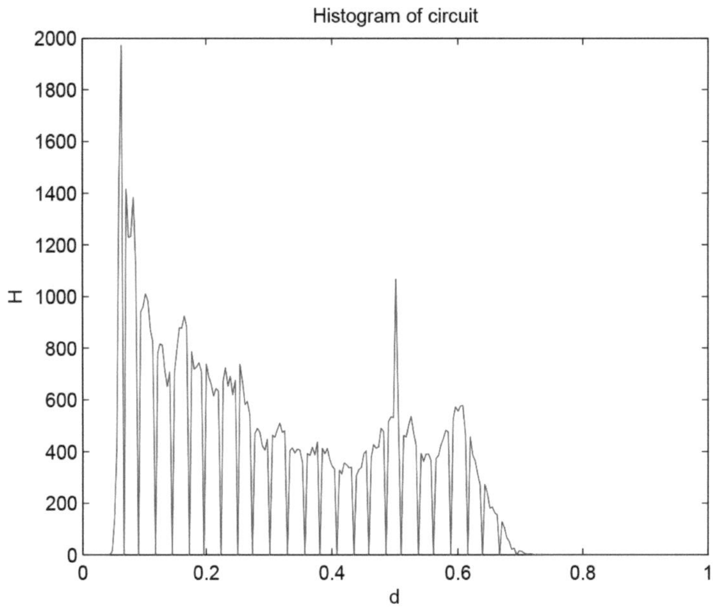

Figure 2. Histogram of circuit.

The histogram represents almost the distribution of the values in the image. To obtain the estimation of the distribution function, it is necessary to normalize the histogram function H to sum equals one [3]:

$$MN = \sum_d H; \qquad H = \frac{H}{MN}; \tag{3}$$

MN = sum (H); %count histogram area;

H = H./MN; %normalize histogram;

figure, plot (d,H); %show normalized histogram;

xlabel ('d');

---

[3] The 0th moment: $\mu_0 = E[(D - E[D])^0] = \sum_i d_k^0 p(d_k) = \sum_k p(d_k)$. The fact that the probability distribution of D is normalized means that the 0th moment is always 1.

http://dx.doi.org/10.5772/63401

ylabel ('probability');

title ('Probability of circuit');

This could be used for many modification (contrast enhancement, frequency evaluation, segmentation, …, etc.).

2.1. Statistical parameters

The distribution function allows us to compute some statistical parameters relevant for the further processing. The distribution is well characterized by two parameters, the location parameter and scaling parameter. The location parameter describes the value around which are all other values.

$$\mu = \frac{\sum_k H_k * d_k}{\sum H_k} \quad (4)$$

%compute mean value from the histogram;

mu = sum (H.*d) / sum(H)

This time, do not write the '$*;'$' symbol at the end of the sentence, to see the result of calculation. This value express the position on the x-axis (d-value), around which is the distribution centered. The value means weighted arithmetic average of all intensity levels. The levels are weighted according to the probability estimated from the histogram function H; The value of the weighted arithmetic average is called mean value[4] μ. Mean is also the first central moment.

figure, plot (d,H);

xlabel ('d');

ylabel ('probability');

title ('Probability of circuit and mean value');

%add mean value to the probability plot;

hold on, plot ([mu, mu], [0, max(H)], 'r');

There is another way how to obtain the mean value directly from the intensity levels of all pixels in the image Im.

%compute mean value from the image;

mu = mean (reshape (Im,size (Im,1)*size (Im,2),1))

The image is reshaped into vector of the size $[MxN, 1]$. No information is lost, only some computations will be simpler to proceed (**Figures 6** and **7**).

[4] There are three Pythagorean means: Arithmetic, Geometric, and Harmonic

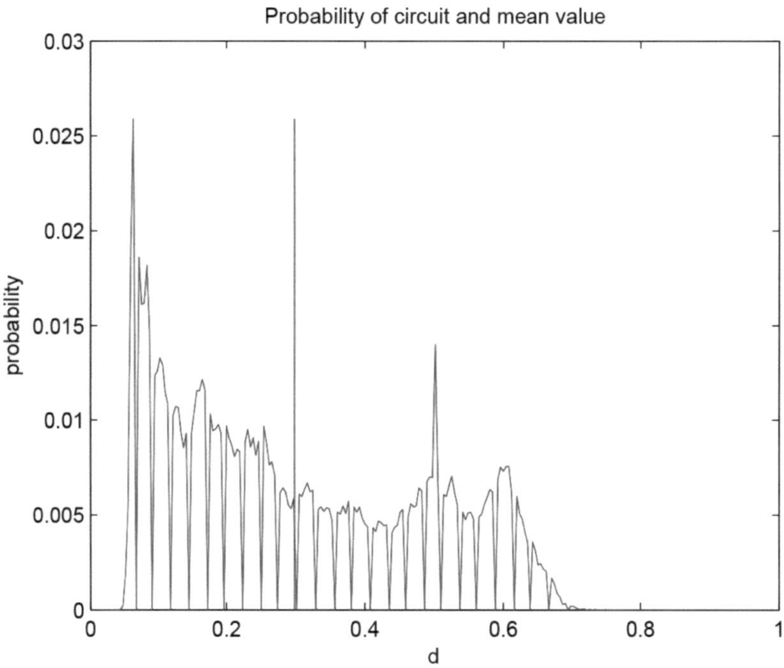

Figure 3. Mean value.

There are two other parameters for the distribution location, median, and mode. The median of the distribution is a value separating the higher half of plot from the lower half, it is a d value. The mode is the value that appears most often in a set of data, the one with highest probability (the d, where is highest H). MATLAB has implemented functions:

```
%compute median from the image;
Me = median ( reshape ( Im,size (Im,1)*size(Im,2),1 ) )
%compute mode from the image;
Mo = mode ( reshape ( Im,size (Im,1)*size (Im,2),1 ) )
figure, plot (d, H);
xlabel ('d');
ylabel ('probability');
title ('Probability of circuit with median and mode values');
%add median value to the probability plot;
hold on, plot ([Me, Me], [0, max(H)], '-.*r');
%add mode value to the probability plot;
hold on, plot ([Mo, Mo], [0, max (H)], ':*g');
```

http://dx.doi.org/10.5772/63401

When plotted, median is dash-dotted red and mode-dotted green. The median often serves instead of mean for the distributions that are not Gaussian. The mode expresses the most frequent value in the distributions that has only one such peak, and thus they are unimodal (**Figures 8** and **9**).

The second parameter of the distribution is the scaling parameter. It describes how far the other d values are from the location parameter μ. The second central moment estimates the variance σ^2, measures how far the d values are spread out (dispersed). An equivalent measure is the square root of the variance, called the standard deviation σ. Standard deviation thus measure dispersion of the d values.

$$\sigma^2 = \sum_k H_k * (d_k - \mu)^2 \quad (5)$$

```
%compute variance from the normalized histogram;
sigma2 = sum (H.*(d-mu). ^2)
%compute standard deviation;
sigma = sqrt (sigma2)
or
%compute variance from the image;
sigma2 = var ( reshape ( Im,size (Im,1)*size (Im,2),1 ) )
%compute standard deviation;
sigma = std ( reshape ( Im,size (Im,1)*size (Im,2),1 ) )
```

In case, that the dispersion is skewed, thus has different dispersions on left and right side of the plot (from the point of view of the location parameter), it is recommended to use the Inter Quartile Range IQR as robust measure of scale. Usage of the IQR also removes the affects of the outliers to the distribution dispersion.

```
%compute inter quartile range;
Q = iqr (reshape (Im,size (Im,1) * size (Im,2),1 ) )
```

The value of the Inter Quartile Range IQR is usually bigger than the standard deviation σ.[5]

However, the basic statistical parameters do not cover the distributions that have more than one mode (multimodal), and also cannot describe the negative exponential distributions without location parameter. In that case, we are using different measure of the distribution, the entropy S. Entropy is a measure of unpredictability of information content:

[5] Approximately 1.349 times for Gaussian distribution

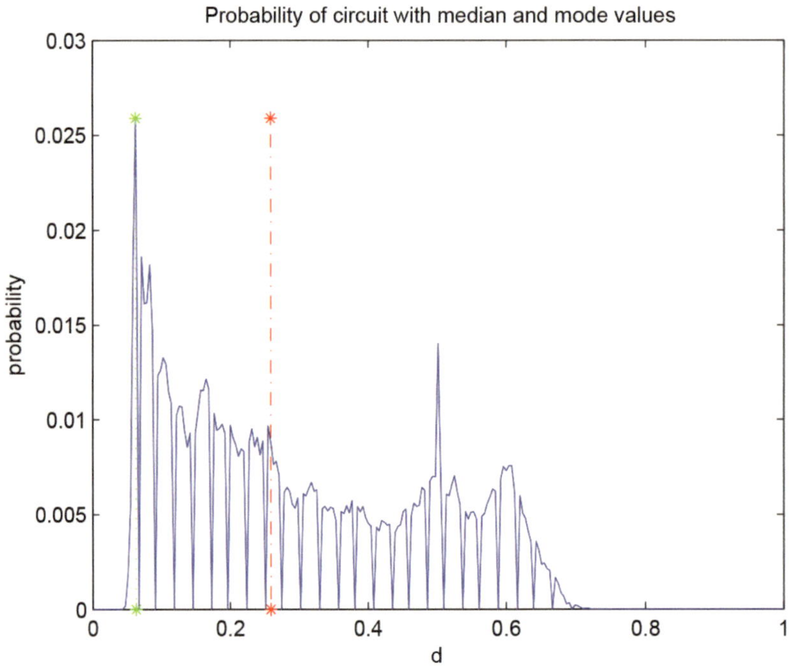

Figure 4. Media and mode values.

```
%compute entropy of the image;

S = entropy (Im)

or

%find where normalized histogram equals zero;

f = find (H==0);

%exclude zero values from computation;

Hx = H;

Hx(f) = [];

%compute entropy from the normalized histogram without zero values;

S = -sum (Hx.*log2 (Hx))
```

http://dx.doi.org/10.5772/63401

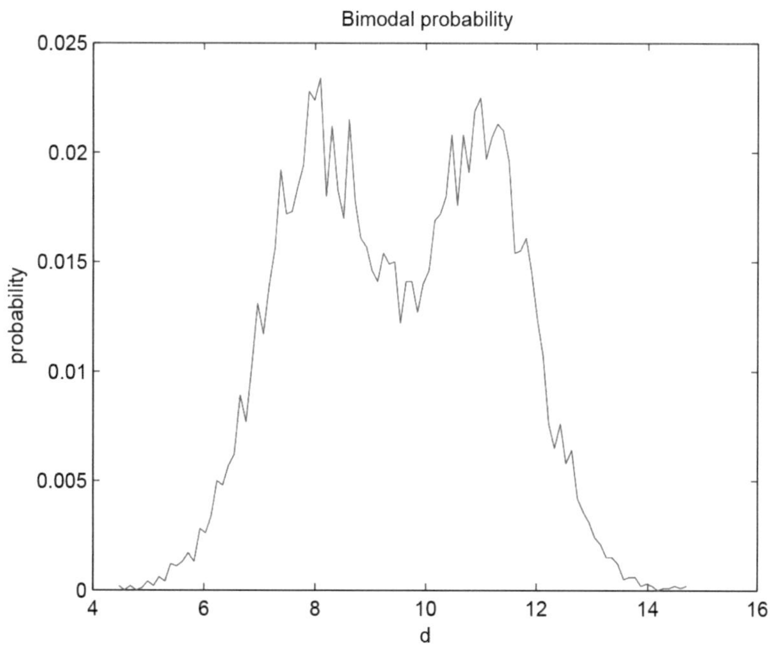

Figure 5. Bimodal distribution.

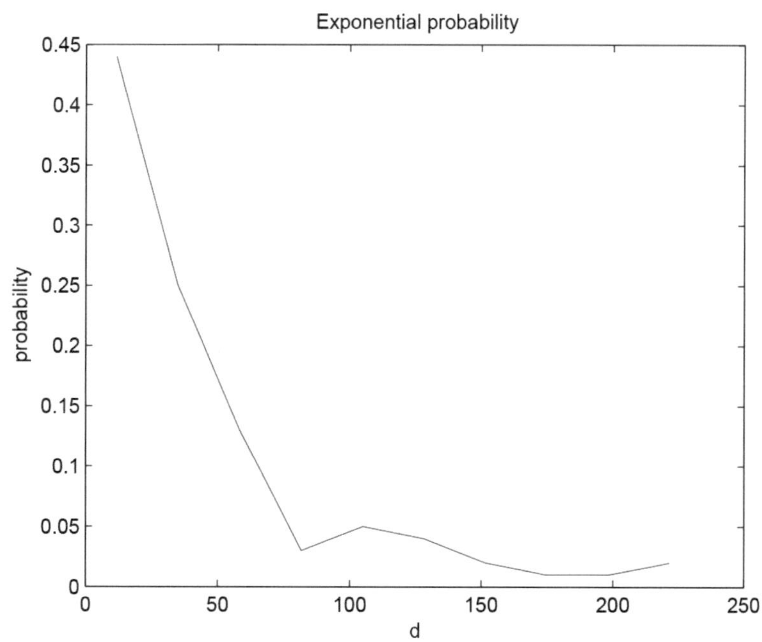

Figure 6. Exponential distribution.

Figure 7. Entropy of the circuit.

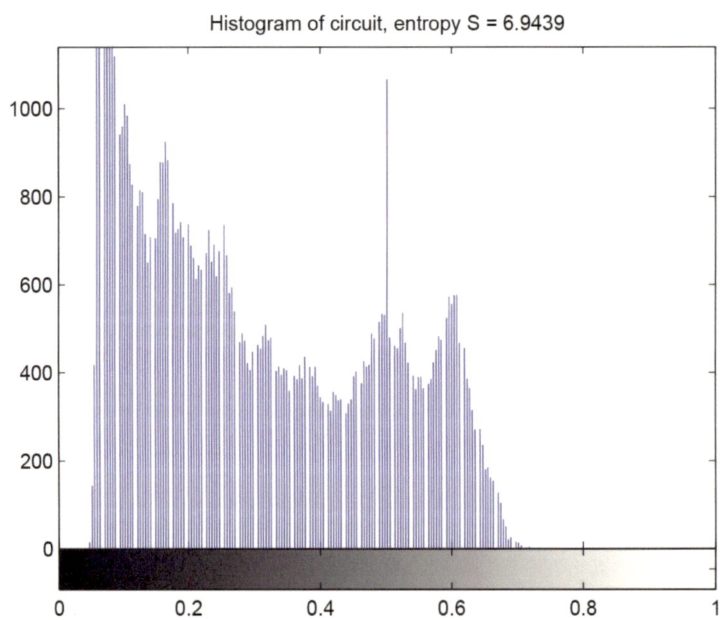

Figure 8. Entropy and histogram of the circuit.

http://dx.doi.org/10.5772/63401

Figure 9. Entropy of the Gaussian distributed intensities, $\mu = 0.5$, $\sigma = 0.1$.

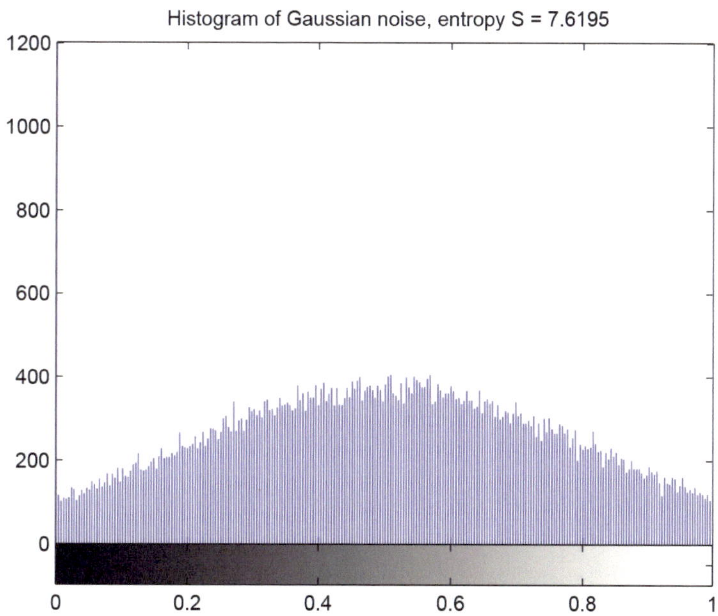

Figure 10. Entropy and histogram of the Gaussian distributed intensities, $\mu = 0.5$, $\sigma = 0.1$.

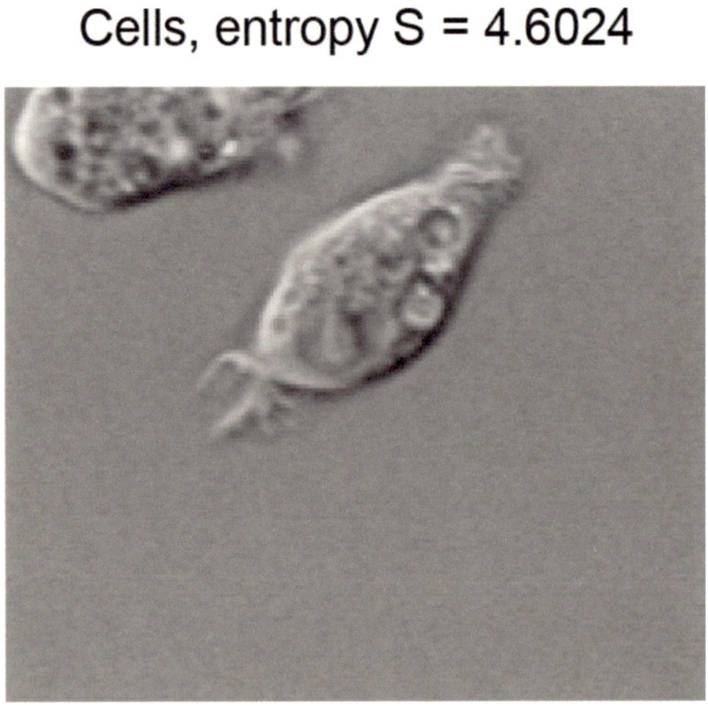

Figure 11. Entropy of the cells.

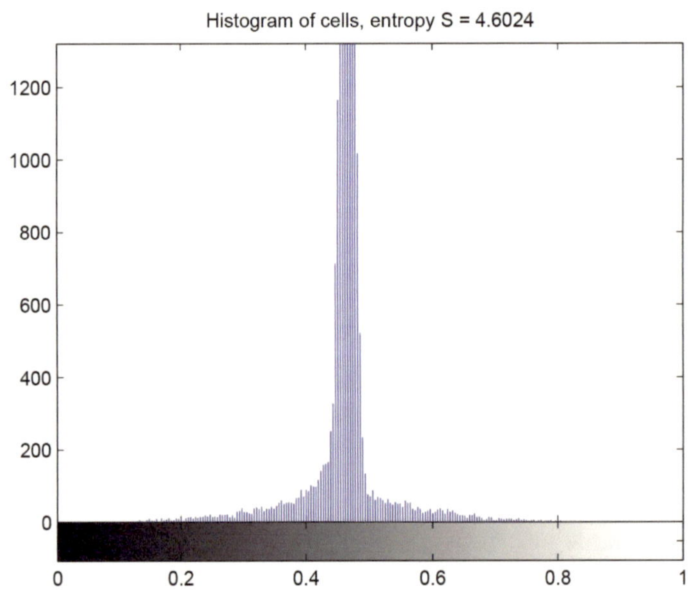

Figure 12. Entropy and histogram of the cells.

http://dx.doi.org/10.5772/63401

Figure 13. Entropy of the unique intensity value for all pixels $d = 0.5$.

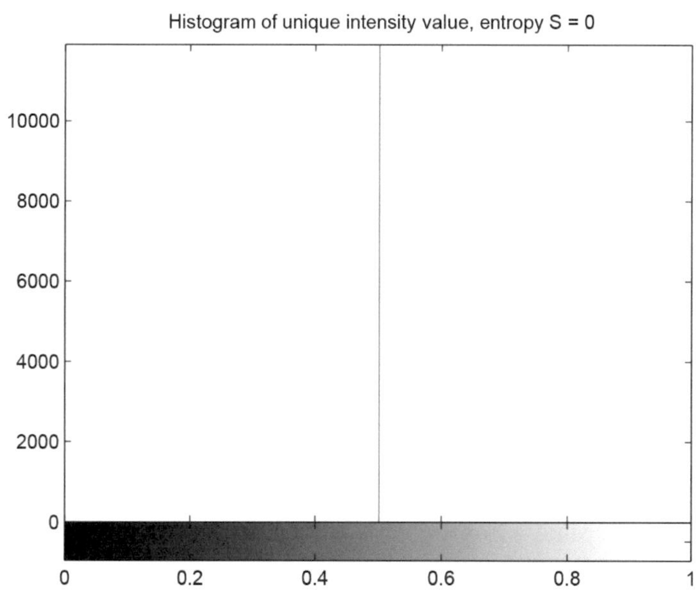

Figure 14. Entropy and histograms of the unique intensity value for all pixels $d = 0.5$.

There will be completely different values of entropy S for images with different distributions/histograms.

```
%show histogram and entropy of circuit image;
figure, imshow (Im);
title (['Circuit, entropy S = ', num2str(S) ] );
figure, imhist (Im);
title (['Histogram of circuit, entropy S = ', num2str(S) ] );
%show histogram and entropy of Gaussian noise;
J = imnoise (zeros (size (Im)), 'Gaussian',.5, .1);
SJ = entropy(J)
figure, imshow(J);
title (['Gaussian noise, entropy S = ',num2str (SJ)]);
figure, imhist(J);
title (['Histogram of Gaussian noise, entropy S = ',num2str(SJ) ] );
%show histogram and entropy of cell image;
C = imread ('cell.tif');
C = double (C) / 255;
SC = entropy (C)
figure, imshow (C);
title (['Cells, entropy S = ', num2str (SC) ] );
figure, imhist (C);
title (['Histogram of cells, entropy S = ',num2str (SC) ] );
%show histogram and entropy of unique value;
U = ones (size (Im))*.5;
SU = entropy (U)
figure, imshow (U);
title (['Unique intensity value, entropy S = ', num2str(SU) ] );
figure, imhist(U);
title (['Histogram of unique intensity value, entropy S = ',num2str(SU) ] );
```

Entropy is a number that somehow characterize the distribution:

http://dx.doi.org/10.5772/63401

Distribution	S
Circuit	6.9439
Gaussian	7.6278
Cells	4.6024
Unique	0
Bimodal	4.2245
Exponential	1.5928

3. Entropy

Let start with a reminder of the form of Shannon entropy from information theory with respect to the image analysis terminology. Any given normalized discrete probability distribution $H * h_1, h_2, \ldots, h_D *$ fulfills the condition:

$$h_d \geq 0$$
$$\sum_{d=1}^{D} h_d = 1. \tag{6}$$

Usually, in an intensity image, there exists an approximation of probability distribution given by the normalized histogram function $H(d)$. H is an intensity function that shows the count of the pixels $\Phi(i,j)$ with intensity equals to d independent on the image position (i,j) [3,4]. The histogram is normalized by the number of pixels to fulfill the conditions.[6]

More conditions are assumed when measuring the information. Information must be additive for two independent events a, b:

$$I(ab) = I(a) + I(b). \tag{7}$$

The information itself should be dependent only on the probability distribution or normalized histogram function in our cases. Equation **7** describes the conditions referred to. This equation is the well-known modified Cauchy's functional equation with unique solution $I(h) = -\kappa \times log_2(h)$. In statistical thermodynamic theory, the constant κ refers to the Boltzman constant [5]. In the Hartley measure of information, κ equals one [6,7]. Let us focus on Hartley measure. If different amounts of information occur with different probabilities, the total

[6] The 0th central moment again.

amount of information is the average of the individual information, weighted by the probabilities of their individual occurrences [7,8]. Therefore, the total amount of information is:

$$\sum_{d}(h_d I_d), \tag{8}$$

which leads us to the definition of Shannon entropy as a measure of information:

$$S = -\sum_{d} h_d log_2(h_d). \tag{9}$$

Thus, entropy is the sum of the individual information weighted by the probabilities of their occurrences.

In image analysis, the unknown probability distribution function of intensity values is approximated via histogram function $H(d)$: The histogram $H(d)$ has to be normalized to the total amount of pixels [9,10]. Shannon entropy allows information content of the whole image or just from the selected part of the image to be measured (**Figures 10** and **11**).

The entropy implemented in MATLAB function

S = entropy(Im)

is Shannon entropy.

4. Entropy filtration

Entropy allows all the information content of the entire image to be measured. However, when we change the number of pixels in the histogram computation, we obtain partial information content that is strictly dependent on the area entering the computation (**Figures 12** and **13**).

Entropy filtering is based on the replacement of pixel values in the image by values of entropy. Entropy is computed in a specified area, usually from the pixel's n-by-n symmetric neighborhood in the input image [4,11]. The shape of the neighborhood should be also defined by the users. The computed entropy is

$$F_{(i,j)} = -\sum h_{d,(se)} log_2(h_{d,(se)}), \tag{10}$$

where $se(i,j)$ is the pixel's $\Phi(i,j)$ neighborhood.

http://dx.doi.org/10.5772/63401

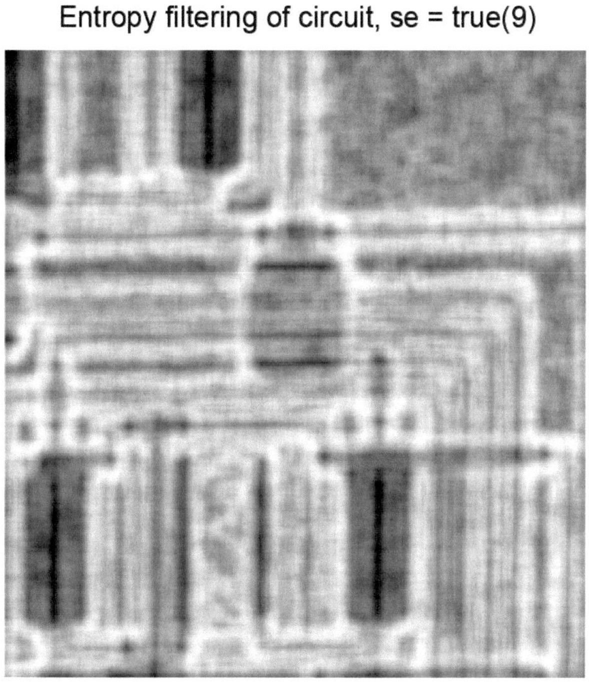

Figure 15. Entropy filtering of circuit image with $se = true(9)$.

Figure 16. Entropy filtering of circuit image with $se = true(41)$.

Figure 17. Entropy filtering of circuit image with $se = true(91)$.

It is clear that the output image (as computed by entropy filtration) is strongly dependent on the area selected. For small *se*, the local disturbances will be given sufficient weight, and the output image will be too noisy. On the other hand, too large an *se* value will not preserve details and the output image will be blurred. Therefore, the key question in the filtration method is how to select a suitable neighborhood. *se* selection is always a compromise between a noisy or blurry image. Of course, filtration can be very useful for decreasing the area and thus allowing further analysis (**Figures 14** and **15**).

```
%compute entropy filtering with small structure element;
F = entropyfilt (Im);
figure, imshow (F,[]);
title ('Entropy filtering of circuit, se = true(9)');
%compute entropy filtering with middle structure element;
F = entropyfilt (Im,true (41));
figure, imshow (F,[]);
title ('Entropy filtering of circuit, se = true(41)');
%compute entropy filtering with large structure element;
F = entropyfilt (Im,true(91));
figure, imshow (F,[]);
title ('Entropy filtering of circuit, se = true(91)');
```

http://dx.doi.org/10.5772/63401

5. Entropy thresholding and segmentation

Thresholding is a time cheap method searching for point in the intensity histogram H for separating image into the objects related to the real objects. It takes from the image parts that corresponding to the threshold parameter(s). Automatic threshold selection using the entropy is based on the maximization of entropy segmentation. The histogram function $H(d)$ is separated into two parts, A and B, iteratively in d. For both parts, the Shannon's entropies are computed

$$S_A = -\sum_{w=1}^{w=k} h_w log_2(h_w) \tag{11}$$

$$S_B = -\sum_{w=k}^{w=D} h_w log_2(h_w), k = d_2 : d_{max-1}. \tag{12}$$

Then, the entropy of part A and B (taken together) is computed as

$$S_V = -log_2(H_A) - log_2(H_B) - \frac{S(A)}{H_A} - \frac{S(B)}{H_B}. \tag{13}$$

A threshold value is set for d, where SV_k is maximized [12,13]. This method uses the global histogram function; therefore, it is not sensitive to the random noise contribution and successfully removes the noise. However, the use of thresholds also ignores local changes in the background, illumination, and non-uniformity. For images with different conditions within the scene, thresholds generally produce loses and artifacts. The use of thresholds without any previous preprocessing, for example,, light normalization, is applicable only with objects that are well separable from the background. Automatic segmentation techniques [3,4,12,14,15] are very powerful tools under easily-separable conditions (**Figures 16** and **17**).

```
HA = zeros(size(H)); %empty lower histogram;

HB = zeros(size(H)); %empty upper histogram;

%empty cumulative distribution function;

C = zeros(size(H));

%cumulative distribution function;

C(1) = H(1);

for k = 2:length(H),

C(k) = C(k-1) + H(k);

end;
```

```
C = double(C);
%cycle through intensity levels;
for k = 1:length(H),
if C(k) > 0, %only for positive cumulation;
for w = 1:k, %from beginning till now;
if H(w) > 0, %only for positive histogram
%compute the lower histogram value
HA(k) = HA(k) - ( H(w)/C(k)) * log2(H(w)/C(k) );
end; %endif;
end; %endfor;
end; %endif;
if ( 1-C(k) ) > 0, %only for positive cumulation residuals;
for w = k + 1:length(H); %from now till end;
if H(w) > 0, %only for positive histogram
%compute the lower histogram value
HB(k) = HB(k) - ( H(w)/(1-C(k))) * log2(H(w)/(1-C(k)) );
end; %endif;
end; %endfor
end; %endif
end; %endfor
%locate the maxima for joined histograms
[co, kde] = max(HA+HB);
%selet threshold
Th = d( kde-1 )
%segment image
II = im2bw(Im, Th);
figure, imshow(II);
title(['Entropy segmentation of circuit, Th = ', num2str(Th)]);
```

The value d where the entropy SV is maximized represents the threshold for segmentation of the image (**Figure 18**).

http://dx.doi.org/10.5772/63401

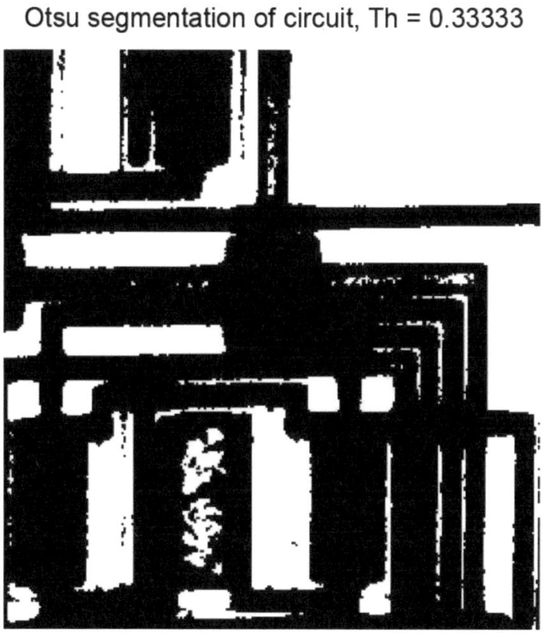

Figure 19. Segmentation of circuit image by Otsu.

Figure 18. Segmentation of circuit image by entropy.

5.1. Grayscale thresholding

The entropy segmentation gives similar results with the Otsu thresholding. Otsu gray level thresholding is a nonparametric method of automatic threshold selection for image segmentation also from the normalized intensity histogram $H(d)$. For separating histogram into two classes, the between class variance is maximized:

```
%cycle through the histogram;

for T=2:length(H)-1,

w(1) = sum( H(1:T) ); %probability of first class

u(1) = sum( H(1:T) .* d(1:T) ); %class mean

%protection against zero;

if w(1) == 0,

u(1) = 0;

else

%class mean recomputation;

u(1) = u(1)/w(1);

end;

w(2) = sum( H( (T+1):end) ); %probability of second class

u(2) = sum( H( (T+1):end) .* d( (T+1):end) ); %class mean

%protection against zero;

if w(2) == 0,

u(2) = 0;

else

%class mean recomputation;

u(2) = u(2)/w(2);

end;

%between class variance;

ut = w*u';

sigmaB(T) = w(1)*(u(1)-ut)^2 + w(2)*(u(2)-ut)^2;

end;

%find maximal between class variance

[e,r] = max(sigmaB);
```

http://dx.doi.org/10.5772/63401

```
TTh(1) = d(r); %set Threshold

or

TTh = graythresh(Im); %compute threshold;

IO = im2bw(Im, TTh); %segment image;

figure, imshow(IO);

title (['Otsu segmentation of circuit, Th = ', num2str(TTh)]);
```

6. Point Information Gain

The most interesting is the point information gain (*PIG*) which asks the question: How important is one pixel for the whole image or for the selected part? In other words, is the occurrence of the value of one single pixel a surprise? It is predictable that for value of background pixels it will not carry a lot of information, if we discard one of them. On the other hand, the objects, especially if they are complicated in structure, will increase the entropy on their position. Shannon equation evaluate total amount of the information entropy from the whole histogram. Let evaluate the normalized image histogram $H(d)$ and compute the Shannon information entropy S:

$$S = -\sum_{d} H_d log_2(H_d), \tag{14}$$

To investigate the contribution of one single pixel with intensity value v to the total entropy, we need to evaluate the second histogram $G(d)$ which is created without this investigated pixel:

$$\begin{aligned} g(i,j,d) &= q(i,j,d), if\ d \neq v; \\ g(i,j,d) &= q(i,j,d) - 1, if\ d = v. \end{aligned} \tag{15}$$

This time we discard the value v of the center investigated $\Phi(i,j)$ from the computation, but only once.

One single pixel of intensity value d will only decrease the histogram value $g(d)$ on its intensity position d. Then, the histogram is again normalized. The probability of intensity value d is slightly lower than the probability $H(d)$ of the primary normalized histogram (with all pixels). The other probabilities $g(d)$, where d is not the value of investigated pixel, are slightly higher than the probability $H(d)$ of the primary normalized histogram (with all pixels). Then, in the second computation of entropy E, computed from the modified normalized histogram $G(r)$:

$$E = -\sum_{d} g_d log_2(g_d), \tag{16}$$

the individual information $log2(g(d))$ as well as their weights $g(d)$ differs according to the computation of whole entropy S. Therefore, we obtained two different entropy values S and E. Entropy S represents the whole measure of information in original image. Entropy E represents the measure of information in the image without the investigated pixel. The difference *PIG* [16]:

$$PIG = S - E, \tag{17}$$

refers to the difference between the entropy of the two histograms, and therefore also difference between the entropy of the two images (the first one with contains our investigated pixel $\Phi(i, j)$ and the second one without this investigated pixel). Recall that the both histograms H and G were normalized, and therefore, any difference in the number of pixels in the images is immaterial. Difference *PIG* represents either the entropy contribution of pixel $\Phi(i, j)$ or the contribution of the value of the pixel $\Phi(i, j)$ to the information content of the whole image. The transformation of each image pixel $\Phi(i, j)$ value to its contribution to the whole image via equation **17** represents the measure of the information carried by that pixel, the Point Information Gain (*PIG*). Repeated computation 17 for every single pixel of the image transforms the original image into the entropy map: the image that shows contribution of every pixel to the whole information content of the image (**Figures 19** and **20**).

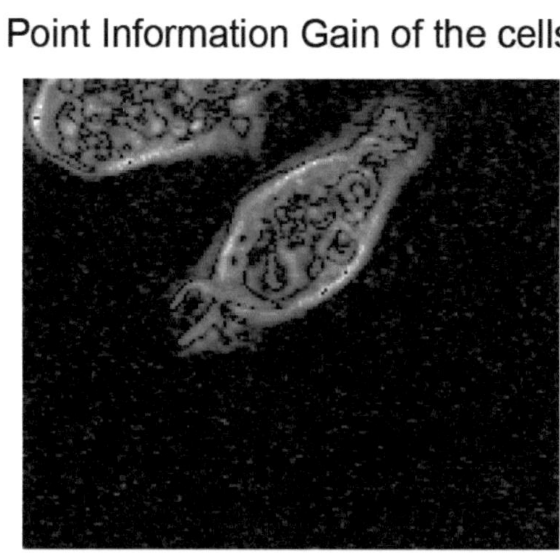

Figure 20. Point information gain of grayscale image cells.

It is predictable that the values of background pixels will not carry a lot of information, even if we discard one of them. On the other, the objects, especially if they are complicated in structure, will increase the entropy in their immediate area. According to the information

http://dx.doi.org/10.5772/63401

theory, the object occurrence produces a bigger surprise than does background occurrence, and the *PIG* quantifies this effect. For this reason, the details in the image are preserved: they are the surprise. For the same reason, random noise is removed: We always know it is presented, and no surprise occurs (**Figures 21** and **22**).

Figure 21. Point Information Gain of grayscale image cameraman.

Figure 22. Point Information Gain of grayscale image circuit.

```
%load images(s)
C = imread('cell.tif');
%C = imread('cameraman.tif');
%C = imread('circuit.tif');
C = double(C)/255;
S = entropy(C); %compute entropy
%compute average probability of one pixel
pomo = 1/numel(C);
[H,d] = imhist(C); %compute histogram
H = H./sum(H); %normalize histogram
IE = zeros(size(C)); %empty result image;
%cycle through intensity levels;
for k=1:length(H);
%precompute second histograms;
G = H;
%remove pixel contribution;
if G(k)>=pomo,
G(k) = G(k) - pomo;
end;
%protection against zero;
f =find(G==0);
G(f) = [];
G = G./sum(G); %renormalization;
%entropy without pixel;
E(k) = -sum(G.*log2(G));
%point information gain;
PIG(k) = S-E(k);
%assign pig to pixels;
f = find(C==k/255);
IE(f) = PIG(k);
```

http://dx.doi.org/10.5772/63401

```
end;

figure, imshow(IE,[]);

title('Point Information Gain of the cells.');

%title('Point Information Gain of the cameraman.');

%title('Point Information Gain of the circuit.');
```

7. Conclusion and discussion

For those, who are interested in the entropy processing, the things are little bit more complicated.

PIG approach is dependent only on pixel $\Phi(i,j)$, there is no information about pixel's position. Therefore, the area *se* of the histogram function computation could include not the whole image, but only some selected area around the investigated pixel. The *se* could be the whole row and whole column in which the pixel is located. Difference $PIG = S - E$ in this case refers to the difference between the information content of the two crosses. Difference *PIG* represents either the entropy contribution of pixel $\Phi(i,j)$ or the contribution of the value of pixel $\Phi(i,j)$ to the cross. Even more derivation from the original *PIG* algorithm were developed recently [17–19].

There also exist different entropies, not only Shannon, namely Tsallis-Havrda-Charvát and Rényi definitions at least. The Rényi entropy:

$$R_\alpha = \frac{1}{1-\alpha}\log_2\left(\sum_d h_d^\alpha\right), \tag{18}$$

is the generalization of the Shannon entropy. For the $\alpha = 0$, the Rényi entropy equals Shannon ($R_0 = S$).

The evaluation of entropy has heavy computational burden; therefore, it is recommended to use parallelization on GPU. For the processing of the color images, it is usual to tread each color channel independently like a grayscale image.

Overall, the entropy is a representative parameter of the image and there is still a lot of potential in its usage for processing and analysis.

The code presented in this chapter could be downloaded at: https://www.mathworks.com/matlabcentral/fileexchange/55493-information-entropy.

Acknowledgements

This work was supported by the Ministry of Education, Youth, and Sports of the Czech Republic - projects "CENAKVA" (No. CZ.1.05/2.1.00/01.0024) and "CENAKVA II" (No. LO1205 under the NPU I program).

Author details

Jan Urban

Address all correspondence to: urbanj@frov.jcu.cz

Laboratory of Signal and Image Processing, Institute of Complex Systems, South Bohemian Research Center of Aquaculture and Biodiversity of Hydocenoses, FFPW, USB, Zámek, Nové Hrady, Czech Republic

References

[1] Katajama, M., Orešic⌣, M. Data processing for mass spectrometry-based metabolomics. Journal of Chromatography A. 1158:318–328, 2007.

[2] Pearson, K. Contributions to the mathematical theory of evolution. II. Skew variation in homogeneous material. Philosophical Transactions of the Royal Society A: Mathematical, Physical and Engineering Sciences. 186:343–414, 1985.

[3] Sonka M., Hlavac V., Boyle R. ĎImage processing, analysis and machine vision. Brooks/ Cole Publishing Company, 1999.

[4] Gonzales R. C., Woods R. E. ĎDigital Image Processing. Addison-Wesley Publishing Company, 1992.

[5] Boublik T. Statistical thermodynamic. Academia, 1996.

[6] Hatley J. V. Bell System Technical Journal. 7:535, 1928

[7] Jizba P., Arimitsu T. The world according to Renyi: thermodynamics of multifractal systems. Annals of Physics. 312:17–59, 2004.

[8] Shannon C. E. A mathematical theory of communication. Bell System Technical Journal. 27:379–423 and 623–656, 1948.

[9] Demirkaya O., Asyali M. H., Sahoo P. K. Image processing with MATLAB: Applications in medicine and biology. CRC Press, 2009.

[10] Nixon M., Aguado A. Feature extraction & image processing. Academic Press, 2002.

[11] Moddemeijer R. On estimation of entropy and mutual information of continuous distributions. Signal Processing. 16(3):233–246, 1989.

[12] Pun T. A new method for grey level thresholding using the entropy of the histogram. Signal Processing. 2:223–237, 1980.

[13] Tzvetkov P., Petrov G., Iliev P. Multidimensional dynamic scene analysis for video security applications. IEEE Computer Science' 2006, Istanbul.

[14] Beucher S. Applications of mathematical morphology in material sciences: a review of recent developments. International Metallography Conference, pp. 41–46, 1995.

[15] Otsu N. A Threshold Selection Method from Gray-Level Histogram. IEEE Transactions on Systems, Man, and Cybernetics 9:62–66, 1979.

[16] Urban J., Vanek J., Stys D. Preprocessing of microscopy images via Shannon's entropy. In Proceedings of Pattern Recognition and Information Processing: pp.183–187, Minsk, Belarus, ISBN 978-985-476-704-8, 2009.

[17] Rychtarikova R., Nahlik T., Smaha R., Urban J., Stys D. Jr., Cisar P., Stys D. Multifractality in imaging: application of information entropy for observation of inner dynamics inside of an unlabeled living cell in bright-field microscopy. In ISCS14, Sanayei et al. (eds.), Springer, pp. 261–267, 2015.

[18] Štys D., Urban J., Vane⌣k J., Císar⌣ P.. Analysis of biological time-lapse microscopic experiment from the point of view of the information theory, Micron, S0968-4328(10)00026-0, 2010.

[19] Štys D., Vane⌣k J., Náhlík T., Urban J., Císar⌣ P.. The cell monolayer trajectory from the system state point of view. Molecular Biosystems, 7:2824–2833, 2011.

Chapter 3

MATLAB for All Steps of Dynamic Vibration Test of Structures

Abdurrahman Sahin and Alemdar Bayraktar

Additional information is available at the end of the chapter

http://dx.doi.org/10.5772/63232

Abstract

With the recent advances in computer technology and digital simulation software, it is now possible to rapidly and accurately build computer models for complex linear and nonlinear dynamic systems. MATLAB is a unique system that can be used for structural and earthquake engineering problems. This study presents MATLAB tools developed for numerical process of all steps of dynamic vibration test of structures. The functions of the tools are processing the signals obtained from forced and ambient vibration tests of structures, determining the dynamic characteristics of structural systems, and automatically updating the analytical finite element (FE) models. The software group is composed of three programs named as SignalCAD, ModalCAD, and FemUP. The SignalCAD program is developed for processing raw measured data obtained from forced and ambient vibration tests of engineering structures. The ModalCAD program is developed for dynamic characteristic identification and validation procedure. The peak picking method, complex exponential method, and polyreference time domain method are used for modal identification process. The FemUP program is developed for automatically updating the numerical models of structures compared to modal testing results. Each program has a unique graphical user interface and is designed as user friendly. The possibilities of the programs are demonstrated with the model vibration test of a steel cantilever beam. The obtained results are compared to the analytical model, and the FE model is automatically updated, whereas the experimental model is considered as the reference model. Finally, it is seen that MATLAB can be used as a scientific programming platform in all vibration test and modal analysis applications.

Keywords: MATLAB, SignalCAD, ModalCAD, FemUP, vibration test of structures, experimental modal analysis, operational modal analysis, FE model updating

INTECH
open science | open minds

© 2016 The Author(s). Licensee InTech. This chapter is distributed under the terms of the Creative Commons Attribution License (http://creativecommons.org/licenses/by/3.0), which permits unrestricted use, distribution, and reproduction in any medium, provided the original work is properly cited. (cc) BY

1. Introduction

The recent developments in computer technology give us the opportunity to construct full-scale models of all kinds of structural systems. Advanced analysis methods can be used to determine the dynamic characteristics of the structures and to simulate the structural behaviors. Although the numerical methods have reached to an advanced level, experimental validations are still necessary to obtain realistic models. Full-scale vibration tests are one of the most reliable and widely used validation techniques. The dynamic vibration tests can be used for dynamic characteristic identification of all structural systems [1–5]. The determined dynamic characteristics are natural vibration frequencies, damping ratios, and mode shapes. These parameters may be used to validate and update the numerical models [6–9].

A complete structural evaluation process, including numerical and experimental studies, consists of some procedures. First, the numerical model of the structural system is constructed. The critical points for vibration test are determined and the structure system is equipped with the accelerometers. Then, the vibration test is performed via artificial or natural excitation sources. Generally, ambient vibration tests are carried out in large civil engineering structures, as it is not easy to record natural exciting sources in real time. After the vibration tests are completed, the raw measured acceleration records are first filtered to clean noise from the signal. Then, the data are processed and spectral functions are produced. These functions are frequency response function (FRF), cross-power spectrum (CPS), power spectral density (PSD), auto power spectrum (APS), and spectrogram. The system identification methods are applied to the produced spectral functions, and the dynamic characteristics of the structure are extracted. The obtained dynamic parameters are natural vibration frequency, damping ratio, and modal vectors of the structure of interest. These parameters are experimental dynamic characteristics of the structures and they are used for validating or updating the numerical models. In the model updating process, all parameters, including material properties, boundary conditions, stiffness distribution, connection details, and damaged parts over the structure, may be considered and the optimal numerical model is obtained, showing the closest behavior to the experimental model.

2. Forced and ambient vibration tests of structures

The dynamic vibration tests on structures are generally subdivided into two groups: (a) forced vibration test and (b) ambient vibration test. In the forced vibration test, the structure is usually excited by artificial means. The excitation force and the response of the structure are recorded at the same time and the spectral functions are developed using these data. In the ambient vibration test, the structure is excited by natural effects, such as wind load and traffic load. The response of the structure is recorded under operational conditions and the spectral functions are developed using these data. The dynamic parameters of the structures are determined from the produced spectral functions.

The modal parameter estimation stage of the forced vibration test is called the experimental modal analysis or input-output modal analysis. On the contrary, the modal parameter estimation stage is called operational modal analysis or output-only modal analysis if the vibration test is carried out under operational conditions (ambient vibration test).

The experimental and operational modal analyses of structures are carried out in four distinct steps. In the first step, data are collected from the test structure. In the second step, digital signal processing is applied to collected raw measured data and the spectral functions are produced. In the third step, modal parameters (natural frequencies, damping ratios, and mode shapes) are extracted and these parameters are visualized and validated. In the last step, the numerical finite element (FE) model is updated by comparing to the experimental model. In the first part, the forced or ambient vibration test is carried out and data are collected from the structural system. This stage is the experimental procedure. The remaining stages are computational procedures and require the development of mathematical algorithms and programming tools. In this study, the developed tools in MATLAB platform for these numerical procedures are presented.

3. Digital signal processing for vibration test of structures

The first step of computational procedure is digital signal processing. In this stage, signals are converted from the time domain to the frequency domain usually through the Fourier transform. In the forced vibration test, FRFs are used to estimate the dynamic properties of a structure. Excitation force and response accelerations are used to obtain these functions. In large-scale civil engineering structures (such as bridges and towers), the structure is under excitation of natural sources such as traffic load and wind load. It is difficult to measure the input to the structure under the operational conditions. The CPSs may be used for output-only modal analysis. The response signals are used to obtain these functions.

3.1. Development of digital signal processing tool

The SignalCAD [10] program is developed for digital signal processing and may be used for forced and ambient vibration tests of structures. In the forced vibration test analysis process, first excitation forces and response signals are collected from the structure as shown in **Figure 1a**. The SignalCAD program reads these records and apply fast Fourier transform (FFT) to these signals using MATLAB Signal Processing Toolbox [11]. Then, coherence functions between input and output signals are generated.

In the ambient vibration spectral analysis process, the acceleration records are collected from the structure as shown in **Figure 1b**. These records may be single signals or signal groups. The ambient vibration test requires more time; therefore, the record time may be much longer. The collected signal may be divided into small signals and the signal series are processed in the system. The SignalCAD program reads these signal groups and applies FFT to these signals using MATLAB Signal Processing Toolbox [11]. The spectrum series, such as CPSs, PSDs, APSs, and spectrograms, are produced. The singular value decomposition (SVD) or averaging methods are applied to the produced spectrum series and the single spectra for each channel are produced. This process is repeated for every channel that collects signal from the structure.

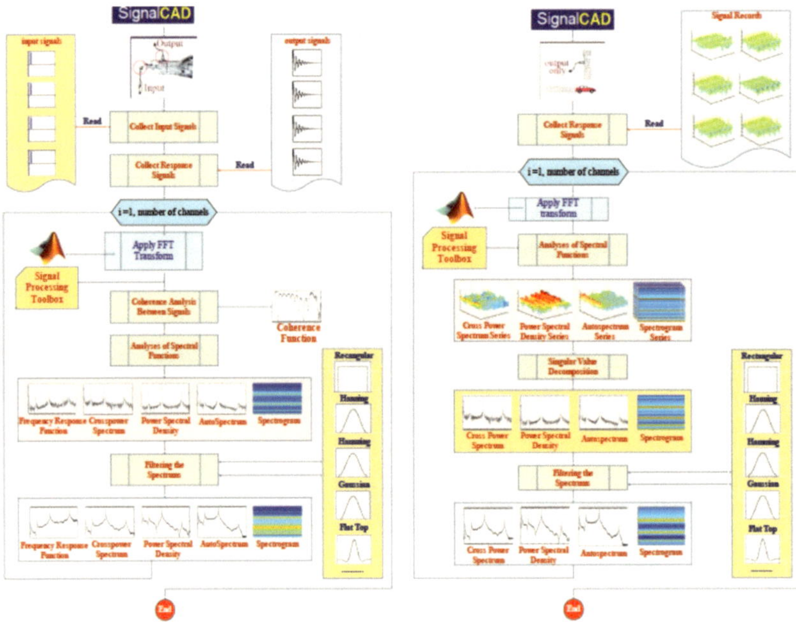

a) Forced vibration test b) Ambient vibration test

Figure 1. Flow chart of digital signal processing procedure with SignalCAD [10]: (a) forced vibration test and (b) ambient vibration test.

As can be seen in **Figure 1**, the leakage errors occur in spectral functions because of the FFT. Windowing functions need be applied to the spectra to eliminate these errors. In SignalCAD, some windowing alternatives may be applied. The main window of SignalCAD program is presented in **Figure 2**.

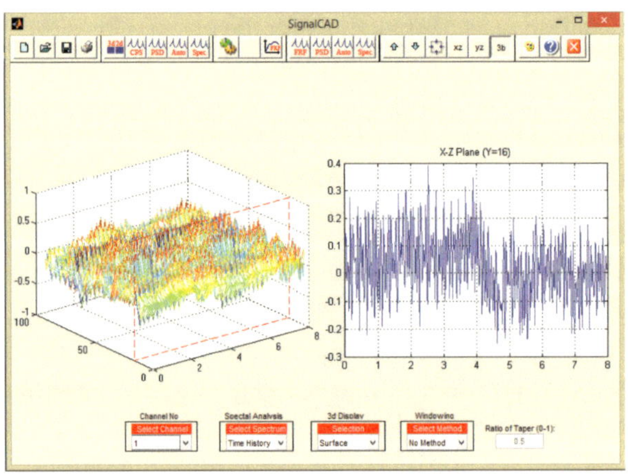

Figure 2. SignalCAD program main window [10].

http://dx.doi.org/10.5772/63232

4. Dynamic characteristic identification

After the collected raw measured acceleration records are processed and spectral functions are produced, dynamic characteristics are extracted from these spectra. MATLAB System Identification Toolbox [12] offers mathematical functions for system identification studies. It identifies time domain models from the data and can be used in modal identification studies. However, it is clear that some postprocessing is needed for the purpose of dynamic characteristic identification of structure. New functions need to be prepared to extract modal parameters from the spectral functions, to produce stabilization diagrams, to visualize

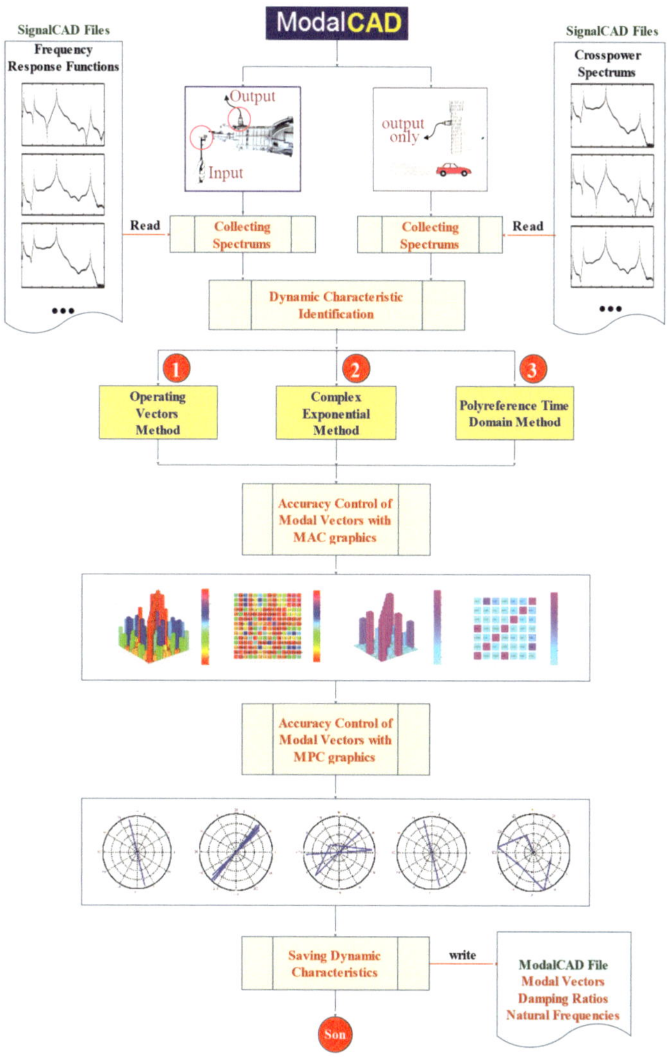

Figure 3. Flow chart of the ModalCAD program [13].

structure's geometry and mode shapes, and to evaluate modal validation tools. From this overview, about 250 new functions have been developed depending on the solution methods and are used together with general System Identification Toolbox functions.

4.1. Development of system identification tool

The ModalCAD [13] program is developed for system identification and may be used for the experimental and operational modal analyses of structures. In ModalCAD, three modal identification methods are used. First is the peak picking method or half-power band method in frequency domain. It may be called the operating vectors (OV) method. The second one is the complex exponential (CE) method in time domain and the polyreference time domain (PTD) method. The detailed explanations of these methods can be found in [13]. The flow chart of the program is given in **Figure 3** and the main window of ModalCAD is presented in **Figure 4**.

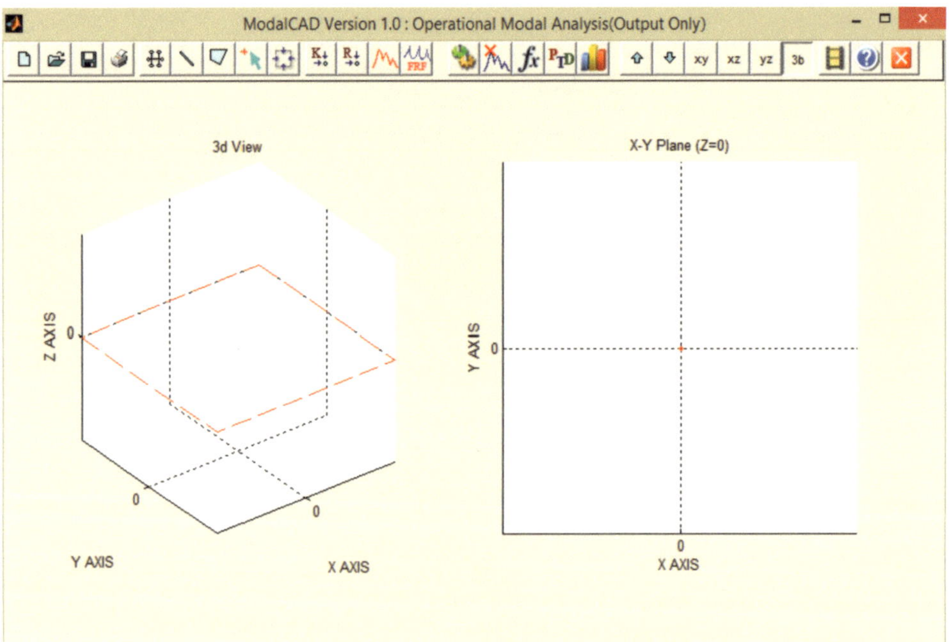

Figure 4. ModalCAD program main window [13].

5. FE model updating procedure

First, the FE model is developed using the initially estimated values for the unknown model parameters. FE modal analysis is then carried out to obtain the FE modal data. ANSYS [14] or any other advanced FE codes may be used for analytical FE modal analysis. For the forced or ambient vibration test of the structure, the optimum points for the placement of sensors are chosen and test data are recorded. The measured raw data are processed with the SignalCAD software. In this process, FRFs are produced for experimental modal analysis and CPSs are produced for operational modal analysis. The experimental and operational modal analyses are then carried out using the OV, CE, and PTD methods to get the modal parameters via the ModalCAD software. For model updating, the modal frequencies and modal vectors are exported from ModalCAD to FemUP. The most common way to compare the analytical and experimental mode shapes is the use of modal assurance criterion (MAC), and it is obtained as follows:

$$\mathrm{MAC}_{\mathrm{j}} = \frac{\left|\Phi_{\mathrm{aj}}^{\mathrm{T}}\Phi_{\mathrm{ej}}\right|^{2}}{\left(\Phi_{\mathrm{aj}}^{\mathrm{T}}\Phi_{\mathrm{ej}}\right)\left(\Phi_{\mathrm{ej}}^{\mathrm{T}}\Phi_{\mathrm{aj}}\right)} \tag{1}$$

where Φ_{aj} is the analytical modal vector that has been paired with the jth experimental modal vector Φ_{ej}. The value of the MAC is bound between 0 and 1. Higher value indicates better correlation between modal vectors. If the MAC value is zero, it is understood that there is not any correlation between the modal vectors. If the MAC value is 1, the highest correlation is obtained.

5.1. Development of computational FE model updating tool

The FemUP [15] program is developed for computational FE model updating automatically. It uses MATLAB Optimization Toolbox [16] for the optimal FE model determination process. A constrained optimization is performed using a sequential quadratic programming (SQP) algorithm. The optimization algorithm is supplied with start values, bounds, constraints, and optimization criterion. The optimization criterion chosen, which is to be minimized, is the sum of the differences in natural frequency within each correlated mode pair. Constraints are used on the correlation between analytical and experimental mode shapes using the diagonal values of the MAC matrix.

The FemUP program can read ANSYS FE models and run this code in batch mode using ANSYS Parametric Design Language. Because natural frequencies and mode shapes must be calculated many times during the updating procedure, ANSYS and MATLAB interact with each other. The objective and constraint functions, taking advantage of MATLAB's ability of reading and writing ASCII files, are used to transfer data between the two different software packages. The main window of FemUP is presented in **Figure 5**. The objective function in FemUP is defined as a sum of experimental and theoretical frequency differences. The constraint function, which includes nonlinear inequality constraints in FemUP, exports a vector that consists of the differences between MAC limit selected by the user and calculated MAC values.

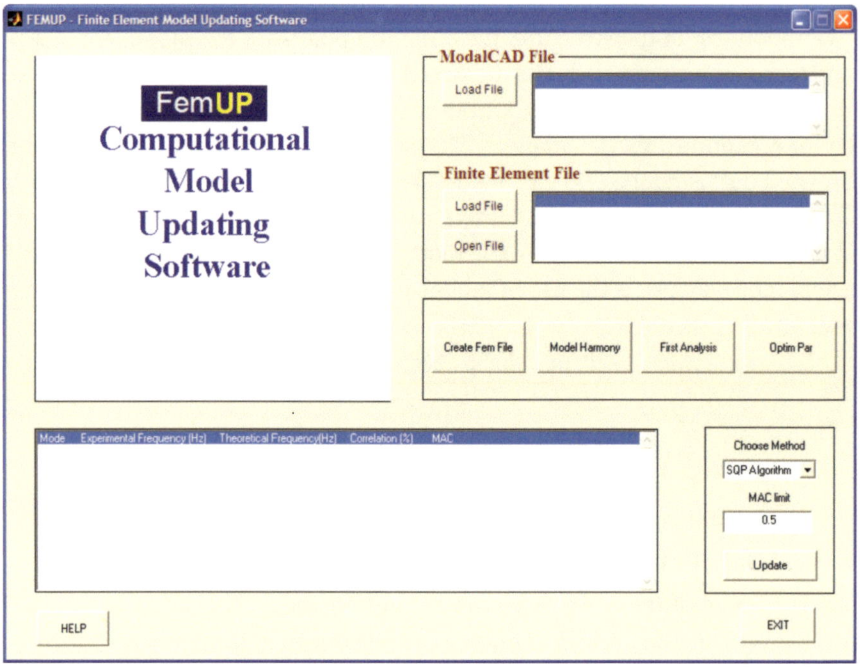

Figure 5. FemUP program main window [15].

6. Interaction between developed tools

As indicated previously, all tools have an interaction with each other and the data developed by a tool are used by others. The raw measured acceleration records are processed with SignalCAD and spectra are produced. The FRFs are produced for input-output modal analysis and the CPSs are produced for output-only modal analysis. These spectra are introduced to ModalCAD and dynamics characteristics are extracted from these spectral functions. The produced dynamic characteristics are input data of the FemUP program. The numerical model produced with ANSYS is also introduced to FemUP and numerical and experimental models are compared to each other. In the comparison process, the summation of natural frequency differences forms the objective function and coherence between modal vectors forms the constraint function. The MAC matrix is used to understand the agreement between experimental and numerical mode shapes. If there is a nontrivial difference between natural frequencies, the system parameters are automatically updated under the defined limits. After the automatic model updating process, the difference is checked again. The model updating process is repeated until the minimal difference is obtained, while the MAC values are about one. Finally, the updated model is presented. The interaction details between developed tools are presented in **Figure 6**.

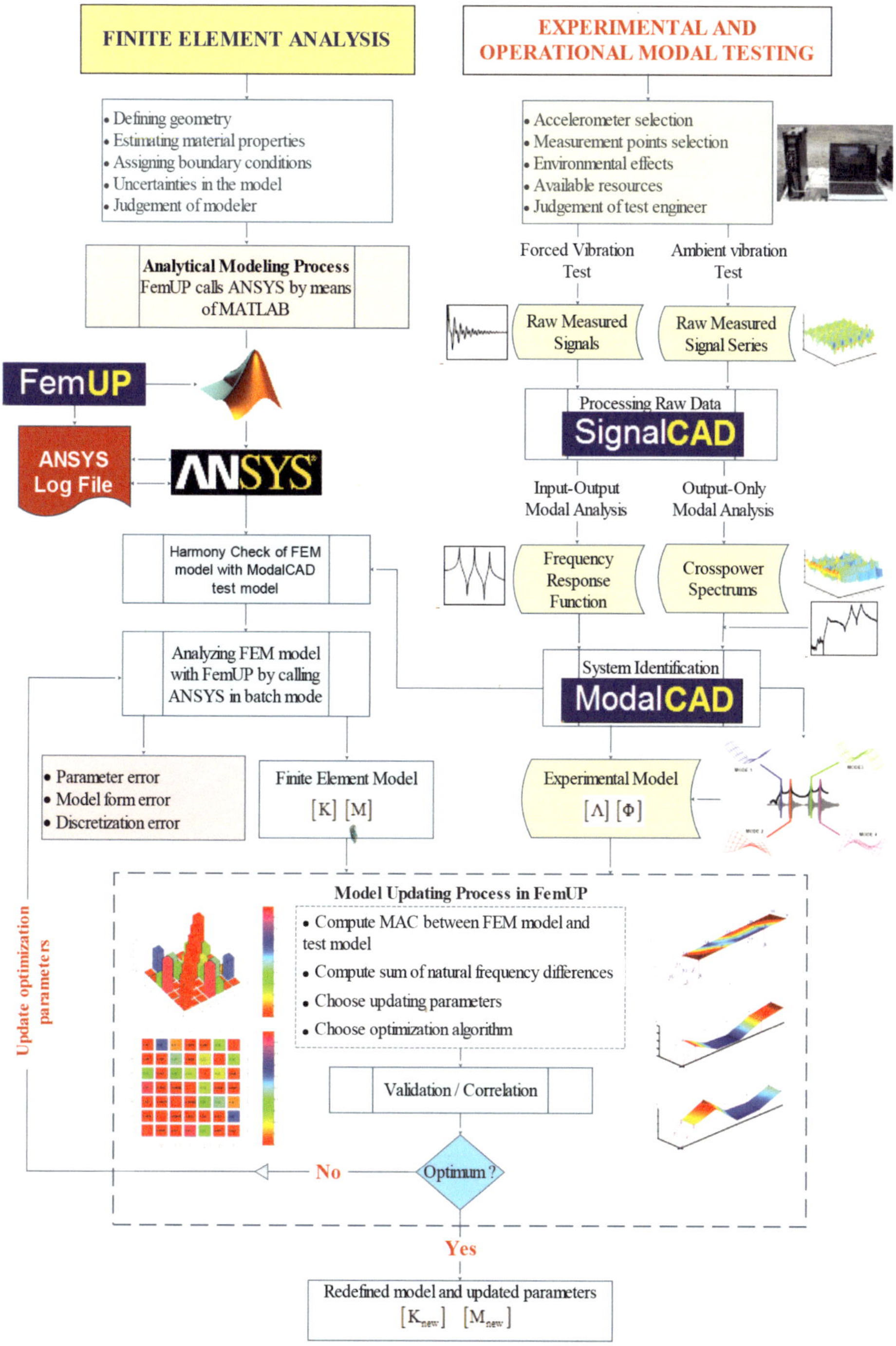

Figure 6. Interaction flow chart between MATLAB programs developed for signal processing, system identification, and FE model updating of structures [15].

7. Numerical application

A simple vibration test is carried out and the capabilities of developed tools are evaluated for a complete vibration test process. The example contains forced and ambient vibration tests, digital signal processing, modal parameter estimation, and automatic FE model updating of a steel cantilever beam model.

7.1. Vibration test and modal analysis

The vibration tests of the steel cantilever beam model are carried out. The beam model and test process are shown in **Figure 7**. The accelerometers are located on the surface of the model. The channel numbers and directions are given in **Figure 7**.

Figure 7. Cantilever beam model, acceleration set-up, and excitation with a hummer.

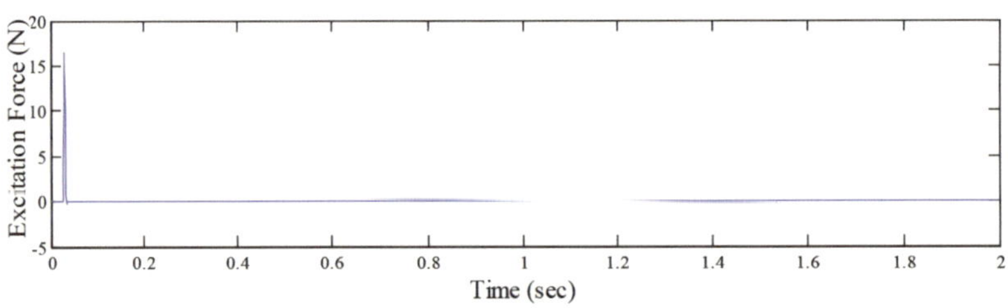

Figure 8. Input force signal collected during the forced vibration test.

First, the forced vibration test is carried out. The excitation force (**Figure 8**) and response of the model (**Figure 9**) are recorded simultaneously. These signals are processed with SignalCAD and the FRFs are developed. These functions are introduced to ModalCAD, and the complex mode identification function (CMIF) is obtained from the developed FRFs as shown in **Figure 10**.

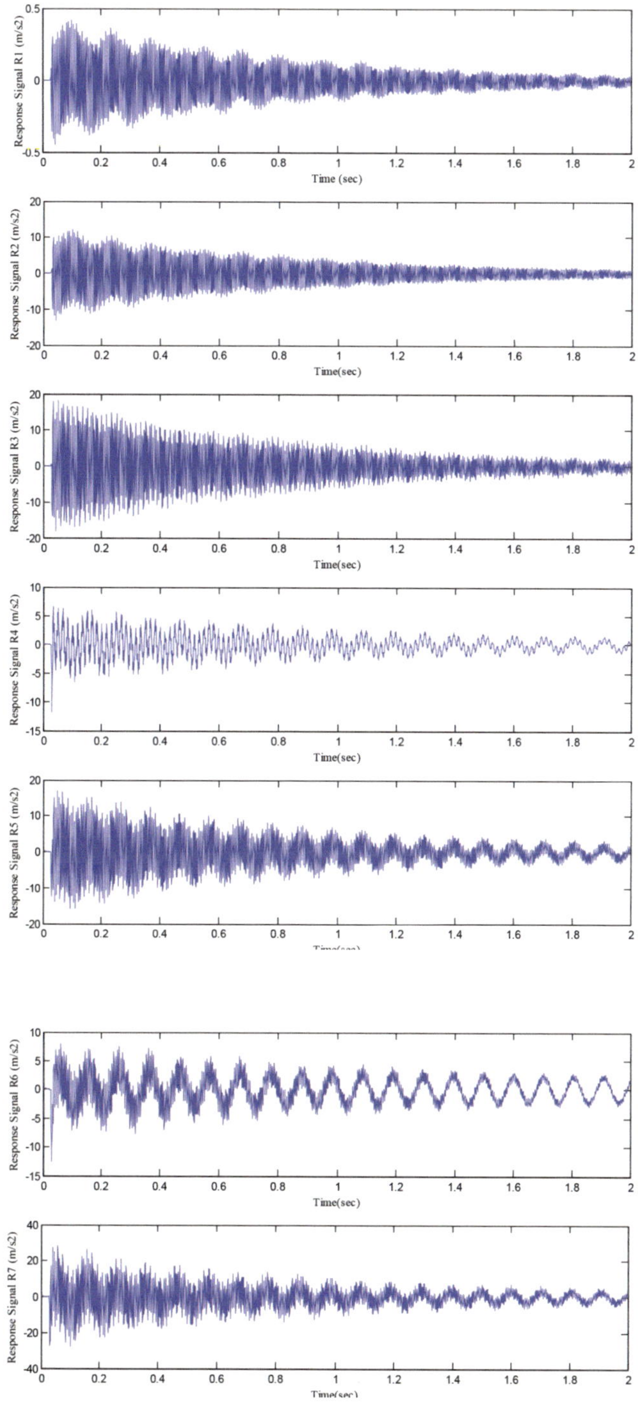

Figure 9. Response accelerations obtained via the forced vibration test.

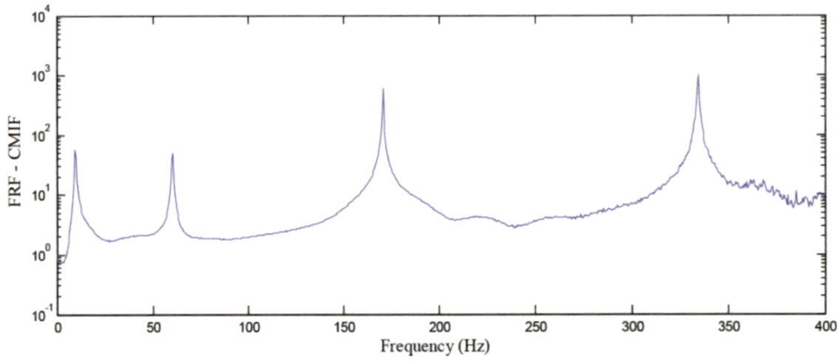

Figure 10. CMIF of calculated FRFs.

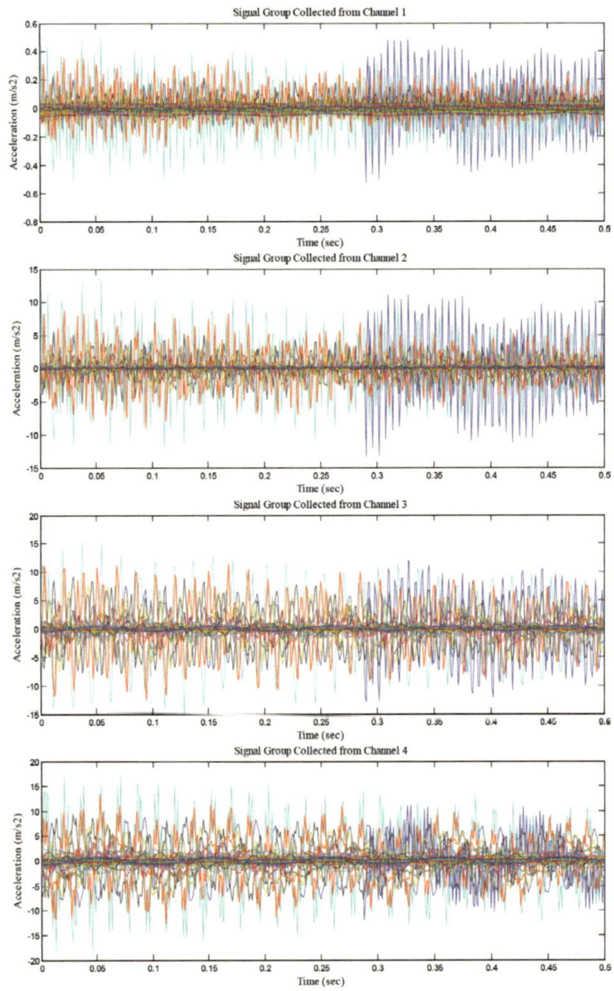

Figure 11. (a) Signal response set from the ambient vibration test (R1–R4).

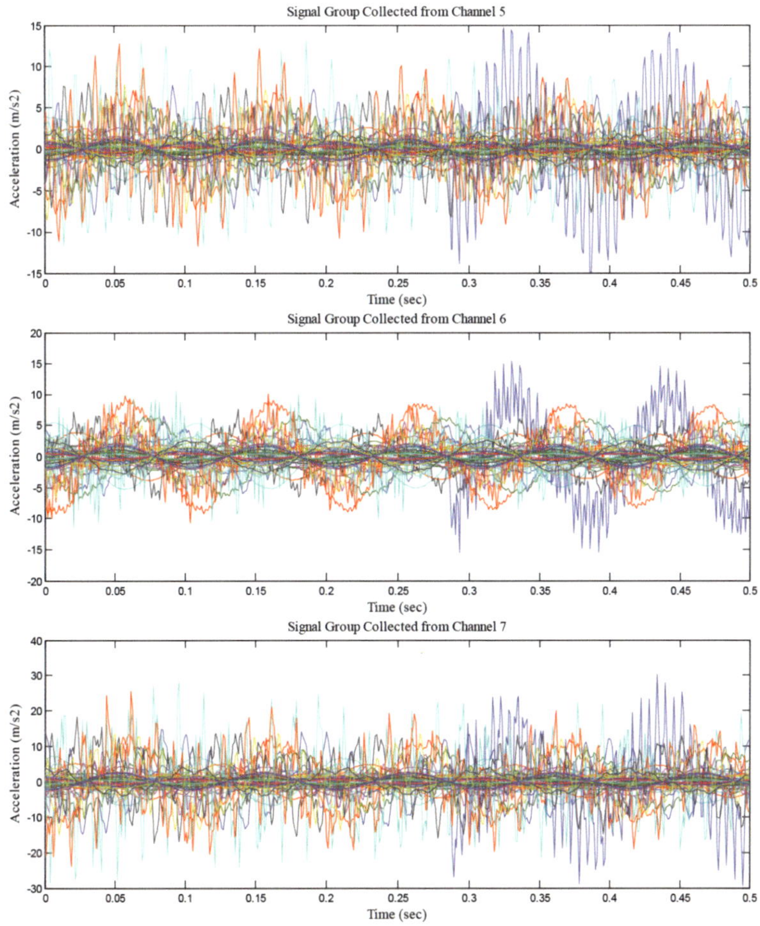

Figure 11. (b) signal response set from the ambient vibration test (R5–R7).

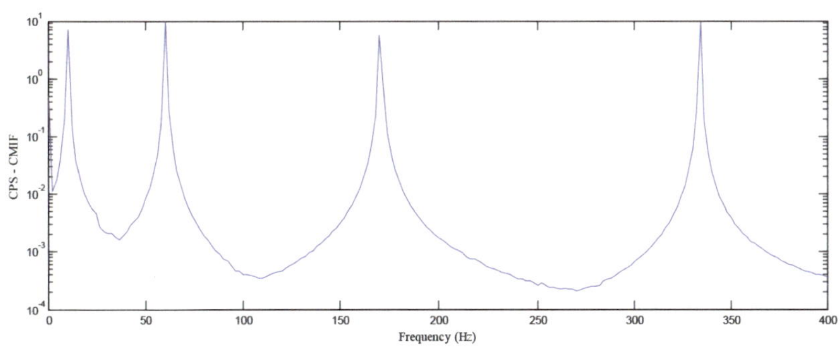

Figure 12. CMIF of calculated CPSs.

Second, the ambient vibration test is carried out and the response of the model is recorded. The collected signals are acceleration series for each channel as shown in **Figure 11**. These signals are processed with SignalCAD and the CPS series are developed. The CPS functions for each channel are produced by applying SVD to the spectrum series. The produced single functions are introduced to ModalCAD and the CMIF is obtained from the developed CPSs as shown in **Figure 12**.

The modal characteristics are then extracted with ModalCAD for input-output and output-only modal analyses. Same mode shapes are obtained from experimental and operational modal analyses with all methods. The obtained modal vectors are given in **Figure 13**.

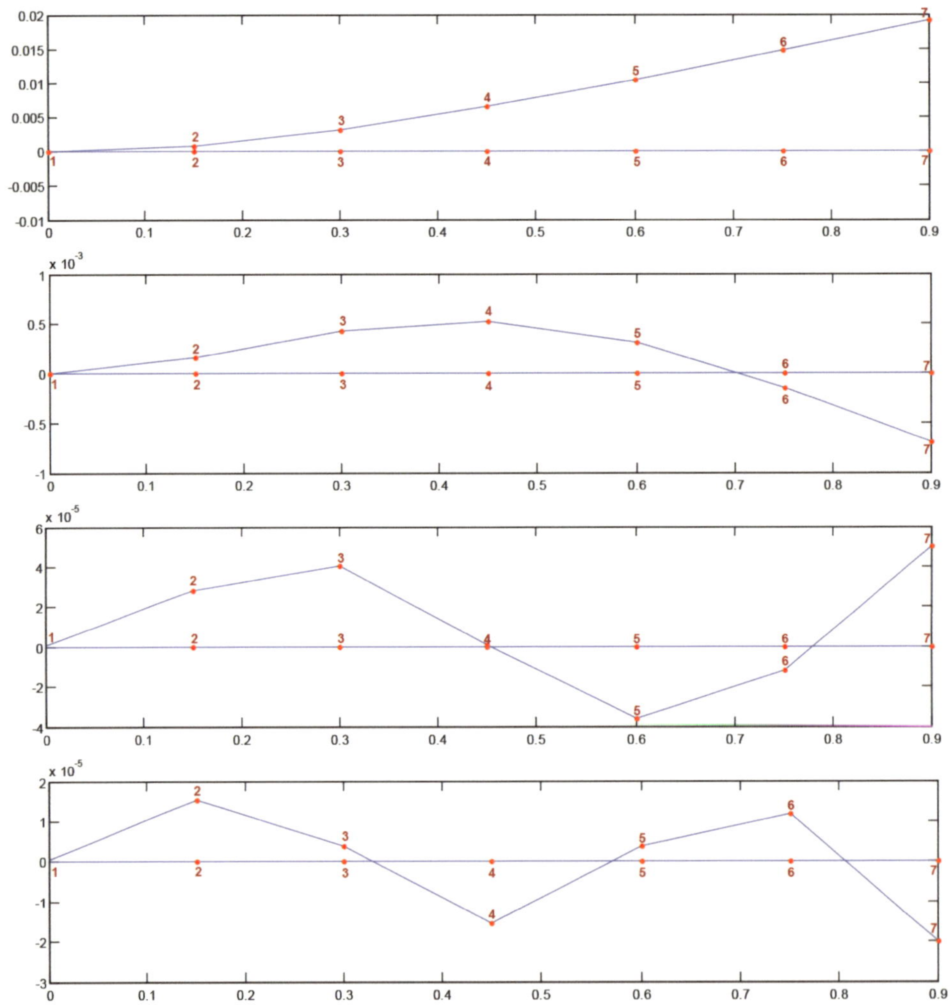

Figure 13. Experimental mode shapes of the cantilever beam model.

The natural vibration frequencies and damping ratios obtained using OV, CE, and PTD methods for input-output and output-only modal analyses are presented in **Tables 1** and **2**, respectively.

Mode no.	Input-output modal analysis (Hz)			Output-only modal analysis (Hz)		
	OV	CE	PTD	OV	CE	PTD
1	9.5	9.71	9.71	10	10	10.19
2	60.5	60.29	60.29	60	60.25	60.01
3	170.5	170.48	170.46	170	170.27	170.23
4	334	333.83	333.85	334	333.83	333.92

Table 1. Modal frequency values obtained from ModalCAD

Mode no.	Input-output modal analysis (%)			Output-only modal analysis (%)		
	OV	CE	PTD	OV	CE	PTD
1	16.3748	0.38409	0.37919	23.9592	0.35837	0.88837
2	2.8235	0.25131	0.2512	3.9965	0.21716	0.16947
3	0.53196	0.10881	0.11048	1.4897	0.12524	0.21411
4	0.38155	0.06087	0.05923	0.71889	0.06135	0.028594

Table 2. Modal damping values obtained from ModalCAD.

7.2. Analytical modal analysis and FE model updating

The analytical model of the cantilever beam is built in ANSYS. The natural frequencies and mode shapes are solved by the Lanczos method. The obtained mode shapes are presented in **Figure 14**. The analytical model is compared to the experimental model. As a reference data, the experimental model results obtained using the PTD method for input-output modal analysis are used because the experimental results are close to each other. The comparison of dynamic characteristics between the initial analytical model and the experimental model shows that the analytical natural frequencies are higher than the corresponding natural frequencies obtained experimentally. The differences in modal frequencies are higher than 20% for all modes as shown in **Table 3**. These differences are based on physical parameters. To achieve an analytical model that correlates better with the experimental results, the material properties are updated. There is no need to add mass and update boundary conditions in this model. The model is automatically updated by running the ANSYS model many times and the iterations are terminated until the aim function reaches the minimum value. The material properties of the beam model before and after the updating process are shown in **Table 4**. As shown in **Table 4**, the modulus of elasticity has been changed by FemUP. This change primarily affects the frequency values and modal vectors. The other parameters such as density and poison ratio have not been changed. In the updating step, three parameters are included in the automated updating procedure. The correlation between mode shapes of the analytical and experimental models is evaluated using the MAC matrix. After the model updating process is completed, it can be said that the correlation is good. All differences in natural frequencies are below 1%. The experimental modal vectors are just same with the analytical modal vectors. This good harmony after the updating process may be observed from the MAC graphics given in **Figure 15**. As a result of the optimization study, it can be said that the most effective physical parameter of the model for model updating is the modulus of elasticity.

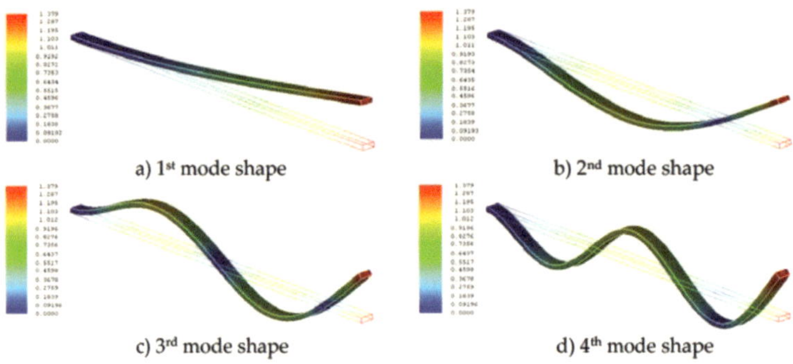

Figure 14. Numerical mode shapes of the cantilever beam model: (a) first mode shape, (b) second mode shape, (c) third mode shape, and (d) fourth mode shape.

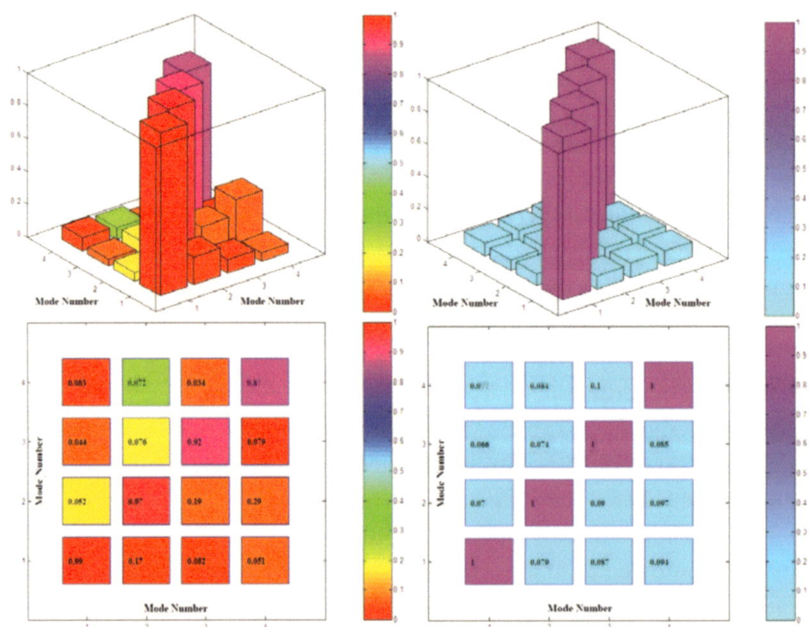

Figure 15. MAC matrices between the experimental model and the numerical model before and after the update process.

http://dx.doi.org/10.5772/63232

Mode no.	Test frequency (Hz)	Analytic frequency before the update (Hz)	Error before the update (%)	MAC before the update	Analytic frequency after the update (Hz)	Error after the update (%)	MAC after the update
1	9.7060	11.8415	−22.00	0.9950	9.7162	−0.11	1.0000
2	60.2896	74.2084	−23.09	0.9746	60.8814	−0.98	0.9995
3	170.4636	207.9209	−21.97	0.9217	170.4305	0.02	0.9963
4	333.8520	408.3915	−22.33	0.8741	333.8636	−0.00	0.9974

Table 3. Initial correlation analysis results between the experimental and analytical models.

Parameter	Before the update	After the update
Modulus of elasticity	$2.75\times10^{11}N/m^2$	$1.85147\times10^{11}N/m^2$
Density	7800 kg/m^3	7800 kg/m^3
Poisson ratio	0.3	0.3

Table 4. Model parameters before and after the update.

8. Conclusion

In this study, the importance of the computational part of vibration tests is highlighted and the capabilities of MATLAB for the possible use of all steps of dynamic vibration test of structures are explained. Three computer programs for these steps have been developed in MATLAB platform. The general properties of these tools are introduced and some flow charts for the general algorithms are also presented. The first tool is an interactive and comparative digital signal processing software developed for vibration test of structures and named as SignalCAD. The Signal Processing Toolbox functions are used for some of the operations. The software provides the capability to simulate vibration tests and perform spectral analysis including FRFs, CPSs, PSDs, coherence functions, transfer functions, and spectrograms. The second tool is the system identification software named as ModalCAD. The System Identification Toolbox functions and new developed functions are used for modal identification process. The software provides the capability to simulate vibration tests, perform experimental and operational modal analyses including structural identification with OV, CE, and PTD methods, and validate/visualize modal analysis results. The last tool is a computational FE model updating software called as FemUP. The SQP algorithm in MATLAB Optimization Toolbox is used to minimize the difference between analytical and experimental natural frequencies. Constraints are used on the correlation between the analytical and experimental mode shapes using the MAC matrix. The natural frequencies and mode shapes are solved by ANSYS. A simple vibration test is carried out and the capabilities of developed tools are evaluated for a complete vibration test process. The example contains forced and ambient vibration tests, signal analyses, system identification, and automatic FE model updating process of a steel cantilever beam model. Beside this simple example, the applications of the developed tools for more detailed civil engineering structures can be seen in [17, 18]. The obtained results show that developed tools work well and can be used for the vibration test of structures.

Author details

Abdurrahman Sahin[1*] and Alemdar Bayraktar[2]

*Address all correspondence to: abdsahin@yildiz.edu.tr

1 Department of Civil Engineering, Yıldız Technical University, Istanbul, Turkey

2 Department of Civil Engineering, Karadeniz Technical University, Trabzon, Turkey

References

[1] Farrar C. R., James G. H. III. System identification from ambient vibration measurements on a bridge. J. Sound Vib. 1997; 205(1): 1–18.

[2] Brownjohn J. M. W., Dumanoglu A. A., Severn R. T. Ambient vibration survey of the Fatih Sultan Mehmet (Second Bosporus) Suspension Bridge. Earthquake Eng. Struct. Dyn. 2004; 21(10): 907–924.

[3] Atamturktur S., Fanning P., Boothby T. Traditional and operational modal testing of monumental masonry structures. International Operational Modal Analysis Conference, Copenhagen, Denmark. 2007.

[4] Gentile C., Saisi A. Ambient vibration testing of historic masonry towers for structural identification and damage assessment. Constr. Build. Mater. 2007; 21(6): 1311–1321.

[5] Ren W.-X., Peng X.-L., Lin Y.-Q. Experimental and analytical studies on dynamic characteristics of a large span cable-stayed bridge. Eng. Struct. 2005; 27(4): 535–548.

[6] Hartley M. J., Pavic A., Waldron P. Investigation of pedestrian walking loads on a cable stayed footbridge using modal testing and FE model updating. 17th International Modal Analysis Conference (IMAC XVII), Kissimmee, FL. 1999; 3727(2): 1076–1082.

[7] Jaishi B., Ren W. X. Structural finite element model updating using ambient vibration test results. J. Struct. Eng. 2005; 131: 617–628.

[8] Foti D., Diaferio M., Giannoccaro N. I., Mongelli M. Ambient vibration testing, dynamic identification and model updating of a historic tower. NDT E. Int., 2012; 47: 88–95.

http://dx.doi.org/10.5772/63232

[9] El-Borgi S., Choura S., Ventura C., Baccouch M., Cherif F. Modal identification and model updating of a reinforced concrete bridge. Smart Struct. Syst. 2005; 1(1): 83–101.

[10] Sahin A., Bayraktar A. SignalCAD—A digital signal processing software for forced and ambient vibration testing of engineering structures. J. Test. Eval. 2010; 38(1): 95–110.

[11] MATLAB Signal Processing Toolbox User's Guide. MathWorks, Natick, MA; 2009.

[12] MATLAB System Identification Toolbox User's Guide. The MathWorks, Natick, MA; 2009.

[13] Sahin A., Bayraktar A. ModalCAD—Interactive dynamic characteristic identification software for experimental and operational modal analysis of engineering structures. J. Test. Eval. 2010; 38(6): 738–758.

[14] ANSYS Finite Element Analysis System. (2007). ANSYS, Inc. 2600 Ansys Drive Canonsburg, Pennsylvania, USA

[15] Sahin A., Bayraktar A. Computational finite element model updating tool for modal testing of structures. Struct. Eng. Mech. 2014; 51(2): 229–248.

[16] MATLAB Optimization Toolbox User's Guide. MathWorks, Natick, MA; 2009.

[17] Sahin A., Bayraktar A. Forced vibration testing and experimental modal analysis of steel footbridge for structural identification. J. Test. Eval. 2014; 42(3): 695–712.

[18] Sahin, A., Bayraktar, A., Ozcan, D. M., Sevim, B., Altunisik, A. C., Turker, T. Dynamic field test, system identification, and modal validation of an RC Minaret: Preprocessing and postprocessing the wind-induced ambient vibration data. J. Perform. Constr. Facil. 2011; 25(4): 336–356.

Chapter 4

Forward and Inverse Dynamics and Quasi-Static Analysis of Mechanizes with MATLAB®

E. Corral, J. Meneses and J.C. García-Prada

Additional information is available at the end of the chapter

http://dx.doi.org/10.5772/63372

Abstract

There are many potential advantages of direct and inverse dynamic and quasi-static analysis of mechanisms, namely control the risk of slippage, improve stability, better adaptation to the environment, obtaining smooth movements and optimizing energy consumption. This chapter proposes new analysis methods and algorithms to bring new solutions to the mechanics of the machines under consideration. The methodology has been developed in modular programs thanks to the flexibility of MATLAB®.

In this chapter, a methodology for the complete kinematic and dynamic study of mechanisms is provided.

The programs have been designed so that all parameters can be modified. It was possible to automate these calculations creating an algorithm implemented in a programming language to easily find the solutions and the results of the analysis.

To test the interest of the methodology, in this chapter, this has been applied to the field of robots, especially the design of the biped robot PASIBOT. The inverse and forward dynamics, accounting for support foot slippage, are encoded in MATLAB®.

In addition, the methodology was applied to another machine, an unmanned ground vehicle (UGV), obtaining navigation optimization results using a numerical program based on a quasi-static half vehicle model.

Keywords: mechanism, dynamics, quasi-static, robot, vehicle

1. Introduction

Nowadays, walking robots, service robotics, and unmanned ground vehicles are considered one of the main areas of research. The employment of robots for dangerous tasks makes its

INTECH
open science | open minds

© 2016 The Author(s). Licensee InTech. This chapter is distributed under the terms of the Creative Commons Attribution License (http://creativecommons.org/licenses/by/3.0), which permits unrestricted use, distribution, and reproduction in any medium, provided the original work is properly cited. (cc) BY

design a crucial point. The interest in the development of humanoid robotics (personal assistance, social task, etc.) is rising, and it is being studied by a great number of research groups. The main issue is current mobile robots are not adapted to be used in domestic environments due to their lack of maneuverability but also to their large volume and/or weight.

These days humanoid biped have a high number of actuators that are used to control the high degrees of freedom (DOF) they possess. Nonetheless, one of the biggest drawbacks in humanoids is that both the weight and the power consumption still make this technology not suitable for many tasks and/or environments. In the majority of cases, around 30% of the total weight is related to the actuators and wires, and more than 25% to the reduction systems. That is why our work is focused on finding a new dynamics analysis to simplify the design of new mechanisms and kinematic chains which, maintaining the robot functionality, does not require such a high number of actuators. This would reduce the robot mass and hence its power consumption and total cost [1–4].

In recent years, different research groups have developed robots based on passive walking techniques. Biped locomotion has been studied from several perspectives. Much effort is devoted to the design of optimal trajectories and stabilized walking cycles via control programs. However, researchers have not focused enough their efforts in solving the slip problem, which has been largely ignored [5, 6].

In this chapter, the kinematics and dynamics analysis of PASIBOT (a biped walking robot designed and built by the Maqlab Groups of the Universidad Carlos III de Madrid, shown in **Figure 2**) are presented. The methodology to do the completed study from a theoretical point of view is explained. The study objective is to calculate all the forces and torques between links, as well as the linear and angular position coordinates, velocities, and accelerations for all links, for any time. The equations have been implemented in MATLAB® code, and the corresponding results have been contrasted [7–12].

The program accepts the initial kinematic state and the motor torque (as a function of time) as inputs and returns the bipedal movement, including the sliding of the supporting foot. The sliding is taken into account by adding one degree of freedom. Thus, we focus on the kinematics and dynamics of the sliding supporting foot [13].

In addition, there is no doubt about all advantages unmanned vehicles have. For this reason, the kinematics and dynamics analysis is one of the principal research lines in robotics. The Tallinn University of Technology is researching in the design and development of the unmanned ground vehicle (UGV) shown in **Figure 20**. This UGV is an all-terrain vehicle equipped with an engine for each of its wheels. The novel aspect of this vehicle is that each wheel is attached to the body by a leg so that the angle between the latter and the body may vary thanks to the use of an attached actuator [14–16].

In this chapter, a parametric quasi-static half vehicle model is implemented on MATLAB® following the explained methodology. The program calculates the variation in configuration angles that optimized desired criteria as the vehicle passes on a particular track profile. This algorithm makes it possible to find the variation of configuration angles along the track profile that keeps the applied torque constant and/or minimized and/or satisfying certain criterion.

http://dx.doi.org/10.5772/63372

2. Methodology

The sketch of the methodology is shown in **Figure 1**.

The first step is to define the mechanism. It is basically naming variables and parameters (with the correct nomenclature the implementation in MATLAB® code is made easier) and classifying the type of movement (degrees of freedom, class of joints, etc.)

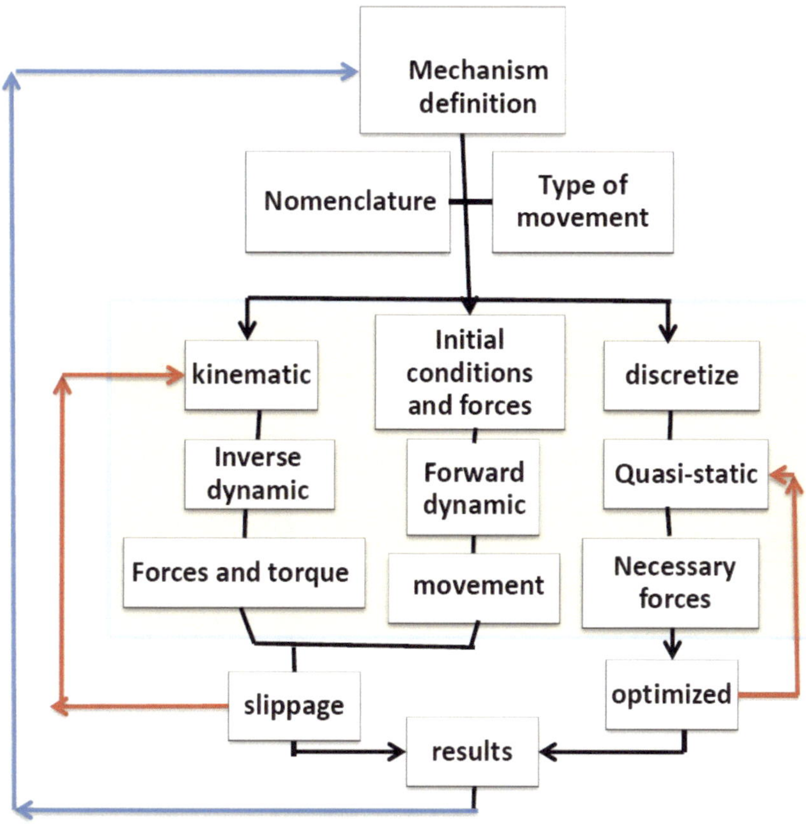

Figure 1. Sketch of the methodology.

It is possible to solve the kinematics and dynamics through the inverse dynamics or the forward dynamics algorithm depending on the type of mechanisms, the known input, and the desired output. Also, if the dynamics are complicated, the quasi-static approach can be useful. The biggest advantage of this approach is that it is easily optimized. This is a valuable tool to improve design and control with mathematics software.

In this chapter, the methodology of inverse and forward dynamics is applied to the biped walking robot PASIBOT and the quasi-static approach to an unmanned ground vehicle.

Note that the input and output of each approach are different and the equations are also different. However, the methodology can be simplified in the **Figure 1** for both, and the correctly chosen nomenclature helps to generate a MATLAB® code. The developed MATLAB® code is totally parametric, giving the possibility of changing the values, adding new analysis and new degrees of freedom (like slippage), or looking for analysis of sensibility.

Another advantage of doing the whole analysis with MATLAB® code is that the result can be used as an input for redesigning or as an optimizing function.

3. Kinematics of the biped robot PASIBOT

Nowadays, certain commercial software of mechanical simulation provides the dynamics of a mechanism with a small error. But, in some cases, like a biped robot actuated by small number of actuators, it is also possible to obtain the kinematics and apply this methodology and obtain the dynamics with a low degree of error. In this chapter, the kinematics of the biped PASIBOT is developed. In next chapters, the inverse and forward dynamics are addressed using the relations obtained in the kinematics.

The biped PASIBOT is a one-degree-of-freedom mechanical system based on a combination of classical mechanisms that emulates human walking. PASIBOT is shown in **Figure 2**.

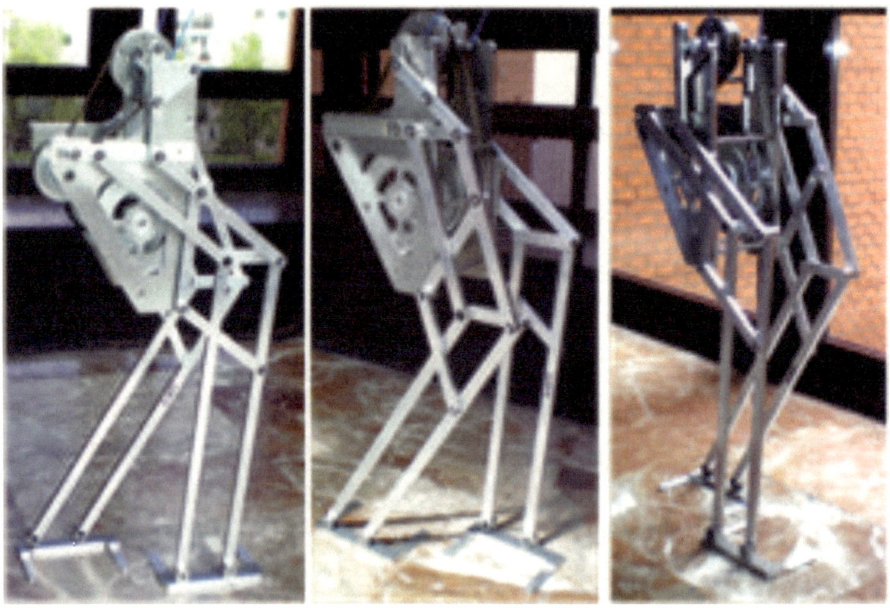

Figure 2. PASIBOT.

The biped PASIBOT (see **Figures 2–4**) is a mechanism composed of three sub-mechanisms of conventional type, each of which is designed to perform a different function:

http://dx.doi.org/10.5772/63372

1. The mechanism "Chebyshev" is responsible for generating a quasi-straight line.
2. A pantograph handles extend the "Chebyshev" coupling curve.
3. The stability of the biped is achieved by parallel extensions.

In **Figure 3**, the sub-mechanisms Chebyshev and pantograph as well as the trajectories for the most relevant points are shown.

The only engine of the biped conveys a full rotation to the crank of the Chebyshev mechanism, so that the end of its connecting rod (point C in **Figure 3**) makes a cyclical movement, one of its tracts being a quasi-straight line. This point is connected to one end of the pantograph, so that its other end (point E in **Figure 3**) carries an inverted and amplified from the previous path. The corresponding amplification ratio depends on the lengths of the links of the pantograph. The amplification ratio is two for the design of PASIBOT presented here.

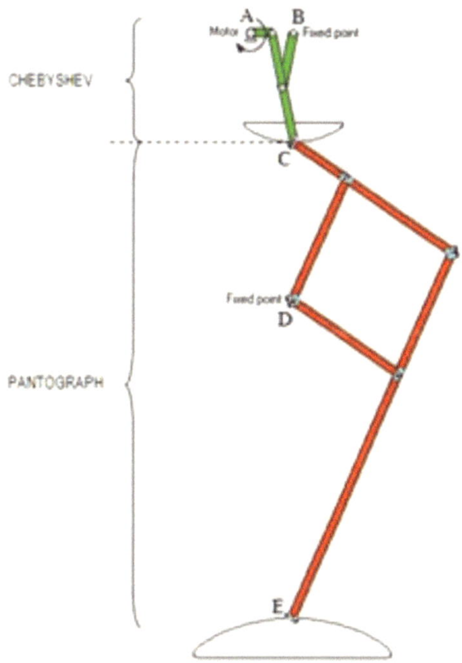

Figure 3. The sub-mechanisms Chebyshev and pantograph with the trajectories of their notable points.

Points A, B, and D in **Figure 3** are attached to the hip, as can be seen in **Figure 4**. The stabilization system consists of a series of articulated parallelograms which are based on the two longest links of the pantograph. These parallelograms guarantee the parallelism between the foot in contact with the floor and the stabilizing link, the end of which slides on a slot at the hip. Since that slot is aligned with the linear segment of the Chebyshev trajectory, the supporting foot remains parallel to the slot during the whole period of support. In order to provide the opposite leg with the appropriate movement, the corresponding crank is phased out π rad (see **Figure 4**) in the same motor axis. In fact, both cranks are part of the same rigid element.

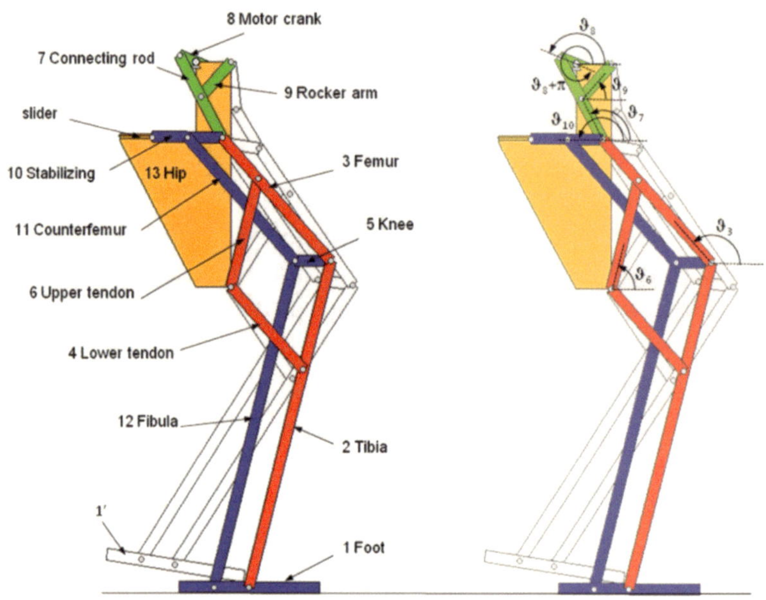

Figure 4. Sub-mechanisms of PASIBOT; nomenclature and numeration for the supporting leg and angular positions for the links.

As shown in **Figure 4**, any link belonging to the flying leg has the same name and number as the corresponding link from the supporting leg, but with a prime to distinguish between them. Each leg comprises 12 links, apart from the engine crank (link number 8), which is shared with both legs (no link number 8′ exists), so the biped PASIBOT has a total of 24 links, including the single hip (link number 13).

Listed below are the parameters and variables that describe the kinematics and dynamics of the biped:

l_i: length of the link i (mm)

m_i: mass of the link i (kg)

$_i$: angle between the link i and the hip (rad)

ω_i: rotational velocity of link i (rad/s)

α_i: rotational acceleration of link i (rad/s^2)

I_i: inertia moment for the link i (kg mm^2)

r_{ij}: position vector of the ij joint from the link i center of mass (mm)

r_{ijx}: x projection of the position vector (mm)

r_{ijy}: y projection of the position vector (mm)

f_{ij}: force exerted by the link i on the link j (N)

f_{ijx}: x projection of the f_{ij} (N)

f_{ijy}: y projection of the f_{ij} (N)

In **Figure 5**, a sequence for one step of PASIBOT is presented, as simulated with a commercial program. Note that one step corresponds to a half rotation (π rad) of the motor crank.

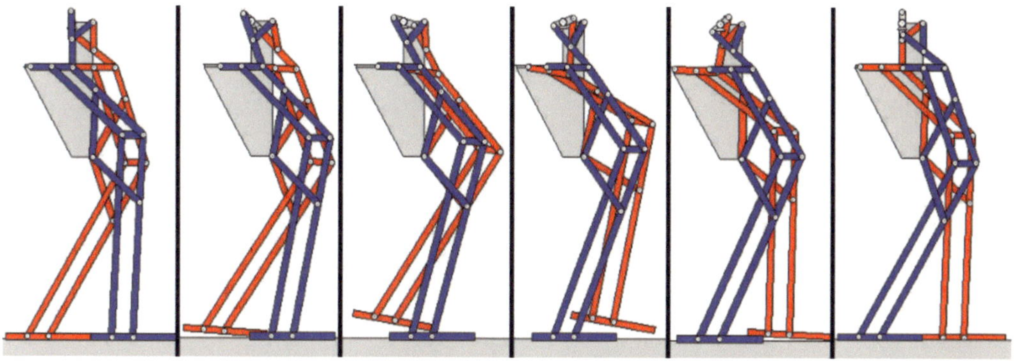

Figure 5. PASIBOT gait along one step (from $_8 = \pi$ to $3\pi/2$ rad).

After defining the whole type of movement and the nomenclature, the kinematical study of one PASIBOT step is presented here. The kinematics is developed for the phase of "simple support," in which the supporting foot is in contact with the horizontal ground, whereas the other leg is flying. First, no sliding between the supporting foot and the ground is considered, so it can be considered part of the ground. Hence, the biped PASIBOT is a one DOF planar mechanism, and we can refer the angular positions of any link to the angular position of the motor crank ($\omega 8$):

$$\theta_i = \theta_i(\theta_8), i = 1,2,\ldots 1',2', \tag{1}$$

Then, the x,y coordinates for its center of mass can be easily expressed with respect to that angle:

$$x_i = x_i(\theta_8); y_i = y_i(\theta_8), i = 1,2,\ldots 1',2', \tag{2}$$

The angular velocities, accelerations and the center of mass linear velocities and accelerations are obtained by taking the first and second derivatives in Eqs. (1) and (2).

Actually, the biped kinematics is divided into three closed-loop kinematic chains:

1. Chebyshev chain (links number 7, 8, 9, and 13)

The distance between motor crank and rocker fixed points (A and B in **Figure 3**, respectively) in a Chebyshev mechanism is $l_{AB} = 2l_8$, the rocker arm length is $l_9 = 2.5l_8$, the connecting rod length is $l_7 = 5l_8$, and the rocker arm and connecting rod are joined at the middle point of the latter. The link lengths have been particularized for the designed biped, and normalized to the crank length, $l_8 = 1$. Taking into account these lengths, the Chebyshev closed-loop kinematic chain provides (see **Figure 6**):

$$2.5e^{j\vartheta_7} - 2.5e^{j\vartheta_9} - e^{j\vartheta_8} + 2 \quad (3)$$

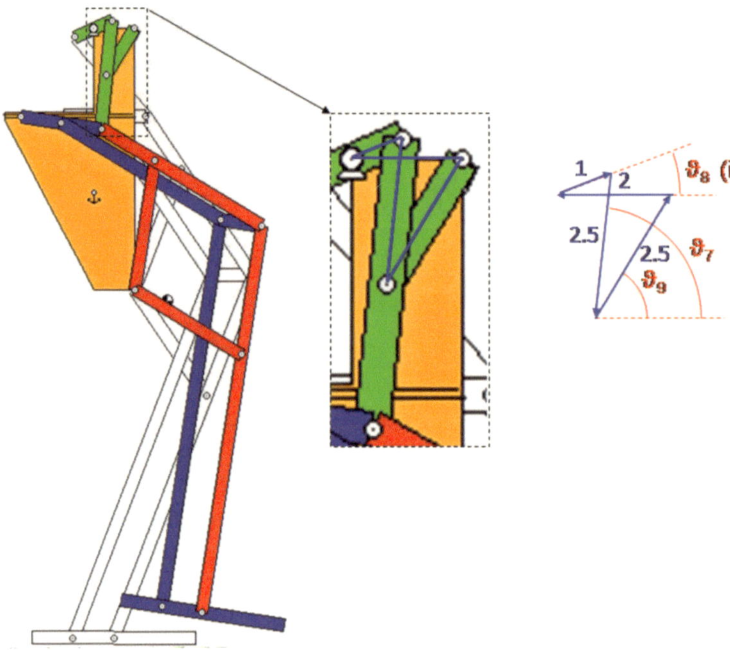

Figure 6. Chebyshev chain (lengths in units of l_8).

In Eqs. (3)–(5), both projections (vertical and horizontal) for each closed-loop equation are written in a compact form following the Euler's formula, where j is the imaginary unit.

2. Pantograph chain (links number 9, 7, 3, 6, and 13)

The tendons length is $l_4 = l_6 = 6l_8$, whereas the distance between the connecting rod-femur and upper tendon-femur joints (points C and F, respectively) is $l_{CF} = 3l_8$, and the distance between rocker arm-hip and upper tendon-hip joints (points B and D, respectively) is $l_{BD} = 12l_8$, so the pantograph closed-loop kinematic chain provides (see **Figure 7**):

$$6e^{j\vartheta_6} + 3e^{j\vartheta_3} + 2.5\left(e^{j\vartheta_7} + e^{j\vartheta_9}\right) - 12j = 0 \quad (4)$$

http://dx.doi.org/10.5772/63372

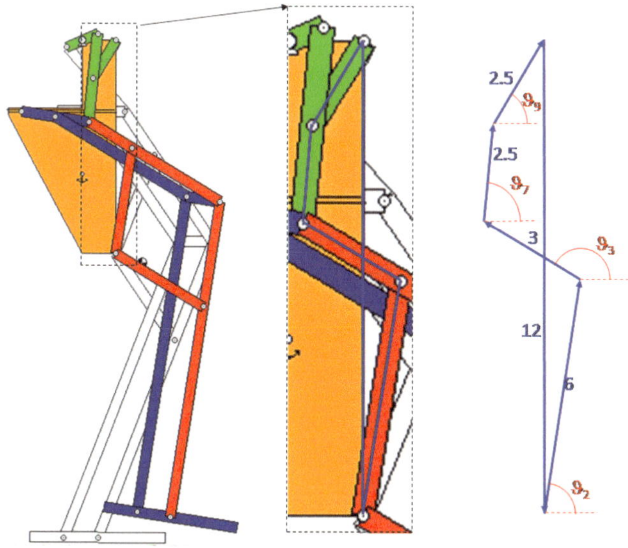

Figure 7. Pantograph chain (lengths in units of l_8).

3. Stability chain (links number 8, 7, 10, and 13)

In our model, the stabilizing link length is $l_{10} = 4.2 l_8$. The vertical distance between the motor crank joint and the slot at the hip is $4l_8$. The horizontal projection distance between the motor crank joint and the end of the stabilizing link is called x. The stability closed-loop kinematic chain is as follows (see **Figure 8**):

$$24.e^{j\vartheta_{10}} - 5e^{j\vartheta_7} + e^{j\vartheta_8} - x + 4j = 0 \tag{5}$$

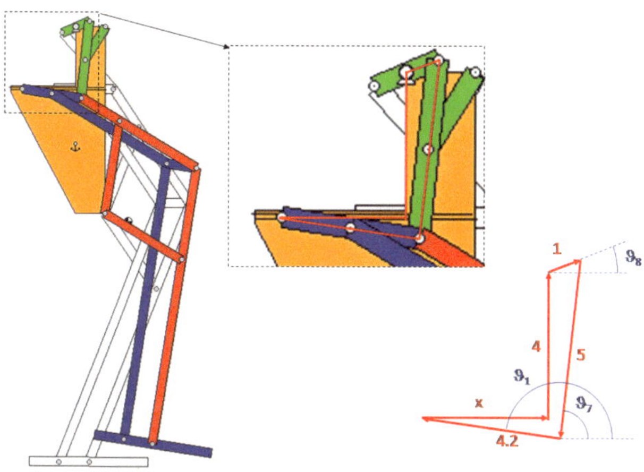

Figure 8. Stabilization chain (lengths in units of l_8).

As stated below, these equations determine the angles for all the links as functions of that for the motor crank, ϑ_8, which is also a function of time. Solving Eq. (3), the following expressions for the connecting rod and rocker arm angles are found:

$$\begin{cases} \vartheta_7 = a\cos\left[\dfrac{-4\cdot\cos^2\vartheta_8 + 13\cdot\cos\vartheta_8 - 10 + \sin\vartheta_8\cdot\sqrt{-16\cdot\cos^2\vartheta_8 - 60\cdot\cos\vartheta_8 + 100}}{25 - 20\cdot\cos\vartheta_8}\right] \\ \vartheta_9 = a\cos\left[\dfrac{-4\cdot\cos^2\vartheta_8 + 13\cdot\cos\vartheta_8 - 10 - \sin\vartheta_8\cdot\sqrt{-16\cdot\cos^2\vartheta_8 - 60\cdot\cos\vartheta_8 + 100}}{-25 + 20\cdot\cos\vartheta_8}\right] \end{cases} \tag{6}$$

From Eq. (4), the femur and tibia angles are found as functions of the previous ones:

$$\begin{cases} \vartheta_6 = a\cos\left[\dfrac{(2.5\cdot(\cos\vartheta_7 + \cos\vartheta_9)\cdot(-27 - A) - 2.5\cdot(\sin\vartheta_7 + \sin\vartheta_9 - 12)\cdot\sqrt{144\cdot A - (-27 - A)^2}}{12\cdot A}\right] \\ \vartheta_3 = a\cos\left[\dfrac{(2.5\cdot\cos\vartheta_7 + \cos\vartheta_9)\cdot(27 - A) + 2.5\cdot(\sin\vartheta_7 + \sin\vartheta_9) - 12)\cdot\sqrt{36\cdot A - (27 - A)^2}}{6\cdot A}\right] \end{cases} \tag{7}$$

where $A = (2.5\cdot(\cos\vartheta_7 + \cos\vartheta_9))^2 + (2.5\cdot(\sin\vartheta_7 + \sin\vartheta_9) - 12)^2$

Finally, Eq. (5) gives the solution for the stabilizing angle:

$$\vartheta_{10} = \text{asin}\left(\frac{5\cdot\sin\vartheta_7 - \sin\vartheta_8 - 4}{4.2}\right) \tag{8}$$

As can be seen in **Figure 3**, the rest of the angles involved are identical to one of the given ones in Eqs. (6)–(8), in particular:

$$\begin{aligned} \vartheta_1 &= \vartheta_5 = \vartheta_{10} \\ \vartheta_{12} &= \vartheta_4 = \vartheta_3 \\ \vartheta_2 &= \vartheta_{13} = \vartheta_6 \end{aligned} \tag{9}$$

For the links belonging to the opposite leg, we apply a phase out of π radians on ϑ_8:

$$\vartheta_{i'}(\vartheta_8) = \vartheta_i(\vartheta_8 + \pi) \tag{10}$$

In order to reference all values to the ground, this corresponding base change must be applied:

$$\vartheta_i^{\text{ground}} = \vartheta_i - \vartheta_1, \tag{11}$$

where $\vartheta_i^{\text{ground}}\vartheta$ is the angle related to the ground system, and ϑ_i is the corresponding one related to the reference system fixed at link 14 (hip).

The positions of the center of mass for every link are obtained using trigonometric relations (e.g. x2=L2cosϑ2/2, y2=L2sinϑ2/2; x3=L2cosϑ2+L3cosϑ3/2, y3=L2sinϑ2+L3sinϑ3/2; etc.). Then, by time differentiating once and then twice, the angular velocity and acceleration as well as linear velocity and acceleration, respectively, for any link are calculated.

Thanks to apply this equations on MATLAB program, the kinematics of the biped robot PASIBOT can be solved for one step, considering a motor crank constant angular velocity,

$$\omega 8 : \vartheta 8(t) \ = \omega 8 \cdot t \tag{12}$$

The PASIBOT possessed a single DOF, so the positions of the center of mass of link *i* can be referred to the angular position of the motor crank (ϑ8):

$$\vartheta_i = \vartheta_i(\vartheta_8), i = 2,3 \ldots 1', 2', \ldots (i \neq 8) \tag{13}$$

$$X_i = X_i(\vartheta_8), i \neq 1 \tag{14}$$

$$y_i = y_i(\vartheta_8), i \neq 1 \tag{15}$$

4. Slipping kinematics of the biped robot PASIBOT

If the supporting foot is allowed to slip, the PASIBOT becomes a 2-DOF mechanism (the biped moves across a plane, and the supporting foot supposedly remains horizontal). Eqs. (13) and (15) remain valid, while Eq. (14) increases by the value of the supporting foot slippage x_1 as follows:

$$\mathrm{x}_i = \mathrm{x}_1 + \mathrm{X}_i(\vartheta_8); \mathrm{i} \neq 1 \tag{16}$$

The first and second time derivatives of Eq. (16) are as follows:

$$\dot{x}_i = \frac{dx_1}{dt} + \frac{dX_i}{d\vartheta_8}\frac{d\vartheta_8}{dt} = \dot{x}_1 + X_i'(\vartheta_8)\dot{\vartheta}_8$$
$$\ddot{x}_i = \ddot{x}_1 + X_i''(\vartheta_8)\dot{\vartheta}_8^2 + X_i'(\vartheta_8)\ddot{\vartheta}_8 \tag{17}$$

where a prime denotes explicit derivative with respect to ϑ_8, and dots denote time derivatives.

5. Non-slipping inverse dynamics of the biped robot PASIBOT

The inputs for the dynamical problem are the kinematic magnitudes (angular acceleration, α_i, and its center of mass acceleration, (a_{ix}, a_{iy})). The dynamical equations for the motion of every link, using Newton action-reaction law, are exposed in Eq. (18):

$$\left.\begin{array}{l} \sum_i \vec{F}_i = m_i \vec{a}_i \\ \vec{f}_{ij} = -\vec{f}_{ji} \\ \sum_i T_{on\ i} = I_i \alpha \end{array}\right\} \Rightarrow \left\{\begin{array}{c} \sum_{j<i} f_{ji_x} - \sum_{k>i} f_{ik_x} = m_i \ddot{x}_i \\ \sum_{j<i} f_{ji_y} - \sum_{k>i} f_{ik_y} = m_i g + m_i \ddot{y}_i \\ T_i + \sum_{j<i}\left(r_{ij_x} f_{ji_y} - r_{ij_y} f_{ji_x}\right) - \sum_{k>i}\left(r_{ik_x} f_{ik_y} - r_{ik_y} f_{ik_x}\right) = I_i \ddot{\theta}_i \end{array}\right.$$
$$i = 2, 3, \ldots, 13, 1', 2', \ldots, 7', 9', \ldots, 12 \tag{18}$$

There are three equations for each link (there are 23 links, excluding the supporting foot), and the system describing the dynamics of the whole mechanism consists of 69 linear equations. The system (Eq. 18) is expressed in a matrix form (Eq. 19), and then solved with a MATLAB® via matrix inversion:

$$\begin{bmatrix} a_{11} & a_{12} & \cdots & \\ a_{21} & a_{22} & \cdots & \\ \vdots & \vdots & \ddots & \vdots \\ & & \cdots & \end{bmatrix} \cdot \begin{bmatrix} f_{12_x} \\ f_{12_y} \\ \vdots \\ T_8 \\ \vdots \end{bmatrix} = \begin{bmatrix} m_2 \ddot{x}_2 \\ m_2 g + m_2 \ddot{y}_2 \\ I_2 \ddot{\theta}_2 \\ \vdots \end{bmatrix}$$
$$[A(\text{coefficient})] \cdot [F(\text{force})] = [I(\text{inertia})]$$
$$[F] = [A]^{-1} \cdot [I] \tag{19}$$

The code of the matrix that must be written in MATLAB® is shown in **Figure 9**.

http://dx.doi.org/10.5772/63372

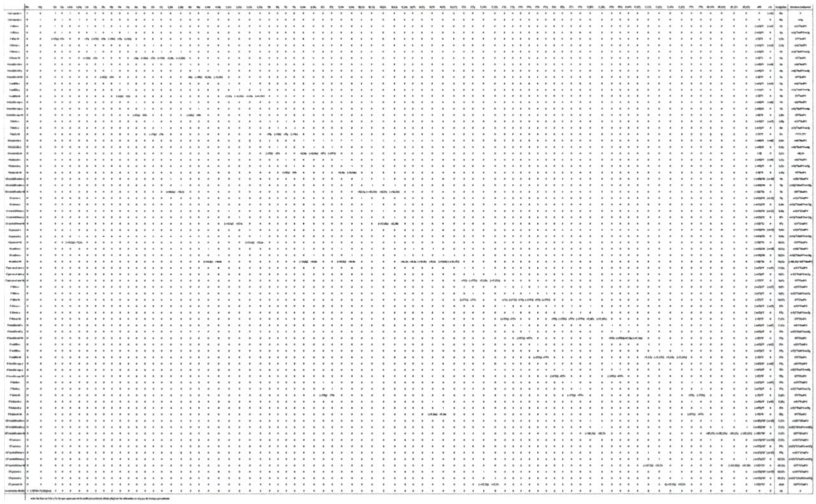

Figure 9. The matrix A (coefficient).

Using MATLAB® code the kinematical and dynamical equations have been implemented in order to obtain solutions depending on a set of parameters (link dimensions, masses and densities, motor angular velocity) entered by the user. In **Figure 10**, the MATLAB flow chart of the kinematics and dynamics algorithm is shown.

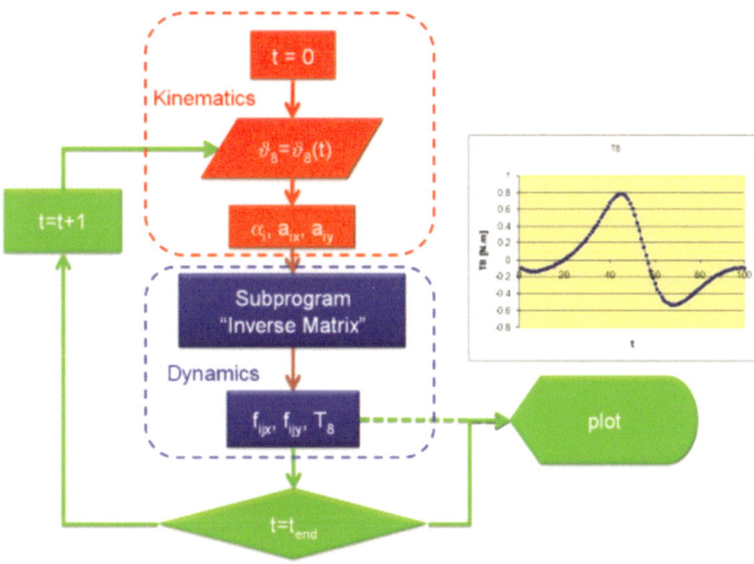

Figure 10. MATLAB® flow chart for the PASIBOT kinematics and dynamics calculus code.

The MATLAB® program first finds the corresponding value of $\vartheta 8(t)$, and using Eqs. (6) to (11), it obtains the corresponding values of the rest of the angles and the positions of the centers of mass. Then, it calculates the kinematics. These data, which define the state of the biped at the time t, form the inertia matrix, (I), in Eq (19). Finally the MATLAB® program inverts the coefficient matrix, (A), by means of a matrix inversion subroutine and multiplies both matrices to provide the forces and torques between links at this time step. These values are stored to be plotted and the calculations are restarted for the next time step.

The results have been validated by comparison with others programs (working model and ADAMS code). The main advantage of the program developed via MATLAB® is that it lets us perform fast modifications, making the final robot design easier by changing parameters.

As the first result, the program implemented in MATLAB® has calculated the motor torque required to perform the movement. **Figure 11** shows the actuator torque in the crank (link number 8) related to time, for different values of the motor angular velocity, $\omega 8$.

In **Figure 11**, the same shape for each case can be appreciated apart from the torque obtained from the highest velocity value ($\omega 8$ = 5 rad/s). With this velocity, the dynamical effect of the inertia forces becomes important. However, for low speeds (below 3 rad/s) torque graphs hardly differ from one to another.

In **Figure 12**, the torque is represented again but for different loads (5, 10, and 15 kg) added to the hip. It is an interesting result. It shows that the required motor torque depends slightly on the added load. This is because the hip remains at almost the same level in a course of a step.

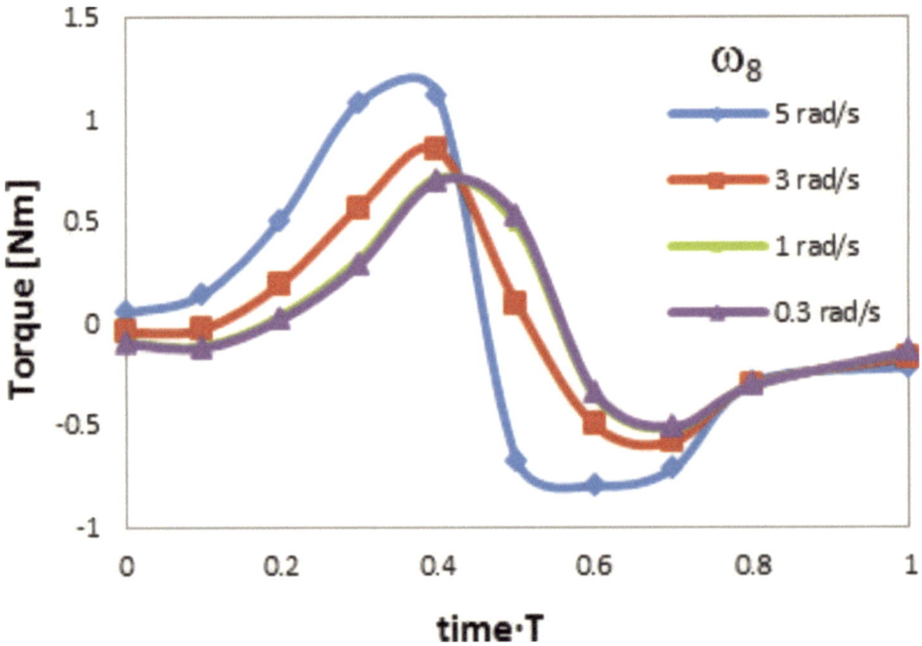

Figure 11. Torque for different crank velocities. T is the period for one step.

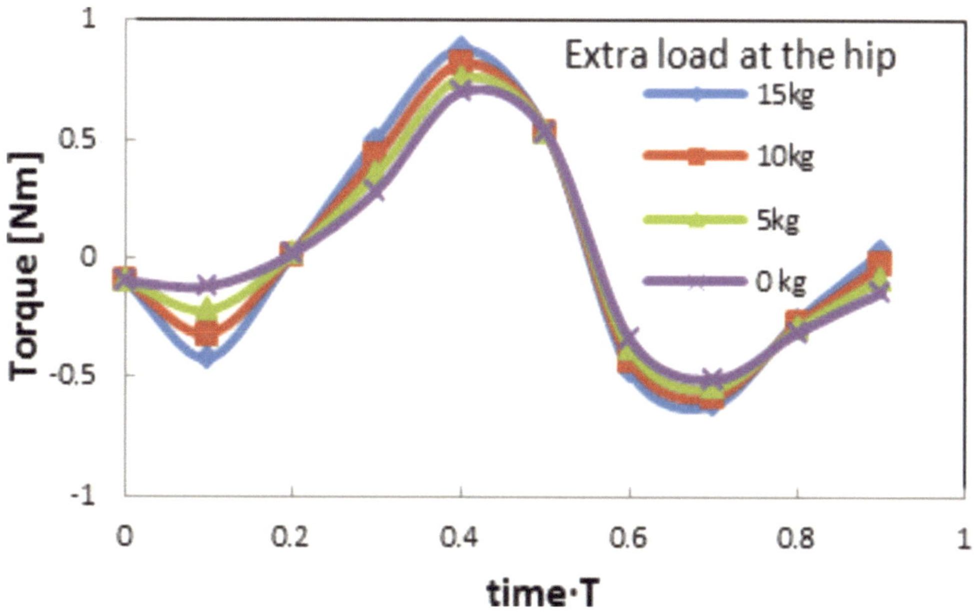

Figure 12. Actuator torque for different hip extra loads.

6. Forward dynamics for biped robot PASIBOT

The dynamics of mechanical systems can be modeled in two ways: inverse dynamics, which calculates the forces and torques that produce kinematics (movement), and forward dynamics, which computes the movement from known applied forces and torques.

When addressing forward dynamics, the kinematics is unknown. However, the angular position of the motor crank, ϑ_8, defines the position of the remaining links by Eqs. (20)–(22). These functions were defined in Eqs. (6)–(12). The corresponding angular velocities and accelerations as well as the center of mass linear velocities and accelerations are obtained from the corresponding first and second time derivatives:

$$\dot{\vartheta}_i = \frac{d\vartheta_i}{d\vartheta_8}\frac{d\vartheta_8}{dt} = \vartheta_i'(\vartheta_8)\dot{\vartheta}_8$$
$$\ddot{\vartheta}_i = \vartheta_i''(\vartheta_8)\dot{\vartheta}_8^2 + \vartheta_i'(\vartheta_8)\ddot{\vartheta}_8 \quad (20)$$

$$\dot{X}_i = X_i'(\vartheta_8)\dot{\vartheta}_8$$
$$\ddot{X}_i = X_i''(\vartheta_8)\vartheta_8^2 + X_i'(\vartheta_8)\ddot{\vartheta}_8 \quad (21)$$

$$\begin{aligned}\dot{y}_i &= y_i'(\vartheta_8)\dot{\vartheta}_8 \\ \ddot{y}_i &= y_i''(\vartheta_8)\dot{\vartheta}_8^2 + y_i'(\vartheta_8)\ddot{\vartheta}_8\end{aligned} \tag{22}$$

When the kinematics is unknown, Eq. (19) becomes a system of second-order differential equations. To solve it numerically, in addition to time discretization, a motor crank angle ϑ_8 discretization is proposed. In this way, the derivatives of the known functions, $\vartheta_i = \vartheta_i(\vartheta_8)$, $X_i = X_i(\vartheta_8)$ and $y_i = y_i(\vartheta_8)$, are computed with respect to ϑ_8 as follows:

$$\begin{cases}\vartheta_i'(\vartheta_8) \cong \dfrac{1}{\Delta\vartheta_8}\left[\vartheta_i(\vartheta_8 + \Delta\vartheta_8) - \vartheta_i(\vartheta_8)\right] \\ \vartheta_i''(\vartheta_8) \cong \dfrac{1}{(\Delta\vartheta_8)^2}\left[\vartheta_i(\vartheta_8 + 2\Delta\vartheta_8) - 2\vartheta_i(\vartheta_8) + \vartheta_i(\vartheta_8)\right]\end{cases} \tag{23}$$

$$\begin{cases}X_i'(\vartheta_8) \cong \dfrac{1}{\Delta\vartheta_8}\left[X_i(\vartheta_8 + \Delta\vartheta_8) - X_i(\vartheta_8)\right] \\ X_i''(\vartheta_8) \cong \dfrac{1}{(\Delta\vartheta_8)^2}\left[X_i(\vartheta_8 + 2\Delta\vartheta_8) - 2X_i(\vartheta_8) + X_i(\vartheta_8)\right]\end{cases} \tag{24}$$

$$\begin{cases}y_i'(\vartheta_8) \cong \dfrac{1}{\Delta\vartheta_8}\left[y_i(\vartheta_8 + \Delta\vartheta_8) - y_i(\vartheta_8)\right] \\ y_i''(\vartheta_8) \cong \dfrac{1}{(\Delta\vartheta_8)^2}\left[y_i(\vartheta_8 + 2\Delta\vartheta_8) - 2y_i(\vartheta_8) + y_i(\vartheta_8)\right]\end{cases} \tag{25}$$

In fact, to implement the forward dynamic problem, Eqs. (23)–(25) are inserted into Eqs. (20)–(22) and then into Eq. (18). Thus, we obtain a system of equations in which the first and second time derivatives of ϑ_8 are unknowns, while the torque is now a known function of time, $T_8 = T_8(t)$. The resulting system of equations is as follows:

$$\begin{cases}\sum\limits_{j<i} f_{ji_x} - \sum\limits_{k>i} f_{ik_x} - m_i X_i'(\vartheta_8)\ddot{\vartheta}_8 = m_i X_i''(\vartheta_8)\dot{\vartheta}_8^2 \\ \sum\limits_{j<i} f_{ji_y} - \sum\limits_{k>i} f_{ik_y} - m_i y_i'(\vartheta_8)\ddot{\vartheta}_8 = m_i g + m_i y_i''(\vartheta_8)\dot{\vartheta}_8^2 \\ \sum\limits_{j<i} T_{ji} - \sum\limits_{k>i} T_{ik} + \sum\limits_{j<i}\left(r_{ij_x} f_{ji_y} - r_{ij_y} f_{ji_x}\right) - \\ -\sum\limits_{k>i}\left(r_{ik_x} f_{ik_y} - r_{ik_y} f_{ik_x}\right) - I_i \vartheta_i'(\vartheta_8)\ddot{\vartheta}_8 = I_i \vartheta_i''(\vartheta_8)\dot{\vartheta}_8^2\end{cases} \tag{26}$$

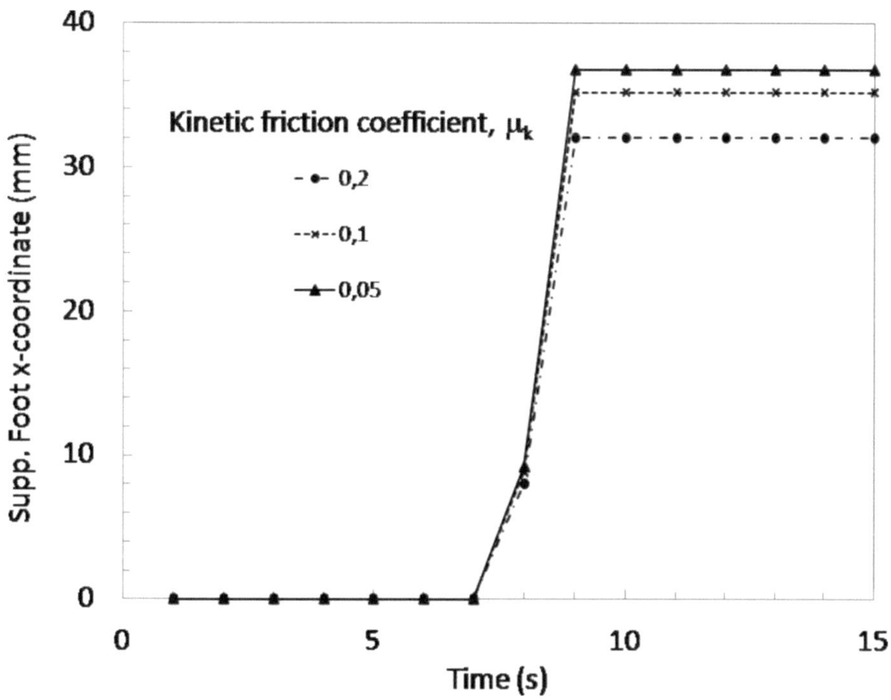

Figure 13. Evolution of the motor crank angle for different motor torques, when the biped starts walking from rest, according to the program described in this chapter (a) and according to Working Model 2D simulations (b).

To solve this system of differential equations, Eq. (26), a time discretization is used. For each time step, a linear inhomogeneous system is calculated, where the forces between links, and the angular acceleration of the motor crank, $\ddot{\vartheta}_8$, are unknowns, while the angular velocity of the motor crank, ϑ_8, is known. In fact, ϑ_8 is assigned an initial input, $\vartheta_8(t=0)$, which is updated after solving Eq. (26) in the previous time step, regarding the determined angular acceleration as constant during Δt. Then the updated angular velocity is as follows:

$$\dot{\vartheta}_8[n\Delta t] = \dot{\vartheta}_8[(n-1)\Delta t] + \ddot{\vartheta}_8 \Delta t \tag{27}$$

Thus, the coefficient matrix is obtained from Eq. (19) by eliminating the column corresponding to the torque coefficients T_8 (previously, it was unknown), and adding a column representing the coefficients of the motor crank angular acceleration, $\ddot{\vartheta}_8$. The torque T_8 must now be included in the right-hand side (RHS) column vector. The forward dynamics system is obtained as

$$A=\begin{bmatrix} a_{11} & a_{12} & \cdots & a_{1,71} & 0 \\ a_{21} & a_{22} & \cdots & a_{2,71} & 0 \\ a_{31} & a_{32} & \cdots & a_{3,71} & -m_2x_2{}'(\vartheta_8) \\ a_{41} & a_{42} & \cdots & a_{4,71} & -m_2y_2{}'(\vartheta_8) \\ a_{51} & a_{52} & \cdots & a_{5,71} & -I_2\vartheta_2{}'(\vartheta_8) \\ \vdots & \vdots & \ddots & \vdots & \vdots \\ a_{71,1} & a_{71,2} & \cdots & a_{71,71} & -I_{12}\vartheta_{12}{}'(\vartheta_8) \end{bmatrix};U=\begin{bmatrix} f_{01x} \\ f_{01y} \\ f_{12x} \\ f_{12y} \\ \vdots \\ . \\ f_{10',12'y} \\ \ddot{\vartheta}_8 \end{bmatrix};C=\begin{bmatrix} 0 \\ m_1g \\ m_2X_2{}''(\vartheta_8)\dot{\vartheta}_8^2 \\ m_2g+m_2y_2{}''(\vartheta_8)\dot{\vartheta}_8^2 \\ I_2\vartheta_2{}''(\vartheta_8)\dot{\vartheta}_8^2 \\ \vdots \\ T_8 \end{bmatrix} \quad (28)$$

$$[A(\text{coeff.})]\cdot\left[U(\text{forces},\ddot{\vartheta}_8)\right]=[C(\text{cts})]\Rightarrow[U]=[A]^{-1}\cdot[C]$$

Note that the torque T_8 now appears in the RHS column vector (constants column). Now some results from the developed forward dynamics model are presented.

As shown in **Figure 13(a)**, the torque above which the biped can start walking is 0.84 Nm. The initial value of ϑ_8 is π/2 (both feet are on the floor).

These results were compared with those obtained with the software Working Model 2D. Comparing **Figure 13(a)** and **(b)**, we can say that the results are similar enough to each other to validate the program described in this chapter.

The MATLAB® program allows changing the density. In **Figure 14**, the motor crank angle is plotted for a constant torque, T_8 = 1 Nm and varying total weight (obtained by varying the density of all links).

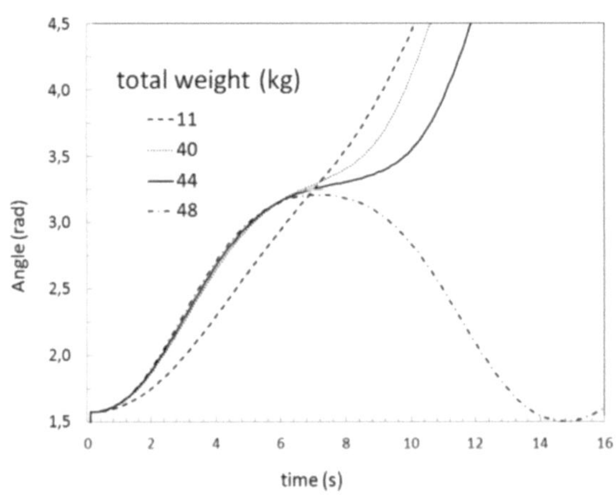

Figure 14. Evolution of the motor crank angle, for a constant motor torque, T_8 = 1 Nm, and for different total weights.

http://dx.doi.org/10.5772/63372

7. Dynamics of the biped robot PASIBOT including slippage between the ground and the supporting foot

7.1. Inverse dynamics with slippage

In the previous sections, we have applied inverse dynamics to parametrically calculate the required torque at the sole motor for PASIBOT to walk at a steady state (constant speed) with no sliding between the supporting foot and the floor. However, when sliding between the supported foot and the floor is allowed the kinematics is unknown and other approaches must be applied. In fact, three more equations regarding the supporting foot dynamics must be considered, as well as the kinematics-statics friction condition.

The forces acting on the supporting foot are

$$f_{01_x} - f_{12_x} - f_{112_x} = m_1 \ddot{x}_1 ; f_{12y} - f_{12y} - f_{112_y} = m_1 g \tag{29}$$

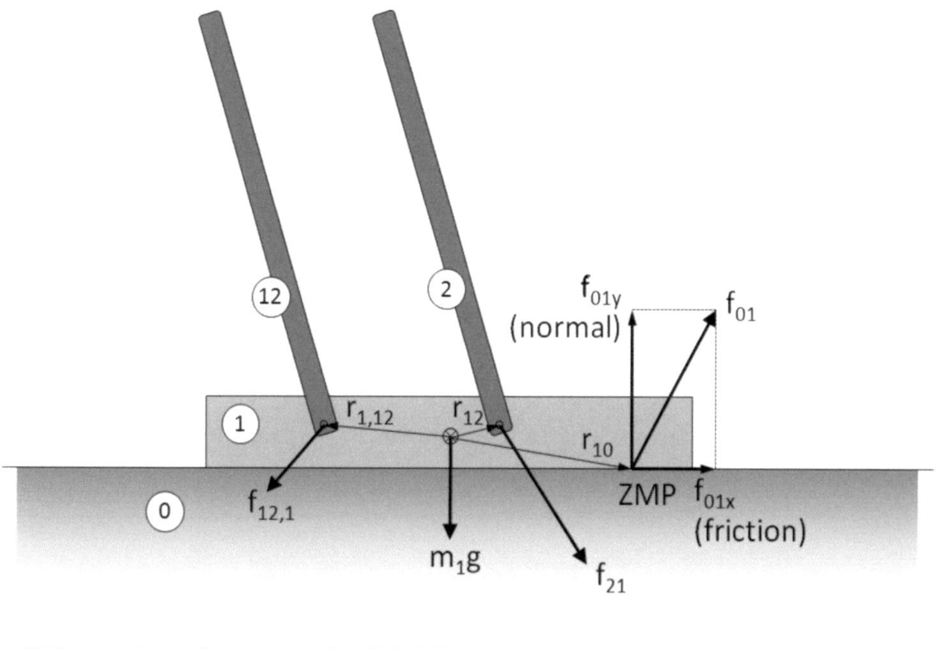

Figure 15. Forces acting on the supporting foot (link 1). Link 1 is connected to links 2 and 12. The floor is considered as link 0.

Since r_{10_x} and $f_{01_y} r$ are both unknown, Eq. (30) is the non-linear torque equation for the supporting foot (link 1; see **Figure 15**):

$$r_{10_x} f_{01_y} - r_{10_y} f_{01_x} - \left(r_{12_x} f_{12_y} - r_{12_y} f_{12_x} \right) - \left(r_{1,12_x} f_{1,12_y} - r_{1,12_y} f_{1,12_x} \right) = 0 \tag{30}$$

Eq. (30) is non-linear. If Eq. (18) is solved without Eq. (30), the latter can be used to obtain the instantaneous zero moment point (ZMP) relative to the center of mass, ZMPx = r_{10_x} r10x, which determines whether the biped topples.

In summary, the "inverse dynamic static friction equation" is obtained as follows in a matrix form:

$$\begin{bmatrix} a_{11} & a_{12} & \cdots & a_{1,71} \\ a_{21} & a_{22} & \cdots & a_{2,71} \\ \vdots & \vdots & \ddots & \vdots \\ a_{71,1} & a_{71,2} & \cdots & a_{71,71} \end{bmatrix} \cdot \begin{bmatrix} f_{01_x} \\ f_{01_y} \\ f_{12_x} \\ f_{12_y} \\ \vdots \\ T_8 \\ \vdots \end{bmatrix} = \begin{bmatrix} 0 \\ m_1 g \\ m_2 \ddot{X}_2 \\ m_2 g + m_2 \ddot{y}_2 \\ I_2 \ddot{\vartheta}_2 \\ \vdots \\ I_{12'} \ddot{\vartheta}_{12'} \end{bmatrix} \tag{31}$$

$$[A(\text{coefficients})]\cdot[F(\text{force})] = [I(\text{inertia})] \Rightarrow$$
$$\Rightarrow [F] = [A]^{-1} \cdot [I]$$

The forces and the motor torque in each time step are computed by solving Eq. (31) via matrix inversion encoded in MATLAB®.

When the supporting foot is allowed to slide, x_1 becomes an independent variable (in general, $x_1 \neq 0$, $\dot{x}_1 \neq 0$, $\ddot{x}_1 \neq 0$). To consider sliding between two bodies involves three possible scenarios: (1) no sliding (static friction), (2) imminent sliding, and (3) actual sliding. To determine the sliding status at each time step, conditional branching was incorporated into the code.

Initially, no sliding is assumed and the state is static friction ($x_1 = 0; \dot{x}_1 = 0; \ddot{x}_1 = 0$). Thus, solving Eq. (31), the values of friction force (f_{01_x}) and normal force (f_{01_y}) are calculated. Then, the static friction condition

$$\left| f_{01_x} \right| \leq \mu_s \left| f_{01_y} \right| \tag{32}$$

is evaluated for a specified static friction coefficient, μ_s. If Eq. (31) is satisfied, the time is incremented by Δt and Eq. (31) is recalculated using the updated values of r_{ij}, $\ddot{x}_i$, $\ddot{y}_i$, $\ddot{\vartheta}_i$. This step closes the "static friction" conditional loop.

If Eq. (32) is false, the PASIBOT enters the state of imminent slipping. This system has the following conditions: First, since the acceleration of the supporting foot, $\ddot{x}_1$, is no longer zero but unknown, it must appear in the column vector of unknowns. Second, the kinetic frictional relationship between normal and tangential components of the floor-foot force must be considered:

$$\left|f_{01_x}\right| = \mu_k \left|f_{01_y}\right|, \tag{33}$$

where μ_k is the kinetic friction coefficient.

The new matrix of coefficients is then obtained from its predecessor by adding the following:

- A column of mi elements in positions corresponding to the x components of Newton's equations, with zeros elsewhere.
- An additional row incorporating Eq. (34).

Therefore, the final matrix form of the "inverse dynamic sliding friction equation" is as follows:

$$\left[\begin{array}{ccccc|c} a_{11} & a_{12} & \cdots & a_{1,71} & & -m_1 \\ a_{21} & a_{22} & \cdots & a_{2,71} & & 0 \\ a_{31} & a_{32} & \cdots & a_{3,71} & & -m_2 \\ \vdots & \vdots & \ddots & \vdots & & \vdots \\ a_{71,1} & a_{71,2} & \cdots & a_{71,71} & & 0 \\ \hline 1 & \pm\mu_k & 0 & \cdots & & 0 \end{array}\right] \cdot \begin{bmatrix} f_{01_x} \\ f_{01_y} \\ f_{12_x} \\ f_{12_y} \\ \vdots \\ T_8 \\ \vdots \\ f_{10',12'_y} \\ \ddot{x}_1 \end{bmatrix} = \begin{bmatrix} 0 \\ m_1 g \\ m_2 \ddot{X}_2 \\ m_2 g + m_2 \ddot{y}_2 \\ I_2 \ddot{\vartheta}_2 \\ \vdots \\ I_{12'} \ddot{\vartheta}_{12'} \\ 0 \end{bmatrix} \tag{34}$$

$$\left[A(\text{Coefficients})\right] \cdot \left[U(\text{Unknowns})\right] = \left[C(\text{Constants})\right] \Rightarrow \left[U\right] = \left[A\right]^{-1} \cdot \left[C\right]$$

The sign of the friction force is depending on the sliding status in the previous calculation. The friction force opposes the horizontal component of the other forces acting on the foot when the previous state was imminent sliding. The friction force opposes the velocity of the supporting foot when the previous state was actual sliding.

With Eq. (34), the MATLAB® program calculates the acceleration with which the supporting foot has begun sliding, $\ddot{x}_1$. In the current time interval ($(n-1)\Delta T - n\Delta t$), the supporting foot is assumed to move with the calculated uniform acceleration. The velocity and position of the supporting foot are then updated by Eq. (35):

$$\begin{aligned} \ddot{x}_1 &= \text{constant in the interval } \Delta t \\ \dot{x}_1[n\Delta t] &= \dot{x}_1[(n-1)\Delta t] + \ddot{x}_1 \Delta t \\ x_1[n\Delta t] &= x_1[(n-1)\Delta t] + \dot{x}_1[(n-1)\Delta t] \cdot \Delta t + \frac{1}{2}\ddot{x}_1 (\Delta t)^2 \end{aligned} \tag{35}$$

The MATLAB® program obtain the kinematics and dynamics data (torque and force data) for all links, and then it increments the time by Δt and re-solves Eq. (34). Note that the square brackets show the dependence.

When the PASIBOT is having a slippage, the friction force is against the supporting foot movement. This force is considered constant during this time interval, and it can stop the sliding of the PASIBOT but not change the direction of the movement. This is obtained with the stopping time, t_s, and compares it with the time increment, Δt, as shown in Eq. (36):

$$t_s = -\frac{\dot{x}_1}{\ddot{x}_1} \tag{36}$$

If t_s is positive and less than Δt, then friction stop the PASIBOT sliding before the end of the time interval. Else, if it becomes negative or exceeds Δt, the PASIBOT continues sliding in the time interval. After that, the MATLAB® program updates the results using t_s instead of Δt and returns to the beginning to solve the case of static friction, as provided in Eq. (31).

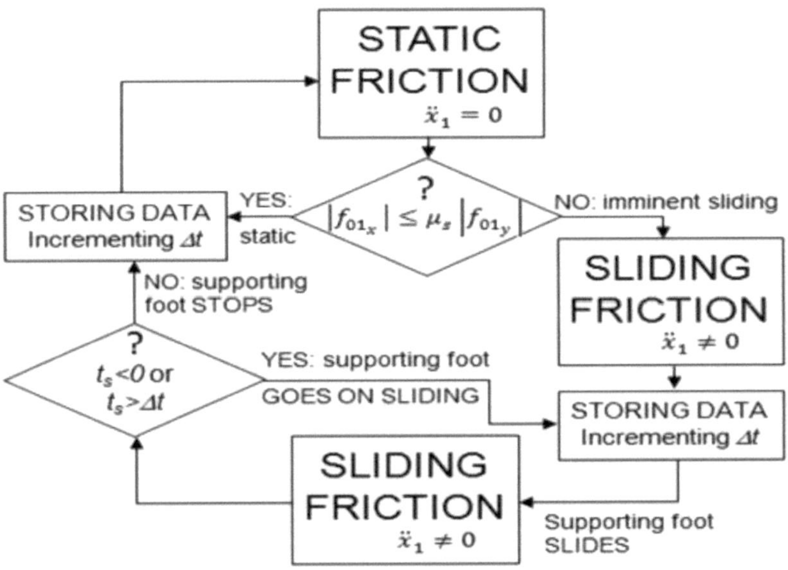

Figure 16. MATLAB® program flowchart with slippage.

http://dx.doi.org/10.5772/63372

In **Figure 16**, it is shown the MATLAB® program inverse dynamics flowchart with slippage. The forces between links and torque (dynamical variables) are calculated during the "STORING DATA" task. The position, velocity, and acceleration (kinematic unknowns) for the supporting foot are updated according to Eq. (34).

7.2. Forward dynamics with slippage

In the previous sections, we have applied this methodology to design the MATLAB® program of inverse dynamics with slippage. To obtain the forward dynamics program, the slippage is treated as in 30, while the dynamics is formulated as in 34. The MATLAB® flowchart showed in **Figure 16** is mostly maintained, but the systems of equations are different:

– The equation system to be calculated in the state of "STATIC FRICTION" is the forward dynamics system of Eq. (28): static system (ST).

– The equation system that describes the slippage of PASIBOT (Eq. 35) in the state of "SLIDING FRICTION," is added to Eq. (28). Also, the motor torque appears in the constants' column and the motor acceleration and the slippage acceleration become the penultimate and final elements of the unknowns' column. Using Eqs. (20)–(25), the first and second derivatives with respect to ϑ_8 of the position, velocity, and acceleration of every link are calculated, with a sufficiently fine discretization of ϑ_8. The resulting system of equations (36) is referred to as the "sliding system (SL)."

$$\left[\begin{array}{cccccc|c} a_{11} & a_{12} & \cdots & a_{1,71} & 0 & & -m_1 \\ a_{21} & a_{22} & \cdots & a_{2,71} & 0 & & 0 \\ a_{31} & a_{32} & \cdots & a_{3,71} & -m_2 x_2^{pf}{}'(\vartheta_8) & & -m_2 \\ a_{41} & a_{42} & \cdots & a_{4,71} & -m_2 y_2{}'(\vartheta_8) & & 0 \\ a_{51} & a_{52} & \cdots & a_{5,71} & -I_2 \vartheta_2{}'(\vartheta_8) & & 0 \\ \vdots & \vdots & \ddots & \vdots & \vdots & & \vdots \\ \cdots & \cdots & \cdots & \cdots & -I_8 & & 0 \\ \vdots & \vdots & \vdots & \ddots & \vdots & & \vdots \\ a_{71,1} & a_{71,2} & \cdots & a_{71,71} & -I_{12''} \vartheta_{12'}(\vartheta_8) & & 0 \\ \hline 1 & \pm\mu_k & 0 & \cdots & 0 & & 0 \end{array}\right] \cdot \begin{bmatrix} f_{01x} \\ f_{01y} \\ f_{12x} \\ f_{12y} \\ \vdots \\ . \\ f_{10',12'y} \\ \ddot{\vartheta}_8 \\ \ddot{x}_1 \end{bmatrix} = \begin{bmatrix} 0 \\ m_1 g \\ m_2 X_2{}''(\vartheta_8)\dot{\vartheta}_8^2 \\ m_2 g + m_2 y_2{}''(\vartheta_8)\dot{\vartheta}_8^2 \\ I_2 \vartheta_2{}''(\vartheta_8)\dot{\vartheta}_8^2 \\ \vdots \\ T_8 \\ \vdots \\ . \end{bmatrix} \tag{37}$$

$$[A(\text{coeff.})]\cdot\left[U(\text{forces}, \ddot{\vartheta}_8, \ddot{x}_1)\right] = [C(\text{cts})] \Rightarrow [U] = [A]^{-1}\cdot[C]$$

– In "STORING DATA" mode, the kinematics of the supporting foot is updated by Eq. (37). The motor crank position and velocity is updated according to Eq. (35).

Some results are presented in the following figures, in which different friction coefficients and motor crank velocities have been considered. **Figure 17** plots the horizontal supporting foot position as a function of time for a constant motor crank angular velocity, $\dot{\vartheta}_8$=3rad/s, and varying friction coefficient (here $\mu_s = \mu_k \equiv \mu$). From this plot, we can deduce the time course of the supporting foot sliding.

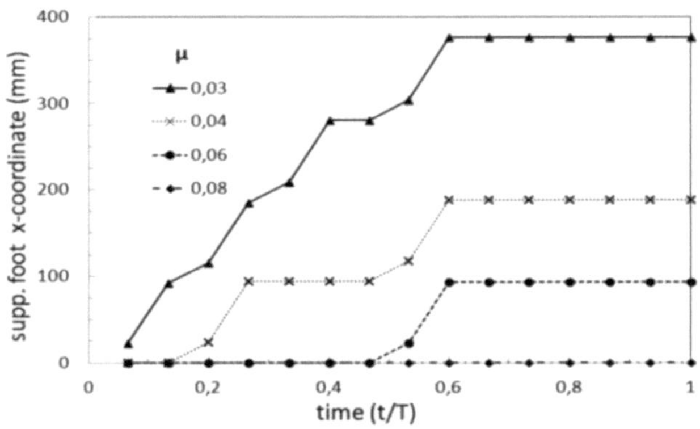

Figure 17. Supporting foot versus time (in units of one period, T) for constant $\vartheta_8 = 3$ rad/s, for a set of different friction coefficient.

In **Figure 17**, it is shown that the minimum friction coefficient that prevents the slippage is 0.08. Also, it can be observed that the slippage occurs during preferred phases. The sliding starts at mid-step until when the swinging leg has reached its highest point. If two slippages occur, one of them is again invoked at mid-step, while the other occurs at the first quarter step. For $\mu = 0.03$, slippage occurs repeatedly at various phases.

Figure 18 shows the sliding characteristics for constant friction coefficient $\mu = 0.1$ but different motor crank angular velocities.

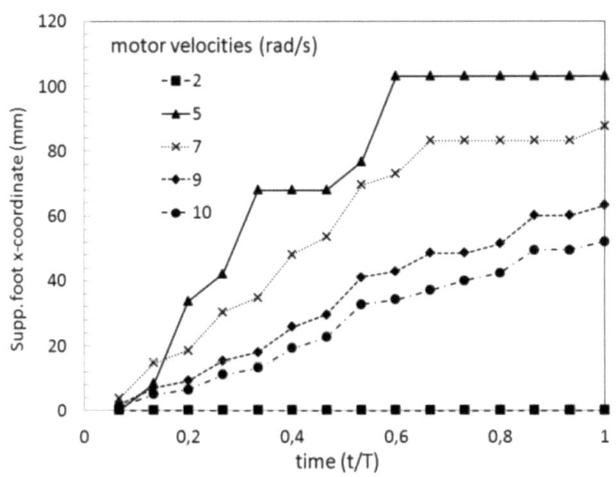

Figure 18. Supporting foot versus time (in units of one period, *T*) for $\mu = 0.1$, varying ϑ_8.

Because the program is parametric it is easy to set different values for static and kinetic friction coefficients (kinetic friction coefficient is smaller than static friction coefficient). **Figure 19** shows the supporting foot of the PASIBOT with slippage for a static friction coefficient, μ_s = 0.2, and three different kinetic friction coefficient, $\mu_k = 0.2$, 0.1, and 0.05.

Note that the bigger the kinetic friction coefficient, the smaller the sliding distance slippage occurs. Also, if there is slippage, it occurs at the same point for all three cases.

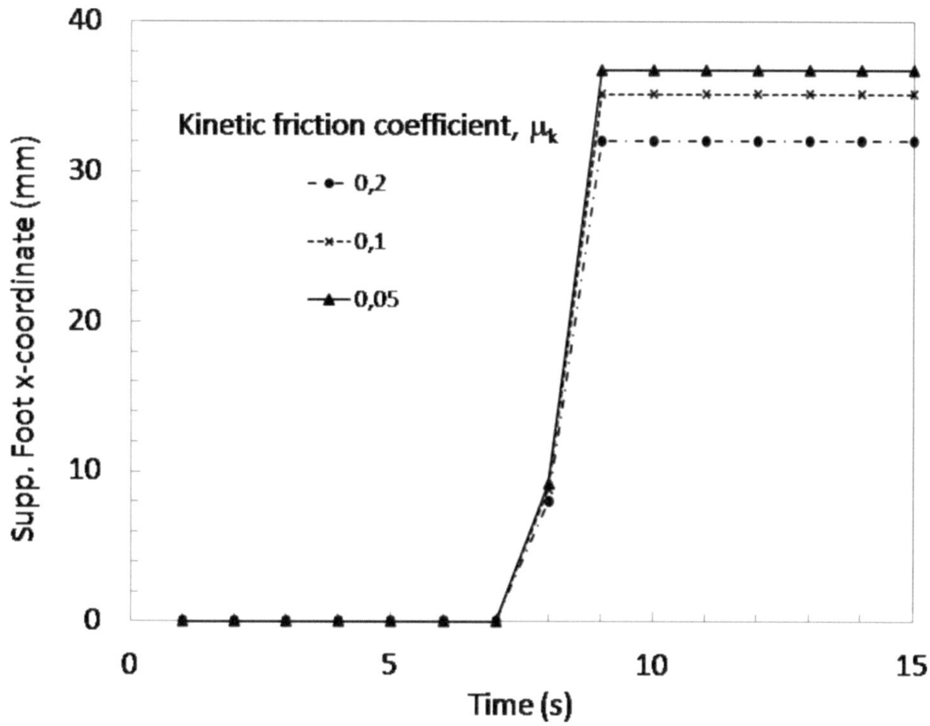

Figure 19. Supporting foot versus time for constant $\dot{\vartheta}_8$ = 5 rad/s, for the same static friction coefficient and for three different kinetic friction coefficients.

8. Applied quasi-static approach methodology to UGV

The quasi-static methodology is applied in this chapter. The main advantage of this approach is that it is easily optimized. It is applied to a vehicle in order to optimize the navigation capabilities. This methodology is applied to an UGV shown in **Figure 20**, which was designed and developed by the Tallinn University of Technology. This unmanned ground vehicle can change the angle between the body and the legs to improve the capabilities of passing obstacles or navigation. It changes the position of the center of mass (CoM) relative to the ground-wheel contacts, as well as the distance between the ground and the body [14].

In order to explain how to apply the methodology to implement this analysis in MATLAB® code, the nomenclature and geometry of the vehicle are presented. The position and/or trajectories of centers of mass, joints, and ground-wheel contact points are defined. Then the quasi-static model is developed and the equations to calculate the forces and torques involved are implemented in MATLAB®. The algorithm with the quasi-static equations obtains the position along the track for any configuration angles, and then calculates the optimal values of those angles that satisfy a given condition. If the vehicle slips or overturns at any point of the track, it is also calculated by the program [15, 16].

Figure 20. The unmanned ground vehicle (UGV) of Tallinn University of Technology.

The nomenclature is shown in the following list:

F_{lw}: force on the rear wheel exerted by the rear leg

F_{wl}: force on the front leg exerted by the front wheel

F_r: friction force exerted by the ground on the rear wheel

F_f: friction force exerted by the ground on the front wheel

N_r: normal force exerted by the ground on the rear wheel

N_f: normal force exerted by the ground on the front wheel

M: torque on the wheels (supposedly the same on front and rear wheels)

D: ground-front wheel contact point; T: ground-back wheel contact point

$L = 0.83$ m: body length; $l = 0.35$m: leg length; C: Center of mass

φ_r: angle between rear leg and body; φ_f: angle between front leg and body

β_r, β_f: rear wheel contact angle, front wheel contact angle

$f(x)$: function defining the track profile

$g(x)$: function defining the trajectory for the centers of the wheels

$m_w = 50$ kg: wheel mass; $m_b = 300$ kg: body mass; $m_l = 20$ kg: leg mass

First, the problem of positions is resolved. For a given ground function, with the front wheel position, x_f and the configuration angles, φ_r and φ_f, the back wheel can be located. The slope of the ground at x is obtained as: $\beta x = \tan\text{-}1[f'(x)]$. After the locus of the centers of the wheels, g(s) are calculated as follows (see **Figure 21**):

http://dx.doi.org/10.5772/63372

$$s = x - r\sin\beta_x$$
$$f(x) \to g(s) = f(x) + r\cos\beta_x \quad (38)$$

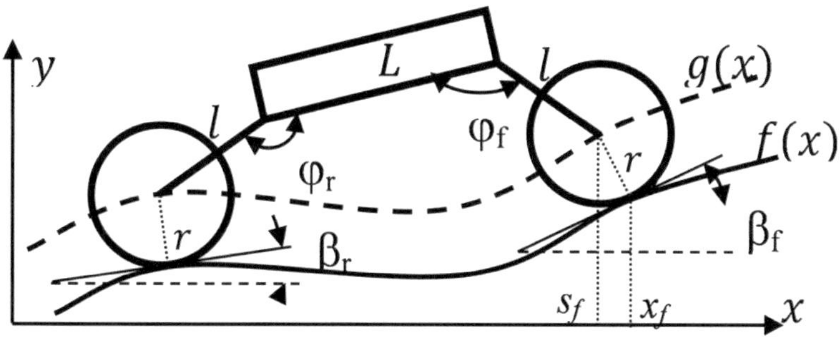

Figure 21. Position problem.

The front wheel center position (sf,g(sf)) is obtained from Eq. (38) and the wheelbase is solved as following:

$$R = \sqrt{\left(L - l\cos\cos\varphi_{\mathrm{r}} - l\cos\cos\varphi_{\mathrm{f}}\right)^2 + l^2\left(\sin\sin\varphi_{\mathrm{r}} - \sin\sin\varphi_{\mathrm{f}}\right)^2} \quad (39)$$

The intersection between the function g(s) and the circumference of radius R centered on the front wheel $(x_{\mathrm{f}} - r\sin\sin\beta_{\mathrm{f}},\ f(x_{\mathrm{f}}) + r\cos\cos\beta_{\mathrm{f}})$ locates the back wheel center (see **Figure 22**).

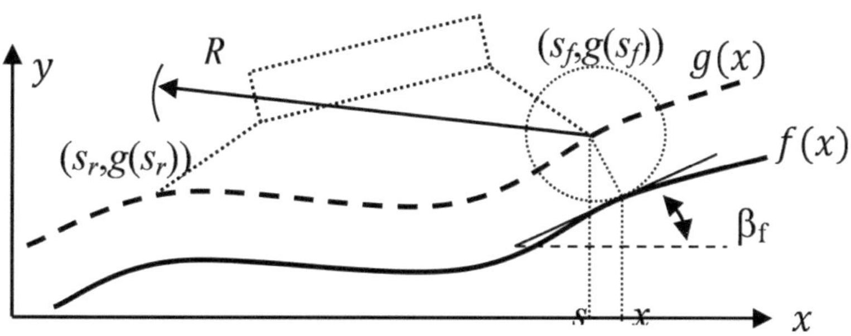

Figure 22. Scheme for locating the back wheel center.

Once the position of the vehicle is established, the locations of the CoMs are solved. The quasi-static approach can be calculated with three subsystems: (see **Figure 23**): (1) back wheel, (2) back wheel, both legs and body, and (3) the whole vehicle.

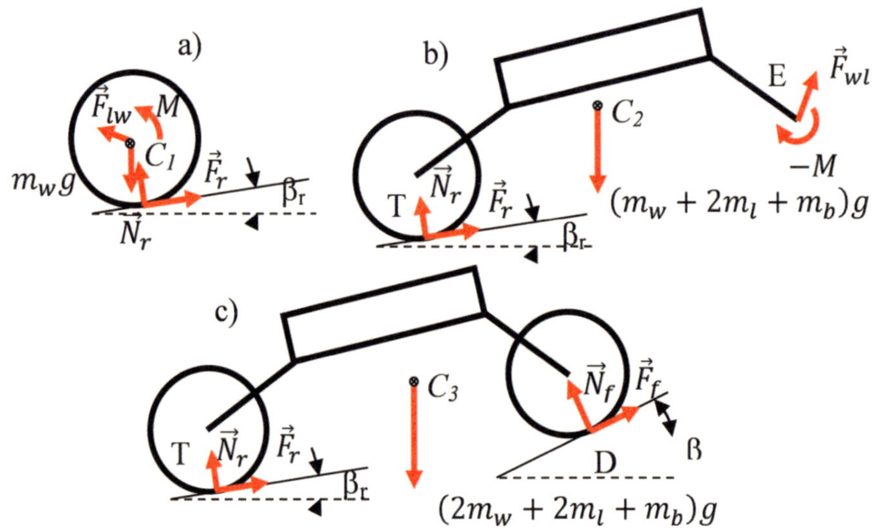

Figure 23. Vehicle subsystems.

For each subsystem, equilibrium requires two force equations and one moment equation:

$$\text{a)}\begin{cases} F_r \cos\cos\beta_r - N_r \sin\sin\beta_r + F_{lw_x} = 0 \\ F_r \sin\sin\beta_r + N_r \cos\cos\beta_r + F_{lw_y} = m_w g \\ F_r r + M = 0 \end{cases} \tag{40}$$

$$\text{b)}\begin{cases} F_r Fr \cos\cos\beta_r Br - N_r Nr \sin\sin\beta_r Br + F_{wl_x} = 0 \\ F_r Frfsinfsin\beta_r Br + N_r Nr \cos\cos\beta_r Br + F_{wl_y} = (m_w + 2m_l + m_b)g \\ (C_2T)_x (F_r \sin\sin\beta_r + N_r \cos\cos\beta_r) - (C_2T)_y (F_r \cos\cos\beta_r \cos\cos\beta_r - N_r \sin\sin\beta_r \sin\sin\beta_r) + \\ +(C_2E)_y F_{wl_x} - (C_2E)_x F_{wl_y} - M = 0 \end{cases} \tag{41}$$

$$c)\begin{cases} F_r \cos\cos\beta_r - N_r \sin\sin\beta_r + F_f \cos\cos\beta_f - N_f \sin\sin\beta_f = 0 \\ F_r \sin\sin\beta_r + N_r \cos\cos\beta_r + F_f \sin\sin\beta_f + N_f \cos\cos\beta_f = (2m_w + 2m_l + m_b)g \\ (C_3T)_x (F_r \sin\sin\beta_r + N_r \cos\cos\beta_r) - (C_3T)_y (F_r \cos\cos\beta_r - N_r \sin\sin\beta_r) + \\ +(C_3D)_x (F_f \sin\sin\beta_f + N_f \cos\cos\beta_f) - (C_3D)_y (F_f \cos\cos\beta_f - N_f \sin\sin\beta_f) = 0 \end{cases} \tag{42}$$

where the unknowns are: F_r, N_r, F_f, N_f, F_{lw_x} Flwx, F_{lwy} Flwy, F_{lw_x} Fwlx, F_{lwy} Fwly and M. The torque is the same on front and back wheels. This system of nine equations can be simplified

http://dx.doi.org/10.5772/63372

into a new system of five equations, where the unknowns are the torque, normal forces, and friction forces. And in a matrix form: A·F = C ⇒ F = A-1 C, where

$$A = \begin{matrix} \cos\beta_r & -\sin\beta_r & \cos\beta_f & -\sin\beta_f & 0 \\ \sin\beta_r & \cos\beta_r & \sin\beta_f & \cos\beta_f & 0 \\ r & 0 & 0 & 0 & 1 \\ C_2T\ _x \sin\beta_r - \ C_2T\ _y \cos\beta_r) & C_2T\ _x \cos\beta_r + \ C_2T\ _y \sin\beta_r & C_2E\ _x \sin\beta_f - \ C_2E\ _y \cos\beta_f & C_2E\ _x \cos\beta_f + \ C_2E\ _y \sin\beta_f & -1 \\ C_3T\ _x \sin\beta_r - \ C_3T\ _y \cos\beta_r & C_3T\ _x \cos\beta_r + \ C_3T\ _y \sin\beta_r & C_3D\ _x \sin\beta_f - \ C_3D\ _y \cos\beta_f & C_3D\ _x \cos\beta_f + \ C_3D\ _y \sin\beta_f & 0 \end{matrix}$$

$$F = \begin{bmatrix} F_r \\ N_r \\ F_f \\ N_f \\ M \end{bmatrix} C = \begin{bmatrix} 0 \\ (2m_w + 2m_l + m_b)g \\ 0 \\ (C_2E)_x (m_b g) \\ 0 \end{bmatrix} \tag{43}$$

MATLAB® code is used to solve the system of five equations. The program calculate for a set of discretized values of the front wheel position, the needed torque for any combination of a set of discretized values of the angles ϕ_r and ϕ_d. Thus, different criterions can be applied: minimize the energy to be supplied to the wheels, minimize the instantaneous torque or maximization the grip, the ground-wheel normal force, etc.

Some results are presented for a soft bump: square exponential profile, $f(x)=0.1e^{-(x-4)^2}$ (in meters). **Figure 24** shows the torque function that must be applied for any static configurations angles passing the soft bump.

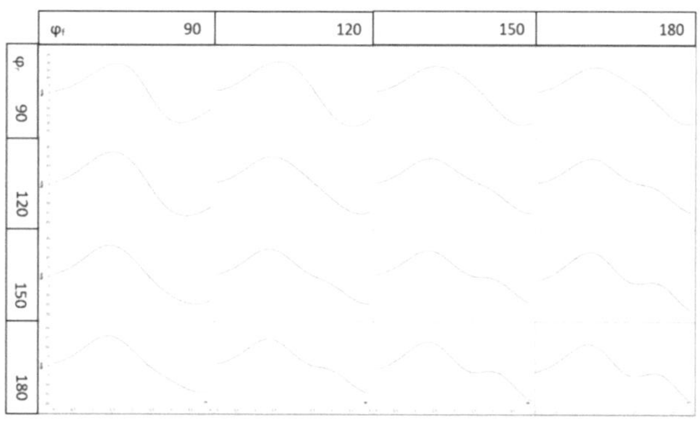

Figure 24. Torque needed passing a soft bump for different static configuration angles.

Figure 25(a) shows configuration angles variation needed to pass over the soft bump, with the minimum variation of torque and the corresponding torque function. **Figure 25(b)** shows the sequence of the UGV passing through the soft bump.

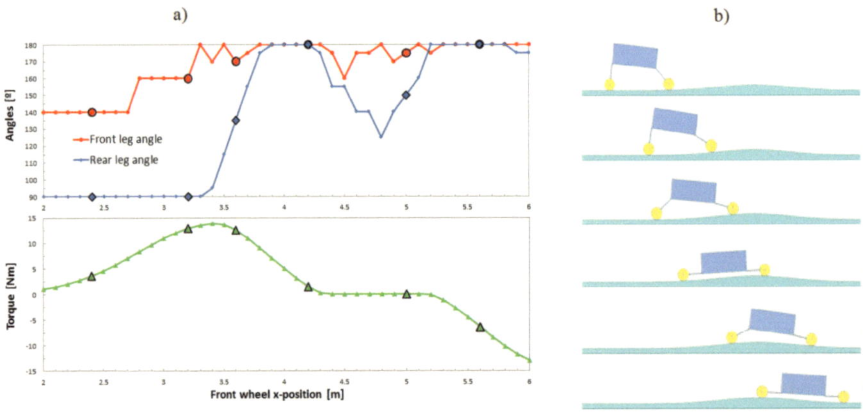

Figure 25. (a) Configuration angles and torque and (b) sequence of the UGV.

9. Conclusions

The methodology provided in this chapter can be applied to mechanisms, vehicles, or robots for the complete mechanical study. The kinematics and dynamics are solved using Newton-Euler equations, from the movement of the actuator to iterating during the time of initial condition as well as external forces, and with the quasi-static approach.

The programs have been designed so that all parameters can be modified. It was possible to automate these calculations creating an algorithm implemented in a programming language to simply find the solutions and the results of the analysis.

The methodology has been applied to design the biped robot PASIBOT. The kinematics and dynamics (both forward and inverse) of the biped robot "PASIBOT," taking into account for support foot slippage are encoded in MATLAB® code.

The great advantage of creating a parametric MATLAB® code following this methodology is that the algorithm can be modify to obtain the results in a parametric way or even changing the conditions easily. For example, it can calculate the motion of the biped from the torque function given by the biped's sole motor or the torques required for starting and braking as well as defining the conditions that prevent or control slippage.

Because the program remains parametric the lengths, densities and masses, motor velocities and torque, friction coefficients and other parameters can be modified by the user.

The methodology was also applied to another machine, a UGV vehicle, obtaining navigation optimization results. A numerical program based on a quasi-static half vehicle model is presented. For a given profile that could be read by sensors the program calculates how the angles between the body and the legs must vary, in order to fulfill the criteria like maintain as constant as possible the torque for example. The program created with this methodology in

MATLAB® code also can calculate the values of normal and friction forces, checking if the UGV rolls over or slip at any point.

In conclusion, this methodology can help to generate MATLAB® programs that will be valuable tools to optimize some navigation capabilities, dynamics analysis, quasi-static analysis, and slippage control among other.

Following this link the reader can find some examples of MATLAB codes done with the methodology of the chapter: http://www.mathworks.com/matlabcentral/profile/authors/7854464-eduardo-corral

The code that calculates the inverse dynamic of the biped PASIBOT with slippage (using the methodology that we explain in the chapter) and the code that calculates the torque of the UGV and that optimized the best route are in the previous links.

Author details

E. Corral*, J. Meneses and J.C. García-Prada

*Address all correspondence to: eduardocorralabad@gmail.com

MAQLAB group, Universidad Carlos III de Madrid, Spain

References

[1] Corral, E., Meneses, J., Castejón, C., García-Prada, J.C. Forward and inverse dynamics of the biped PASIBOT. Int J Adv Robot Syst, 2014, 11:109. doi: 10.5772/58537

[2] Meneses, J., Castejón, C., Corral, E., Rubio, H., García-Prada, J.C. Kinematics and dynamics of the quasi-passive biped "PASIBOT". Strojniški vestnik J Mech Eng, 2011, 57, 12:879–887.

[3] Corral, E., Meneses, J., Rubio, H., Castejón, C., García-Prada, J.C. A configuration optimization algorithm based on quasi-static approach for a UGV. 17th International conference on climbing and walking robots, CLAWARS 2014, University of Technology, Poznan, Poland, 2014.

[4] Corral, E., Meneses, J., Garcia-Prada, J.C. Inverse and forward dynamics of the biped PASIBOT. International Symposium on Multibody Systems and Mechatronics, MUSME 2011, Valencia, España, 2011.

[5] Fujimoto, Y. Minimum Energy Trajectory Planning for Biped Robots, Humanoid Robots: New Developments, Armando Carlos de Pina Filho (Ed.), InTech, Rijeka, Croatia, 2007, ISBN: 978-3-902613-00-4, Available from: http://www.intechopen.com/

books/humanoid_robots_new_developments/minimum_energy_trajectory_planning_for_biped_robots

[6] Kappaganthu, L., Nataraj, C. Optimal Biped Design Using a Moving Torso: Theory and Experiments, Biped Robots, Prof. Armando Carlos Pina Filho (Ed.), InTech, 2011, ISBN: 978-953-307-216-6, Available from: http://www.intechopen.com/books/biped-robots/optimal-biped-design-using-a-moving-torsotheory-and-experiments

[7] Garcia de Jalon, J., Bayo, E. Kinematic and Dynamic Simulation of Multibody Systems – The Real-Time Challenge," Springer-Verlag, New York, 1993.

[8] Shabana, A.A., Computational Dynamics, Wiley, New York, United States, 2001.

[9] Shabana, A.A., Dynamics of Multibody Systems, 2nd ed., Cambridge University Press, New York, United States, 1998.

[10] Castejón, C., Carbone, G., García-Prada, J.C., Cecarelli, M. A methodology to design robotic arms for service tasks since early design stage, Int J Mech Control, 13, 02:73–83, 2012. ISSN: 1590-8844

[11] Castejón, C., Carbone, G., García-Prada, J.C., Ceccarelli, M. A multi-objective optimization of a robotic arm for service tasks. Strojniški vestnik – J Mech Eng, 2010, 56, 5:316–329.

[12] Gómez, M.J., Castejón, C., García-Prada. J.C., (2010). Evaluación de la adaptabilidad mecánica de los robots en entornos humanos (*Evaluation of Mechanical Adaptability of Robots in Human Environments*), in language spanish. Anales de Ingeniería Mecánica. Vol 01, Pages 187. ISSN: 0212-5072.

[13] Tokiwadai, Hodogayaku, Yokohama. Maintaining floor-foot contact of a biped robot by force constraint position control. Proceedings of the 2011 IEEE International Conference on Mechatronics, 2011.

[14] Universal Ground Vehicle , Research Project L523. Tallinn University of Technology , Department of Mechatronics , 2005–2008.

[15] Corral, E., Meneses, J., Aryassov, G. A quasi-static approach to optimize the motion of a UGV depending of the track profile. 9th International Conference, MSM, Vilnius, Lithuania, 2013.

[16] Corral, E., Aryassov, G., Meneses, J. A quasi-static approach to optimize the motion of an UGV depending on the track profile. Solid State Phenomena, 2015, 220–221:774–780. doi:10.4028/www.scientific.net/SSP.220-221.774

Chapter 5

Design, Simulation, and Control of a Hexapod Robot in Simscape Multibody

Claudio Urrea, Luis Valenzuela and John Kern

Additional information is available at the end of the chapter

http://dx.doi.org/10.5772/63388

Abstract

In this chapter, we present the design, simulation, and control of a hexapod robot using tools available in MATLAB software. In addition, we design and implement a dynamic model (using the Simscape Multibody™ toolbox) as well as a three-dimensional model of the robot, using Virtual Reality Modeling Language (VRML), that help to visualize the robot's walking sequence. This three-dimensional model is interconnected with the Simscape Multibody™ blocks using MATLAB's virtual reality blocks. Apart from this, and following specific requirements, we design and implement a Proportional–Integral–Derivative controller in order to obtain a pre-established displacement for the robot that, thanks to the developed computer simulations, proved to be satisfactory. Special emphasis is put in obtaining a modular representation of the dynamic model of the studied robot because it will permit to design more sophisticated nonlinear controllers in future works, allowing a good dynamic behavior of the robot in front of environmental perturbations, an issue that will become evident through computer simulations of its displacement.

Keywords: Mobile Hexapod Robot, Robot control, Modeling, Simscape Multibody, Virtual reality

1. Introduction

Research on multi-legged walking robots, which are created to mimic the structure of limbs and movement control in insects and arthropods, has been carried out for decades. Among many multi-legged robots, the hexapod robot is one of the most employed robots for a wide range of tasks [1, 2].

INTECH
open science | open minds

© 2016 The Author(s). Licensee InTech. This chapter is distributed under the terms of the Creative Commons Attribution License (http://creativecommons.org/licenses/by/3.0), which permits unrestricted use, distribution, and reproduction in any medium, provided the original work is properly cited. (cc) BY

Hexapod robots have many advantages over other kinds of multi-legged walking robots: they can easily get and keep their equilibrium while moving (they are statically stable); they have the ability to adapt to irregular surfaces of different nature; they have redundancy of legs (it allow them to continue their task even if they lose a limb); they are omnidirectional and are less affected by environmental conditions than robots with wheels [3, 4].

Their advantages make them suitable for tasks requiring some degree of autonomy and high levels of reliability. Among the possible fields of application for hexapod robots, we have volcanic exploration, rescue procedures, detection of antipersonal landmines, undersea operations (marine floor), as well as sample collection, search for life, recognition missions in extraterrestrial exploration. The most of those tasks are hazardous and are usually accompanied by harsh environments, not compatible with human operation [5–7].

2. Hexapod robot

Success in designing a hexapod robot lies fundamentally in the structure of chosen legs. The main aspects of a hexapod robot's displacement are ruled by physical limitations of their legs. It is of paramount importance to choose a leg whose design provides the maximum possible range of movements and that does not pose unnecessary constraints that can affect the movement of the robot [5, 6].

2.1. Direct kinematics of a hexapod robot

In order to obtain the kinematics of the studied robot, it is necessary to use the Denavit-Hartenberg algorithm, applying it to a leg of the hexapod robot. This robot is formed by a symmetrical structure composed of six identical legs, having three degrees of freedom (DOF)

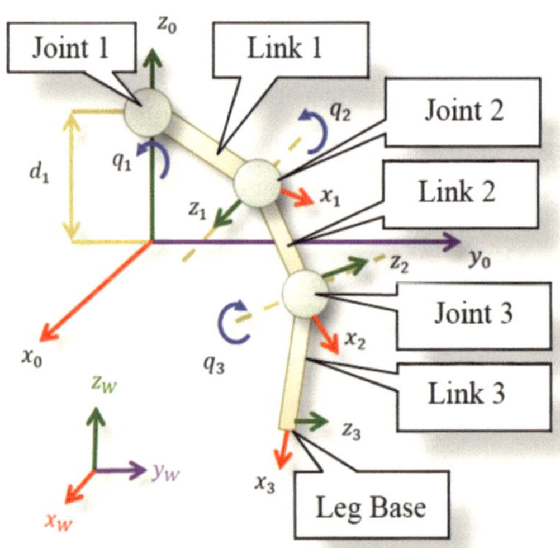

Figure 1. Model of the hexapod robot leg.

of rotational type in each leg. Thanks to its symmetry, this analysis can be done in one single leg [4, 7], as shown in **Figure 1**.

According to **Figure 1**, joint 1 is the point where the leg unites with the body of the robot (which is called "thorax"), link 1 is called "coxa," link 2 is called "femur," and link 3 is "tibia." Parameters obtained through the application of the Denavit-Hartenberg method are displayed in **Table 1**. Those parameters were obtained from the study of Olaru [7].

Link	a_i	α_i	d_i	θ_i
1	L1	90°	$d1$	$\theta 1$
2	L2	0°	0	$\theta 2$
3	L3	180°	0	$\theta 3$

Table 1. Denavit-Hartenberg parameters.

Those parameters originate the homogeneous transformation matrices that relate link i-1 with link i. It is possible to find the homogeneous transformation matrix for each link by means of equation (1), the which is presented in the study of Pullteap [4] and Olaru [7].

$$ {}^{i-1}A_i = \begin{bmatrix} \cos\theta_i & -\cos\alpha_i \cdot sen\theta_i & sen\alpha_i \cdot sen\theta_i & a_i \cdot \cos\theta_i \\ sen\theta_i & \cos\alpha_i \cdot \cos\theta_i & -sen\alpha_i \cdot \cos\theta_i & a_i \cdot sen\theta_i \\ 0 & sen\alpha_i & \cos\alpha_i & d_i \\ 0 & 0 & 0 & 1 \end{bmatrix} \tag{1} $$

The matrix that relates the first link with the reference system defined in **Figure 1** is shown in equation (2); the matrix that relates the second link with the first one is shown in equation (3); and finally, the matrix that relates the second link with the base of the robot's leg is given by equation (4).

$$ {}^{0}A_1 = \begin{bmatrix} \cos\theta_1 & 0 & sen\theta_1 & L_1 \cdot \cos\theta_1 \\ sen\theta_1 & 0 & -\cos\theta_1 & L_1 \cdot sen\theta_1 \\ 0 & 0 & 0 & d_1 \\ 0 & 0 & 0 & 1 \end{bmatrix} \tag{2} $$

$$ {}^{1}A_2 = \begin{bmatrix} \cos\theta_2 & sen\theta_2 & 0 & L_2 \cdot \cos\theta_2 \\ sen\theta_2 & -\cos\theta_2 & 0 & L_2 \cdot sen\theta_2 \\ 0 & 0 & -1 & 0 \\ 0 & 0 & 0 & 1 \end{bmatrix} \tag{3} $$

$$^{2}A_{3} = \begin{bmatrix} \cos\theta_{3} & -sen\theta_{3} & 0 & L_{3}\cdot\cos\theta_{2} \\ sen\theta_{3} & \cos\theta_{3} & 0 & L_{3}\cdot sen\theta_{2} \\ 0 & 0 & 1 & 0 \\ 0 & 0 & 0 & 1 \end{bmatrix} \tag{4}$$

The total transformation is obtained by multiplying expressions (2)–(4), as pointed in equation (5), and the resulting expression represents the relationship between the system of coordinates of the robot's base with the base of the leg (6)–(9) [4, 7].

$$^{0}A_{3} = {}^{0}A_{1}\cdot{}^{1}A_{2}\cdot{}^{2}A_{3} \tag{5}$$

$$x = \cos\theta_{1}\cdot\left(L_{1} + L_{2}\cdot\cos\theta_{2} + L_{3}\cdot\cos\left(\theta_{2}-\theta_{3}\right)\right) \tag{6}$$

$$y = sen\theta_{1}\cdot\left(L_{1} + L_{2}\cdot\cos\theta_{2} + L_{3}\cdot\cos\left(\theta_{2}-\theta_{3}\right)\right) \tag{7}$$

$$z = d_{1} + L_{2}\cdot sen\theta_{2} + L_{3}\cdot sen\left(\theta_{2}-\theta_{3}\right) \tag{8}$$

2.2. Inverse kinematics

Inverse kinematics is the process of determination of the angles in terms of the coordinates for the leg's desired position in the Cartesian system. Unlike the problem posed by direct kinematics, the procedure for getting the equations is strongly dependent on the robot's configuration, making it a complex procedure because it is very difficult to obtain systematically those equations, even plainly impossible. Inverse kinematics, in this case, is obtained through geometrical considerations based on the leg's shape. Considering **Figure 2**, the obtained equations are shown in (8)–(11):

$$\theta_{1} = \arctan\left(\frac{y_{1}}{x_{1}}\right) \tag{9}$$

$$\theta_{2} = \arccos\left(\frac{L_{2}^{2} + x_{3}^{2} + y_{3}^{2} - L_{3}^{2}}{2\cdot L_{2}\cdot\sqrt{x_{3}^{2} + y_{3}^{2}}}\right) + \arctan\left(\frac{y_{3}}{x_{3}}\right) \tag{10}$$

$$\theta_{3} = \pi - \arccos\left(\frac{L_{2}^{2} + L_{3}^{2} - \left(x_{3}^{2} + y_{3}^{2}\right)}{2\cdot L_{2}\cdot L_{3}}\right) \tag{11}$$

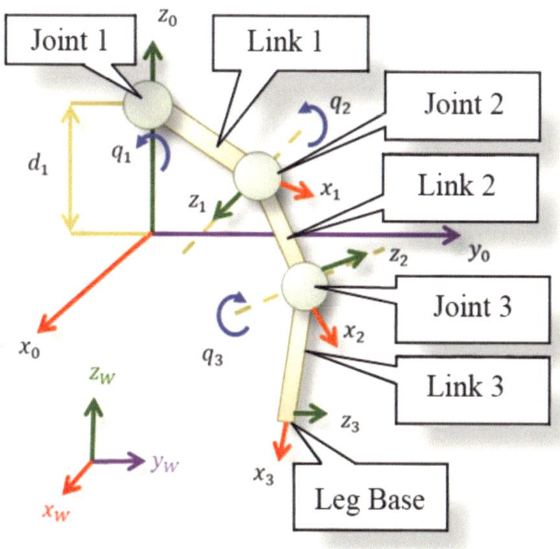

Figure 2. Model of the leg for the hexapod robot.

3. Dynamics of the hexapod robot

The problem of obtaining a robot's dynamic model is one of the more complex aspects in the field of robotics, and it is necessary for achieving the following objectives: design and evaluation of robot's dynamic control, sizing of actuators, evaluation of the robot's mechanical structure, and motion simulation of the robot design [4].

The dynamic model of the studied hexapod robot can be obtained through the application of Lagrange-Euler or Newton-Euler algorithms. Even if the Newton-Euler method is more efficient from the point of view of computer processing, we can also employ Lagrange-Euler method, because this robot has few DOF per leg. The obtained equations are shown in (12)–(14), and they also include masses of actuators—in this case, servo motors of mass M. Besides, the analysis is simplified by assuming that the masses of the first and the last link are identical [7].

$$\tau_1 = \ddot{\theta}_1 \cdot \left(I_1^{'} + I_1^{"} + M \cdot \left(l_1^2 + R_3^2 \right) + m_2 \cdot \left(r_2^2 + r_3^2 \right) \right) \tag{12}$$

$$\tau_2 = \ddot{\theta}_2 \left(I_2^{'} + I_2^{"} + M l_2^2 + m_3 r_4^2 \right) - g \left(l_3 \cos(\theta_2 + \theta_3) \left(3M + m_1 + \frac{3m_2}{2} \right) + l_2 \cos\theta_2 \left(2M + m_1 + \frac{m_2}{2} \right) \right) \tag{13}$$

$$\tau_3 = \ddot{\theta}_3 \cdot \left(I_3^{'} + I_3^{''}\right) - g \cdot l_3 \cdot \cos\left(\theta_2 + \theta_3\right) \cdot \left(3M + m_1 + \frac{3m_2}{2}\right) \tag{14}$$

where:

$I_1^{'}$, $I_2^{'}$, $I_3^{'}$: moment of inertia associated to servo motors 1, 2, and 3, respectively.

$I_1^{''}$, $I_2^{''}$, $I_3^{''}$: moment of inertia associated to links 1, 2, and 3, respectively.

r_2, r_3, r_4: radius of rotation of the mass center associated to links 1, 2, and 3, respectively.

R_3: radius of the rotation circle of servo motor 3.

4. Hexapod robot model and simulations

4.1. Hexapod robot model

In order to carry out a modeling and further simulation of a hexapod robot, it is necessary to take into account the robot's physical characteristics (mass, dimensions of thorax, measures of links, and the inertia matrix). In this case, we will employ the model developed in Ref. [9], which details the robot's size, as well as the other parameters. However, some parameter modifications will be made, trying to get as close as possible to real conditions. Basically, we will employ the robot geometry shown in **Figure 3** and **4**.

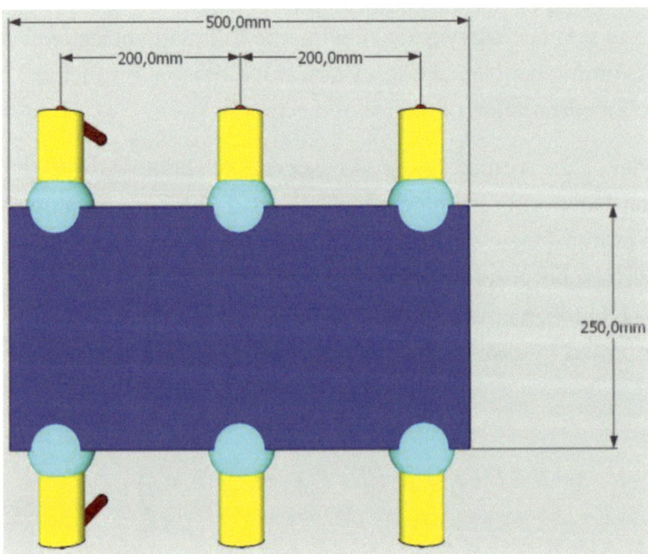

Figure 3. Top view of the hexapod robot.

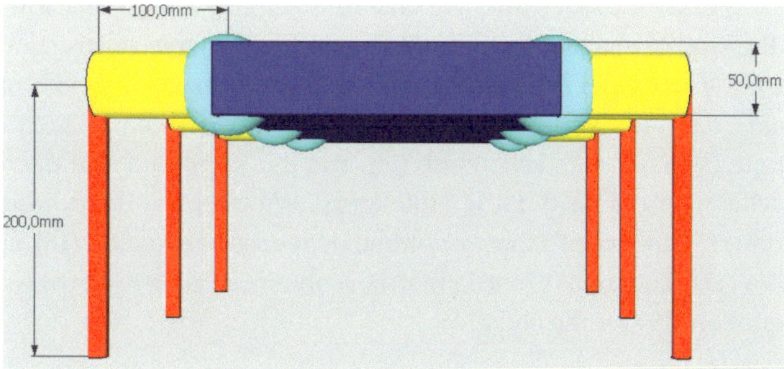

Figure 4. Front view of the hexapod robot.

To obtain the three-dimensional (3D) model of the hexapod robot, we will employ the VRML language, developing a robot model using simple geometrical figures [8]. This language allows to obtain a complex model, simply using a group of basic 3D bodies (cubes, spheres, cones, etc.). There are many alternatives to develop a 3D model using VRML language: one of them consists in programming it directly using its commands or employing a graphical editor that eases the design. In this last case, a *script* is developed containing the instructions that model the robot (**Figure 5**).

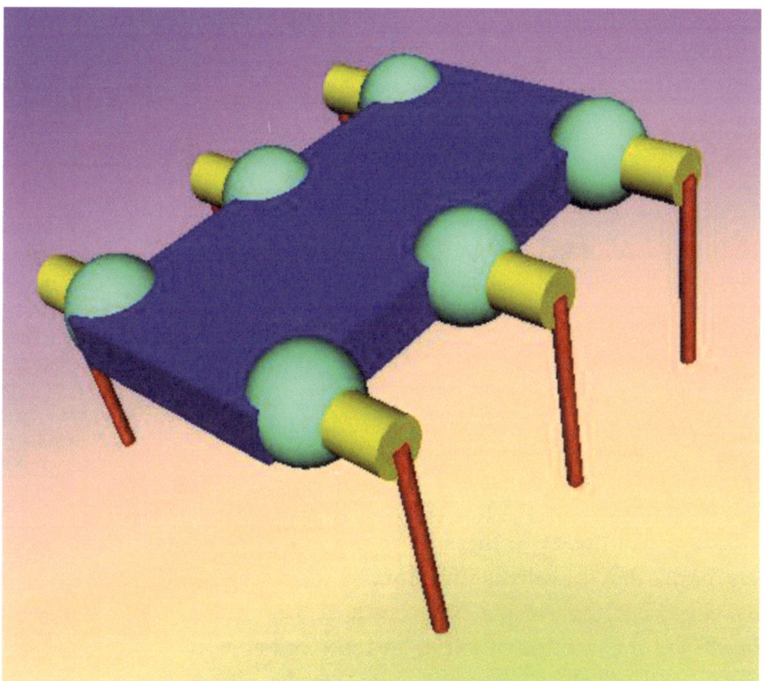

Figure 5. Perspective view of the three-dimensional model of the hexapod robot.

To obtain mass (m) of each robot's link, we take into account the geometrical considerations of the link and the kind of material that would be employed in the construction of this type of robot; for example, we consider (for simplicity's sake) that the robot legs are composed of two cylinders with different radius (R) and height (H); the thorax (the central body of the hexapod robot) has a length (l), height (h), and width (w), and it is supposed that the robot is built in transparent acrylic, whose density (p) is 1190 kg/m^3. We calculate the cylinder's volume by means of equation (15), the robot's thorax volume by means of equation (16), and the mass by means of formula (17). The robot's inertia matrix is obtained using the expression (18) for the cylinder and equation (19) for the body.

$$V_C = \iiint_S dV = \pi \cdot R^2 \cdot H \tag{15}$$

$$V_P = \iiint_S dV = h \cdot w \cdot l \tag{16}$$

$$m = V \cdot \rho \tag{17}$$

$$I_C = \begin{bmatrix} \frac{1}{12} \cdot M_C \cdot \left(3R^2 + H^2\right) & 0 & 0 \\ 0 & \frac{1}{2} \cdot M_C \cdot R^2 & 0 \\ 0 & 0 & \frac{1}{12} \cdot M_C \cdot \left(3R^2 + H^2\right) \end{bmatrix} \tag{18}$$

$$I_C = \begin{bmatrix} \frac{1}{12} \cdot M_C \cdot \left(3R^2 + H^2\right) & 0 & 0 \\ 0 & \frac{1}{2} \cdot M_C \cdot R^2 & 0 \\ 0 & 0 & \frac{1}{12} \cdot M_C \cdot \left(3R^2 + H^2\right) \end{bmatrix} \tag{19}$$

It is important to calculate those parameters, because they will be employed in the simulation section. In Simscape Multibody™, this information must be entered in each corresponding block. We must notice that the calculation of masses does not includes additional loads which, in real terms, represent the robot's electronics, sensors, batteries, actuators, and cables, therefore simplifying the number of variables to be considered. The calculation of volumes and masses is shown in **Table 2**, and the corresponding inertia matrices for each link are obtained by means of expressions (20)–(22).

Parameter	Description	Value
HM	Thigh length	10 (cm)
HP	Leg length	20 (cm)
RM	Thigh radius	2.5 (cm)
RP	Leg radius	0.75 (cm)
h	Thorax height	5 (cm)
w	Thorax width	25 (cm)
l	Thorax length	50 (cm)
VT	Thorax volume	6250 (cm^3)
VM	Thigh volume	196.35 (cm^3)
VP	Leg volume	35.34 (cm^3)
MT	Thorax mass	7437.5 (g)
MM	Thigh mass	233.66 (g)
MP	Leg mass	42.06 (g)

Table 2. Hexapod robot parameters.

$$I_{THIGH} = \begin{bmatrix} 2{,}312.26\,(g\cdot cm^2) & 0 & 0 \\ 0 & 730.19\,(g\cdot cm^2) & 0 \\ 0 & 0 & 2{,}312.6\,(g\cdot cm^2) \end{bmatrix} \tag{20}$$

$$I_{LEG} = \begin{bmatrix} 1{,}407.92\,(g\cdot cm^2) & 0 & 0 \\ 0 & 11.83\,(g\cdot cm^2) & 0 \\ 0 & 0 & 1{,}407.92\,(g\cdot cm^2) \end{bmatrix} \tag{21}$$

$$I_{THORAX} = \begin{bmatrix} 1{,}564{,}973.96\,(g\cdot cm^2) & 0 & 0 \\ 0 & 1{,}936{,}848.96\,(g\cdot cm^2) & 0 \\ 0 & 0 & 402{,}864.58\,(g\cdot cm^2) \end{bmatrix} \tag{22}$$

The center of mass for each link can be obtained making a simple analysis on each link. We can observe that they are symmetrical bodies, and their mass is homogeneous all over their structure, so the center of mass coincides with the geometric center of each element.

4.2. Simulations

When observing the complexity of obtained expressions, it becomes evident that the greater the number of DOF a robot has, the more difficult is to find the equations, more computer resources are consumed, and longer time and greater effort are spent trying to obtain them. As previously mentioned, an expression for the individual dynamics of a single leg of the hexapod robot is relatively easy to obtain, nevertheless the hexapod robot has six legs, that is a total of 18 DOF, therefore making the simulation more complex. That is why we employed a MATLAB tool called Simscape Multibody™, which has the advantage to perform simulations using blocks that represent links and joints (rotational or prismatic), as if the robot was being assembled. The advantage of this is that we do not need to obtain previously the dynamic model, because those blocks simulate it by configuring parameters on each block separately. Those parameters are inertia matrix, masses, center of mass, and geometry of the robot. In order to do that, we proceed as follows: we start by implementing a leg, and next, we convert it into a block, easing handling and replication for the robot's simulation. Each leg has three associated PID control blocks, provided by MATLAB. **Figure 6** shows the blocks composing the hexapod: the blocks representing the legs, the block of virtual reality, and the block for robot trajectory.

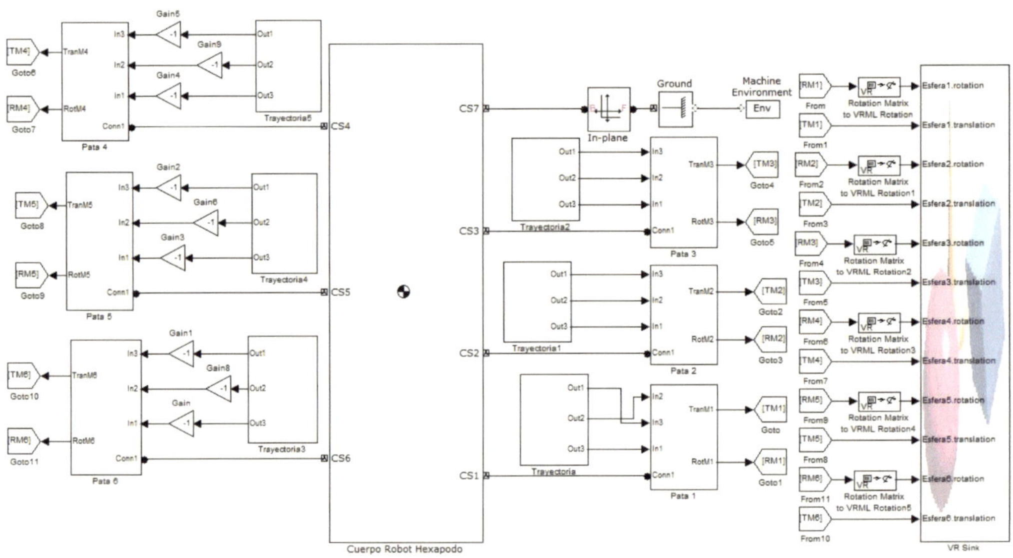

Figure 6. Model of the hexapod robot.

Despite the fact that the hexapod robot is clearly modeled through a nonlinear system, a PID control was implemented in each DOF of the robot. We started by tuning one leg (it has three PID controllers) and then replicated those parameters in the rest of the legs. This procedure was possible because in this work we did not intend to design a controller that able to perform a precise control for this robot but rather a controller that responded in a quick and acceptable manner to input references. In order to implement the controller, we used the PID block available in Simulink, which eases the process of designing and tuning the controller.

Trajectory planning is made through sinusoidal functions, according to the robot's sequence for straight-line displacement, and the work space. We developed a block containing the positions that the hexapod robot must follow in time (see **Figure 7**). For displacements, we considered the joint that unites femur and tibia is fixed at 0° (it is not necessary that this link moves in rectilinear displacements), also considered that the joint uniting coxa and thorax will cover between −50° and 50°, and finally, that the joint uniting coxa and femur will vary from −30° to 30°. The displacement speed can be modified by manipulating the angular frequency (fixed at 1 (rad/s) in this case). The displacement sequence is detailed in **Figure 8**.

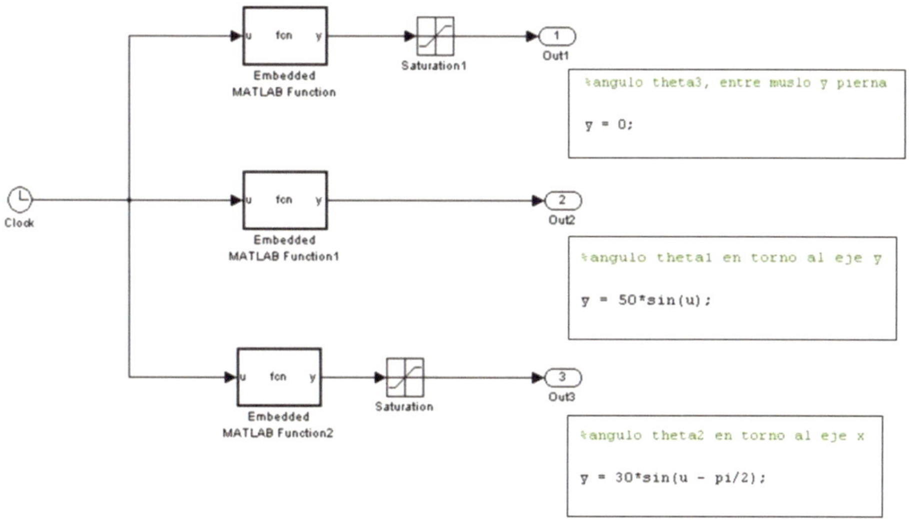

Figure 7. Trajectory planning block for each joint.

For tuning the PID controllers, we do not use a conventional method, but we do this process by varying parameters in the following way (trial and error): we vary the proportional gain without intervening the rest of the gains, and when reaching an adequate value, we continue varying the integrative gain until the stationary state error becomes zero (or near to zero), and finally we modify the derivative gain until it reaches a proper value. The proportional action delivers power enough to arrive with speed to the setpoint, the integral action eliminates the stationary state error, and the derivative action responds to the error's change speed and produces a significant correction before the magnitude of the error becomes too great. Due to the nonlinearity of the hexapod robot, the PID control is not suitable.

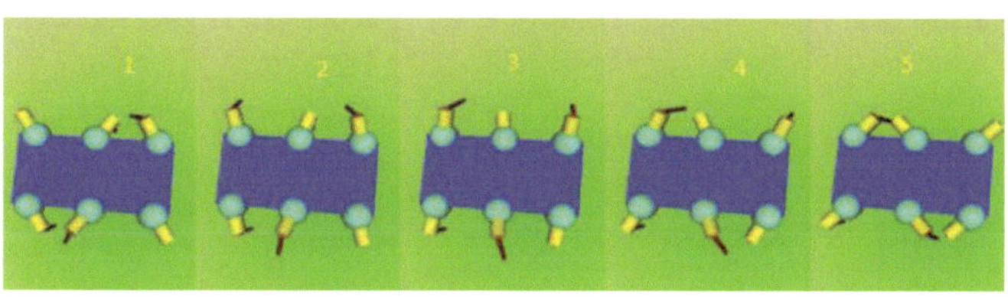

Figure 8. Simulation of the hexapod's walking sequence.

The main file that contains the folders with the programming codes of the computational simulations presented in this chapter can be downloaded directly from: http://www.mathworks.com/matlabcentral/fileexchange/56184-hexapod-robot

5. Conclusions and future development

Obtaining a dynamic model for a hexapod robot can be a laborious and complex task (especially when the robot has several DOF), which makes Simscape Multibody™ a powerful and easy-to-use tool for this purpose. We do not need to obtain an explicit dynamic model when using Simscape Multibody™ because such model is elaborated by means of blocks that represent links and joints, therefore consuming little time in the implementation of computer simulations. The development of a model in three dimensions and its further simulation help to visualize the design and possible problems that a real robot could confront (if the robot already exists or if it is going to be built).

PID controllers are not the most suitable devices to perform position control for this kind of robots; however, it is necessary to remark that the aim of our work was not to design a controller that could allow precise control, but getting the robot to respond in a quick and acceptable manner to input references. Special emphasis has been put in obtaining a modular representation of the dynamic model of the studied robot because it will permit to design more sophisticated nonlinear controllers in future works, allowing a good dynamic behavior of the robot in front of environmental perturbations, an issue that will become evident through computer simulations of its displacement.

In the near future, a robot of this kind will be designed and built, which will permit to implement algorithms for intelligent control, such as neural nets, fuzzy logic, and/or adaptive control. Additionally, not only the locomotion of the hexapod robot will be developed but also its artificial vision systems.

Acknowledgements

This work was supported by Proyectos Basales and the Vicerrectoría de Investigación, Desarrollo e Innovación of the Universidad de Santiago de Chile, Chile.

Author details

Claudio Urrea*, Luis Valenzuela and John Kern

*Address all correspondence to: claudio.urrea@usach.cl

Grupo de Automática, Departamento de Ingeniería Eléctrica, Universidad de Santiago de Chile (USACH), Santiago, Chile

References

[1] Mohiuddin A. A novel navigation algorithm for hexagonal hexapod robot. American Journal of Engineering and Applied Sciences. 2010;3(2):320–327.

[2] Bo J. Design and Configuration of a Hexapod Walking Robot. In: Third International Conference on Measuring Technology and Mechatronics Automation, IEEE Computer Society; 2011. pp. 863–866.

[3] Duan X. Tripod Gaits Planning and Kinematics Analysis of a Hexapod Robot. In: IEEE International Conference on Control and Automation; Christchurch, New Zealand. 2009. p. 1850–1855.

[4] Pullteap S. Development of a hexapod robot controlling by fuzzy logic controller. International Journal of Artificial, Intelligence, and Mechatronics. 2013;1(6):141–146.

[5] Nonami K., Kumar R., Irawan A., and Razali M. Hydraulically Actuated Hexapod Robots. Kelly Bennett, In Design, Implementation and Control. Japan: Springer; 2014.

[6] Fedák V., Ďurovský F., and Üveges R. Analysis of Robotic System Motion in SimMechanics and MATLAB GUI Environment. In: MATLAB Applications for the Practical Engineer, Chapter 20; New York, USA., Kelly Bennett InTech; 2014. [Internet]. Available from: http://www.intechopen.com/books/matlab-applications-for-the-practical-engineer/analysis-of-robotic-system-motion-in-simmechanics-and-matlab-gui-environment [Accessed: March 14, 2016]

[7] Olaru M. Hexapod robot. Mathematical support for modeling and control. In: System Theory, Control, and Computing (ICSTCC), 2011 15th International Conference on, 14–16 October, Sinaia. IEEE; 2011. p. 1–6.

[8] Barai R. K., Saha P., and Mandal A. SMART-HexBot: a Simulation, Modeling, Analysis and Research Tool for Hexapod Robot in Virtual Reality and Simulin. In: AIR '13 Proceedings of Conference on Advances in Robotics, July 4th–6th, Pune, India. New York, NY, USA: ACM; 2013.

[9] MathWorks. MathWorks - MATLAB and Simulink for Technical Computing [Internet]. Available from: http://www.mathworks.com/?requestedDomain=www.mathworks.com [Accessed: January 12, 2016].

Chapter 6

Case Studies in Using MATLAB to Build Model Calibration Tools for Multiscale Modeling

Ricolindo L. Carino and Mark .F. Horstemeyer

Additional information is available at the end of the chapter

http://dx.doi.org/10.5772/62348

Abstract

This chapter illustrates the versatility of MATLAB for building interactive end-user software applications to support the pedagogy of a multiscale modeling approach to computational materials engineering. The case studies presented here demonstrate how preexisting codes that model complex material behavior, even if written in compiled computer languages such as Fortran or C++, may be utilized as computational libraries for model calibration software tools built with MATLAB. Intended for students in computational engineering (mechanics and materials), these tools execute on personal computers without MATLAB if the MATLAB Runtime shared libraries are installed. Publications coauthored by students using these tools to calibrate material models and to investigate the performance of engineering materials indicate that the tools enable advances in engineering design from a computational engineering perspective.

Keywords: multiscale modeling, interactive model calibration, parallel optimization, mixed-language programming, MATLAB

1. Introduction

The book "Integrated Computational Materials Engineering (ICME) for metals: using multiscale modeling to invigorate engineering design with science" by Mark F. Horstemeyer [1] aims to educate the next generation of practitioners of a simulation-based approach for the understanding, design, development, and manufacturing of load-bearing structural products. Intended as a textbook for senior undergraduate and graduate students of computational materials engineering, the book contains lecture notes, questions and solutions manual, and tutorials on the model codes at each length scale. The book has a companion website [2] with a

INTECH
open science | open minds

© 2016 The Author(s). Licensee InTech. This chapter is distributed under the terms of the Creative Commons Attribution License (http://creativecommons.org/licenses/by/3.0), which permits unrestricted use, distribution, and reproduction in any medium, provided the original work is properly cited.

section each dedicated to the classes of materials (metals, ceramics, polymers, biomaterials, etc.) and to material models at the different length scales. Many of the model codes discussed in the book have been incorporated into compiled MATLAB [3] applications for students to run on personal computers and research workstations with or without MATLAB installed. The design of these MATLAB applications and examples of their use as computational tools to investigate materials for engineering products is the subject of this chapter.

Section 2 provides an overview of the multiscale modeling approach to the study material behavior. Section 3 describes the general design considerations and requirements for model calibration tools built on top of the preexisting model codes for multiscale modeling. The first MATLAB application built by the authors based on these requirements is DMGfit [4] for calibrating the internal state variable (ISV) damage and plasticity model [5, 6] written as a Fortran subroutine. Section 4 describes DMGfit in some detail as its support for user interactivity and its exploitation of multiprocessing capability in hardware heavily influenced the development of subsequent applications built by the authors. Section 5 describes TPgui [7], a graphical user interface (GUI) and calibration tool for a thermoplastic model of polymers [8]. TPgui was developed at about the same time as the underlying model; hence, flexibility was built into the interface to accommodate model revisions. Section 6 focuses on VPSCgui [9], a GUI to the viscoplastic self-consistent (VPSC) model of polycrystalline aggregates [10]. VPSC is a self-contained Fortran program, raising the issue of information exchange with the interface. Section 7 provides screenshots and summaries of the calibration tool for the multistage fatigue (MSF) model of crystal plasticity [11] and the modified embedded atom method (MEAM) parameter calibration (MPC) tool [12] that embeds LAMMPS-MEAM (large-scale atomic/molecular massively parallel simulator with the MEAM package for many-body potentials) [13–15]. Section 8 summarizes some lessons learned in building MATLAB applications for pedagogy and research in the multiscale modeling of materials.

2. Multiscale modeling of materials

Consider an engineering metallic product that is a component of a larger system. Of particular interest is a reliable prediction for the failure of the component. The simulation-based design of the component to satisfy specified engineering objectives would use information provided by material models at all involved length scales. See **Figure 1** for an illustration.

The larger system is the vehicle, with the automotive control arm as the component of interest. Pertinent questions regarding the component may include the following: As designed, where will failure occur, and what is the expected lifetime of the component? Can the component design be optimized and/or can the component be built using a different material such that the component will cost less, weigh less, and last longer? These questions may be investigated using a hierarchical multiscale model. Based on the illustration in **Figure 1**, the length scales and some of the computational models that have been used at each scale are listed in **Table 1**.

http://dx.doi.org/10.5772/62348

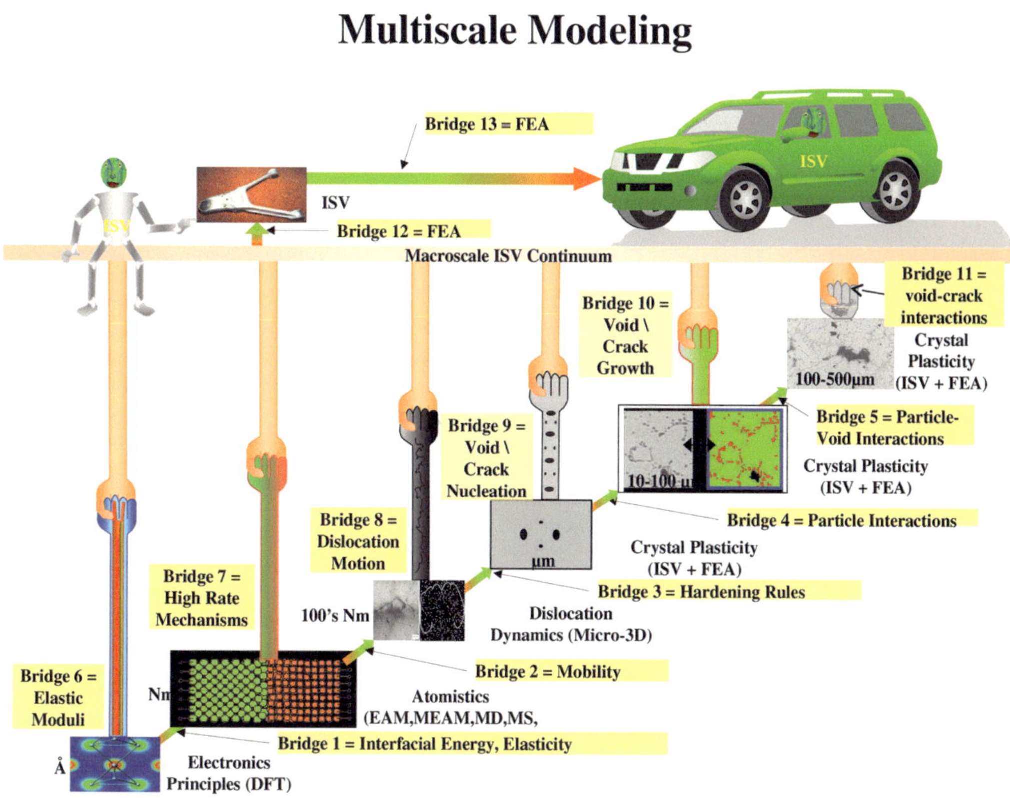

Figure 1. Multiscale modeling example of an automobile component made from metal (from [1], p. 11).

Length scale	Computational model
L1: Electrons (Å)	M1: Electronics principles (DFT)
L2: Atoms (nm)	M2: Atomistic (EAM, MEAM, MD, MS)
L3: Dislocations (100 nm)	M3: Dislocation dynamics
L4a: Grains (1 μm)	M4a: Crystal plasticity (1 μm ISV+FEA)
L4b: Grains (10–100 μm)	M4b: Crystal plasticity (10–100 μm ISV+FEA
L4c: Grains (100–500 μm)	M4c: Crystal plasticity (100–500 μm ISV+FEA)
L5: Macroscale continuum	M5: Macroscale ISV
L6: Component	M6: ISV
L7: Whole system	M7: ISV

FEA, finite element analysis; MD, molecular dynamics; MS, molecular statics.

Table 1. Multiscale modeling length scales and computational models.

The computational material codes typically solve complicated physics-based formulas for material behavior and are written in procedural computer languages, such as Fortran, C, or C++, or may even be mixed-language programs. These material model codes usually require an input file containing values of the model parameters and computational settings. Output files generated by these model codes are typically postprocessed or visualized by other software.

Computational simulations at lower-length scales generate information that will be used by material models at the higher-length scales (upscaling). Alternatively, models at higher-length scales may specify information that imposes boundary conditions on simulations at the lower-length scales (downscaling). The upscaling and downscaling calculations form "bridges" between material models and simulations. **Table 2** lists the model-bridging calculations based on the illustration in **Figure 1**.

Model #1	Model #2	Bridging calculation	Model #1	Model #2	Bridging calculation
M1	M2	Bridge 1=Interfacial energy; elasticity	M1	M5	Bridge 6=Elastic moduli
M2	M3	Bridge 2=Mobility	M2	M5	Bridge 7=High rate mechanisms
M3	M4a	Bridge 3=Hardening rules	M3	M5	Bridge 8=Dislocation motion
M4a	M4b	Bridge 4=Particle interaction	M4a	M5	Bridge 9=Void/crack nucleation
M4b	M4c	Bridge 5=Particle-void interactions	M4b	M5	Bridge 10=Void/crack growth
M4c	M5	Bridge 11=Void-crack interactions	M5	M6	Bridge 12=FEA
			M6	M7	Bridge 13=FEA

Table 2. Model-bridging calculations in multiscale modeling.

3. Design considerations for model calibration tools

The applications described here are intended to support pedagogy and research in a multiscale modeling approach to computational materials engineering. Because students who are learning complex models of material behavior will use the applications, interactivity is an important consideration. In addition, automation is also important so that the applications can save time for busy researchers who are already familiar with the models and just need to calculate a few sets of model parameters. Students may be using personal computers running Microsoft Windows or Mac OS or research workstations running Linux. Whatever is the operating system, most modern laptops and workstations already have built-in multiprocessing capabilities that may be harnessed to speed up intensive computations. In addition, the model codes may undergo revisions as research progresses. Finally, the application may need to be shared with collaborators for exchange of ideas. Thus, many issues pertaining to students, research collaborators, computing platforms, and the certainty of incremental model revisions need to be addressed in the design of applications for both pedagogy and research in multiscale modeling.

http://dx.doi.org/10.5772/62348

At the core of the multiscale modeling approach are mathematical constitutive models representing material behavior at various length scales. These models are typically expressed as complex mathematical functions with several parameters. For a specific material, some of these model parameters may be known from the scientific literature or from the material data sheet prepared by the manufacturer, whereas other parameters are to be determined from material characterization experiments or from results of other computational simulations. The process of determining model parameters from experimental or simulation data is referred to here as model calibration.

Figure 2 depicts an interactive model calibration process. The model parameters produced as outputs of the process may be used in the model-bridging calculations in **Table 2** or by models in the higher-length scales. The model calibration tools described here were initially developed for students of computational engineering. A student may use a tool to complete an assignment, to model experimental data that are collected during a research project, or to learn about and revise its underlying material model.

Interactivity in a model calibration tool is a requirement so that end-users are able to immediately visualize the effect of changing a model parameter. This is important, as an incremental and heuristic strategy to calibration is sometimes necessary, owing to the complexity of a

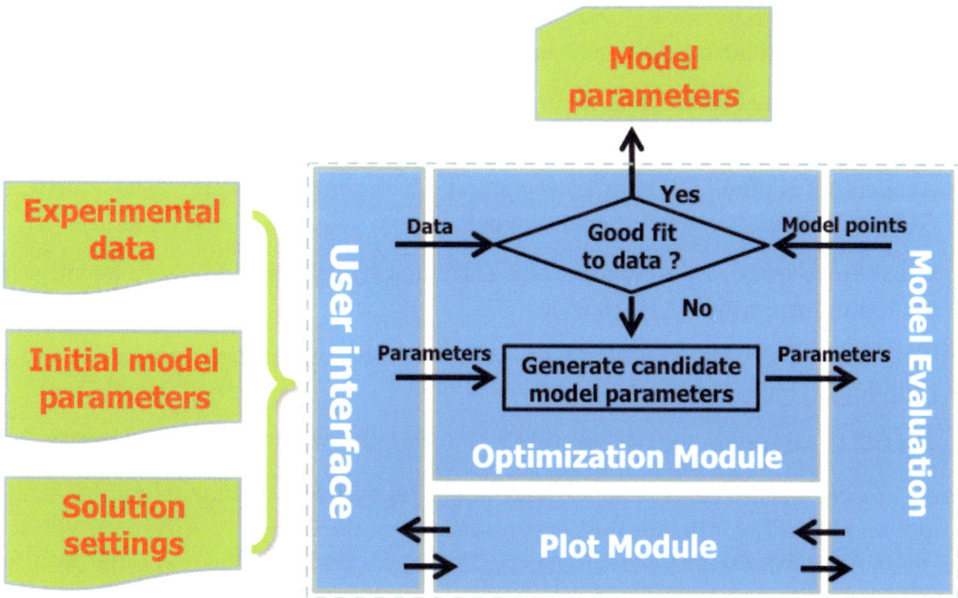

Figure 2. Interactive model calibration to determine model parameters from experimental data. The user specifies the experimental data, initial model parameters, and solution settings (the inputs) through the User interface. The Plot Module invokes the Model Evaluation module (the model code) to calculate a model curve from the model parameters currently on display. The model points are plotted alongside the experimental data. Individual parameters may be manually edited on the User interface to change the shape of model curve. The Optimization Module attempts to automatically find values for a set of parameters (the output) that will generate model curves that are "close" to the experimental data.

material model. Another requirement is that a calibration tool must run on stand-alone personal computers commonly used by students (usually Microsoft Windows or Mac OS) and on research workstations (typically Linux). Further, because modern personal computers and workstations typically have built-in multiprocessing capabilities, another design requirement is that the tool must be able to exploit parallelism available in the runtime system for the faster execution of applicable steps in the interactive model calibration process.

The scientific theory underlying a material model is always a work in progress. Revisions to theory translate into changes in the constitutive model code, such as the addition of model parameters or extended formulas to better capture material behavior. Therefore, another design requirement for the tool is that code changes to accommodate additional model parameters or updates to model formulas should be confined to the Model Evaluation module. This will enable students who are doing research on improving the underlying material model to concentrate on the model code with very minimal changes in the Model Evaluation module and the User Interface.

Research collaborations typically involve the transmission of software for evaluation or trial use by interested parties. In many cases, constitutive model codes written as part of sponsored research have disclosure restrictions. To facilitate the exchange of novel ideas embedded in material models without disclosing source codes, the binary executable for a model calibration tool will have to be transmitted. Thus, the programming environment for the tool must be capable of building a binary executable that is royalty free when redistributed.

MATLAB was selected as the programming environment for building the model calibration tools because of the following features:

1. Availability of numerical libraries, graphical functions, parallel code development, and GUI-building tools in a single environment;
2. Constitutive model codes written in other languages (Fortran, C/C++) can be integrated without rewrite with MATLAB code;
3. The same MATLAB application source code runs on multiple operating systems (Windows, Linux, and Mac OS); and
4. The MATLAB application can be compiled into an executable that is freely redistributable.

The succeeding sections describe some of the model calibration tools built using MATLAB by the authors primarily for graduate research assistants in the Center for Advanced Vehicular Systems (CAVS), Mississippi State University. These tools are interactive and at the same time support a semiautomated process of model calibration. The tools run on personal laptops and desktop workstations with or without MATLAB and can exploit multiprocessing capabilities provided by hardware. For some model codes that are subroutines written in Fortran only or in C/C++ with Fortran, MATLAB gateway functions (mexfunctions) were written to facilitate the invocation of the subroutines as library calls from the Plot and Optimization modules of the tool. For other single-program model codes that read input decks and write output to text files, MATLAB functions were written to generate the input decks from entries in the User Interface and to extract relevant values from the program outputs. MATLAB-generated binary executables of the tools have been used by collaborators and other interested researchers. Each tool also has a website that provides usage instructions and links to download the executable or the sources if made publicly available.

4. DMGfit—damage and plasticity model-fitting tool

DMGfit is an interactive calibration tool for the ISV damage and plasticity model [5, 6]. The model is written in Fortran as an ABAQUS User Material subroutine (UMAT or VUMAT) [16]. DMGfit executes the UMAT/VUMAT as a library routine, not as a separate external process. DMGfit inputs comprise experimental stress-strain data to determine "material properties" that are subsequently used along with the UMAT/VUMAT by an ABAQUS simulation in length scale L6. **Figure 3** depicts the component modules of DMGfit, its interface to the model code UMAT/VUMAT, and how a finite element simulation consumes the DMGfit output. The source codes of DMGfit are online [17].

The damage and plasticity model is specified by 55 parameters (material properties) at the time of this writing. Some properties, such as bulk modulus, shear modulus, and melting temperature, are fixed constants for a given material and may be obtained from the literature. Other properties, such as average radius of voids, average size of particles, and average grain

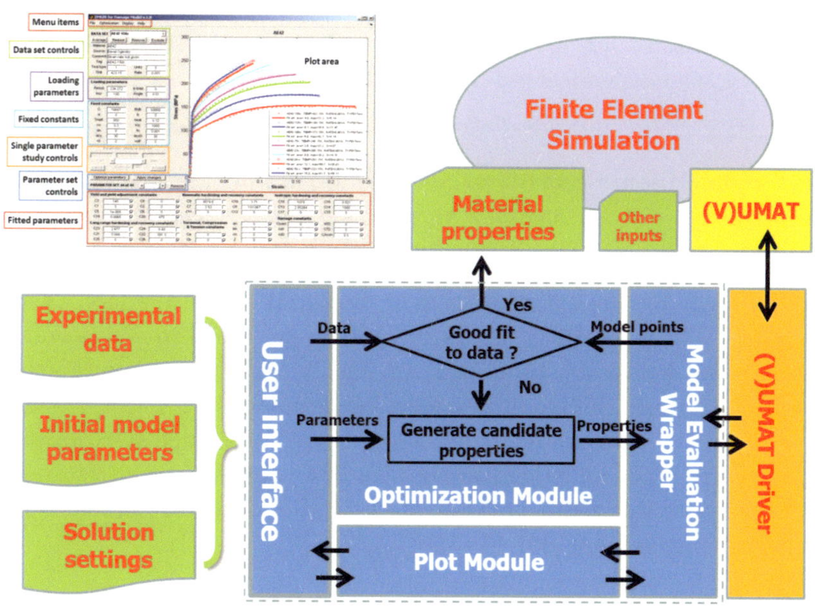

Figure 3. DMGfit screenshot, component modules (blue boxes, in MATLAB), damage and plasticity model subroutine (yellow, in Fortran), and model driver (orange, in Fortran). Experimental data inputs to DMGfit are stress-strain curves. The Material properties output by DMGfit and the model subroutine are inputs to a finite element simulation in ABAQUS. The bridge between MATLAB and Fortran is a mexfunction in the Model Evaluation Wrapper.

size, are measured from characterization experiments on samples of the material. DMGfit calibrates the remaining properties using stress-strain data collected from tension, compression, and shear experiments on the samples at various combinations of strain rates and temperatures.

The interactive calibration of the damage and plasticity model using DMGfit typically proceeds as follows:

1. Load all experimental data sets. For each data set, establish the experiment settings (initial temperature, strain rate, stress units, etc.), loading parameters, and fixed constants.
2. Start by fitting the experimental data set with the lowest temperature and lowest rate. Temporarily exclude the rest of the data sets. If there are different tests, fit the compression data sets first followed by tension data sets and then torsion data sets.
3. For the first data set, adjust the parameters as follows: yield C3; kinematic hardening C9 and dynamic recovery C7; isotropic hardening C15 and dynamic recovery C13.
4. Restore second data set. If it has a different temperature than the first, adjust the parameters as follows: {C3, C4} if yield is temperature dependent, then {C10, C8, C16, C14}. If the data set has a different strain rate, adjust C1 and C5 if yield is strain rate dependent, then {C9, C7, C11} and {C15, C13, C17}.
5. Repeat step 4 for the rest of the data sets. If adjusting the temperature dependence parameters (even Cs) does not produce good models for high temperature data, adjust C19 and C20. Adjust torsion, compression, and tension differentiation parameters, if adding stress state-dependent experimental data.
6. Adjust damage parameters. Readjust parameters in other boxes as necessary.
7. Create a "restart" file to record calibration session for resumption later. Merge the material constants with an existing ABAQUS input deck if one has been prepared previously or write results to text files for postprocessing by other applications such as Microsoft Excel.

The user may specify the number of plots to be displayed on the interface. There are three plotting strategies: a single plot for all data sets, which may result in an overcrowded plot area; one data set per plot, which may produce many small plots; and, as a compromise, one plot per data set type (i.e., one plot for tension data sets, another plot for compression data sets, etc.). After a data set is loaded into the application, it may be included or excluded from plots and from participating in the calibration process. See [4] for details about all features of DMGfit. **Figure 4** depicts a sample screenshot of DMGfit when used to calibrate the material properties for a 7075-T651 aluminum plate [18].

DMGfit provides three methods of adjusting the model parameters. First, a user can manually adjust model parameters by directly editing their values and clicking the "Apply changes" button to regenerate the model curves. Second, a user can activate the "Parameter study" slider by a right click on a parameter. A click or drag on the slider will vary the parameter and regenerate the model curves. The third method allows two or more parameters to be adjusted

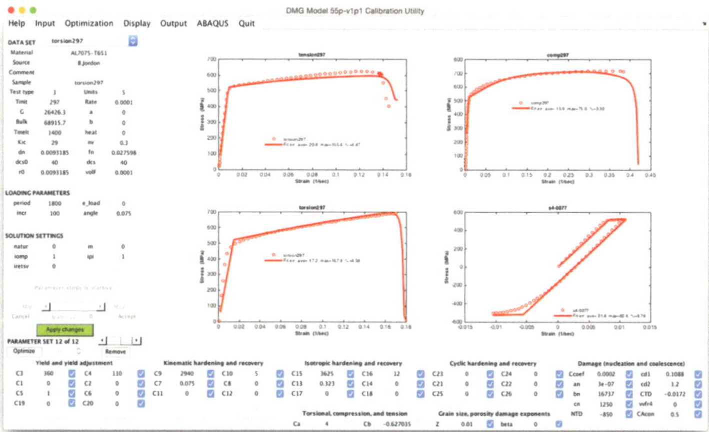

Figure 4. DMGfit screenshot showing the material properties for an aluminum 7075-T651 plate [18]. The damage and plasticity model parameters calibrated by DMGfit predict the strength, failure, and other mechanical characteristics of the plate.

simultaneously using optimization. The optimization objective is to minimize the distance between the model curve and the experimental stress-strain data. The optimization variables are the unchecked parameters. Clicking the "Optimize" button runs the optimization using the displayed values of the unchecked parameters as the starting solution. The optimization methods available in DMGfit are the MATLAB functions **fminsearch** (simplex search), **lsqnonlin** (nonlinear least squares) **fmincon** (constrained minimization), **patternsearch** (pattern search optimization), and **ga** (genetic algorithm).

DMGfit uses multiple computational cores depending on the settings of the menu item "Optimization | Enable parallelism" and pop-up menu beside the Optimize button. This pop-up determines the number of starting solutions when the Optimize button is clicked. If one starting solution is specified (i.e., "Optimize 1") and the optimization method is **fmincon** or **patternsearch** or **ga**, then DMGfit will use the multiple cores. These optimization methods have parallel implementations in MATLAB; hence, the optimization process will benefit from the multiple cores. The methods **fminsearch** and **lsqnonlin** do not have parallel implementations (in MATLAB R2012a), so optimization with these methods will not benefit from multiple cores with "Optimize 1"; however, **fminsearch** and **lsqnonlin** will still find final solutions. If "Optimize N" is specified for a small value of *N*, then DMGfit will automatically generate a number of starting solutions as follows. Let *K* be the number of parameters that are unchecked in the DMGfit user interface. The "global" search space for the optimization is the *K*-dimensional hyperrectangular region *R*:

$$R = [\text{min\_1}, \text{max\_1}] * [\text{min\_2}, \text{max\_2}] * \ldots * [\text{min\_K}, \text{max\_K}],$$

where [min_i, max_i] is the range for the *i*th optimization variable. DMGfit will divide each range into N subintervals so that there will be N^K (N to the power K) hyperrectangular subregions. DMGfit will generate a random starting solution within each subregion and run an optimization from the random starting point. The optimization variables will be bounded by the limits of the subregion (except if the method is **fminsearch**). The "spmd…end" (single program, multiple data) MATLAB statement will be used to execute the N^K optimization runs in parallel. Because one run might take several seconds or a few minutes, the parallel run may still require a significant wait. DMGfit will collect a number of "locally good" results along with the limits of the subregions returning such results. When all N^K searches are complete, the results can be browsed manually to decide which are "really good". Not all subregions will produce "good" results; hence, much less than N^K results will be returned.

5. TPgui—a flexible GUI and fitting tool for a thermoplastic polymer model

Many engineering products include components made from polymers. A modern automotive vehicle, for example, has polymer parts such as plastics, rubbers, fibers, foams, and adhesives. Thus, it is important to predict the mechanical responses of polymer components, as these may be subjected to high strain rates during crash scenarios. In general, there are three groups of polymers: thermosets, which are rigid materials that do not flow under the action of heat; thermoplastics, which become fluid when heat is applied; and, elastomers, which can be easily deformed but will return to the original size when the loading is released. This section briefly describes TPgui, a GUI and calibration tool for an ISV model for thermoplastics. **Figure 5** provides a TPgui screenshot. The model equations are described in [8], and a TPgui tutorial may be downloaded from [19].

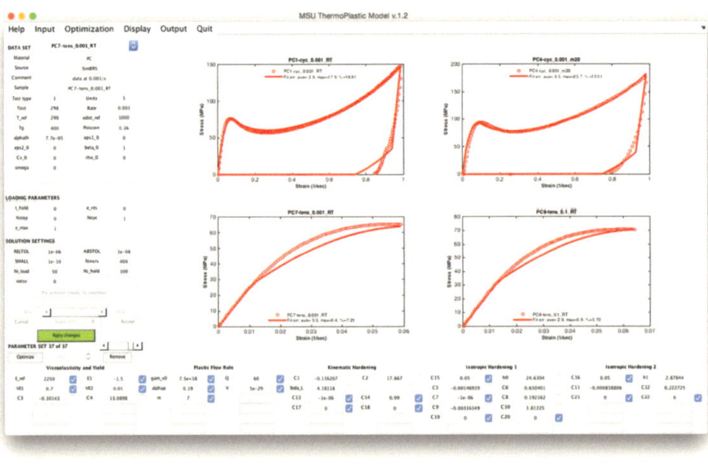

Figure 5. TPgui screenshot showing the material properties for a polycarbonate.

http://dx.doi.org/10.5772/62348

The TPgui user interface code is derived from DMGfit; hence, TPgui inherits all the interactive and parallel-enabled features of DMGfit. Unlike the model code of DMGfit that is a Fortran subroutine, the ISV thermoplastic model code is written as a MATLAB function; therefore, a mexfunction is not necessary in TPgui. A theoretician was developing the thermoplastic model code at the same time the authors were building the user interface. Therefore, to accommodate additional model parameters, experimental data, and computational settings, the TPgui interface was designed with placeholders for items that were yet to be specified by the theoretician. These placeholders are the gray (disabled) textboxes in **Figure 5** under the "DATA SET" label for experimental data, under the "SOLUTION SETTINGS" label for computational settings, and on the lower portion of the user interface for model parameters. The interface allows up to 60 model parameters arranged in a 6×10 grid. More placeholders for model parameter may be added if necessary by copy-pasting the bottom row in MATLAB's GUIDE (GUI Design Environment). To activate, for example, the placeholder in grid positions (4,1) and (4,2) (below C3 and C4, respectively) for new model parameters "C3a" and "C4a", the initialization routine only have to be edited like the highlighted lines in following code fragment:

```
% Property fields (for fitted model parameters)
% Format: 'handle', 'gui_string', 'prop. name', 'init fixed? min max',
'description/tooltip', 'TeX annotation'
% An empty handle or gui_string means it will not appear in the GUI
property_strings = { ...
     % columns 1 & 2    (Viscoelasticity and Yield)
    'p1',  'E_ref',  'E_ref', '0 0 0 1.0e6', 'Reference elastic
modulus (MPa)', 'E_{ref}'; ...
    'p2',  'E1',      'E1',    '0 0 0 10.0', 'Activation term for
elastic modulus temperature dependence (MPa)', 'E1'; ...
    'p11',  'VE1',     'VE1',  '0 0 0 5.0', 'Viscoelastic parameter
(numerator) (MPa)', 'VE1'; ...
    'p12',  'VE2',     'VE2',  '0 0 0 1.0', 'Viscoelastic parameter
(denomenator) (MPa)', 'VE2'; ...
    'p21',  'C3',    'Yref',   '0 0 -0.9 0',  'Activation term for
yield temperature dependence (MPa)', 'C_3'; ...
    'p22',  'C4',      'Y1',   '0 0 0 100',  'Temperature independent
yield (MPa)', 'C_4'; ...
    'p31',  'C3a',       ' C3a ', '0 0 1 0', 'New parameter C3a', '
C_{3a}'; ...
    'p32',  '',       '', '', '', ''; ...
    'p41',  'C4a',       ' C4a ', '0 0 1 0', 'New parameter C4a', '
C_{4a}'; ...
    'p42',  '',       '', '', '', ''; ...
    % ''
    'p51',  '', '', '', '', ''; ...
    'p52',  '', '', '', '', ''; ...
    % columns 3 & 4    (Plastic Flow Rule)
```

Similar edits may be used to activate placeholders for experimental data and computational settings. Column labels for related model parameters are also customizable. To use the new parameters "C3a" and "C4a" in the thermoplastic model, the initializations in model code only have to be edited like in the following fragment:

```
function [time strain stress statev] = TP_Model_Uniaxial(dataset,
property, option)
% ISV model for Thermoplastics.

%----------- Y
C3 = property.Yref(1);      % Yref  [...]
C4 = property.Y1(1);        % Y1  [...]
%----------- New parameters C3a, C4a
C3a = property.C3a(1);      % C3a [...]
C4a = property.C4a(1);      % C4a [...]
```

TPgui demonstrates the versatility of MATLAB in facilitating the development of dual-purpose model calibration tools. The TPgui code is a result of a strategy for building a flexible user interface that supports interactive calibration of model parameters by student researchers and at the same time serves as a test environment for theoreticians investigating alternate formulations of the underlying model. Just like an end-user being able to immediately visualize the effect of changing the value of a model parameter on the model curve, a theoretician can revise a model formula and immediately visualize its effect on the model curve.

6. VPSCgui—VPSC model calibration interface

VPSC is a Fortran 77 program that simulates the plastic deformation of polycrystalline aggregates subjected to external strains and stresses. VPSC stands for viscoplastic self-consistent and refers to the particular mechanical regime addressed (VP) and to the approach used (SC). VPSC accounts for the following material behavior: full anisotropy in properties and response of the single crystals; the hardening, reorientation, and shape change of individual grains; and grain interaction effects. In addition to providing the macroscopic stress-strain response, VPSC predicts the evolution of hardening and texture associated with plastic forming. The simulation procedure can be applied to deformation of metals, intermetallics, and geologic aggregates [10].

As of version 7b, the VPSC code is text-based and is executed from a command line. One or more of four input files have to be manually edited before a computational deformation experiment can be started. The program produces up to 10 output files; the files containing results of interest have to be postprocessed and transformed as inputs for other applications for visualization. In addition, manual calibration of the model parameters to produce a stress-strain curve that will match an experimental stress-strain data set is a very tedious, mechanical, and error-prone undertaking. Such was the experience of graduate students when they first used the VPSC to model deformation of magnesium and thus motivated the development of a user-friendly GUI to VPSC that incorporates a model-fitting functionality.

VPSCgui, a GUI to the VPSC executable, was built by the authors with the following requirements: it must be "point and click"; it must incorporate an interactive model calibration functionality; and revisions to the VPSC source code must be minimal, with no changes to the program logic. The source code, sample input, and documentation for VPSCgui are online [9], excluding the VPSC sources. The only changes to the VPSC code to make it work with the interface involved the renumbering some of the I/O units, and the addition of write statements at several places in the code so that VPSC will write "STOPPED" to standard output just before it ends as a completion signal to the interface. **Figure 6** is a screenshot of VPSCgui in modeling the behavior of magnesium AM30 undergoing channel die compression [20].

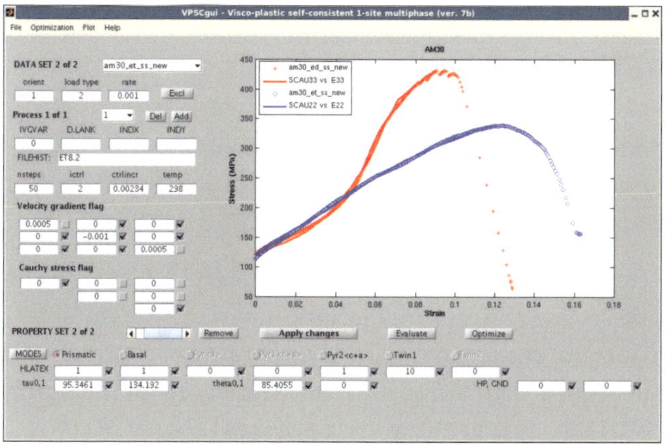

Figure 6. VPSCgui screenshot: experimental data controls (top left), deformation simulation settings (middle left), model parameters (bottom), experimental stress-strain data plots (discrete points), and VPSC model plots (solid lines).

VPSCgui implements the interactive model calibration process outlined by **Figure 2**. Unlike DMGfit and TPgui that execute their underlying models via library calls, VPSCgui invokes the VPSC program as a separate external process, and the two processes communicate through the relevant input and output files of VPSC. The input files are initially loaded into VPSCgui where a user can edit the model parameters and specify the settings for a deformation simulation. When the user clicks the "Evaluate" button, the input files are updated with the changes made on the interface, and the VPSC executable is invoked to run the deformation simulation. When the VPSC simulation completes, the interface retrieves and displays the model curves from the output files. The "Optimize" button follows the same sequence, where the optimization algorithm automatically adjusts user-selected model parameters.

VPSCgui demonstrates how MATLAB can be used to build a model calibration interface for preexisting model code (VPSC) that is a self-contained program. In this case, a mexfunction is not applicable, as VPSC has to execute as a process that is separate from VPSCgui. Data must be exchanged through the input and output files of VPSC; therefore, VPSCgui includes routines to read/write the input files of VPSC and to read the relevant output files for the model curves. Developing these routines for VPSCgui required much effort, as the Fortran subroutines in VPSC to read the input files were practically translated into MATLAB.

VPSCgui also exploits multiprocessing capability provided by hardware. Because one deformation simulation is required to model a single data set, parallelism occurs when there are several data sets being modeled. The VPSC program is inherently serial; however, several VPSC instances can run in parallel, one instance per data set. VPSCgui invokes the VPSC instances in separate directories to avoid collisions when writing the output files, as the file unit numbers will be the same across instances. After parallel invocation, VPSCgui periodically checks the files that are piped from the standard output of each VPSC instance for the "STOPPED" signal.

7. Other model calibration tools

Experience gained in building the model calibration tools described in the previous sections guided the development of more tools for other length scales. This section briefly describes the calibration tools for the MSF model and the MEAM.

Figure 7 shows a screenshot of the MSF model calibration tool [11]. The MSF model predicts the amount of fatigue cycling required for the appearance of a measurable crack, the crack size as a function of and loading cycles. The model incorporates microstructural features that affect the fatigue life predictions for incubation, microstructurally small crack growth, and long crack growth stages in both high-cycle and low-cycle regimes [21].

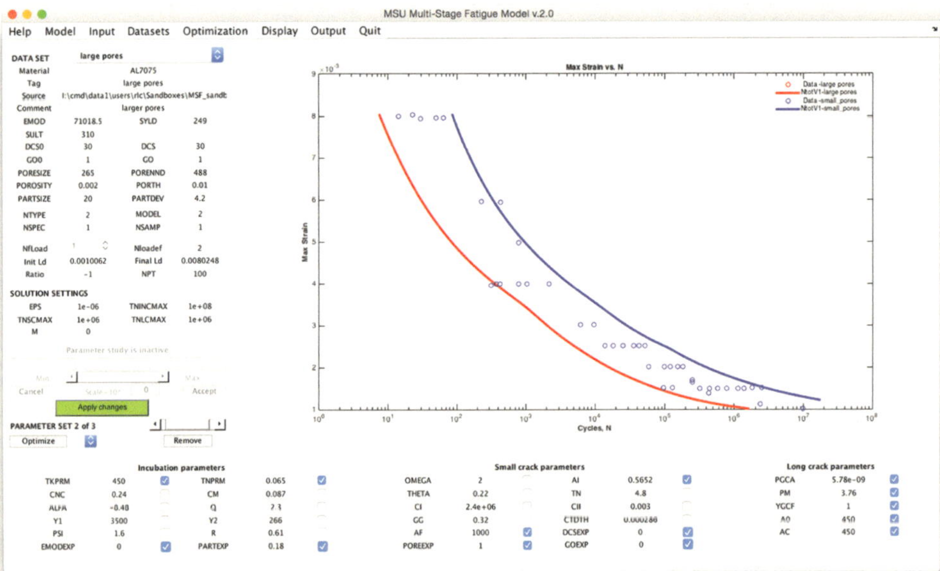

Figure 7. Screenshot of the MSF model calibration tool with model parameters to predict the fatigue life for aluminum 7075-T651 [18].

The MSF model code is an ABAQUS VUMAT written in Fortran, similar to the damage and plasticity model used by DMGfit. The MSF interface implements the same interactive and parallel features of DMGfit.

http://dx.doi.org/10.5772/62348

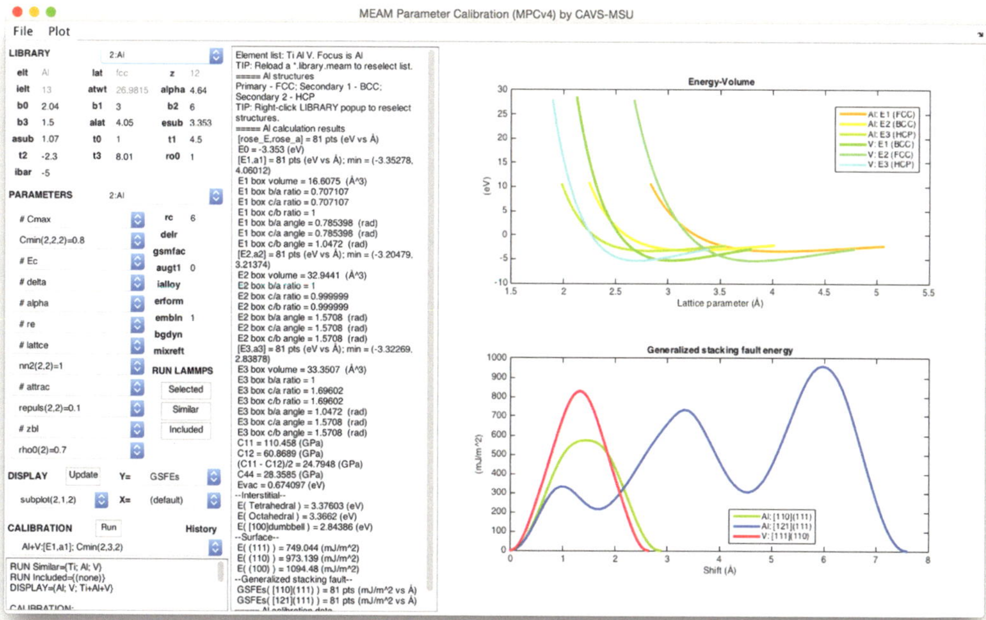

Figure 8. Screenshot of MPC tool.

Figure 8 shows a screenshot of MPC tool [12] for the interactive editing of MEAM library and parameter files and for the semiautomated calibration of MEAM parameters. The calibration targets may be density functional theory (DFT) simulation data and/or experimental data. Similar to VPSCgui, MPC reads and writes the LAMMPS input files; however, unlike VPSCgui, MPC does not execute the model code as a separate external process. Instead, MPC executes LAMMPS-MEAM, the large-scale atomic/molecular massively parallel simulator (in C++/C) with the MEAM package for many-body potentials (in Fortran) [15] as a library call such as in DMGfit.

A prior version of MPC [22,23] invokes a Python script that in turn executes LAMMPS-MEAM as a separate external program. The Python script also retrieves the relevant information to be returned to MPC from the LAMMPS-generated log file. This strategy of using Python as an intermediary between MPC and LAMMPS incurs significant file I/O overhead. Further, it was cumbersome to revise the Python scripts to set up additional LAMMPS calculations. As a consequence, the current MPC version is designed to use mexfunctions for invoking LAMMPS-MEAM as a library call, eliminating the need to run the Python interpreter and significantly reducing file I/O overhead.

8. Concluding remarks

Several issues need to be addressed when building a model calibration tool for a preexisting material model code. A potential end-user of the tool may be a student learning about the model, a researcher who needs the tool to model experimental data for some new material, or a theoretician seeking to improve the underlying model formulas so that it better captures material behavior. In each case, interactivity is a very important feature of the tool. A user may have a choice between a Microsoft Windows and a Mac OS personal machine to run the tool, or only a Linux workstation may be available. The model code may be written as a Fortran subroutine, a MATLAB script, or as a complete stand-alone mixed-language program.

The following MATLAB features were found to be sufficient in addressing all of the aforementioned issues. MATLAB GUIDE enables the creation of interfaces that support an interactive and semiautomated model calibration process. MATLAB Optimization Toolbox provides a variety of optimization techniques for automatically adjusting selected model parameters to fit experimental data. MATLAB Parallel Computing Toolbox enables the writing of parallel code that exploits multiprocessing features of modern personal computers to accelerate the model calibration process. MATLAB MEX files enable model codes written as Fortran subroutines or C/C++ functions to be invoked directly by MATLAB. In addition, model codes that are stand-alone programs can be executed as external processes through the MATLAB **system()** command. The model calibration tools described in this chapter demonstrate the versatility of MATLAB as a programming environment for building such tools.

Author details

Ricolindo L. Carino[1*] and Mark .F. Horstemeyer[1,2]

*Address all correspondence to: carino@cavs.msstate.edu

1 Center for Advanced Vehicular Systems, Mississippi State University, Mississippi, USA

2 Department of Mechanical Engineering, Mississippi State University, Mississippi, USA

References

[1] Horstemeyer MF. Integrated Computational Materials Engineering (ICME) for Metals: Using Multiscale Modeling to Invigorate Engineering Design with Science. Hoboken: John Wiley & Sons; 2012. 472 p. DOI: 10.1002/9781118342664p.

[2] Mississippi State University Center for Advanced Vehicular Systems. Engineering Virtual Organization for CyberDesign [Internet]. 2011 [Updated 2014]. Available at:

https://icme.hpc.msstate.edu/mediawiki/index.php/Main_Page [Accessed: 2016-01-14].

[3] MathWorks. MathWorks—MATLAB and Simulink for Technical Computing [Internet]. 1994 [Updated 2016]. Available at: http://www.mathworks.com [Accessed: 2016-01-14].

[4] Cariño RL. DMGfit User Guide [Internet]. 2012 [Updated 2015]. Available at: https://icme.hpc.msstate.edu/mediawiki/index.php/DMGfit_55p_v1p1 [Accessed: 2016-01-14].

[5] Bammann DJ, Chiesa ML, Horstemeyer MF, Weingarten LI. Failure in ductile materials using finite element methods. In: Jones N, Wierzbicki T, editors. Structural Crashworthiness and Failure. Barking (England): Elsevier Science Publishers Ltd.; 1993. pp. 1–54.

[6] Horstemeyer MF, Lathrop J, Gokhale AM, Dighe M. Modeling stress state dependent damage evolution in a cast Al-Si-Mg aluminum alloy. Theoretical and Applied Fracture Mechanics. 2000;33(1):31–47. DOI: 10.1016/S0167-8442(99)00049-X.

[7] Bouvard JL, Cariño RL. CMD Codes Repository—TPgui [Internet]. 2010 [Updated 2012]. Available at: https://icme.hpc.msstate.edu/viewvc/CMD%20Codes%20Repository/TPgui/ [Accessed: 2016-01-14].

[8] Bouvard JL, Ward DK, Hossain D, Marin EB, Bammann DJ, Horstemeyer MF. A general inelastic internal state variable model for amorphous glassy polymers. Acta Mechanica. 2010;213(1):71–96. DOI: 10.1007/s00707-010-0349-y.

[9] Cariño RL. CMD Codes Repository—VPSC7b_gui [Internet]. [2009]. Available at: https://icme.hpc.msstate.edu/viewvc/CMD%20Codes%20Repository/VPSC7b_gui/ [Accessed: 2016-01-14].

[10] Tomé CN, Lebensohn RA. Manual for Code Visco-Plastic Self-Consistent (VPSC), Version 7b [Internet]. 2007. Available at: https://icme.hpc.msstate.edu/viewvc/CMD%20Codes%20Repository/VPSC7b_gui/trunk/doc/VPSC7b_manual.pdf?view=log [Accessed: 2016-01-14].

[11] Cariño RL. Multistage Fatigue Model Calibration Tool (v2) User Guide [Internet]. 2012. Available at: https://icme.hpc.msstate.edu/mediawiki/index.php/MSF_v2 [Accessed: 2016-01-14].

[12] Cariño RL. MEAM Parameter Calibration Tool (Version 4) User Guide [Internet]. 2015. Available at: https://icme.hpc.msstate.edu/mediawiki/index.php/MPC [Accessed: 2016-01-14].

[13] Sandia Corporation. LAMMPS Molecular Dynamics Simulator [Internet]. 1997 [Updated 2015]. Available at: http://LAMMPS.sandia.gov [Accessed: 2016-01-14].

[14] Sandia Corporation. pair_style MEAM command [Internet]. 2013. Available at: http://LAMMPS.sandia.gov/doc/pair_MEAM.html [Accessed: 2016-01-14].

[15] Baskes MI, Johnson RA. Modified embedded atom potentials for HCP metals. Modelling and Simulation in Materials Science and Engineering. 1994;2(1):147–163. DOI: 10.1088/0965-0393/2/1/011.

[16] Dassault Systèmes. Abaqus Analysis User's Manual [Internet]. 2007. Available at: http://www.egr.msu.edu/software/abaqus/Documentation/docs/v6.7/books/usb/default.htm?startat=pt05ch20s08abm59.html [Accessed: 2016-01-14].

[17] Horstemeyer MF, Cariño RL, Hammi Y, Solanki KN. CMD Codes Repository: DMG [Internet]. 2009 [Updated 2012]. Available at: https://icme.hpc.msstate.edu/viewvc/CMD%20Codes%20Repository/DMG/ [Accessed: 2016-01-14].

[18] Jordon JB, Horstemeyer MF, Solanki KN, Bernard JD, Berry J, Williams TN. Damage characterization and modeling of 7075-T651 aluminum plate. Materials Science and Engineering A. 2009;527(1):169–178. DOI: 10.1016/j.msea.2009.07.049.

[19] Bouvard JL, Cariño RL. Tutorial on the thermoplastic model calibration tool [Internet]. 2014. Available at: https://icme.hpc.msstate.edu/mediawiki/index.php/File:TPgui-1.2-Tutorial.zip [Accessed: 2016-01-14].

[20] Ma Q, Marin EB, Antonyraj A, Hammi Y, El Kadiri H, Wang PT, Horstemeyer MF. On predicting the channel die compression behavior of HCP magnesium AM30 using crystal plasticity FEM. In: Sillekens WH, Agnew SR, Neelameggham NR, Mathaudhu SN, editors. Magnesium Technology 2011. Hoboken: John Wiley & Sons, Inc.; 2011. pp. 583–587. DOI: 10.1002/9781118062029.ch107.

[21] McDowell DL, Gall K, Horstemeyer MF, Fan J. Microstructure-based fatigue modeling of cast A356-T6 alloy. Engineering Fracture Mechanics. 2003;70(1):49–80. DOI: 10.1016/S0013-7944(02)00021-8.

[22] Cariño RL, Kim S. MEAM Parameter Calibration Tool (Version 3) User Guide [Internet]. 2014 [Updated 2015]. Available at: https://icme.hpc.msstate.edu/mediawiki/index.php/MPCv3 [Accessed: 2016-01-14].

[23] Horstemeyer MF, Hughes JM, Sukhija N, Lawrimore WBII, Kim S, Carino RL, Baskes MI. Hierarchical bridging between ab initio and atomistic level computations: calibrating the modified embedded atom method (MEAM) potential (part A). Journal of Materials. 2015;67(1):143–147. DOI: 10.1007/s11837-014-1244-0.

Chapter 7

Virtual Instrument for the Analysis of Vibrations in Rotary Machines

Claudio Urrea, Rodrigo Cisterna and John Kern

Additional information is available at the end of the chapter

http://dx.doi.org/10.5772/63736

Abstract

In this chapter, the implementation of a "Virtual Instrument" developed in MATLAB/Simulink® that allows the analysis of the measurement of mechanical vibrations in rotating machines is presented. To accomplish this, we identified the main rotating machines used in industry, the parameters that can be relevant when an analysis of vibration is made, the typical vibration frequency spectra of certain electrical and mechanical failures, the most common regulations employed by the industry with respect to vibration levels in rotating machinery, the tools that are used for vibration analysis, and tools for developing MATLAB software that includes features for storing and managing data from a database, also allowing an analysis and diagnosis of vibration in rotating machines.

The development cost for this virtual instrument is very low compared with the tens of thousands of dollars of their equivalents now available in the market.

Keywords: virtual instrument, rotating machines, predictive maintenance, vibration analysis, vibration diagnostic

1. Introduction

Machine maintenance is one of the most important issues in any industry, since good maintenance procedures avoid catastrophic failures that threaten the productive process, and most important of all, the life of the workers involved [1].

Due to catastrophic failures, industrial maintenance has been evolved to prevent machines from failures, which looks for symptoms in machines that allow determining the most appropriate time for doing maintenance, and even more important, determining the exact failure occurring in a machine [2, 3].

INTECH
open science | open minds

© 2016 The Author(s). Licensee InTech. This chapter is distributed under the terms of the Creative Commons Attribution License (http://creativecommons.org/licenses/by/3.0), which permits unrestricted use, distribution, and reproduction in any medium, provided the original work is properly cited.

This new form of industrial maintenance development, called "predictive maintenance," requires new methodologies and expert analysis, which can act as "machine physicians," able to determine a machine's health condition based on those symptoms [4].

One of the most accurate predictive methods is vibration analysis [5–7], which implies the study of machine vibration signals as a symptom allowing to determine eventual failures in an incipient state [8], thus avoiding a possible catastrophic failure. A significant problem associated with this study has to do with cost, currently ranging from US$ 12,000 to US$ 40,000 [5]. On the other hand, MATLAB is a very powerful calculation tool that, among many other remarkable features, can be used to create matrix-type databases, perform complex calculations, and generates graphs, allowing the creation of graphical interfaces, etc., so undoubtedly we can use it to develop a software for storing vibration analysis data in a database and tools that permit the analysis of data stored in the same software, this being a first step toward the creation of a low-cost "virtual instrument" [9]. This software is limited, in this first development stage, to data acquisition from an Excel spreadsheet, along with the recording and analysis of the acquired data, leaving aside for the time being the capture of the machine's vibrations stage through a transducer, the conditioning of the captured vibrations, as well as the subsequent data acquisition [10, 11].

2. Software development for vibration analysis

In this chapter, we present the development of a virtual analyzer of mechanical vibrations to be used in industry. This software was developed on MATLAB/Simulink due to that software's calculation capacity and because it has a visual programming tool called GUIDE, which allows an easy development of a graphical interface for vibration analysis [12].

The database is called "basedatos," and it is created as a variable in MATLAB's Workspace and stored in the same place. To access it, we must load the database through the command "Load" at the time of starting the program.

The database is a structure where we include operation conditions and measurement data, such as date, observations, etc., and inside this structure, one of the fields is an arrangement called "signal," where we include width, frequency, phase, and harmonics attenuation coefficient of the vibrational signal.

Another important feature of MATLAB is a compiler that creates an ".exe" file that allows the execution of the program without the need to have it previously installed, therefore allowing to run the vibration analyzer on any PC.

Several screens are created for the different "analyzer features" and for the "implementable tools" that can be accessed through buttons arranged on a main screen called "Main" for the program root, and "Vibration analysis" for the developed tools, as shown in **Figure 1**.

Those screens or graphical interfaces have many components, such as buttons, selection boxes, dialog boxes, etc., that must be named first. In order to do that, inside the option "property" of the "tag" section of the interface elements, the names that those components will have are

http://dx.doi.org/10.5772/63736

entered by the user. The names should be easy to remember, so we commonly use abbreviations referring to names of the corresponding functions or components. The importance of naming the components is that, at the time of creating the program's code, those components are called through the "Callbacks" function, for editing or capturing their values through the "set" and "get" functions, respectively.

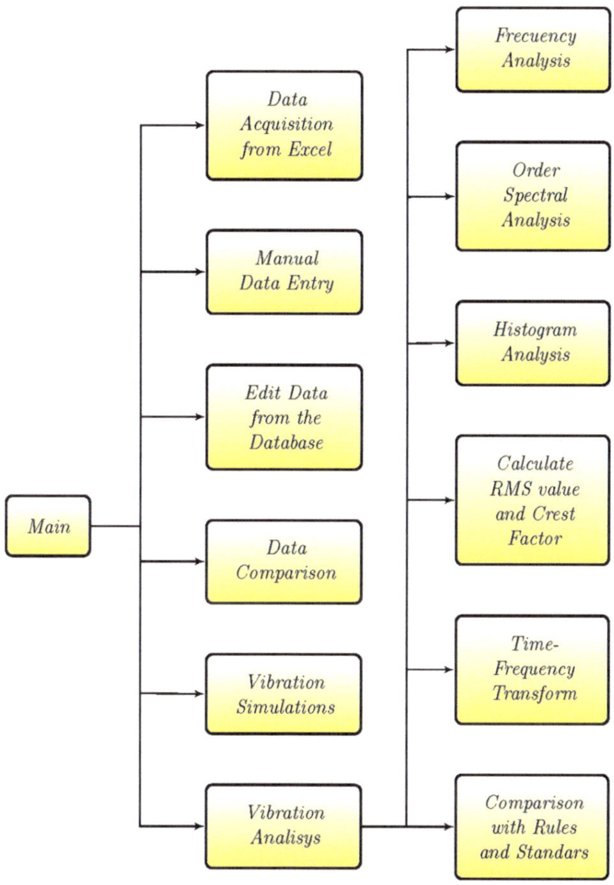

Figure 1. Vibration analysis software structure.

2.1. Analyzer features

2.1.1. Data acquisition from Excel

This function allows importing vibration data from an Excel spreadsheet, in this way filling the database more quickly than entering the data one by one.

2.1.2. Manual data entry

Manual entry allows entering specified data step by step with respect to the machine, the measurement point, sensor arrangement, the values of the measurement's representative peaks, etc.

2.1.3. Editing data from the database

With this function, we can look for the already existing data inside the database and modify them, allowing the correction of possible errors.

2.1.4. Data comparison

Two measurements can be compared in parallel, to see their frequency spectra and the operation conditions at the time the measurement was made.

2.1.5. Vibration simulations

This function makes it possible to see how entering another vibration with a different phase and/or damping coefficient will affect the frequency spectrum of a given signal, as well as to simply see the frequency spectrum of a designed signal.

2.1.6. Vibration analysis

This is the software's main function, where we can access different kinds of vibration analysis that can be carried out with discrete data, as is the case of these data.

The machines that can be analyzed with this software are as follows: DC motors, AC motors, rotodynamic pumps, hydraulic generators, steam generators, and SAG mills.

3. Implementable tools

This software's basic tools allow capturing data from an Excel spreadsheet, store the data manually in the database, edit the data, compare fast Fourier transform (FFT) graphics, and simulate vibrations, looking at how they affect the data previously stored in the database. All those tools are part of the main features of the analyzer.

The fact that this software works with data entered in a discrete way limits the kind of vibration analysis tools that can be adapted to MATLAB. The tools that could be adapted to MATLAB are the following:

3.1. Frequency analysis

With this analysis, we can see the frequency spectrum of a vibration signal stored in the database, by varying the sampling frequency, and we can also see the spectrum in the form of a bar graph with a frequency error of 10^{-3}, which allows a very good resolution and shows the peaks clearly. This technique uses the Fast Fourier Transform (FFT) [9, 13].

The "frequency analysis" screen has a signal finder, a sector where the values of operational conditions are printed once the "Load" button is pressed, and a sector where the kind of graph is chosen and the sampling frequency in the case of choosing an FFT graph is determined.

3.2. Order spectral analysis

To carry out this kind of analysis, we must take a reference value that will be 1X, and, from this reference, the other frequencies will be expressed as multiples of it, where this value is usually the machine speed [13].

To do this, we will take a reference value in (KCPM) by which every frequency of the spectrum to be analyzed will be divided.

This screen is very similar to that of the "frequency analysis," but instead of entering the sampling frequency, we can choose a reference frequency to generate the orders, and those frequencies can be the speed or the net frequency stored for that datum in the database, or any other that can be written and selected.

3.3. Histogram analysis

With this function, we can see the evolution over time of a given frequency value in a specific machine, at a specific measurement point, and with a specific sensor arrangement.

Because of this, it is necessary to determine which are the machine, the point, and the arrangement from which we want to extract a given frequency to see its evolution in time. Hence, on this screen, there is a sector for determining each of those parameters, and another sector for determining the central frequency in (KCPM) that we are searching, along with a tolerance value in this same unit allowing a search range around the central frequency. There is also another sector for determining whether we want to look for frequencies from all the existing measurements in the database, or if we only want to graph the last "X" data from the database, with respect to date and time from the last measurement to the first stored measurement.

On this screen, we can search for data stored in the database and determine the RMS value of the vibration rate and the crest factor (CF), a value allowing to see the influence of the complete vibration signal over the signal's highest peak [14].

3.4. Time-frequency transform

Through this analysis, we can see the evolution in time of the complete vibration signal [13], and it is similar to the histogram analysis, but considering all the frequencies of the signals.

In order to do that we arrange data in the same way as on the "histogram analysis" screen, only varying the way the chart is created, since we must capture all the frequency-width pairs of all the data or of the last "X" data, which can be selected at will, and graph them next to one another to form a three-dimensional (3D) surface.

For this analysis, we considered two kinds of charts, a two-dimensional (2D) one that permits a simpler analysis of vibration evolution, and a 3D one that allows the signal peaks to be seen, but making the determination of the coordinates of the points more complex. The 2D chart is generated after pressing the "CONTOUR GRAPH" button and the 3D chart by pressing the "3D TFT CHART."

3.5. Comparison with rules and standards

On this screen, we can make comparisons with ISO2372, ISO2373, and ISO10816 standards, which require RMS values of the vibration rate. These standards were chosen because they are widely used in industry [15, 16].

4. Software operation

In order to see the operation of this analyzer based on real measurements, we invented a series of measurements to test the performance of the analysis tools in order to see the evolution in time of the measurements.

The data exported from Excel have a structure that facilitates their storage in the software's database. This structure is shown in **Figure 2**.

	DATOS DE LA MEDICIÓN			SEÑAL		
				Nº	AMPLITUD (mm/s)	FRECUENCIA (KCPM)
1	FECHA	DIA	1	1	0.1616	0.391
		MES	1	2	0.6818	0.656
		AÑO	2009	3	0.0760	1.114
	HORA	HORA	20	4	0.0812	3.511
		MINUTOS	0	5	0.1842	5.505
	MEDICIÓN	MÁQUINA	1	6	0.1818	6.001
		PUNTO	1	7	0.1197	6.339
		DISPOSICIÓN	1	8	0.1413	10.541
		CÓDIGO PIEZA	123	9	0.0722	10.808
	INYECTORES	INYECTOR 1	1	10	0.0805	11.054
		APERTURA INY1	40	11	0.0737	11.254
		INYECTOR 2	1	12	0.0842	11.502
		APERTURA INY2	40	13	0.0704	11.763
		INYECTOR 3	1	14	0.0748	16.564
		APERTURA INY3	40	15	0.0900	18.005
		INYECTOR 4	1	16	0.1511	21.017
		APERTURA INY4	40	17	0	0
		INYECTOR 5	1	18	0	0
		APERTURA INY5	40			
		INYECTOR 6	1			
		APERTURA INY6	40			
	CONDICIONES DE OPERACIÓN	POTENCIA ACTV.	200			
		POTENCIA REACT.	0			
		VELOCIDAD	500			
		Nº DE INYECTORES	6			
		Nº DE ÁLABES	21			
		Tº MÁQUINA	40			
		Tº AMBIENTE	33			
		VOLTAJE GENERADO	220			
		SALTO	0			
		VOLTAJE APLICADO	0			
		CORRIENTE APLICADA	0			
		POT. SUMINISTRADA	0			
		TORQUE GENERADO	0			
		Nº DE DELGAS	0			
		FRECUENCIA DE LA	50			
		Nº DE POLOS	0			
		Nº DE BOLAS	0			

Figure 2. Worksheet for data exportation to the analysis software.

From the "Main" screen, we access, pressing the corresponding button, the "Vibration Analysis" screen, as shown in **Figure 3**.

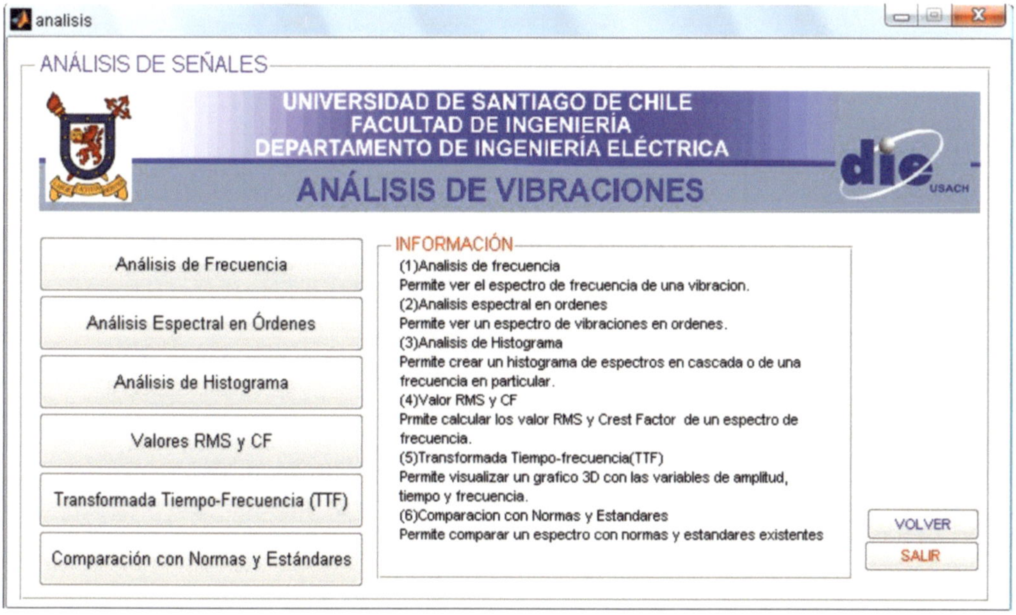

Figure 3. "Vibration Analysis" screen.

By means of the "Frequency Analysis" tool, we can get an FFT graph of a specific datum, or a representation of this FFT on a bar graph, as shown in **Figures 4** and **5**.

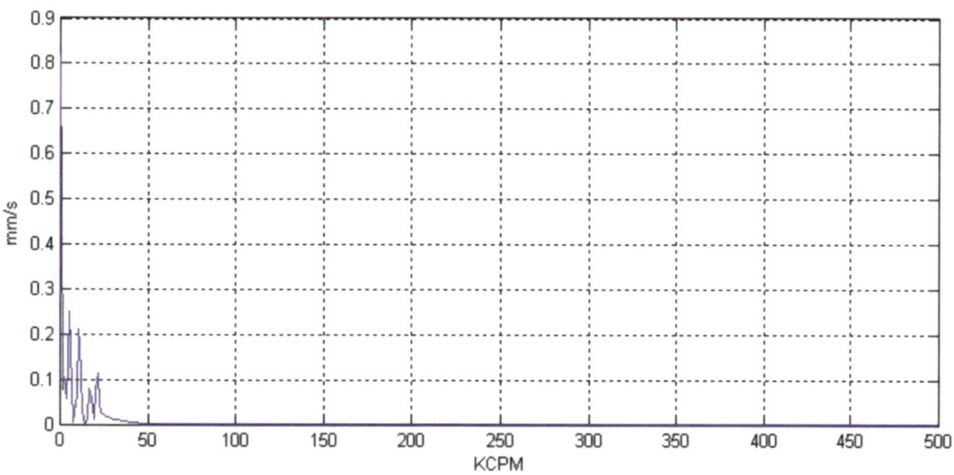

Figure 4. FFT chart of data to be analyzed.

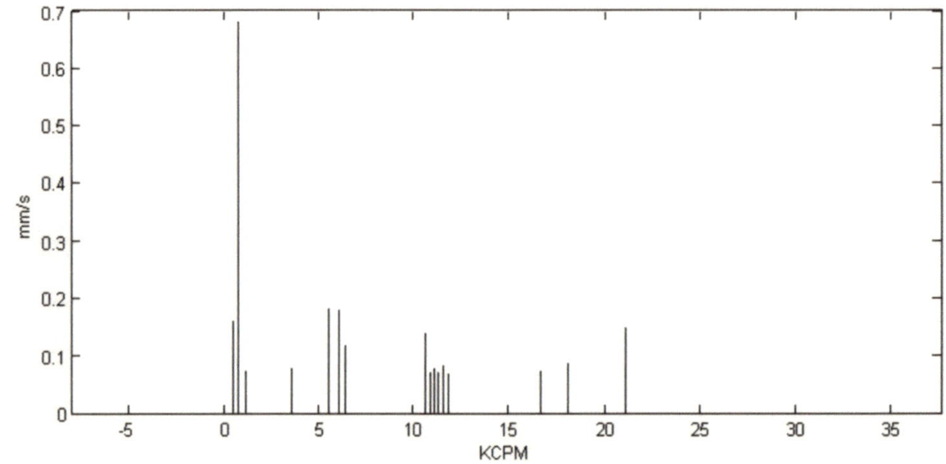

Figure 5. Bar chart of frequency analysis.

The tool "Spectral Analysis in Orders" allows the generation of a chart in orders taking as base frequency the machine's recorded speed, the net frequency, or any desired value, and the graph obtained is an FFT chart or a representation of the FFT on a bar graph, as shown in **Figure 6**.

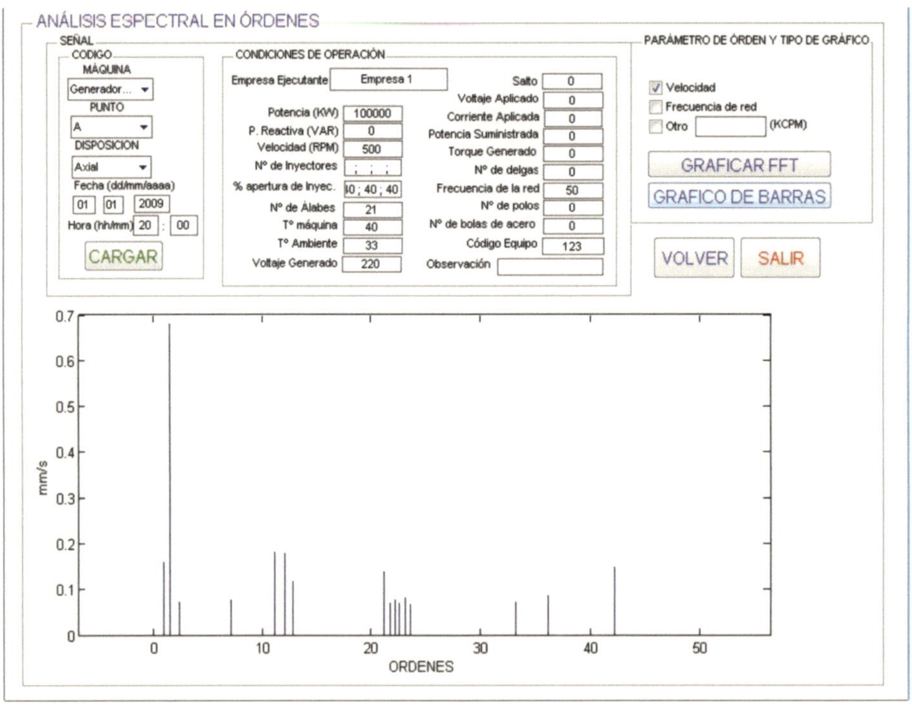

Figure 6. Bar graph of orders taking as base frequency the machine's recorded speed.

The "Histogram Analysis" tool allows seeing the evolution of a given frequency of the vibration spectrum. Here, we choose the machine, the point and the sensor arrangement, when the measurement was made, selecting the frequency we want to survey, along with a tolerance range in case the exact desired value is not found. **Figure 7** shows this screen, where we are looking for the 12 KCPM with a frequency tolerance of 0.5 KCPM.

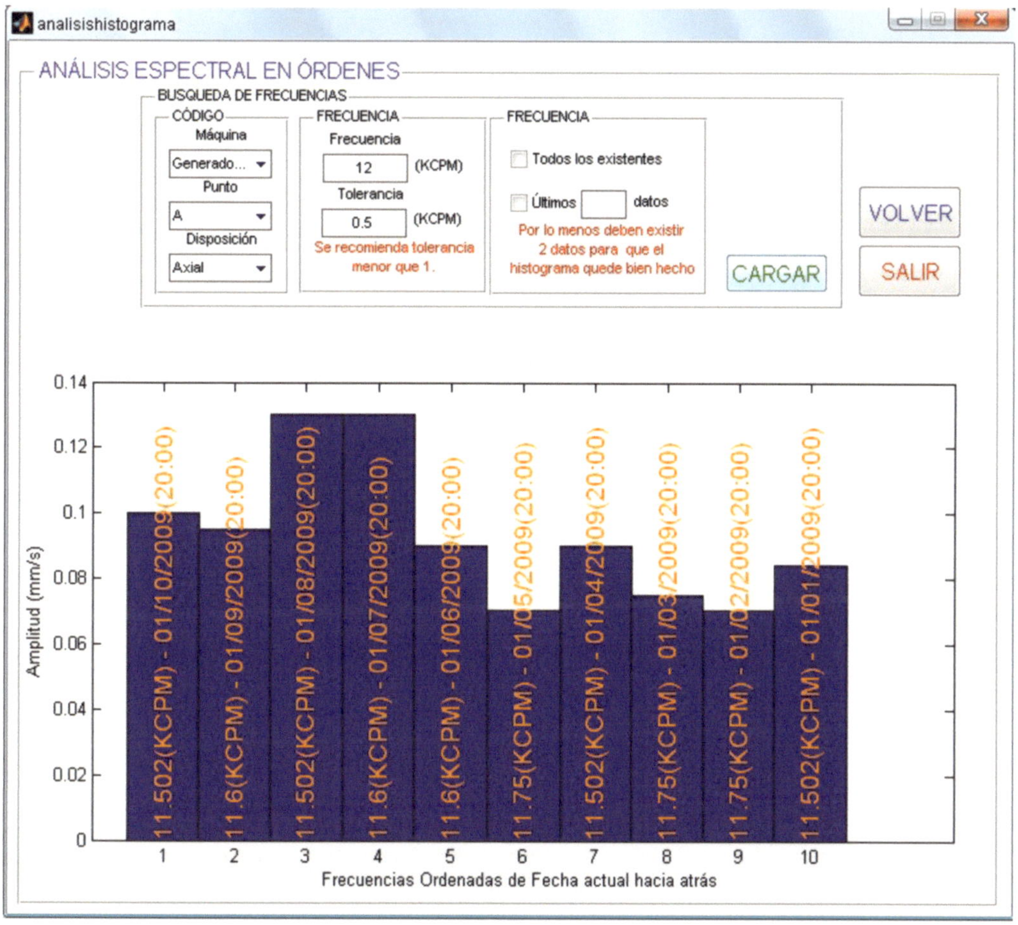

Figure 7. "Histogram Analysis" screen. Searching 12 KCPM frequency.

The exact frequency obtained and the dates of the measurement are shown above the histogram bars.

With the "RMS and CF value" tool, we can calculate the RMS value and the CF, displaying the signal's FFT or the signal as a function of time, so we can see the location of those values inside the vibration spectrum, as shown in **Figure 8**.

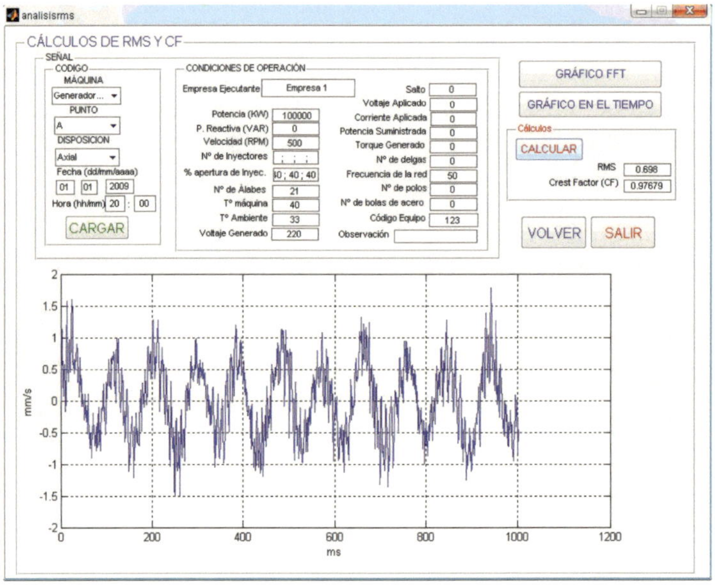

Figure 8. "RMS Value and CF" screen.

The "Time-Frequency Transform (TFT)" tool allows getting two kinds of graphs that represent the frequency, width, and time variables of the measured vibration spectra. One of the graphs is a 3D presentation of those variables (see **Figure 9**), and the other is a 2D contour line presentation of the 3D image, allowing a better analysis (see **Figure 10**).

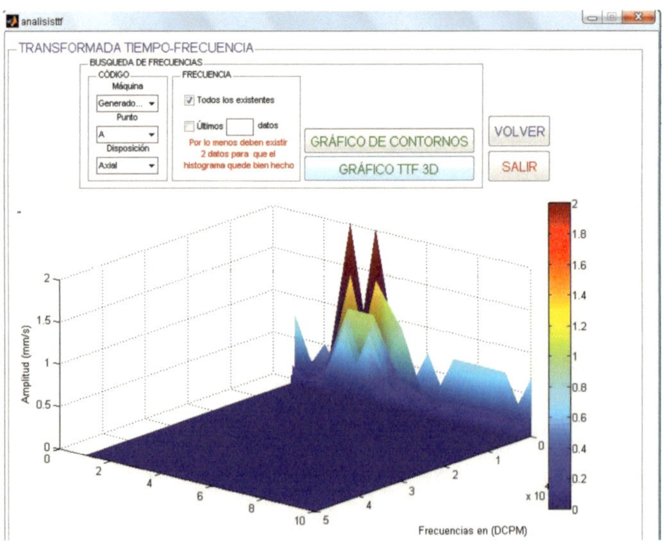

Figure 9. 3D and 2D TFT graphs.

http://dx.doi.org/10.5772/63736

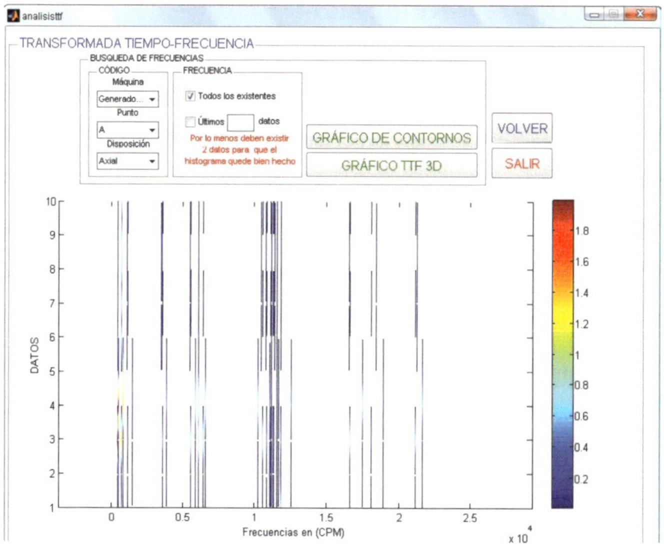

Figure 10. 2D TFT graphs.

With the tool "Comparison with Rules and Standards," we can, after calculating the rms value, get a vibration severity evaluation, according to ISO 2372, ISO 2373, and ISO10816 standards. In this function, we select the rule with which we want the data to be compared, selecting the machine's classification in accordance with the chosen rule, and then pressing the "Compare" button. This gives an evaluation of the vibration severity of the machine, according to the selected standard. This is shown in **Figure 11**.

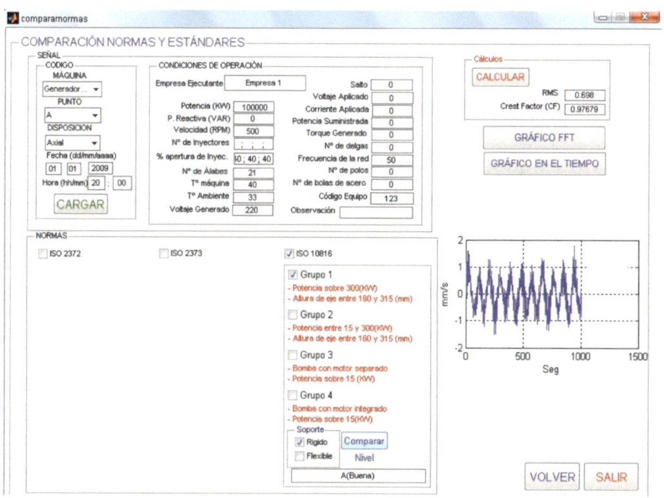

Figure 11. Screen "Comparison with Rules and Standards."

5. Conclusions and future development

A powerful software for vibration analysis was developed, with a very low cost compared with the tens of thousand dollars that a system for acquisition and analysis of mechanical vibrations can effectively cost.

This software, developed in MATLAB, has powerful tools like the creation of FFT graphs or bar graphs allowing to see more clearly the FFT peaks, order charts, histograms of some frequencies in a given time period, calculation of the RMS value and CF of a given frequency spectrum, creation of TFT graphs in 3D and 2D, and comparison of frequency spectra with ISO 2372, ISO 2373, and ISO 10816 standards.

This is a first stage in the development of this kind of "virtual instrument," since many parts still remain unsolved, like direct data acquisition from the machine, capturing and conditioning vibration signals for further storage in the database of the designed software, and this is an actual challenge to be faced in the short term.

Another interesting point for further development is the creation of an intelligent system (expert system, neural net, artificial intelligence, etc.) able to determine which is the possible failure appearing with vibration as a symptom.

The main file that contains the folders with the programming codes of the computational simulator (virtual instrument) presented in this chapter can be downloaded directly from the following website: http://www.mathworks.com/matlabcentral/fileexchange/56693-virtual-instrument-for-the-analysis-of-vibrations-in-rotary-machines

Acknowledgements

This work was supported by Proyectos Basales and the Vicerrectoría de Investigación, Desarrollo e Innovación of the Universidad de Santiago de Chile, Chile.

Author details

Claudio Urrea*, Rodrigo Cisterna and John Kern

*Address all correspondence to: claudio.urrea@usach.cl

Grupo de Automática, Departamento de Ingeniería Eléctrica, Universidad de Santiago de Chile (USACH), Santiago, Estación Central, Santiago, Chile

http://dx.doi.org/10.5772/63736

References

[1] Afefy I. H. Maintenance planning based on computer-aided preventive maintenance policy. In: International MultiConference of Engineers and Computer Scientists; 14–16 March, 2012; The Royal Garden Hotel, Kowloon, Hong Kong. Hong Kong: Newswood Limited; 2012. p. 1378–1383.

[2] Yan H.-C., Zhou J.-H. and Pang C. K. Gamma process with recursive MLE for wear PDF prediction in precognitive maintenance under aperiodic monitoring. Mechatronics. 2005;31:68–77.

[3] Widodo A., Yang B.-S., Gu D.-S. and Choi B.-K. Intelligent fault diagnosis system of induction motor based on transient current signal. Mechatronics. 2009;19(5):680–689.

[4] Bittencourt A., Saarinen K., Sander-Tavallaey S., Gunnarsson S. and Norrlöf M. A data-driven approach to diagnostics of repetitive processes in the distribution domain – applications to gearbox diagnostics in industrial robots and rotating machines. Mechatronics. 2014;24(8):1032–1041.

[5] San Román O. and Herrera J. Predictive fault system for critical equipment in the SAG plant of CODELCO Chile, Andina division [thesis]. Santiago, Chile: Universidad de Santiago de Chile, Departamento de Ingeniería Eléctrica; 2000.

[6] Czmochowski J., Moczko P., Odyjas P. and Pietrusiak D. Tests of rotary machines vibrations in steady and unsteady states on the basis of large diameter centrifugal fans. Maintenance and Reliability. 2014;6(2):211–216.

[7] Zarei J., Tajeddini M. A. and Karimi H. R. Vibration analysis for bearing fault detection and classification using an intelligent filter. Mechatronics. 2014;24(2):151–157.

[8] Xuejun L., Lingli J. and Fulei C. Design and implementation of the hardware and software of portable displacement-acceleration vibration signal measurement system. Journal of Electronic Measurement and Instrument. 2008, 2, pp. 56–61.

[9] Estupiñán P. E., San Martín C. and Canales M. L. Development of a virtual instrument for the dynamic balancing of rotors. Ingeniare – Revista Chilena de Ingeniería. 2006;14(2):146–152.

[10] Lakhoua M. N. Surveillance of pump vibrations using a supervisory control and data acquisition system. Journal of Control Engineering and Applied Informatics. 2010;12(1):15–20.

[11] Sanz F. A., Ramirez J. M. and Correa R. E. Hybrid method for the diagnosis of electrical rotary machines by vibration signals. In: North American Power Symposium (NAPS); 26–28 September; Arlington, TX; 2010. p. 1–6.

[12] MathWorks. MathWorks – MATLAB and Simulink for Technical Computing [Internet]. Available from: http://www.mathworks.com/?requested-Domain=www.mathworks.com [Accessed: Jan 12, 2016].

[13] Saavedra P. Monitoring and diagnosis of mining critical machines' mechanical condition. In: Conferencia Latinoamericana. Gestión Mantención y Confiabilidad Operacional, 13° Congreso Iberoamericano de Mantenimiento. Valparaiso, Chile. 2005.

[14] Moreno R., Pintado P., Alonzo F., Chicharro J., Morales A. and Nieto A. Assessment and comparison of fault diagnosis in gears using mechanical vibration signals. In: 8° Congreso Iberoamericano de Ingeniería Mecánica; 23–25 October; Cusco, Perú 2007. Código 585.

[15] A-Maq S.A. Machinery analysis: a tutorial on vibrations for mechanical maintenance. Medellín, Colombia. Jorge Marcel. 2005. 41 p.

[16] International Standard ISO. ISO 10816-1: Mechanical vibration – evaluation of machine vibration by measurements on non rotating part. Nicola Perou. Berlin, Germany. 2005.

Chapter 8

Application of MATLAB in *-Omics* and Systems Biology

Arsen Arakelyan, Lilit Nersisyan and Anna Hakobyan

Additional information is available at the end of the chapter

http://dx.doi.org/10.5772/62847

Abstract

Biological data analysis has dramatically changed since the introduction of high-throughput *-omics* technologies, such as microarrays and next-generation sequencing. The key advantage of obtaining thousands of measurements from a single sample soon became a bottleneck limiting transformation of generated data into knowledge. It has become apparent that traditional statistical approaches are not suited to solve problems in the new reality of "big biological data." From the other side, traditional computing languages such as C/C++ and Java, are not flexible enough to allow for quick development and testing of new algorithms, while MATLAB provides a powerful computing environment and a variety of sophisticated toolboxes for performing complex bioinformatics calculations.

We have used MATLAB to develop the pathway signal flow (PSF) algorithm for assessment of pathway activity changes based on high-throughput gene expression and pathway topologies. Additionally, we have created a KEGGParser tool for parsing, editing, and visualizing Kyoto Encyclopedia of Genes and Genomes (KEGG) pathway maps. We have used these tools to obtain a collection of KEGG pathways and evaluate their activity changes in different clinical forms of pulmonary sarcoidosis (PS). The application of PSF provided an extended systems view on pathway deregulation states and implicated several new pathways in sarcoidosis that had not been identified using other analysis approaches.

Keywords: biological data mining/visualization, *-omics* data analysis, pathway visualization, pathway flow analysis, KEGG pathway database

1. Introduction

Biology and biomedicine have always been quantitative scientific disciplines and data collection has been an important part of biological knowledge inference. Biological data types

INTECH
open science | open minds

© 2016 The Author(s). Licensee InTech. This chapter is distributed under the terms of the Creative Commons Attribution License (http://creativecommons.org/licenses/by/3.0), which permits unrestricted use, distribution, and reproduction in any medium, provided the original work is properly cited. (cc) BY

are very diverse and their nature has dramatically changed since introduction of new measurement technologies starting from the mid-twentieth century. DNA/RNA/protein sequencing [1, 2], X-ray crystallography [3], antibody-based assays [4, 5], and various modifications of polymerase chain reaction (PCR) [6, 7], allowed for collection of data about various aspects of cell function in normal and diseased conditions. A few of the most common biodata types include but are not limited to:

- Sequences—the one-dimensional orderings of monomers (DNA/RNA/proteins).
- Graphs—representation of a set of objects and pairwise interactions between them (pathway maps, protein–protein interaction nets).
- High-dimensional data—each sample is defined by hundreds or thousands of measurements, usually concurrently obtained (e.g., high-throughput gene expression data; see below).
- Geometric information—information about 3D structure of proteins, lipids, and nucleic acids.
- Patterns—regularities that characterize biological entities (transcription factor binding sites, network motifs, etc.).
- Models—mathematical or visual representations of dynamic or static behavior of biological entities.
- Literature—biological literature itself can be regarded as data to be exploited via data/text mining for revealing findings that would otherwise go undiscovered.

Traditionally, statistics has played significant role in biological data analysis [8]. It is used in biomarker identification [9–11], testing new drugs [12], analysis of genetic associations [13, 14], understanding associations between the levels of different biomolecules, experiment planning, etc. This has been made possible due to several key factors brought together. First of all, introduction of the "data analysis" concept was made by Tukey [15], implying that there is no need to be a statistician to be able to analyze and interpret the data. Next, the active penetration of computers into various research fields, as well as development of computer software and data analysis packages that can be used by "non-statisticians," has greatly enforced the progress in biomedical data analysis.

A new era of biomedical research has started in the twenty-first century with the advent of massively parallel measurement technologies. Traditional data collection approaches (low-throughput) are mainly focused on measurement of a few carefully selected parameters from a large number of samples, while high-throughput methods, such as microarrays, next-generation sequencing, and proteomics approaches, allow for acquiring dozens or hundred thousand observations from a single sample. Low-throughput techniques still remain an important tool in biomedical research; however, only high-throughput approaches provide global outlook on complex biological processes occurring at cellular, tissue, or even organismal level [16, 17]. This breakthrough has also changed the main paradigm in biological data representation, shifting from datasets containing large number of observations with few

http://dx.doi.org/10.5772/62847

variables (i.e., attributes or entries in the data vector) to datasets containing more variables than observations (high-dimension, low-sample size data (HDLSS)). HDLSS data is generated via various technologies measuring protein activity/abundance levels, gene expression levels (the amount of transcripts generated from each gene), ribonucleic acids (RNA) abundances, etc. For example, a typical high-throughput measurement of gene expression is performed for about 20,000 genes per subject, while the number of subjects rarely exceeds 10–20.

With this new data type, classical statistical approaches frequently fail to produce meaningful results because they are not designed to cope with this growth of dimensionality in datasets [18–20]. Thus, a demand for new algorithms and software for data analysis and visualization has emerged. From the other side, traditional computing languages, such as C/C++ and Java, are not flexible enough to allow for quick development and testing of new algorithms. This is because in contrast to scripting languages they require compilation of the whole code before execution, definition of variable types, etc. The limitations of compiled languages pose the challenge of having professional software engineers (or dedicated persons with programming skills) for writing software. In contrast, scripting languages allow for execution of separate lines of the script, without caring for variable type definitions and memory allocation beforehand. They are commonly at higher language level and additionally are supported by a wide range of packages for specific scientific purposes.

In this sense, MATLAB provides a powerful computing environment and a variety of sophisticated toolboxes for performing complex bioinformatics calculations. In this chapter, we discuss the examples of MATLAB application for high-throughput gene expression data analysis and visualization based on the algorithms and software developed by our research group.

2. Analysis of gene expression data

Gene expression is the realization of the information stored in genes through synthesis of ribonucleic acids (RNA) and proteins that perform functional and structural activities in a cell and an organism [21]. Genes are DNA fragments that code for products such as proteins and functional RNA, including ribosomal RNA (rRNA), transfer RNA (tRNA), or small nuclear RNA (snRNA). According to the central dogma of molecular biology, protein coding genes are expressed in a two-stage process involving synthesis of a messenger RNA (mRNA) (transcription) and synthesis of a protein on the mRNA template (translation) (**Figure 1**) [21]. However, in biomedical research the term "gene expression" is often used to refer only to the transcription stage, and the gene expression value usually indicates the amount of mRNA produced from each gene.

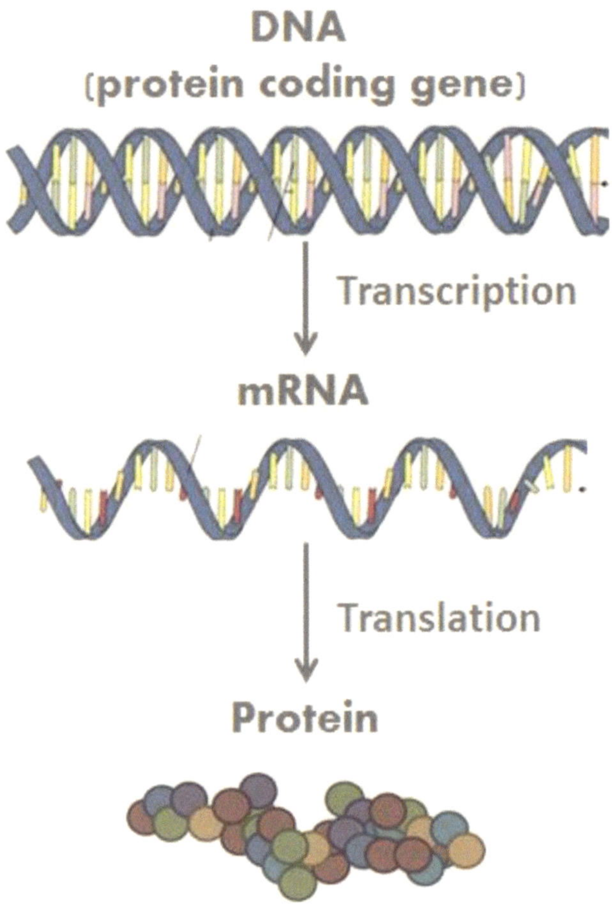

Figure 1. The synthesis of proteins from protein coding genes, according to the central dogma of molecular biology.

High-throughput analysis of gene expression is one of the cornerstones of systems biology [16]. The study of gene expression signatures has largely contributed to better understanding of molecular pathology of lung diseases [22, 23] and to identification of new disease subclasses/entities [24]. It has also provided new approaches to diagnostics [25] and helped to suggest novel therapeutic compounds [26].

There are two main techniques that allow for massively parallel measurement of gene expression in cells and tissues: microarrays and next-generation RNA sequencing (RNA-seq). The technology details of these approaches are summarized in **Figure 2** and are described in a number of publications elsewhere [2, 27–29]. The raw gene expression data for microarray and RNA-seq gene experiments are usually presented in a form of expression matrix. Each column represents all the gene expression levels for a single sample, and each row represents the expression of a gene across all the samples. This matrix serves as the source for subsequent analysis steps.

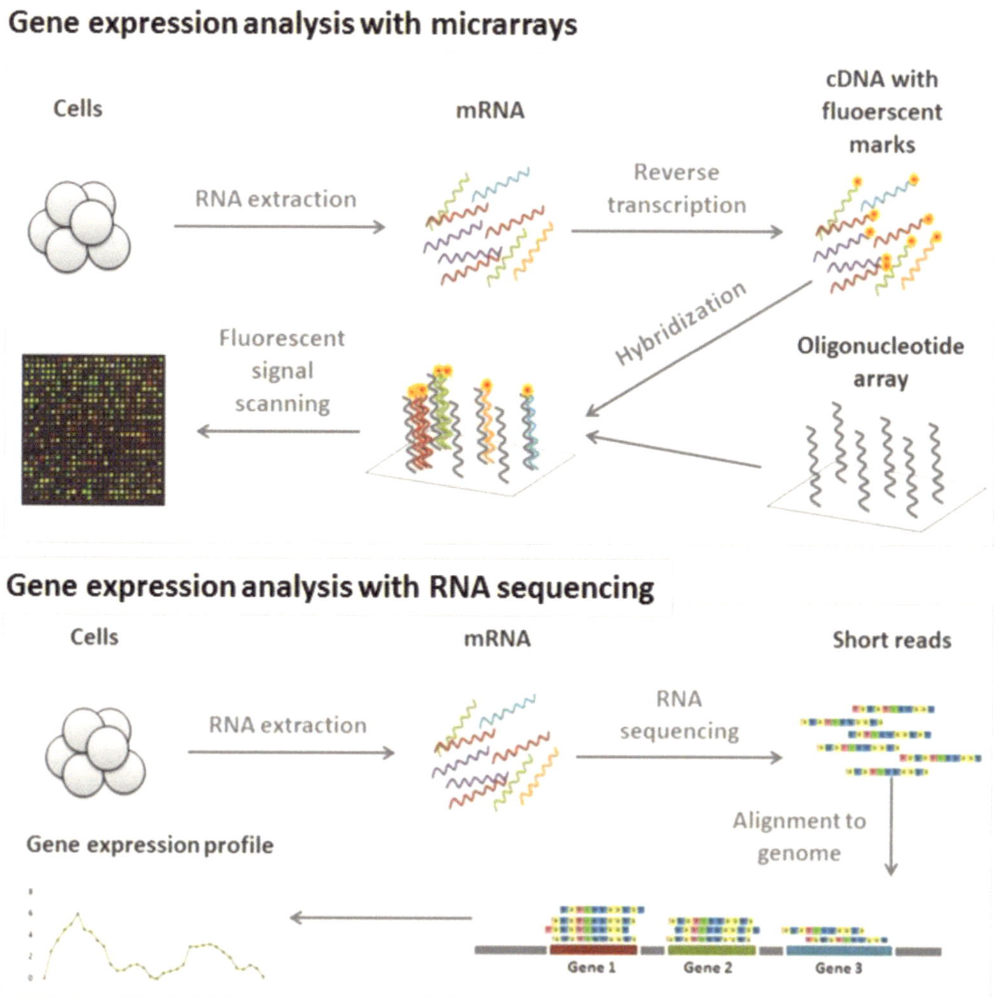

Figure 2. A general summary of two main techniques for gene expression assessment. Microarray-based techniques (at the top) are based on hybridization of complementary DNAs, obtained from RNA extracted from the cells, to specially designed oligonucleotide arrays and subsequent capturing of fluorescent signals coming from hybridized probes. The more the signal, the more RNA was produced from the gene corresponding to the respective oligonucleotide. RNA sequencing (at the bottom) utilizes next-generation sequencing technologies to obtain short sequencing reads from RNA extracted from the cells. These short reads are then aligned to the reference genome to determine the corresponding genes and to compute RNA abundance for each gene.

There are many different algorithms, also implemented in MATLAB, that are aimed at analysis of global gene expression [30–32]. MATLAB Bioinformatics toolbox demos are excellent start points to become acquainted with microarray and RNA-seq gene expression analysis. Most of these algorithms exploit a common gene-centered analysis pipeline, which identifies genes differentially expressed between studied conditions, and further annotates the gene lists by assessment of their relative abundance in predefined functional categories available in biological databases [33], such as Gene Ontology (GO) [34], Kyoto Encyclopedia of Genes and Genomes (KEGG) [35], and others. A shortcoming of these approaches is that they overlook the interactions that exist between gene products in a cell. These interactions define the actual behavior of biological systems, along with expression values of the interacting agents. The information on interactions occurring between gene products is depicted in topologies of biological pathways, and thus, gene expression analysis that also accounts for topology information would be more informative about the state of pathways and activities of associated biological processes. Biological pathways are directed and spatially defined sequences of biomolecular physical and regulatory interactions that represent molecular signal propagations leading to functional realizations of biological processes. The behavior of a given pathway highly depends on both gene expression and its topology [36]. It is known that a significant portion of genes may be involved in more than one pathway, while perturbation of a single pathway may be conditioned by differential expression of multiple member genes. Moreover, a single disease may be characterized by orchestrated deregulation of several pathways. Finally, profiles of pathway deregulations may be common for different diseases. Thus, based on gene expression and pathway topology data, it is possible to identify common and specific pathways among diseases.

3. KEGGParser

KEGGParser is a MATLAB graph-based graphical user interface tool for parsing, editing, visualization, and analysis of biological pathway maps from Kyoto Encyclopedia of Genes and Genomes (KEGG) pathway database. It is based solely on functions contained in MATLAB, MATLAB Bioinformatics toolbox version 3.x, and Image Processing Toolbox 2.x. KEGGParser is freely available at http://www.mathworks.com/matlabcentral/fileexchange/37561.

KEGG pathways are stored in a collection of manually curated pathway maps. Each pathway is represented by an image and accompanying xml (KGML) file, which stores an xml tree structure containing information about nodes and edges. The KGML files are created from the map images with "KegSketch" program.

KEGG pathways can be accessed from MATLAB using KEGG REST interface implemented in MATLAB Bioinformatics toolbox. However, KEGG REST functions are very limited and intended for very basic operations, such as retrieval of pathway images, node information, and mapping of gene expression data via coloring of nodes on top of the map images, and are not suited for much wider range of pathway analysis needed. In contrast, KEGGParser uses information stored in pathway KGML files to convert them directly to MATLAB biograph objects (a graph representation of the pathways), which then allows for performing advanced pathway analysis. Biograph is a MATLAB data structure for implementation of directed graphs. Graph nodes can represent diverse biological agents, such as genes and proteins, and edges depict directed interactions between the agents, which can represent physical, regulatory interactions, dependencies, etc. The biograph object also stores graphical properties, such as color, labels, and sizes, used for 2D visualization.

http://dx.doi.org/10.5772/62847

Although the biograph object is ideally suited for storing and manipulating biological pathways, its severe limitation is the absence of generic methods for adding or deleting edges on already created graphs. This can seriously impede downstream analyses, because KGML files do not contain all the information depicted in the pathway map (Figures 3 and 4).

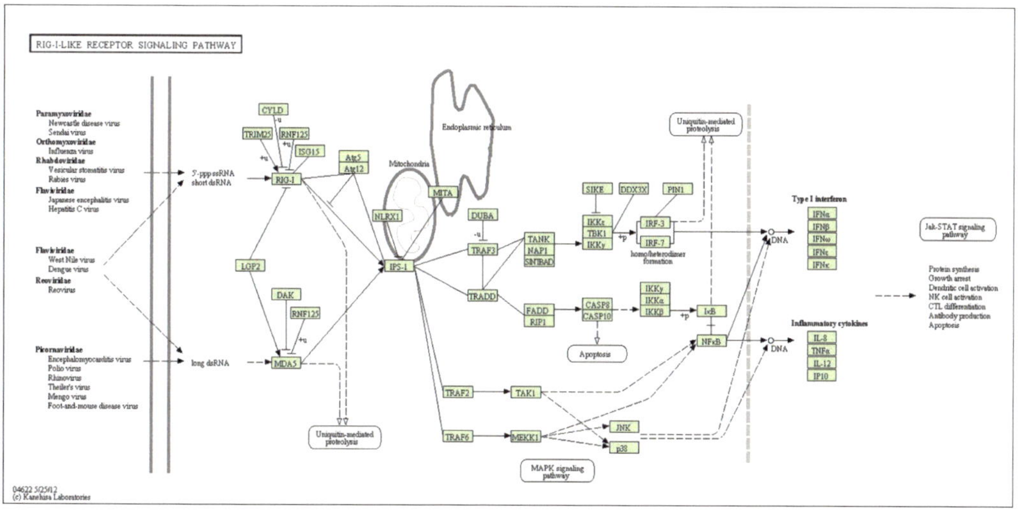

Figure 3. The RIG-I-like signaling pathway map image obtained from KEGG pathway database.

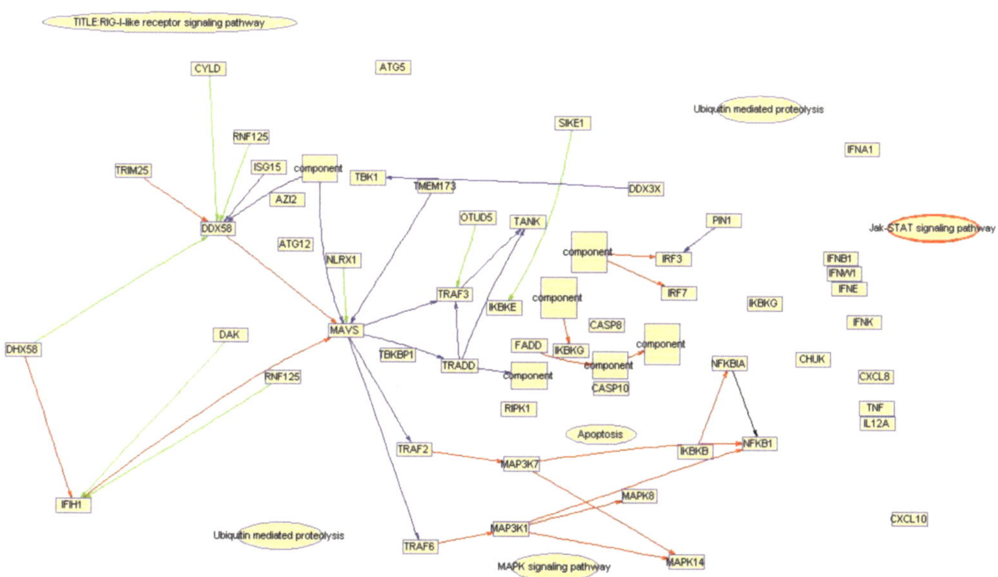

Figure 4. The RIG-I-like pathway map obtained by parsing the pathway KGML file.

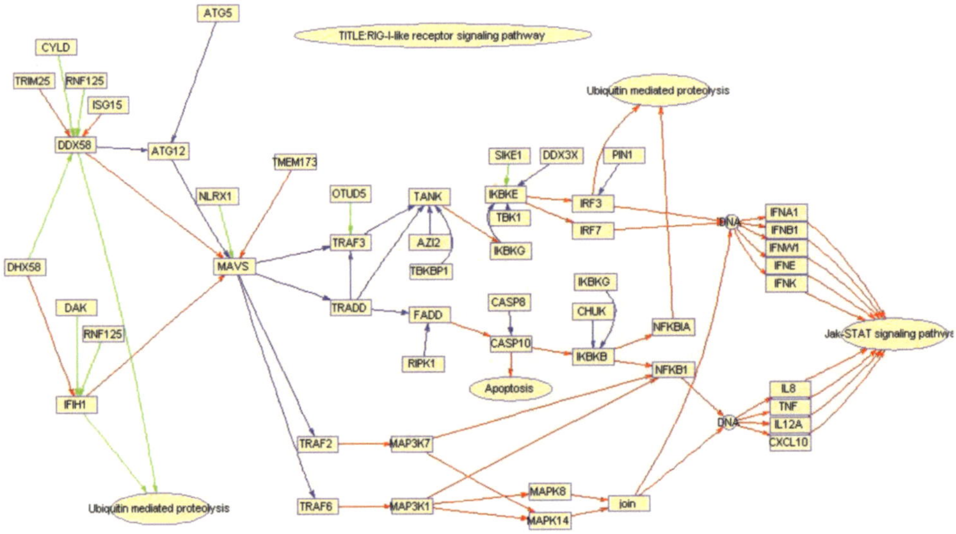

Figure 5. Manipulation of a sample biograph object with graph manipulation tools. The process of node and edge addition and deletion is depicted. See the main text for the respective example code.

Moreover, it is known that pathways can change their topology (i.e., interactions between nodes in a pathway) due to mutations, regulation of gene expression, , etc. In order to overcome these limitations, we have developed several functions that allow for graph manipulations on pre-calculated graphs. They are accessible from the link http://www.mathworks.com/matlabcentral/fileexchange/37475. The following example and **Figure 5** demonstrate the biograph object editing process using graph manipulation tools.

```
% Create an adjacency matrix
cm = [0,0,1; 1,0,0; 0,1,0];
%convert adjacency matrix to biograph object
bg = biograph(cm);
%plot graph object
view(bg);
%add new node to existing graph
bg = node_add(bg);
%change node label
bg.Nodes(4).ID = 'Node 4';
view(bg);
%add new edge from node 4 to node 1
bg = edge_add(bg, 4, 1);
view(bg);
% delete created edge
bg = edge_del(bg, 4,1);
view(bg);
% delete node 4
bg = node_del(bg, 4);
view(bg);
```

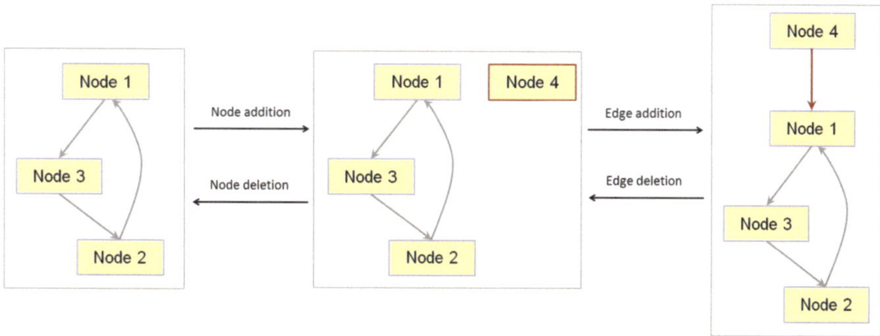

Figure 6. The RIG-I-like pathway map obtained by KGML file parsing and further corrections and recovery of missing information using KEGGParser.

The graph manipulation tools are used by KEGGParser for parsing KGML files, creating and editing biograph objects that represent KEGG pathway graphs. Along with creation of pathway graphs, KEGGParser automatically handles and respectively edits part of inconsistencies between KGML files and map images. The overall KEGGParser workflow and usage examples are described in detail in the original publication [37]. In this chapter we present two different use cases for this software.

The first example refers to retrieval, editing, and visualization of KEGG pathways using KEGGParser. As an example we have chosen RIG-I (retinoic acid-inducible gene 1) - like receptor signaling pathway. RIG-I-like receptors and downstream signaling are key elements in sensing viral pathogens and generating innate immune responses [38, 39]. Activation of this pathway is essential for production of various cytokines, mediators of inflammation, and proliferation of immune system cells. Deregulation of RIG-I-like pathway activity is implicated in many autoimmune disorders, such as systemic lupus erythematosus and Aicardi–Goutières syndrome [40]. In order to access the basic characteristics of the pathway topology, we used KEGGParser for retrieving and editing the corresponding KGML file. The pathway map from KEGG pathway database, as well as the native graph object parsed using KEGGParser, is presented in Figures 3 and 4 (static image and parsed without automatic corrections). As can be noticed, the parsed graph in MATLAB has many missing edges and unconnected nodes, making subsequent analysis improper. This is because KGML file contains information only about protein–protein interactions and the information about other types of interactions present in the map images is lost after KGML parsing. Using KEGGParser, we manually edited the pathway graph object and restored missing edges (**Figure 6**).

In order to perform graph theory-based analyses, we stored unedited and edited pathway graphs in rig_like.mat and rig_corr.mat files, respectively (available at [41]). Using graph theory functions implemented in MATLAB Bioinformatics toolbox, we performed some basic comparisons of unedited and manually edited pathway graphs. First we compared connectivities of nodes in the graphs:

```
%Comparison of edited and unedited KEGG graphs using MATLAB
%graph theory functions: node degrees
%
% Load the unedited graph, use load rig_cor for the edited one
load rig_like.mat
bgtemp = bg.deepCopy;
n = length(bgtemp.nodes);
mat = zeros(n,3);
for i = 1:n
        % all nodes connected to the given node
tot = length(getrelatives(bgtemp.nodes(i)))-1;
up = length(getancestors(bgtemp.nodes(i)))-1;
down = length(getdescendants(bgtemp.nodes(i)))-1;
mat(i,:) = [tot,up, down];
end

% Plot the histogram of node degrees
hist(mat(:,1))
clear all
```

Analysis of node degree histograms in the unedited graph shows significant skew toward 0-degree nodes, compared to the edited graph (**Figure 7A** and **B**).

```
%Comparison of edited and unedited KEGG graphs using MATLAB
%graph theory functions: analysis of connected components
%
% Load the unedited graph, use load rig_cor for the edited one
load rig_like.mat
bgtemp = bg.deepCopy;
[S, C] = conncomp(bgtemp, 'Directed', false)

% Plot the histogram of nodes in connected components
hist(C, unique(C))
clear all
```

The results showed that there are five strongly connected multi-node components (with four nodes on average) in the unedited pathway graph, while the edited graph identifies six components containing on average seven nodes (**Figure 7C** and **D**). These components correspond to nodes that form separate pathway branches and lead to different functional outcomes associated with pathway activation.

Finally, the distributions of all lengths of shortest paths between pairs in the unedited and edited graphs were significantly different, showing longer average path in the edited graph consistent with the static pathway map image (**Figure 7E** and **F**). Thus, KEGGParser can facilitate the better representation of biological pathways in MATLAB and contribute to the adequate analyses of pathway topologies. Manual/automatic editing options help to restore correct topologies of the pathways. Using KEGGParser, we have created a collection of signaling biological pathways that were further used for analysis of pathway activity perturbations in various diseases (see pathway signal flow (PSF) section).

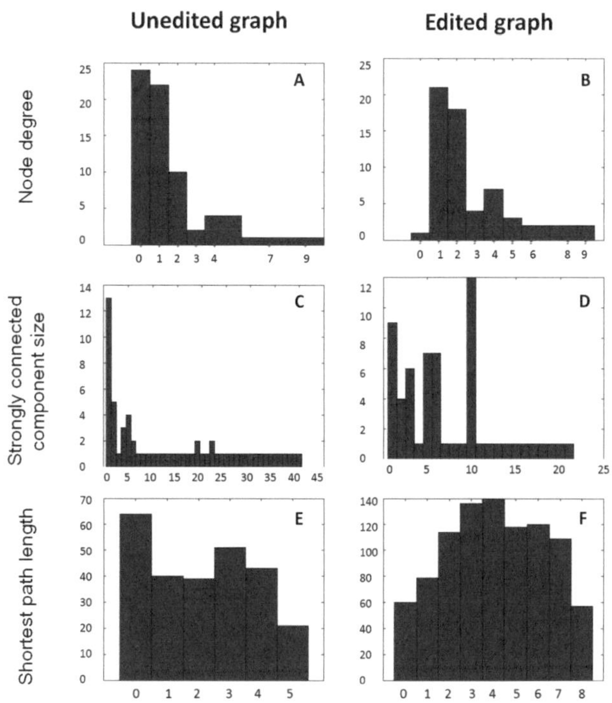

Figure 7. Graph characteristics of RIG-I-like signaling pathway after initial KGML parsing (unedited graph) and further editing to correct for missing nodes and edges (edited graph). (A and B) Node degree distributions; (C and D) the distributions of sizes of strongly connected components; and (E and F) the distribution of shortest path lengths.

4. Pathway signal flow

The PSF algorithm can be used to assess the changes in activity of a given biological pathway depending on the pathway topology and relative gene expression [42]. In contrast to the traditional gene-centered approaches for expression data analysis, PSF also takes into account the interactions between gene products (i.e., proteins, RNA, etc.) and other biological entities and, thus, provides richer outlook on actual molecular events associated with pathways.

This algorithm calculates how the activating signal is propagated from pathway input nodes, through interactions between intermediate node pairs, to the output nodes, leading to functional realization of associated biological processes. The amount of signal approaching the output nodes is called PSF. The extent of changes in the pathway flow is indicative of the likeliness of the given pathway to be involved in the biological processes underlying the phenotypic differences between the studied conditions. The detailed description of PSF is given in a number of publications [42, 43]. Here we will bring an example of PSF usage for analysis of pathway flow perturbations in pulmonary sarcoidosis (PS) and its different clinical forms.

PS is a systemic granulomatous disease with unknown cause [44]. It is characterized by massive influx of activated T-lymphocytes and macrophages into the lungs, formation of granulomas, and lung function failure. The immune disturbances and and granulomatous deposits resolve spontaneously in 60–70% of PS patients; the rest follow a chronic course [44]. Though significant advances have been made in understanding of immunological features of this disease, the central pathomechanisms of its development are yet unknown. In this study, we aimed at identification of differentially deregulated pathways in sarcoidosis, as well as in different clinical forms of the disease, compared with healthy lung. We have used two microarray gene expression datasets from Gene Expression Omnibus public repository (dataset IDs: GDS3580 and GDS3705). The gene expression data and PSF scripts are available for download from [41].

The results of PSF analysis indicate that inflammation-related pathways are significantly upregulated in sarcoidosis compared to healthy lung, while pathways interfering with cell proliferation and fibrosis are downregulated (**Table 1**). Moreover, compared to self-limiting PS, the progressive form of the disease is characterized by more prominent deregulation of pathways associated with proinflammatory response and fibrotic conversion of the tissue (**Table 2**).

Pathway	PSF	*p* value
PPAR (Peroxisome proliferator-activated receptor) signaling pathway	0.98	0.0000
Chemokine signaling pathway	33.05	0.0000
NF-kappa B signaling pathway	1.62	0.0000
Apoptosis	0.98	0.0000

Table 1. Pathway activity deregulation in pulmonary sarcoidosis compared to healthy lung.

Pathway	PSF	*p* value
Fc gamma R-mediated phagocytosis	13.72	0.0000
Chemokine signaling pathway	12.65	0.0000
Fc epsilon RI signaling pathway	7.27	0.0000
Ras signaling pathway	6.55	0.0000
PI3K (Phosphoinositide 3-kinase)-Akt signaling pathway	2.98	0.0000
HIF-1 (Hypoxia-inducible factor 1) signaling pathway	2.62	0.0000
B-cell receptor signaling pathway	2.18	0.0000
NF-kappa B signaling pathway	2.17	0.0000
NOD (Nucleotide-binding oligomerization domain)-like receptor signaling pathway	1.81	0.0339

http://dx.doi.org/10.5772/62847

Pathway	PSF	*p* value
VEGF (Vascular-endothelial growth factor) signaling pathway	1.71	0.0000
MAPK (mitogen-activated protein kinases) signaling pathway	1.69	0.0000
p53 signaling pathway	1.33	0.0000
Apoptosis	1.26	0.0000

Table 2. Pathway activity deregulation in progressive versus self-limiting sarcoidosis.

These findings are in compliance with the existing knowledge on sarcoidosis pathogenesis. Numerous experimental studies, including our own, have implicated immune/inflammatory pathways, such as Toll-like receptor signaling, phagocytosis, and chemokine signaling in sarcoidosis [45–47]. However, application of PSF provided an extended systems view on pathway deregulation states. Moreover, PSF implicated several new pathways that were not detected using gene-centered analysis approaches in the original publications [48, 49].

5. Conclusions

This chapter demonstrates the advantages of MATLAB for performing bioinformatics research. The powerful scripting language combined with various toolboxes makes it a valuable tool for creation of complete pipelines for -*omics* data analysis and visualization. We have contributed to MATLAB Bioinformatics toolbox with the PSF algorithm for assessment of pathway activity changes, and KEGGParser for fine-tuned pathway editing and visualization. MATLAB GUI support allows for visualization of the results, making it easy to use for the general scientific audience. Combining our tools with the rest of the MATLAB Bioinformatics toolbox has the power of having various complete pipelines for high-throughput data analyses.

Finally, MATLAB scripting language allows for easy development and testing of various algorithms that can later be translated into other scripting and programming languages. It should be noted that KEGGParser and PSF, originally developed in MATLAB, were then ported to various programming and scripting environments, such as Java and R [43, 50].

Author details

Arsen Arakelyan[1,2*], Lilit Nersisyan[1,2] and Anna Hakobyan[1]

*Address all correspondence to: aarakelyan@sci.am

1 Bioinformatics Group, Institute of Molecular Biology MAS RA, Yerevan, Armenia

2 College of Science and Engineering, American University of Armenia, Yerevan, Armenia

References

[1] Moorthie S, Mattocks CJ, Wright CF. Review of massively parallel DNA sequencing technologies. Hugo J. 2011;5(1–4):1–12. DOI: 10.1007/s11568-011-9156-3.

[2] Ozsolak F, Milos PM. RNA sequencing: advances, challenges and opportunities. Nat Rev Genet. 2011;12(2):87–98. DOI: 10.1038/nrg2934.

[3] Shi Y. A glimpse of structural biology through X-ray crystallography. Cell. 2014;159(5): 995–1014. DOI: 10.1016/j.cell.2014.10.051.

[4] Kahlert H, Cromwell O. Monoclonal antibodies. Methods Mol Med. 2008;138:183–96.DOI: 10.1007/978–1–59745–366–0_15.

[5] Zhu K, Dietrich R, Didier A, Doyscher D, Märtlbauer E. Recent developments in antibody-based assays for the detection of bacterial toxins. Toxins (Basel). 2014;6(4): 1325–48. DOI: 10.3390/toxins6041325.

[6] Lo YM, Chan KC. Introduction to the polymerase chain reaction. Methods Mol Biol. 2006;336:1–10.

[7] Fakruddin M, Mannan KS, Chowdhury A, Mazumdar RM, Hossain MN, Islam S, Chowdhury MA. Nucleic acid amplification: alternative methods of polymerase chain reaction. J Pharm Bioallied Sci. 2013;5(4):245–52. DOI: 10.4103/0975-7406.120066.

[8] Bang H, Davidian M. In: Bang H, Zhou XK, van Epps HL, Mazumdar M, editors. Statistical Methods in Molecular Biology. 1st ed. Humana Press; 2010. 636 p. DOI: 10.1007/978-1-60761-580-4.

[9] Wang IM, Stone DJ, Nickle D, Loboda A, Puig O, Roberts C. Systems biology approach for new target and biomarker identification. Curr Top Microbiol Immunol. 2013;363:169–99. DOI: 10.1007/82_2012_252.

[10] Rajcevic U, Niclou SP, Jimenez CR. Proteomics strategies for target identification and biomarker discovery in cancer. Front Biosci (Landmark Ed). 2009;14:3292–303.

[11] Vandenbogaert M, Li-Thiao-Té S, Kaltenbach HM, Zhang R, Aittokallio T, Schwikowski B. Alignment of LC–MS images, with applications to biomarker discovery and protein identification. Proteomics. 2008;8(4):650–72. DOI: 10.1002/pmic.200700791.

[12] Ahuja V, Sharma S. Drug safety testing paradigm, current progress and future challenges: an overview. J Appl Toxicol. 2014;34(6):576–94. DOI: 10.1002/jat.2935.

[13] Srivastava K, Srivastava A. Comprehensive review of genetic association studies and meta-analyses on miRNA polymorphisms and cancer risk. PLoS One. 2012;7(11):e50966. DOI: 10.1371/journal.pone.0050966.

[14] Lee YH. Meta-analysis of genetic association studies. Ann Lab Med. 2015;35(3):283–7. DOI: 10.3343/alm.2015.35.3.283.

[15] Tukey JW. The future of data analysis. Ann Math Stat. 1962;33(1):1–67. DOI: 10.1214/aoms/1177704711.

[16] Braun R. Systems analysis of high-throughput data. Adv Exp Med Biol. 2014;844:153–87. DOI: 10.1007/978-1-4939-2095-2_8.

[17] Reuter JA, Spacek DV, Snyder MP. High-throughput sequencing technologies. Mol Cell. 2015;58(4):586–97. DOI: 10.1016/j.molcel.2015.05.004.

[18] Li L. Dimension reduction for high-dimensional data. Methods Mol Biol. 2010;620:417–34. DOI: 10.1007/978-1-60761-580-4_14.

[19] Huang H, Liu Y, Yuan M, Marron JS. Statistical significance of clustering using soft thresholding. J Comp Graph Stat. 2015;24(4):975–93.

[20] Ibrahim M, Jassim S, Cawthorne MA, Langlands K. Multidimensionality of microarrays: statistical challenges and (im)possible solutions. Mol Oncol. 2011;5(2):190–6. DOI: 10.1016/j.molonc.2011.01.002.

[21] Weinzierl ROJ. Mechanisms of Gene Expression. Imperial College Press; 1999. 436 p. DOI: 10.1142/9781848160606_fmatter.

[22] Thakur RK, Yadav VK, Kumar A, Basundra R, Kar A, Halder R, Singh A, Kumar P, Baral A, Kumar MM, Pal K, Banerjee R, Chowdhury S. Functional genomics of lung cancer progression reveals mechanism of metastasis suppressor function. Mol Cytogenet. 2014;7(Suppl 1 Proceedings of the International Conference on Human):I9. DOI: 10.1186/1755-8166-7-S1-I9.

[23] Cancer Genome Atlas Research Network. Comprehensive genomic characterization of squamous cell lung cancers. Nature. 2012;489(7417):519–25. DOI: 10.1038/nature11404.

[24] Bhattacharjee A, Richards WG, Staunton J, Li C, Monti S, Vasa P, Ladd C, Beheshti J, Bueno R, Gillette M, Loda M, Weber G, Mark EJ, Lander ES, Wong W, Johnson BE, Golub TR, Sugarbaker DJ, Meyerson M. Classification of human lung carcinomas by mRNA expression profiling reveals distinct adenocarcinoma subclasses. Proc Natl Acad Sci U S A. 2001;98(24):13790–5.

[25] DePianto DJ, Chandriani S, Abbas AR, Jia G, N'Diaye EN, Caplazi P, Kauder SE, Biswas S, Karnik SK, Ha C, Modrusan Z, Matthay MA, Kukreja J, Collard HR, Egen JG, Wolters PJ, Arron JR. Heterogeneous gene expression signatures correspond to distinct lung pathologies and biomarkers of disease severity in idiopathic pulmonary fibrosis. Thorax. 2015;70(1):48–56. DOI: 10.1136/thoraxjnl-2013-204596.

[26] Gerber DE, Oxnard GR, Govindan R. ALCHEMIST: bringing genomic discovery and targeted therapies to early-stage lung cancer. Clin Pharmacol Ther. 2015;97(5):447–50. DOI: 10.1002/cpt.91.

[27] Slonim DK, Yanai I. Getting started in gene expression microarray analysis. PLoS Comput Biol. 2009;5(10):e1000543. DOI: 10.1371/journal.pcbi.1000543.

[28] Roberts PC. Gene expression microarray data analysis demystified. Biotechnol Annu Rev. 2008;14:29–61. DOI: 10.1016/S1387-2656(08)00002-1.

[29] Vikman P, Fadista J, Oskolkov N. RNA sequencing: current and prospective uses in metabolic research. J Mol Endocrinol. 2014;53(2):R93–101. DOI: 10.1530/JME-14-0170.

[30] Ye N, Yin H, Liu J, Dai X, Yin T. GESearch: an interactive GUI tool for identifying gene expression signature. Biomed Res Int. 2015;2015:853734. DOI: 10.1155/2015/853734.

[31] Taylor A, Steinberg J, Andrews TS, Webber C. GeneNet Toolbox for MATLAB: a flexible platform for the analysis of gene connectivity in biological networks. Bioinformatics. 2015;31(3):442–4. DOI: 10.1093/bioinformatics/btu669.

[32] Ibrahim M, Jassim S, Cawthorne MA, Langlands K. A MATLAB tool for pathway enrichment using a topology-based pathway regulation score. BMC Bioinformatics. 2014;15:358. DOI: 10.1186/s12859-014-0358-2.

[33] Hung JH. Gene set/pathway enrichment analysis. Methods Mol Biol. 2013;939:201–13. DOI: 10.1007/978-1-62703-107-3_13.

[34] Gene Ontology Consortium. Gene Ontology Consortium: going forward. Nucleic Acids Res. 2015;43(Database issue):D1049–56. DOI: 10.1093/nar/gku1179.

[35] Kanehisa M, Goto S. KEGG: Kyoto encyclopedia of genes and genomes. Nucleic Acids Res. 2000;28(1):27–30.

[36] Yuryev A. Introduction to pathway analysis. In: Yuryev A, editor. Pathway Analysis for Drug Discovery: Computational Infrastructure and Applications. Hoboken, NJ, USA: John Wiley & Sons, Inc.; 2008. DOI: 10.1002/9780470399279.ch1.

[37] Arakelyan A, Nersisyan L. KEGGParser: parsing and editing KEGG pathway maps in Matlab. Bioinformatics. 2013;29(4):518–9. DOI: 10.1093/bioinformatics/bts730.

[38] Zeng W, Sun L, Jiang X, Chen X, Hou F, Adhikari A, Xu M, Chen ZJ. Reconstitution of the RIG-I pathway reveals a signaling role of unanchored polyubiquitin chains in innate immunity. Cell. 2010;141(2):315–30. DOI: 10.1016/j.cell.2010.03.029.

[39] Kaneda Y. The RIG-I/MAVS signaling pathway in cancer cell-selective apoptosis. Oncoimmunology. 2013;2(4):e23566.

[40] Kato H, Fujita T. RIG-I-like receptors and autoimmune diseases. Curr Opin Immunol. 2015;37:40–5. DOI: 10.1016/j.coi.2015.10.002.

[41] ArakelyanA. MATLAB chapter supplement: PSF scripts and gene expression data [Internet]. 2016 [updated: 16.01.16]. Available from: https://www.dropbox.com/sh/ni26ga5t0nn4kzy/AADY5XDcheAV2jBqY5XAh1Jua [Accessed: 16.01.16].

[42] Arakelyan A, Aslanyan L, Boyajyan A. High-throughput gene expression analysis concepts and applications. In: Sequence and Genome Analysis II – Bacteria, Viruses and Metabolic Pathways. Hong Kong: iConcept Press; 2013.

[43] Nersisyan L, Johnson G, Riel-Mehan M, Pico A, Arakelyan A. PSFC: a pathway signal flow calculator app for cytoscape. F1000Research. 2015;4:480. DOI: 10.12688/f1000research.6706.1.

[44] Valeyre D, Bernaudin JF, Jeny F, Duchemann B, Freynet O, Planès C, Kambouchner M, Nunes H. Pulmonary sarcoidosis. Clin Chest Med. 2015;36(4):631–41. DOI: 10.1016/j.ccm.2015.08.006.

[45] Kriegova E, Fillerova R, Tomankova T, Hutyrova B, Mrazek F, Tichy T, Kolek V, du Bois RM, Petrek M. T-helper cell type-1 transcription factor T-bet is upregulated in pulmonary sarcoidosis. Eur Respir J. 2011;38(5):1136–44. DOI: 10.1183/09031936.00089910.

[46] Arakelyan A, Kriegova E, Kubistova Z, Mrazek F, Kverka M, du Bois RM, Kolek V, Petrek M. Protein levels of CC chemokine ligand (CCL)15, CCL16 and macrophage stimulating protein in patients with sarcoidosis. Clin Exp Immunol. 2009;155(3):457–65. DOI: 10.1111/j.1365-2249.2008.03832.x.

[47] Pabst S, Bradler O, Gillissen A, Nickenig G, Skowasch D, Grohe C. Toll-like receptor-9 polymorphisms in sarcoidosis and chronic obstructive pulmonary disease. Adv Exp Med Biol. 2013;756:239–45. DOI: 10.1007/978-94-007-4549-0_30.

[48] Crouser ED, Culver DA, Knox KS, Julian MW, Shao G, Abraham S, Liyanarachchi S, Macre JE, Wewers MD, Gavrilin MA, Ross P, Abbas A, Eng C. Gene expression profiling identifies MMP-12 and ADAMDEC1 as potential pathogenic mediators of pulmonary sarcoidosis. Am J Respir Crit Care Med. 2009;179(10):929–38. DOI: 10.1164/rccm.200803-490OC.

[49] Lockstone HE, Sanderson S, Kulakova N, Baban D, Leonard A, Kok WL, McGowan S, McMichael AJ, Ho LP. Gene set analysis of lung samples provides insight into pathogenesis of progressive, fibrotic pulmonary sarcoidosis. Am J Respir Crit Care Med. 2010;181(12):1367–75. DOI: 10.1164/rccm.200912-1855OC.

[50] Nersisyan L, Samsonyan R, Arakelyan A. CyKEGGParser: tailoring KEGG pathways to fit into systems biology analysis workflows. F1000Res. 2014;3:145. DOI: 10.12688/f1000research.4410.2.

Chapter 9

Small Molecule LC-MS/MS Fragmentation Data Analysis and Application to Siderophore Identification

Oliver Baars and David H. Perlman

Additional information is available at the end of the chapter

http://dx.doi.org/10.5772/63018

Abstract

Rapid developments in tandem liquid chromatography-mass spectrometry (LC-MS/MS) have created wide interest in applications for the analysis of small molecule mixtures. MS/MS spectra can contain rich structural information, but because of the structural diversity of small molecules and different data acquisition methods, analysis algorithms and workflows frequently need to be tailored to individual research questions. This chapter shows how MATLAB can be used for LC-MS/MS-based structural characterization of small molecules. Starting with the import of raw data, ways for visualization and the creation of graphical user interfaces (GUIs) for individual applications are demonstrated. A selection of frequently used algorithms for pre-processing and data analysis is reviewed in context of their MATLAB implementation. The approaches are then tailored and applied to the analysis of iron-binding peptides (peptidic siderophores) by high-resolution LC-MS/MS. The method uses a database with siderophore structures to exploit prior knowledge about siderophore structural diversity for the interpretation of MS/MS spectra from known and new siderophores.

Keywords: small molecules, metabolomics, fragmentation spectra, LC-MS/MS, liquid chromatography tandem mass spectrometry, neutral-loss, fragment-ion, auto-convolution spectra, molecular networks, secondary metabolites, siderophores, iron, nonribosomal peptides, MATLAB

1. Introduction

Liquid chromatography-mass spectrometry (LC-MS) enables the analysis of complex mixtures of small molecules and is applied widely in diverse research areas, such as metabolomics analysis in biology [1] and medicine [2, 3] and molecular characterization of samples in

INTECH
open science | open minds

© 2016 The Author(s). Licensee InTech. This chapter is distributed under the terms of the Creative Commons Attribution License (http://creativecommons.org/licenses/by/3.0), which permits unrestricted use, distribution, and reproduction in any medium, provided the original work is properly cited.

environmental chemistry [4] and combinatorial chemistry [5], among many other applications. Recent advances in LC-MS instrumentation with respect to speed and sensitivity, coupled with improved computational methods to extract information from complex datasets, have translated into falling costs of analyses and have created wide interest in LC-MS applications. As instruments have become able to explore samples at very high sensitivity and resolution (e.g., nano-flow LC coupled to high-resolution MS detectors, such as Orbitraps or Q-TOFs), the computational analysis of the generated raw data has become more challenging. In untargeted, 'discovery type' LC-MS experiments, the analysis of the raw data may include the following steps [6–8]:

1. Extraction of features from a raw LC-MS dataset. LC-MS features are defined by unique, characteristic combinations of retention time and mass-to-charge ratio. Associated with the chromatographic peak of a feature is a peak intensity or area, which serves as a relative measure of the abundance of the compound producing the feature. These parameters represent a fingerprint of compounds in a given sample.

2. Comparison of corresponding features in different sample sets and evaluation of significant differences.

3. Compound identification and structural characterization of unknown compounds of interest.

Soft ionization methods in LC-MS, most commonly electrospray ionization (ESI), generate mass spectra with minimal compound fragmentation and facilitate the extraction of LC-MS features associated with the intact molecular ion. Nevertheless, extraction of features for subsequent statistical analysis is non-trivial when complex mixtures of small molecules are analyzed [6]. Fortunately, open-source (e.g., mzMine2 [9], XCMS2 [10]) and commercial (e.g., Agilent MassHunter, Waters ProGenesis QI, ABSciex XCMSPlus, ThermoFisher Scientific SIEVE) software tools for this task have been developed and have become increasingly powerful and user-friendly.

With the extraction of features from LC-MS data becoming more readily achievable, the identification or structural characterization of small molecules has become a major bottleneck [11, 12]. Insight into chemical sum formulas and chemical interaction with the LC stationary phase (e.g., hydrophobicity in reversed phase chromatography) may be gained from LC-MS data because it contains information about molecular masses, isotope patterns, and retention times. However, even at ultra-high mass accuracies (<1 ppm), it is usually not possible to assign unique sum formulas to chromatographic features from MS1 data [13]. In addition, for any given sum formula, there are typically many theoretically possible isobaric compounds with different structures. Therefore, structural assignment of a compound is generally not possible based on MS1 data alone. Direct structural information can be obtained by measurement of fragmentation spectra (MS/MS, tandem MS, MS2, or for multiple rounds of fragmentation MS^N). LC-MS/MS datasets are composed of time series of individual full scan MS1 spectra, interspersed by one or more MS/MS spectra derived from the fragmentation of one or more species present in the MS1 (**Figure 1**).

http://dx.doi.org/10.5772/63018

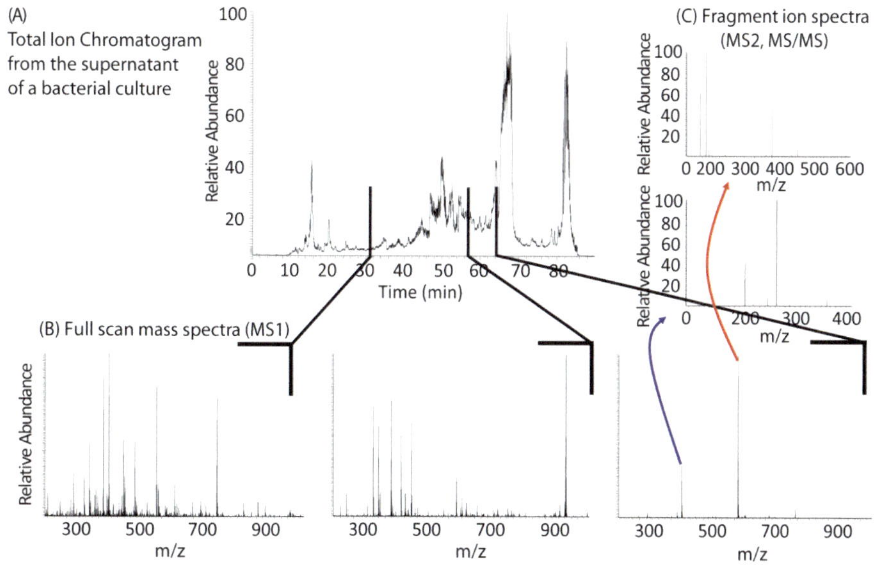

Figure 1. LC-MS/MS data is composed of time series of individual full scan MS1 spectra, interspersed by one or more MS/MS spectra. Shown are high-resolution LC-MS data for a bacterial culture supernatant collected with an Orbitrap XL mass analyser: (A) Total ion chromatogram (TIC, sum of MS1 intensities over time), (B) full scan MS1 spectra at three different retention times, and (C) fragment-ion spectra (MS2, MS/MS) for the two major peaks in the third MS1 spectrum.

Because of the vast diversity of small molecule structures, MS/MS-based structural characterization of compounds represents a great challenge [11, 12]. Identification by direct comparison of an experimental MS/MS spectrum to a library of MS/MS spectra is often limited by unavailable authentic standards. Even if MS/MS spectra for a compound (or a structurally closely related analogue) exist in a library, algorithms may not return the best match in the database, particularly if spectra are noisy or incomplete (e.g., contain contaminant ions, few fragments, minor fragments below detection limit, etc.) [14]. Complementary to these MS/MS spectral library-based approaches, de novo methods use known structures to calculate in-silico fragmentation spectra (random or rule based). Observed fragments are matched to possible substructures to reconstruct the observed MS/MS spectrum. The success of these methods depends on the chosen fragmentation rules and database search space [11]. Thus, the final success of attempts for structural characterization usually depends on a combination of prior knowledge about the compounds in the sample, adequate computational tools, and manual inspection of the raw data.

In addition to the identification of individual compounds, MS/MS structural information may be used at different stages in the interrogation of the samples. For example, at an early stage, it is possible to obtain an overview of structural diversity in a sample by clustering the MS/MS spectra into similarity networks [15], while at a later stage, once specific unknown features of interest have emerged, a more detailed interpretation of individual MS/MS spectra for compound characterization can be undertaken. MS/MS spectra can also be used to direct further targeted LC-MS/MS approaches aimed at deeper exploration of species possessing common fragments or fragmentation patterns of interest. This approach is commonly employed to specifically characterize molecules with certain functional groups or chemical modifications that produce characteristic patterns in their MS/MS spectra [14].

To make the best use of the rich structural information contained in LC-MS/MS datasets, there is a large need for MS/MS analysis algorithms that are tailored to many different individual research applications [11, 16]. As we demonstrate in this chapter, MATLAB provides an accessible and convenient platform for the interactive analysis and visualization of LC-MS/MS data and the implementation of customized algorithms and workflows. Tools are introduced for basic tasks, such as neutral-loss searches, as well as for more complex workflows, such as for the generation of MS/MS similarity networks or for the application of auto-convolution spectra to the structural characterization of peptides. We then apply these tools in the context of a specific basic research application: the discovery and structural characterization of peptidic siderophores. Siderophores are a class of secondary metabolites that are released by many bacteria and fungi to bind and take up iron (Fe), an essential and often growth-limiting micronutrient [17]. Using a siderophore structural database to exploit considerable prior knowledge about siderophore structural diversity, an effective workflow is shown for the LC-MS/MS-based analysis of known and new siderophores.

2. Importing raw data into MATLAB

The LC-MS raw data generated by the MS instrumentation is stored in vendor-specific binary file formats. For access by non-vendor software, the raw data file first needs to be converted to an open file format, such as the common mzXML format [7]. The program msconvert, which is part of the open-source proteomics package ProteoWizard (http://proteowizard.sourceforge.net/tools.shtml), can be used to convert from most raw data formats to mzXML [18]. At this point, LC-MS data recorded in profile mode can also be centroided by vendor supported algorithms built into msconvert. During centroiding, the centroid is determined for each mass spectral peak, which consists of multiple m/z—intensity measurements across the profile of the detected ion at any given time, and the peak is replaced by a single m/z and intensity pair at its center [18]. Centroiding reduces the data file size and is required for the subsequent analysis steps in this chapter.

MATLAB's bioinformatics toolbox provides several functions applicable to the processing of LC-MS data. For this study, we will use the functions mzxmlread and mzxml2peaks. The function mzxmlread can be used to import LC-MS data from mzXML files into a MATLAB structure array: mzXMLstruct = mzxmlread(mzXMLFilename). The returned structure contains the LC-MS/MS data and relevant metadata from the mzXML file, such as scan number, MS level, ionization mode, MS/MS collision energy, and MS/MS precursor information (**Figure 2**).

http://dx.doi.org/10.5772/63018

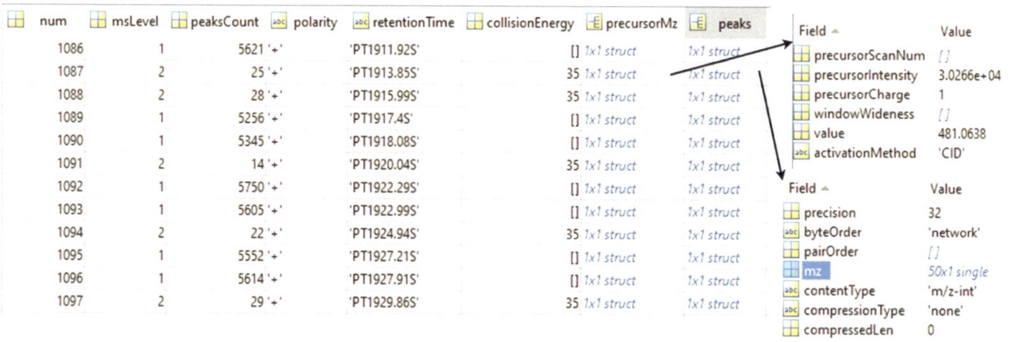

num	msLevel	peaksCount	polarity	retentionTime	collisionEnergy	precursorMz	peaks
1086	1	5621	'+'	'PT1911.92S'	[]	1x1 struct	1x1 struct
1087	2	25	'+'	'PT1913.85S'	35	1x1 struct	1x1 struct
1088	2	28	'+'	'PT1915.99S'	35	1x1 struct	1x1 struct
1089	1	5256	'+'	'PT1917.4S'	[]	1x1 struct	1x1 struct
1090	1	5345	'+'	'PT1918.08S'	[]	1x1 struct	1x1 struct
1091	2	14	'+'	'PT1920.04S'	35	1x1 struct	1x1 struct
1092	1	5750	'+'	'PT1922.29S'	[]	1x1 struct	1x1 struct
1093	1	5605	'+'	'PT1922.99S'	[]	1x1 struct	1x1 struct
1094	2	22	'+'	'PT1924.94S'	35	1x1 struct	1x1 struct
1095	1	5552	'+'	'PT1927.21S'	[]	1x1 struct	1x1 struct
1096	1	5614	'+'	'PT1927.91S'	[]	1x1 struct	1x1 struct
1097	2	29	'+'	'PT1929.86S'	35	1x1 struct	1x1 struct

Field	Value
precursorScanNum	[]
precursorIntensity	3.0266e+04
precursorCharge	1
windowWideness	[]
value	481.0638
activationMethod	'CID'

Field	Value
precision	32
byteOrder	'network'
pairOrder	[]
mz	50x1 single
contentType	'm/z-int'
compressionType	'none'
compressedLen	0

Figure 2. A selection of fields in the MATLAB structure array returned after the import of an mzXML file with LC-MS/MS data.

The function mzxml2peaks can be employed to extract the mass spectra (*m*/*z* values and intensities), together with their corresponding retention times, for a selected MS level (MS1, MS2, etc.) from mzXMLstruct: [Spectra, Times] = mzxml2peaks(mzXMLstruct, MSLevel, LevelValue), where Spectra is a cell array in which each element contains a two-column matrix of *m*/*z*—intensity pairs corresponding to one mass spectrum collected at a specific retention time, and Times is a vector with the corresponding retention time for each mass spectrum. To analyze MS/MS spectra, it is usually necessary to retrieve additional information from mzXMLstruct. Information about MS/MS precursor ions (precursor *m*/*z*, intensity, and charge) can be accessed in mzXMLstruct.scan.precursorMz :

```
% Number of peaks (Peak Count) for each spectrum
PC = arrayfun(@(x) x.peaksCount, mzXMLstruct.scan);
% MS level of each spectrum
level = arrayfun(@(x) x.msLevel, mzXMLstruct.scan);
h = find(PC & ismember(level,2));  % select only MS2 spectra
% extract precursor m/z, intensity, and charge
prec_mz = arrayfun(@(x) x.precursorMz.value, mzXMLstruct.scan(h));
prec_Int = arrayfun(@(x) x.precursorMz.precursorIntensity, ...
   mzXMLstruct.scan(h));
prec_z = arrayfun(@(x) x.precursorMz.precursorCharge, mzXMLstruct.scan(h));
```

If mass spectra are collected in positive and negative ionization modes during the same run, it may be useful to process positive and negative modes separately. To extract one ionization mode only, a filter can be applied to the data in mzXMLstruct:

```
Pol = '+';  % only positive mode data
pol_select = arrayfun(@(x) strcmp(x.polarity, Pol), mzXMLstruct.scan);
mzXMLstruct.scan = mzXMLstruct.scan(pol_select);
```

These loops through scan metadata in mzXMLstruct can be added to the mzxml2peaks function together with optional output and input arguments. In the following, we will use an optional output matrix called Precursors which contains precursor information for each MS/MS scan in three columns: *m/z*, intensity, and *z*.

3. Visualization and graphical-user-interface implementation

When analyzing LC-MS/MS data, it is helpful to be able to visualize spectra and chromatograms in order to display significant features, evaluate spectral noise, consider potential interferences, or evaluate fragmentation patterns, and so on. The two common projections of the three-dimensional LC-MS data (retention time, *m/z*, intensity) into two-dimensional space are chromatograms (intensity vs. retention time) and mass spectra (intensity vs. *m/z*). Note that a chromatogram with intensities of a selected range of *m/z* values is called an extracted ion chromatogram (EIC), whereas a chromatogram that shows the sum of all ions is known as a total ion chromatogram (TIC). The *m/z* tolerance $\Delta m/z$ is often given in ppm of the *m/z* value or as an absolute error in amu.

To plot an MS/MS spectrum for a given precursor *m/z*, the matrix Precursors can be used to find precursor *m/z* values within a specified error tolerance. The corresponding elements in Spectra represent the MS/MS spectra recorded for this *m/z* value:

```
mz = 419.142;  % find MS/MS spectra for precursor with m/z = 419.142
% ppm error or minimum absolute error
error = max(minerror, ppmerror * 10^-6 * mz);
MS2idx = find(abs(Precursors(:,1) - mz) <= error);
if ~isempty(MS2idx)
  MS2Peaks = Spectra{MS2idx(1)};   % select the first found MS2 spectrum
end

% To plot the centroided mass spectrum:
plotms(2:3:3 * size(MS2Peaks,1),2) = MS2Peaks (:,2);
plotms(1:3:3 * size(MS2Peaks,1),1) = MS2Peaks (:,1);
plotms(2:3:3 * size(MS2Peaks,1),1) = MS2Peaks (:,1);
plotms(3:3:3 * size(MS2Peaks,1),1) = MS2Peaks (:,1);
plot(plotms(:,1), plotms(:,2));
```

Graphical-user-interfaces (GUIs) can aid in efficiently browsing and evaluating the LC-MS/MS data and can serve as a platform for data manipulation and analysis. GUIs are also particularly helpful for users who are not familiar with MATLAB and can be shared as stand-alone applications. MATLAB facilitates the creation and programming of GUIs with the tool GUIDE (graphical user interface design environment). GUIDE provides an interface for designing the layout, while creating the code for the GUI, including the implementation of callbacks for a number of standard User Interface (UI) controls, such as 'pushbuttons', 'popup menus', and 'listboxes'. The callback functions can then be filled with user-defined code to provide the intended functionality. A GUI for LC-MS/MS data analysis created with MATLAB is shown in **Figure 3**.

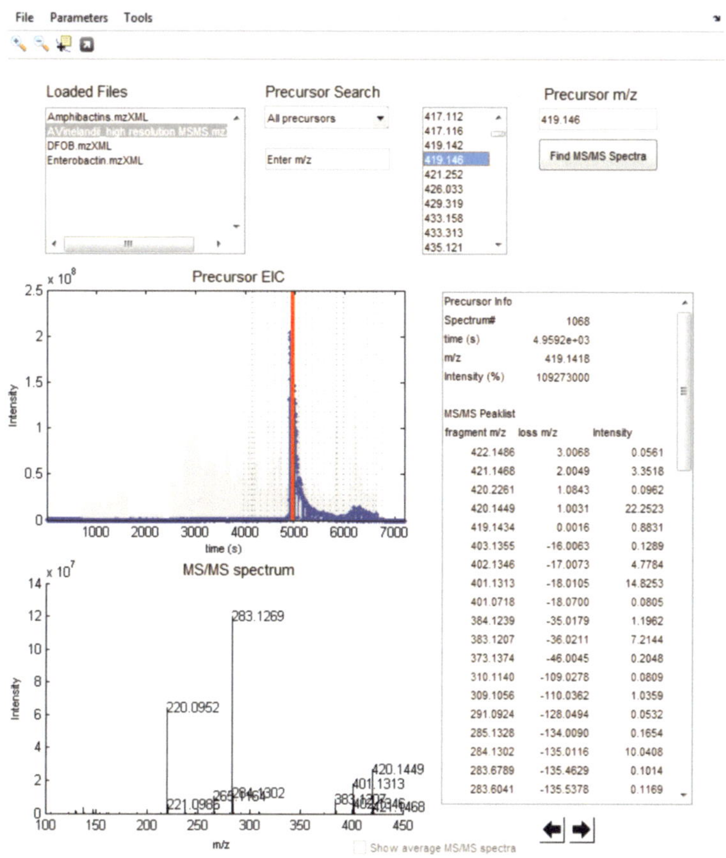

Figure 3. Graphical User Interface (GUI) for visualization, pre-processing, and analysis of LC-MS/MS data. The main window allows the user to select or search MS/MS precursor *m*/*z* values. When a precursor *m*/*z* value is selected, a corresponding EIC is generated with the MS1 data and the MS/MS spectrum is shown in this figure. The retention time corresponding to the MS/MS spectrum is indicated by a red line in the EIC figure. A table to the right shows the precursor information and a table of the MS/MS peaks. A menu bar provides functionality to import LC-MS data from mzXML files, open or save files, enter *m*/*z* error tolerances and other parameters, and select from a range of pre-processing and analysis tools.

4. Pre-processing of MS/MS spectra

Before analysis of LC-MS/MS data, pre-processing can be employed to increase signal-to-noise ratios, remove contaminant peaks, and reduce the data for the following analysis steps. Pre-processing and analysis algorithms are often tailored to individual data acquisition methods, data quality, and analytical goals.

4.1. Noise removal

The ratio of maximum-to-median peak intensities in MS/MS spectra has been used as an estimate of signal-to-noise ratios [14]. In order to remove noise and reduce the amount of data in MS/MS spectra, filters have been applied to retain only the most intense peaks within a given mass spectral bracket (e.g., five most intense peaks in a 50 Da window) [19, 20]. If several fragment-ion spectra are available for the same precursor, noise can be removed by retaining only those fragments that are present in a majority of the MS/MS spectra [21] or the spectra can be summed or averaged, which may minimize the noise contribution if it is random (see Section 4.3). For high-resolution MS/MS spectra, exact masses can also be used to determine possible fragment-ion sum formulas in order to remove noise or satellite peaks that possess m/z values leading to possible compositions that are completely incongruent with the precursor [21]. Similarly, MS/MS peaks with masses larger than the precursor mass can be removed.

Interfering signals are not only due to random noise but frequently a consequence of relatively wide precursor ion isolation windows (usually > 1 Da) utilized by the instruments' ion optics during ion selection prior to MS/MS. For this reason, the selection of minor features that may be well resolved in MS1 can result in the co-isolation of significant quantities of unrelated species, which, in turn, produce significant contaminant peaks in the corresponding MS/MS spectra. Spectral deconvolution algorithms to remove possible contaminant peaks or to determine multiple precursors from unintentional or intentional wide-window ion isolation (such as that achieved in recently developed data-independent acquisition methods) have been published [22, 23].

4.2. Removal of ^{13}C-isotopologue peaks

Another consequence of wide precursor isolation windows is that fragment ions may be accompanied to some degree by their ^{13}C-isotopologues. To de-isotope a high-resolution MS/MS spectrum, an algorithm can proceed from the lowest to the highest intensity fragment ion. For each ion peak, it is evaluated whether it may represent a ^{13}C isotopologue of a more abundant peak, by searching for another peak with the exact mass difference of a ^{13}C isotope ($\Delta m/z$ = -1.0034 Da for z = 1), within the defined error tolerance (e.g., ±0.0035 Da). If this mass difference is detected, the ^{13}C isotopologue peak is removed from the spectrum. This process is repeated for all relevant charge states, for example, all charge states up to the precursor charge. At the same time, if ^{13}C isotopologue peaks are detected, this procedure can be used to assign charge states to individual fragment ions.

4.3. Consensus spectra

If several MS/MS spectra of the same precursor have been acquired, the construction of consensus spectra can increase signal-to-noise ratios and significantly speed up the downstream analysis. To select which MS/MS spectra are to contribute to one consensus spectrum, the Spectra cell array can be filtered by identifying the elements with the same precursor m/z (within the specified m/z error tolerance) and charge state z in the Precursor matrix. In many situations, a number of different possible precursor structures can exist for the same m/z value (isobaric compounds) or indistinguishable *m/z* values within specified *m/z* tolerances. In such cases, the retention time can be used as an additional filter, that is, only those MS/MS spectra are clustered that are recorded during elution of the corresponding parent ion in MS1. It is also possible to combine only those MS/MS spectra in a consensus spectrum that show high pairwise similarity [20, 21]. The calculation of MS/MS spectral similarity is described in detail in Section 5.2.

To calculate a consensus spectrum for each cluster of MS/MS spectra, all *m/z*-intensity pairs of the individual contributing MS/MS spectra are combined in a common matrix [21]. All peaks within the defined *m/z* tolerance around the most intense peak are determined and an intensity-weighed mean *m/z*, and an intensity value can be calculated and then refined iteratively, as follows. If any additional peaks are within the bin around the intensity-weighed average *m/z*, a new intensity-weighed average is calculated until no further peaks fall within the bin. The peaks within the bin are then replaced by the intensity-weighed average *m/z* and intensity value and the process is repeated with all peaks in order of decreasing peak intensity.

5. Analysis of fragmentation spectra

In this section, three relevant LC-MS/MS analysis approaches are reviewed that can be applied for a wide range of analytical questions. In Section 6, we illustrate an example application for each approach (Sections 6.2–6.4) that is specifically tailored to the discovery and structural characterization of siderophores.

5.1. Fragment-ion and neutral-loss search

Fragment-ion or neutral-loss searches can be utilized to mine LC-MS/MS data for molecules with characteristic substructures or fragmentation behavior, such as certain lipid headgroups [24] or metabolite conjugates (e.g., GSH or phosphate) [25]. In targeted analysis, a defined fragment-ion or neutral-loss can be exploited to increase specificity for detection of the target compound.

Simple algorithms can loop through the MS/MS cell array (Spectra) to search for fragment-ion peaks within the defined *m/z* tolerance. To detect defined neutral-losses, 'neutral-loss peaks' can be computed as differences between the *m/z* values of the precursor ion and the fragment-ions (precursor neutral-loss search) or all pairwise differences between the measured ions (including the precursor and all fragment-ions). The algorithm can be refined by taking into account the charge state of the precursor ion and the fragment-ions to calculate fragment-ion and neutral-loss masses instead of *m/z* values (see Section 4.2 for fragment-ion charge state determination).

5.2. Pairwise similarity of MS/MS spectra

Given the task to find a best match for an experimental MS/MS spectrum among members of a spectral library, the experimental spectrum needs to be compared to each spectrum in the database and a pairwise similarity score needs to be computed. A common approach is to calculate a normalized dot product (cosine similarity) between pairs of MS/MS spectra S_A and S_B [14]:

$$cosine\,similarity\,score = \frac{\sum_{i=1}^{n} A_i B_i}{\sqrt{\sum_{i=1}^{n} A_i^2}\sqrt{\sum_{i=1}^{n} B_i^2}} \quad (1)$$

A and **B** are two vectors that contain the peak intensities from the MS/MS spectra S_A or S_B. The intensities of two peaks that occur at the same *m/z* in S_A and S_B (within the defined *m/z* tolerance) are corresponding elements A_i and B_i. To match fragment-ions in S_A and S_B, the algorithm can proceed from high to low intensities and identify corresponding peaks within a defined absolute or relative *m/z* tolerance in the corresponding other spectrum [20, 21]. If a peak is present in only one of the two spectra, its intensity is added to the respective vector **A** or **B** while the corresponding element in the other vector is set to 0. A similarity score of 1 indicates identical spectra, whereas a value of 0 indicates that no fragments with a common *m/z* are present. An implementation of this approach in MATLAB is as follows:

If a matching structure is not present in the database, the information may nevertheless be used for the identification of potential common substructures of a structurally related com-

```
% calculate normalized intensities for each MS2 spectrum
Spectra_norm = arrayfun(@(x) [x{1}(:,1) x{1}(:,2) ./ max(x{1}(:,2))],...
  Spectra, 'UniformOutput', false);
error = 0.005;  % m/z tolerance
% select the first two MS2 spectra for calculation of cosine similarity
MS2_A = sortrows(Spectra_norm{1}, 2);  % sort with ascending peak intensity
MS2_B = sortrows(Spectra_norm{2}, 2);
% matched_AB will contain intensities of matched peaks from MS2_A and MS2_B
% in columns 1 and 2
matched_AB = [MS2_A(:,2) zeros(size(MS2_A,1),1)];
for i = size(MS2_A,1):-1:1  % in order of decreasing peak intensity in MS_A
  if ~isempty(MS2_B)
    common = abs(MS2_B(:,1) - MS2_A(i,1)) <= error;  % matching m/z in MS_B?
    common = common .* MS2_B(:,2);  % corresponding intensities in MS_B
    % if more than 1 match is found, select the one with highest intensity
    if sum(common) > 0
      maxB_row = find(common, 1, 'last');
      matched_AB(i,2) = MS2_B(maxB_row,2);
      MS2_B(maxB_row,:) = [];  % delete matched peak in MS2_B
    end
  end
end
% add unmatched peaks from MS2_B to matched_AB
matched_AB = [matched_AB; [zeros(size(MS2_B,1),1) MS2_B(:,2)]];
A = matched_AB(:,1); B = matched_AB(:,2);
similarity_AB = dot(A,B) / (norm(A) * norm(B));  % cosine similarity
```

pound. For such applications, the matching of fragments in **A** and **B** can be modified to include not only common fragment-ions in both spectra but also common neutral-losses, that is, pairs of peaks in S_A and S_B that have *m/z* values which differ by a common *m/z* value. In a simple implementation this difference can be the mass difference of the parent ions of S_A and S_B (see **Figure 4** for an example) [25, 26].

Another useful application of similarity calculations is found in the generation of MS/MS similarity networks as described previously [15]. Calculating all pairwise similarities between consensus LC-MS/MS spectra yields a table that can be visualized in a molecular network using freeware tools such as Cytoscape (www.cytoscape.org). In the MS/MS network, each node represents one consensus spectrum (precursor information) and each edge between two nodes illustrates the relatedness. Cytoscape provides functionality to create edge-weighed force-directed layouts to cluster closely related nodes in order to obtain an overview of structural diversity in a sample.

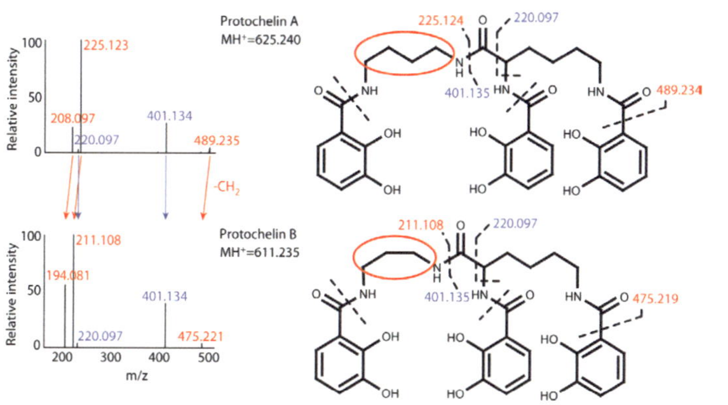

Figure 4. MS/MS spectra of the siderophore protochelin A and its related analogue protochelin B. Protochelin A and B have the same structures except for an exchange of a 1,4- diaminobutane linker group in protochelin A with 1,3-diaminopropane in protochelin B (red circles). Accordingly, parent ion *m/z* ratios differ by a CH_2 group and fragment peaks that include the modification are shifted by the *m/z* of CH_2 ($\Delta m/z$ = 14.0157). To calculate similarities between such structurally related compounds, the shifted peaks can be matched in addition to the peaks that both spectra have in common. Figure modified from [27].

5.3. MS/MS convolution and auto-convolution

De-novo sequencing of peptides is most widely performed by the analysis of fragmentation spectra that are acquired by positive-mode collision-induced dissociation (CID) [28]. With positive-mode CID, major MS/MS peaks result from dissociation of the molecule at the peptide bonds, yielding b- and y- type ions (**Figure 5**) [29, 30]. In addition, the spectra regularly include other related fragments. For example a-ions have a mass difference corresponding to a CO group relative to b-ions (Δm = 27.9949) and, if present, can be used to distinguish b-ions from y-ions. In addition, neutral-losses of H_2O or NH_3 are often observed.

As illustrated in **Figure 5**, the mass differences between fragments include the mass of individual peptide monomers (amino acid residues). Spectral convolution between two spectra S_A and S_B calculates the *m*/*z* difference between each peak in S_A and each peak in S_B. The multiplicity of each observed *m*/*z* difference, within the given *m*/*z* tolerance, is then counted to yield the convolution spectrum with the multiplicity for each *m*/*z* versus the observed *m*/*z* differences. The convolution spectrum between unrelated spectra S_A and S_B is close to 0 or 1 for most *m*/*z* values, whereas the convolution spectrum for structurally related peptides (i.e., peptides with shared sequences) will show significant peaks for some *m*/*z* values [26]. The following MATLAB code shows a basic implementation of spectral convolution.

```
% select two MS2 spectra for convolution and get the m/z of all peaks
mz_A = Spectra{1}(:,1);   mz_B = Spectra{2}(:,1);
error = 0.005;   % m/z tolerance
PC_A = numel(mz_A); PC_B = numel(mz_B); n_AB = PC_A * PC_B;
diffAB = zeros(n_AB,1);   % diffAB will be a vector with all m/z differences
MS2_conv = nan(n_AB,2);   %  MS2_conv will be the convolution spectrum
for i = 1:PC_B
  diffAB((i - 1) * PC_A + 1:i * PC_A) = abs(mz_B(i,1) - mz_A(:,1));
end
n = 0;
% group m/z within m/z tolerance in diffAB
while ~isempty(diffAB)
  n = n + 1;
  bin_idx = abs(diffAB - diffAB(1)) <= error;
  % mean of m/z differences and multiplicity
  MS2_conv(n,:) = [mean(diffAB(bin_idx)) sum(bin_idx)];
  diffAB(bin_idx) = [];   % delete processed m/z values in diffAB
end
MS2_conv(isnan(MS2_conv(:,1)),:) = [];
```

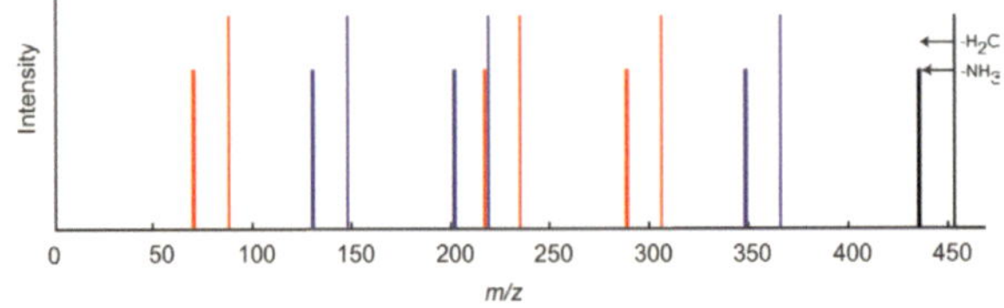

Figure 5. Theoretical LC-MS spectrum for a peptide with the sequence Ser-Phe-Ala-Glu. The spectrum shows the position of expected b- and y-ions together with neutral-losses of H_2O or NH_3.

Auto-convolution spectra are generated by calculating the *m/z* differences between all peaks within one single spectrum. These have been used for the identification of possible peptide monomers in cyclic nonribosomal peptides (NRPs) [19]. NRPs are secondary metabolite peptides synthesized by nonribosomal peptide synthetases (NRPS), and include antibiotics, toxins, and siderophores. The structures of NRPs contain unusual non-proteinogenic amino acids, which increase the number of possible monomers from the canonical 20 found in most proteins to several hundred. Possible peptide monomer species in cyclic NRPs are revealed by matching peaks in the auto-convolution spectrum to masses in a database of possible peptide monomers [19]. The NORINE database with NRPs and corresponding peptide monomers can be used for this purpose and is freely accessible at http://bioinfo.lifl.fr/norine/ [31].

6. Application to siderophore analysis

In this section, the LC-MS/MS analysis methods discussed above are applied to the discovery and structural characterization of peptidic siderophores. Siderophores are secondary metabolites that are released by many bacteria and fungi to bind and take up iron (Fe), an essential and often growth-limiting micro-nutrient [17]. Using a siderophore structural database to exploit considerable prior knowledge about siderophore structural diversity, an effective workflow is presented for the LC-MS/MS-based analysis of known and new siderophores.

6.1. Workflow

6.1.1. Overview

Previously, we described an algorithm for the discovery of siderophores in high-resolution LC-MS1 data by screening for the natural stable isotope pattern of iron (^{54}Fe and ^{56}Fe) bound to siderophores and by searching for related iron-free siderophores [32]. Here, we complement this method by analysis of high-resolution LC-MS/MS data for discovery and structural characterization of siderophores (**Figure 6**).

To obtain a list of siderophore candidates, Fe can be added to the sample extract before injection onto the LC-MS system, which facilitates the generation of Fe-ligand complexes and the recognition of the Fe isotope patterns associated with Fe-bound siderophores (**Figure 6-1a**). Independent of isotope patterns, fragmentation spectra can be mined for siderophore-characteristic substructures by fragment-ion and neutral-loss searches (**Figure 6-1b**, Section 6.2). Both approaches yield a table with *m/z* ratios of candidate siderophore Fe complexes and associated free siderophores. The tables are combined to create a parent-ion-list for a replicate run with data-dependent LC-MS/MS acquisition.

For the replicate run, no Fe is added to the sample extract, maximizing the signal for the free siderophore species, which are preferentially selected for structural characterization in subsequent analytical steps (at the same time, differences in peak abundances between the extracts with and without added Fe can give further confidence to the assignment of siderophores). MS/MS spectra of unbound siderophore candidates are selected to generate an MS/MS molecular network which provides an overview of structurally distinct groups of siderophores (**Figure 6-2a**, Section 6.3). Representative species in the network are selected for structural characterization by calculation of auto-convolution spectra (**Figure 6-2b**, Section 6.4). By matching peaks in the auto-convolution spectra to masses in a database of siderophore peptide monomers, possible siderophore substructures are assigned. Combinations of peptide-monomers are then used as a signature to find possible related known structures in the database, aiding in the reconstruction of the original MS/MS spectrum (**Figure 6-2c**). Iterations with structurally related compounds in the MS/MS network can refine the structure suggestions and be used to efficiently evaluate structures of derivatives. Depending on the

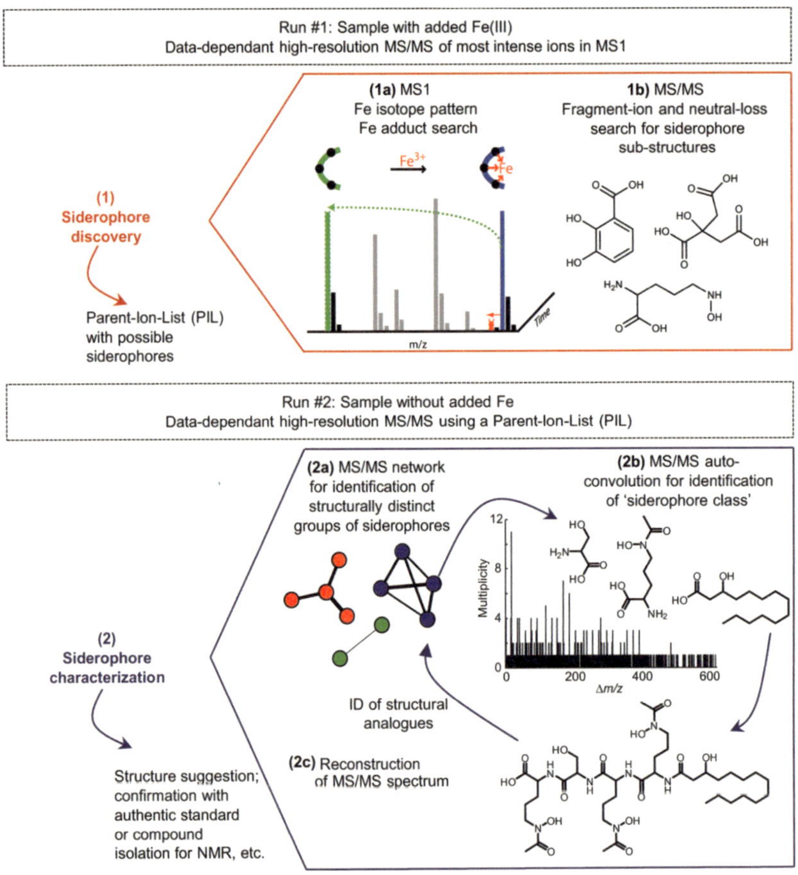

Figure 6. Schematic workflow for discovery (**6–1**) and structural characterization (**6–2**) of siderophores by high-resolution LC-MS/MS. Two complementary approaches may be used for siderophore discovery: mining for characteristic iron-isotopic patterns of iron siderophore complexes as well as for peaks corresponding to unbound siderophore species (**6–1a**), and searches for fragment-ions or neutral-losses associated with characteristic siderophore substructures (**6–1b**). To characterize siderophore structures, MS/MS similarity networks (**6–2a**) can be used to identify groups of structurally distinct siderophores. MS/MS auto-convolution in combination with a siderophore database may reveal sub-structures and 'siderophore class' (**6–2b**) to aid in the reconstruction of the original MS/MS spectrum (**6–2c**). The analysis results may then inform iterations with structurally related siderophores in the MS/MS network.

http://dx.doi.org/10.5772/63018

analysis outcomes, the putative structures can be confirmed with authentic standards or by isolation of the compound for characterization by orthogonal means (e.g., by nuclear magnetic resonance spectroscopy, etc.).

6.1.2. Experimental methods and data pre-processing

The samples for this study include the siderophore standards desferrioxamine B (DFOB, Aldrich), enterobactin (EMC Biochemicals), amphibactins (kindly provided by A. Butler, UC Santa Barbara), and extracts of iron-limited *Azotobacter vinelandii* culture supernatants. *A. vinelandii* culture conditions and sample preparation were described previously [27].

LC-MS analyses were performed on a high-performance liquid chromatography (HPLC)-MS platform, using a C18 column coupled to an LTQ-Orbitrap XL hybrid mass spectrometer (ThermoFisher). Samples were separated under a gradient of solutions A and B (solution A consisted of water, 0.1% FA, and 0.1% acetic acid; solution B consisted of acetonitrile, 0.1% FA, and 0.1% acetic acid; gradient, 0 to 100% B; flow rate, 50 μl/min). Full-scan mass spectra were acquired in positive-ion mode with a resolving power (R) of 60,000 ($m/z = 400$). MS/MS spectra were simultaneously acquired using collision-induced dissociation (CID; 35 V collision voltage) in the Orbitrap, a parent ion intensity threshold of 10,000, and targeting the three most abundant species in the full-scan spectrum or targeting selectively only predefined species on a parent ion list.

LC-MS/MS raw data are converted to mzXML, centroided, and imported into MATLAB as described in Section 2. Spectra in which the maximum-to-median intensity ratio is below 3 are removed. Spectra are de-isotoped with an m/z tolerance for ^{13}C isotopes of $\Delta m/z = 0.0035$, and only the top five most intense peaks in a 50 Da window are retained. The user-defined m/z tolerance for neutral-loss and parent-ion searches is set to $\Delta m/z = 0.0050$. For the generation of MS/MS molecular networks and auto-convolution spectra, consensus spectra are calculated using an m/z bin width of 0.01 Da ($\Delta m/z = 0.0050$). A siderophore database with >300 known siderophore structures was assembled in ChemBioFinder™ to determine siderophore-characteristic substructures, and to aid in the structural characterization of known and new siderophores.

6.2. Fragment-ion and neutral-loss searches

Utilizing a database with >300 known siderophore structures, the most frequently occurring iron binding substructures in siderophores are identified (**Table 1**, **Figure 7**). The specificity of these structures for siderophore discovery by fragment-ion or neutral-loss searches is evaluated by searching the NORINE database of nonribosomal peptides (NRPs) with >1,100 NRP structures (http://bioinfo.lifl.fr/norine/). With the exception of N-hydroxyornithine and N-cyclo-hydroxyornithine, the peptide monomers have unique masses in NORINE (±0.005 Da, Table 1). In addition, the iron binding substructures are not observed in non-siderophore structures in the database, with the exception of two putative NRPS products that are predicted to include compounds 10 and 11. Corresponding neutral-loss searches in the METLIN library with >70,000 small molecule CID MS/MS spectra reveal 39–232 false positive neutral-loss hits (i.e., matching neutral-loss mass within ±0.005 Da despite siderophore-unrelated structures), representing less than 1% of the MS/MS spectra in the database.

#	Monomer name	Monoisotope mass	Neutral loss mass	Unrelated isobaric structures in NORINE(*)	Occurrence in non-siderophore structures in NORINE (**)	False-positive neutral-loss hits in METLIN (***)
1	N-acetyl-hydroxy-ornithine (Ac-OH-Orn)	190.0954	172.0848	0	0	122
2	N-formyl-hydroxy-ornithine (Fo-OH-Orn)	176.0797	158.0691	0	0	107
3	N-hydroxy-ornithine (OH-Orn)	148.0848	130.0742, 148.0848	2	0	93, 159
4	N-hydroxy-cyclo-ornithine (OH-cOrn)	130.0742	130.0742	2	0	93
5	N-hydroxy-lysine (OH-Lys)	162.1004	144.0898, 162.1004	0	not in NORINE	114, 232
6	5-Amino-N-hydroxypentan-1-amine (5AHA)	118.1106	118.1106	0	Not in NORINE	93
7	4-Amino-N-hydroxybutan-1-amine (4AHA)	104.095	104.095	0	Not in NORINE	48
8	3-Amino-N-hydroxypropan-1-amine (3AHA)	90.0793	90.0793	0	Not in NORINE	69
9	Citric acid (Cit)	192.0270	174.0164	0	Not in NORINE	44
10	Hydroxy-aspartic acid (OH-Asp)	149.0324	131.0218	0		45
11	2,3-Dihydroxy-benzoic acid (di-OH-Bz)	154.0266	136.0160	0		39
12	Pyoverdine chromophore (ChrP)	277.1063	259.0957	0		52

(*) NORINE database with >1,100 nonribosomal peptides (NRPs): http://bioinfo.lifl.fr/norine/.
(**) putative NRPS products.
(***) METLIN MS/MS database with >70,000 high-resolution MS/MS spectra: https://metlin.scripps.edu.

Table 1 Common iron-binding peptide monomers in known siderophores. Corresponding neutral-loss and fragment-ion searches can be used to mine LC-MS/MS datasets for siderophores. The mass for fragment ion searches can be obtained by adding a proton to the given neutral loss masses (+1.00783). Database searches in NORINE and METLIN were performed using a mass tolerance of ±0.005 Da. Corresponding compound structures are shown in **Figure 7**.

http://dx.doi.org/10.5772/63018

Application of neutral-loss and fragment-ion searches with the standards DFOB (containing 5AHA, compound 6), enterobactin (containing di-OH-Bz, compound 11), and amphibactin (containing Ac-OH-Orn, compound 1) readily reveal the parent ion *m/z* values of the standards. Application with a supernatant sample from the bacterium *A. vinelandii* yield a large number of siderophores related to its known catechol siderophores aminochelin, azotochelin, and protochelin as well as vibrioferrin, in agreement with previously reported results that were based on Fe stable isotope pattern screening of LC-MS data [27]. However, the *A. vinelandii* extract also contains a number of neutral-losses corresponding to siderophore substructures in Table 1, which upon further structural characterization are identified as false positives, originating from noise in the spectra. This further demonstrates that neutral-loss or fragment-ion searches alone are not sufficient for identification of siderophores. Nevertheless, they can provide a shortlist of candidate siderophore *m/z* values for structural characterization. If siderophore structures in a sample are known or expected (e.g., from genomic analyses), structure-specific fragments or neutral-losses can also be used to find related analogues. For example, the amphiphilic amphibactin siderophores yield fragmentation spectra with a common headgroup fragment: *m/z* = 450.219 [33]. This *m/z* may be used to screen suspect samples for the presence of amphibactin-related siderophore species.

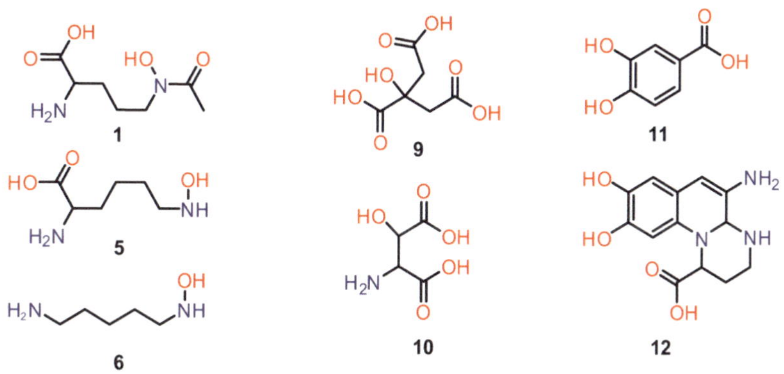

Figure 7. Common iron-binding substructures in siderophores, including hydroxamic acids (**1, 5, 6**), α-hydroxycarboxylic acids (**9, 10**), and catechols and related structures (**11, 12**).

6.3. Siderophore MS/MS similarity networks

Bacteria are known to often produce suits of structurally closely related siderophores [17]. MS/MS similarity networks can give an overview of which precursors in a list of candidate siderophores are structurally independent, potentially originating from separate siderophore gene clusters, and which are likely to be structural analogues. An MS/MS similarity network for *A. vinelandii* distinguishes the three main independent siderophore structures that this bacterium produces: dihydroxybenzoic acid containing siderophores, vibrioferrin-type citrate containing siderophores, and azotobactin related siderophores as reported previously [27] (**Figure 8**). The MS/MS network facilitates efficient structural assignments and structural refinement (see below).

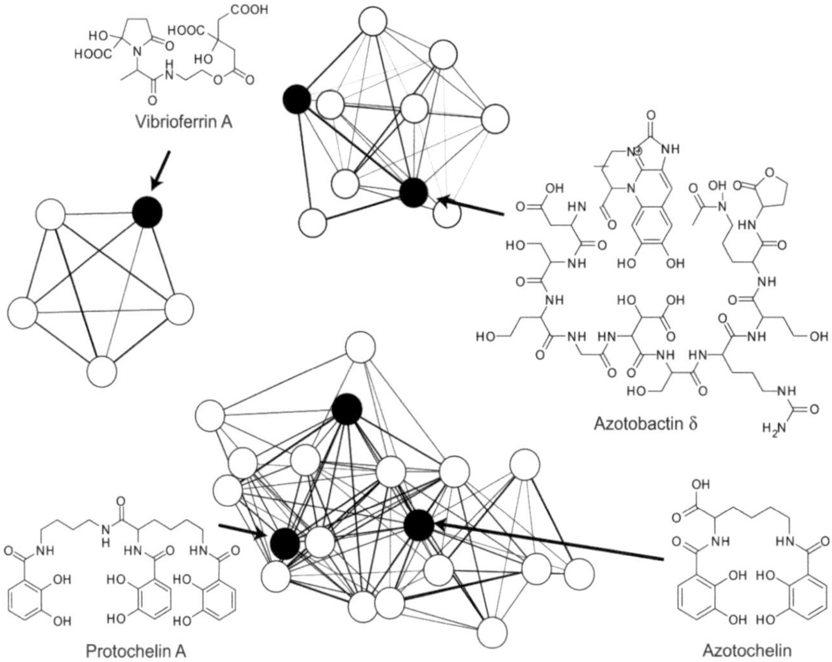

Figure 8. Siderophore MS/MS molecular network from the supernatant of *A. vinelandii* cultures, modified from [27]. Each node represents an individual siderophore and a corresponding consensus MS/MS spectrum; edge thicknesses represent the cosine similarity. An edge weighted-force directed layout in Cytoscape was used to cluster closely related nodes.

6.4. Application of MS/MS auto-convolution to siderophore analysis

The success of de novo structural analysis of nonribosomal peptides (NRPs) using spectral auto-convolution depends on the identification of most or all amino acids involved in the structure, thus requiring a database that contains all involved peptide monomers as well as a good coverage of fragments in the MS/MS [19, 34]. To use auto-convolution for siderophore analysis, a database with >300 siderophore structures was compiled along with a database of the peptide-monomers occurring in these structures (160 different structures with 51 different Fe binding monomers), most of which are not present in the NORINE database of nonribosomal peptides (http://bioinfo.lifl.fr/norine/). Auto-convolution spectra were previously applied to cyclic NRPs (see Section 5.3), in which an MS/MS experiment leads to ring opening, and MS3 creates additional fragmentation [19]. Because ring opening may occur at any peptide bond, the theoretical MS3 spectra are a superposition of spectra derived from all possible linear peptides (circular permutations).

A modified auto-convolution approach is used here for analysis of peptidic siderophores and applied to siderophore structures that can also be linear, branched, or partly cyclic. Before auto-convolution, the algorithm adds the parent ion as a peak to the MS/MS spectrum and its intensity is set equal to the most intense peak in the spectrum. This ensures that the all precursor neutral loss *m*/*z* values occur in the auto-convolution spectrum, even if the precursor ion is not present as a peak in the MS/MS spectrum. In addition to the auto-convolution spectrum, the algorithm calculates the sum of the relative intensities of all fragment-ions associated with each *m/z* in the auto-convolution spectrum. The *m/z* values in the auto-convolution spectrum are then matched to masses in the siderophore database, taking into account possible neutral-losses of one or two H_2O or NH_3. Finally, neutral-charge masses of fragment-ions in the original MS/MS spectrum are calculated and also matched to the database of siderophore peptide monomers.

The relevance of database hits is judged by the multiplicity in the auto-convolution spectrum and the corresponding relative intensities of the MS/MS peaks involved. Illustrative results from the analysis of the siderophore amphibactin B are shown in **Figure 9**. The auto-convolution peaks with the highest multiplicity and highest relative intensities reveal all structural features of the molecule: the iron binding N-acetyl-hydroxyornithines, a serine, and the fatty acid tail. Combinations of monomers are then used as a fingerprint to search for possible related structures in the siderophore database. Four families of siderophores in the database contain the three possible substructures: amphibactins, aquachelins, marinobactins, and loihichelins. With this information, the amphibactin can be readily identified by reconstruction of the original MS/MS spectrum. A number of *m/z* differences shown in **Figure 9** have database matches with low multiplicity and relative intensity and do not relate to peptide monomers in the structure. One cause of false identifications of monomers can be spectral noise and contaminant peaks. To eliminate noise in the auto-convolution spectra, the analysis can be repeated with other related compounds in the siderophore MS/MS network and only those monomers prominent in a majority of spectra may be considered for structure proposals.

The approach was also successfully applied to the other siderophore standards used in this study: DFOB showed the iron-binding monomer 5AHA (Table 1) together with the succinic acid linker among the three substructures with the highest intensity and multiplicity. One potential peptide monomer (N^1,N^1-dimethyl-N^5-acetyl-N^5-hydroxy-ornithine, m = 200.1161) was a false match as it has the same sum formula as the sum of 5AHA (m = 118.1106) and succinic acid (m = 82.0055 for succinic acid-2H_2O). Searching the siderophore database for these monomers revealed ferrioxamines as most likely related structure. The cyclic enterobactin showed a prominent fragment with a mass corresponding to the iron binding dihydroxybenzoic acid groups in the structure as well as high multiplicity and intensity for the serines in the structure. The *A. vinelandii* supernatant contains three groups of structurally unrelated siderophores (**Figure 8**). Vibrioferrins were associated with a strong auto-convolution peak for the iron-binding citric acid monomer in the molecule among a number of unrelated peptide monomers that were also matched. Protochelin, azotochelin, and related structures produced by *A. vinelandii* showed the characteristic dihydroxybenzoic acid together with the lysine or putrescine linkers contained in the structures. In contrast, azotobactin-related compounds in the supernatant did not show a clear siderophore signature, due to poor peptide fragmentation around the iron binding groups in the molecule.

When analyzing an unknown siderophore, the described auto-convolution approach can give confidence in the siderophore assignment: siderophores often contain three characteristic iron chelating peptide monomers for hexadentate iron coordination, which cause high multiplicities and relative intensities. A combination of peptide monomers in the structure can be used as a fingerprint to search the siderophore database for possible related structures, giving insight into the possible 'siderophore class' and aiding in the reconstruction of the original MS/MS spectrum to make a structure suggestion.

(A)

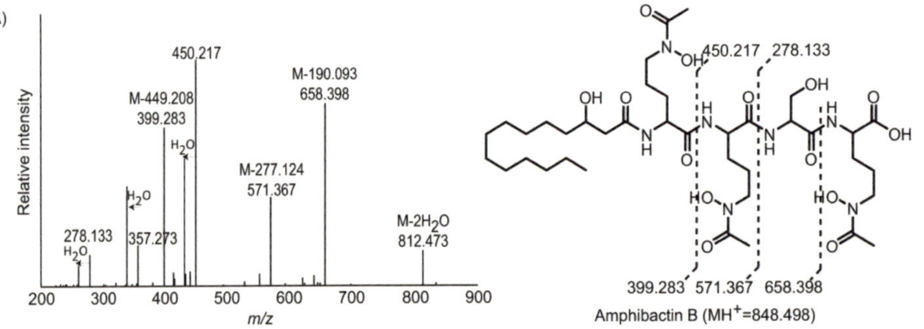

(B)

found *m/z*	multiplicity	relative intensity	Monomer mass	ID
172.084	7	55	190.095	N-acetyl-hydroxyornithine or N-formyl-hydroxylysine
42.009	4	30	60.021	Acetic acid
208.181	3	41	226.193 or 244.204	FA-C14:1 $-H_2O$ or FA-C14:0-OH $-2H_2O$
130.075	2	19	130.074 or 148.085	Hydroxy-cycloornithine or hydroxy-ornithine $-H_2O$
69.020	2	9	105.043	Serine
244.201	1	14	244.204	FA-C14:0-OH
136.064	1	3	136.067	2-(2-aminoethylthio)-N-hydroxyethanamine
111.028	1	1	147.053	Glutamic acid $-2H_2O$
		...		

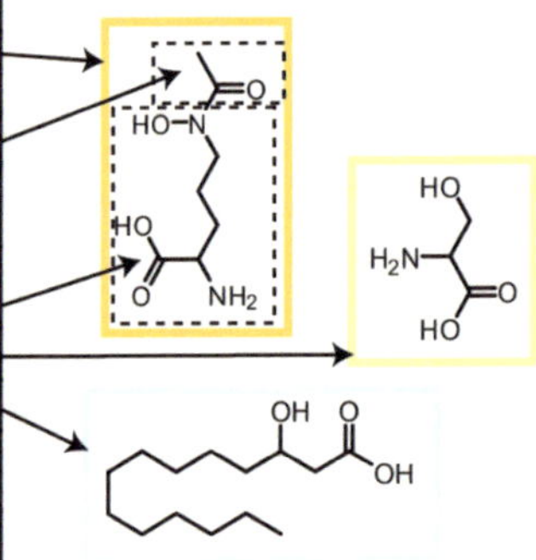

Figure 9. (A) MS/MS spectrum of the siderophore amphibactin B. (B) Results after application of a modified auto-convolution approach. Only auto-convolution *m/z* values are shown in the table that correspond to masses in a siderophore peptide monomer database. The *m/z* values with highest multiplicity and relative intensity reveal the structural features of this siderophore: the iron-binding N-acetyl-hydroxyornithines (orange), a serine (green), and a fatty acid tail (blue). A number of *m/z* values have database matches with low multiplicity and relative intensity and do not relate to peptide monomers in the structure (white).

7. Conclusions

The basic tools and considerations introduced in this chapter provide insight into the systematic analysis of LC-MS/MS fragmentation data for the structural characterization of small molecules and demonstrate how this can be performed within MATLAB. Since many researchers are familiar with MATLAB, this environment provides a low-barrier entry point and facilitates the creation of new strategies and tools to exploit the full power of modern high-resolution LC-MS/MS for structural interrogation. MATLAB facilitates data handling, manipulation, and the implementation of graphical user interfaces to serve as a platform for the visualization, pre-processing, and analysis of LC-MS/MS data.

The discussed methods were applied in a new workflow for the discovery and structural characterization of siderophores by high-resolution LC-MS/MS. Using a database with siderophore structures, characteristic neutral-loss and fragment-ion masses were identified to mine LC-MS/MS data for potential siderophores. MS/MS siderophore networks in combination with a modified MS/MS auto-convolution approach revealed siderophore peptide monomers and corresponding siderophore families. This information was key tostructure assignments by reconstruction of the original MS/MS spectrum. The tools and approaches outlined here may also be adapted to explorations of other classes of complex small molecules.

Acknowledgements

We thank Yubo Li for helping with the assembly of the siderophore database and Alison Butler (UC Santa Barbara) for providing the amphibactin samples. Financial support for O.B. was provided by the Grand Challenge Program of the Princeton Environmental Institute.

Supporting information

The MATLAB siderophore analysis software ('MS2Browser') and the siderophore database are available for download on SourceForge (https://sourceforge.net/projects/ms2browser/).

Author details

Oliver Baars[1*] and David H. Perlman[2]

*Address all correspondence to: obaars@princeton.edu

1 Department of Geosciences, Princeton University, Princeton, NJ, USA

2 Department of Chemistry, Princeton University, Princeton, NJ, USA

References

[1] Patti GJ, Yanes O, Siuzdak G. Metabolomics: the apogee of the omics trilogy. Nature Reviews Molecular Cell Biology. 2012;13(4):263–9.

[2] Mastrangelo A, Armitage EG, Garcia A, Barbas C. Metabolomics as a tool for drug discovery and personalised medicine. A review. Current Topics in Medicinal Chemistry. 2014;14(23):2627–36.

[3] Beger R. A review of applications of metabolomics in cancer. Metabolites. 2013;3(3): 552.

[4] Zwiener C, Frimmel FH. LC-MS analysis in the aquatic environment and in water treatment technology—a critical review. Part II: Applications for emerging contaminants and related pollutants, microorganisms and humic acids. Analytical and Bioanalytical Chemistry. 2004;378(4):862–74.

[5] Cheng X, Hochlowski J. Current application of mass spectrometry to combinatorial chemistry. Analytical Chemistry. 2002;74(12):2679–90.

[6] Castillo S, Gopalacharyulu P, Yetukuri L, Orešič M. Algorithms and tools for the preprocessing of LC–MS metabolomics data. Chemometrics and Intelligent Laboratory Systems. 2011;108(1):23–32.

[7] Sugimoto M, Kawakami M, Robert M, Soga T, Tomita M. Bioinformatics tools for mass spectroscopy-based metabolomic data processing and analysis. Current Bioinformatics. 2012;7(1):96–108.

[8] Wolfender JL, Marti G, Thomas A, Bertrand S. Current approaches and challenges for the metabolite profiling of complex natural extracts. Journal of Chromatography A. 2015;1382:136–64.

[9] Pluskal T, Castillo S, Villar-Briones A, Oresic M. MZmine 2: modular framework for processing, visualizing, and analyzing mass spectrometry-based molecular profile data. BMC Bioinformatics. 2010;11:395.

[10] Benton HP, Wong DM, Trauger SA, Siuzdak G. XCMS2: processing tandem mass spectrometry data for metabolite identification and structural characterization. Analytical Chemistry. 2008;80(16):6382–9.

[11] Scheubert K, Hufsky F, Böcker S. Computational mass spectrometry for small molecules. Journal of Cheminformatics. 2013;5:12.

[12] Xiao JF, Zhou B, Ressom HW. Metabolite identification and quantitation in LC-MS/MS-based metabolomics. Trends in Analytical Chemistry. 2012;32:1–14.

[13] Kind T, Fiehn O. Metabolomic database annotations via query of elemental compositions: mass accuracy is insufficient even at less than 1 ppm. BMC Bioinformatics. 2006;7(1):1–10.

[14] Stein SE. Mass spectral reference libraries: an ever-expanding resource for chemical identification. Analytical Chemistry. 2012;84(17):7274–82.

[15] Watrous J, Roach P, Alexandrov T, Heath BS, Yang JY, Kersten RD, et al. Mass spectral molecular networking of living microbial colonies. Proceedings of the National Academy of Sciences. 2012;109(26):E1743–E52.

[16] Kind T, Fiehn O. Advances in structure elucidation of small molecules using mass spectrometry. Bioanalytical Reviews. 2010;2(1–4):23–60.

[17] Hider RC, Kong XL. Chemistry and biology of siderophores. Natural Product Reports. 2010;27(5):637–57.

[18] Holman JD, Tabb DL, Mallick P. Employing ProteoWizard to convert raw mass spectrometry data. Current Protocols in Bioinformatics. 2014;46:13.24.1–9.

[19] Ng J, Bandeira N, Liu W-T, Ghassemian M, Simmons TL, Gerwick WH, et al. Dereplication and de novo sequencing of nonribosomal peptides. Nature Methods. 2009;6(8): 596–9.

[20] Frank AM, Bandeira N, Shen Z, Tanner S, Briggs SP, Smith RD, et al. Clustering millions of tandem mass spectra. Journal of Proteome Research. 2008;7(1):113–22.

[21] Yang X, Neta P, Stein SE. Quality control for building libraries from electrospray ionization tandem mass spectra. Analytical Chemistry. 2014;86(13):6393–400.

[22] Tsugawa H, Cajka T, Kind T, Ma Y, Higgins B, Ikeda K, et al. MS-DIAL: data-independent MS/MS deconvolution for comprehensive metabolome analysis. Nature Methods. 2015;12(6):523–6.

[23] Stein SE. An integrated method for spectrum extraction and compound identification from gas chromatography/mass spectrometry data. Journal of the American Society for Mass Spectrometry. 1999;10(8):770–81.

[24] Brown NL, Stoyanov JV, Kidd SP, Hobman JL. The MerR family of transcriptional regulators. FEMS Microbiology Reviews. 2003;27(2–3):145–63.

[25] Stein SE. Chemical substructure identification by mass spectral library searching. Journal of the American Society for Mass Spectrometry. 1995;6(8):644–55.

[26] Pevzner PA, Dančík V, Tang CL. Mutation-tolerant protein identification by mass spectrometry. Journal of Computational Biology. 2000;7(6):777–87.

[27] Baars O, Zhang X, Morel FM, Seyedsayamdost MR. The siderophore metabolome of *Azotobacter vinelandii*. Applied and Environmental Microbiology. 2015;82(1):27–39.

[28] Brodbelt JS. Ion activation methods for peptides and proteins. Analytical Chemistry. 2016;88(1):30–51.

[29] Chaturvedi KS, Henderson JP. Pathogenic adaptations to host-derived antibacterial copper. Frontiers in Cellular and Infection Microbiology. 2014;4:3.

[30] Roepstorff P, Fohlman J. Proposal for a common nomenclature for sequence ions in mass spectra of peptides. Biomedical Mass Spectrometry. 1984;11(11):601.

[31] Caboche S, Pupin M, Leclère V, Fontaine A, Jacques P, Kucherov G. NORINE: a database of nonribosomal peptides. Nucleic Acids Research. 2008;36:D326–D31.

[32] Baars O, Morel FMM, Perlman DH. ChelomEx: isotope-assisted discovery of metal chelates in complex media using high-resolution LC-MS. Analytical Chemistry. 2014;86(22):11298–305.

[33] Martinez JS, Carter-Franklin JN, Mann EL, Martin JD, Haygood MG, Butler A. Structure and membrane affinity of a suite of amphiphilic siderophores produced by a marine bacterium. Proceedings of the National Academy of Sciences. 2003;100(7):3754–9.

[34] Mohimani H, Liu W-T, Yang Y-L, Gaudêncio SP, Fenical W, Dorrestein PC, et al. Multiplex de novo sequencing of peptide antibiotics. Journal of Computational Biology. 2011;18(11):1371–81.

Chapter 10

Intelligent Sliding Surface Design Methods Applied to an IBVS System for Robot Manipulators

Tolga Yüksel

Additional information is available at the end of the chapter

http://dx.doi.org/10.5772/63046

Abstract

The controller of an image-based visual servoing (IBVS) system is based on the design of the kinematic velocity controller which guarantees exponentially decreasing feature errors. In fact, this controller is using the sliding surface approach of classical Sliding Mode Control (SMC). In SMC, the system dynamics are taken into consideration and the sliding surface is designed according to the physical limitations and desired convergence time. Different design methods are proposed in the literature using adaptive gain, time variations, nonlinear functions, and intelligent methods like fuzzy logic (FL) and genetic algorithms (GA). In this study, five different sliding surface designs with analytical and intelligent methods are modified and applied to an IBVS system to expand these designs to visually guided robot manipulators. The design methods are selected by their convenience and applicability to these types of manipulator systems. To show the performance of the design methods, an IBVS system with six-DOF manipulator is simulated using MATLAB *Simulink, Robotics Toolbox, Machine Vision Toolbox,* and *Fuzzy Logic Toolbox*. A comparison of these design methods according to convergence time, error cost function, defined parameters, and motion characteristics is given.

Keywords: Sliding surface, visual servoing, robot manipulators, fuzzy logic, Simulink

1. Introduction

Visual servoing (VS) uses the camera image to control the motion of a robot, and it needs points or important pixels named as features in an image. In VS, image plane is used to define these k feature points and the coordinates of these features in image plane form, the vector s. Error signal vector is derived from the difference between the desired vector s^* and s, and these signals are used to obtain velocity control law. By using these definitions, VS methods are mentioned

INTECH
open science | open minds

© 2016 The Author(s). Licensee InTech. This chapter is distributed under the terms of the Creative Commons Attribution License (http://creativecommons.org/licenses/by/3.0), which permits unrestricted use, distribution, and reproduction in any medium, provided the original work is properly cited. (cc) BY

in two main titles. Image-based visual servoing (IBVS) uses s vector obtained from the image directly but position-based visual servoing (PBVS) needs s obtained from 3D parameter estimations of image and robot pose [1]. This advantage and robustness against depth estimation errors make IBVS more attractive and applicable in VS. Here, it must be noted that featureless visual servoing approaches like kernel-based or luminance-based methods are becoming more popular [2, 3], but feature-based methods will continue their royalty. Besides these features, the configuration of the camera and the end effector should be taken into consideration in VS. Eye-in-hand configuration, as the most popular configuration in VS, is chosen for this study. This configuration is also a step of VS for unmanned air vehicles (UAV).

Studies on IBVS mostly focus on different feature extraction methods [4], different camera geometries and types [5], hybrid VS methods [6] or other problems of VS like singularity avoidance or field of view (FOV) keeping [7] but the controller design doesn't draw too much attention because the linear velocity controller design approach of VS is assumed as the sufficient controller as the errors are decreasing exponentially. Besides this common sense, other performance parameters like convergence time, velocity limits, and error magnitudes are actually real-time metrics. For robot applications in a production line, these parameters become dominant to speed up process to increase accuracy and repeatability. Some other control approaches like visual predictive control [8] fusing predictive control with VS are promising but the controller should be applicable in real-time.

To design a new IBVS controller, the velocity controller design approach of IBVS should be examined. As explained in details in the following section, the linear controller of IBVS is using sliding surface design of sliding mode control (SMC). In SMC, two design steps are defined. The first one is designing a sliding surface that represent desired stable states of the system, and the second one is designing a control law that guarantee states reaching to the sliding surface and sliding on this surface [9]. A sliding slope is defined in SMC and this slope is named as gain in IBVS. The rule of thumb of an appropriate slope in SMC is choosing a slope small enough in order not to exceed control limits and conversely, choosing a slope big enough to reach the sliding slope faster and slide on this surface faster. This is interpreted by IBVS as choosing gain small enough in order not to exceed velocity limits and choosing gain big enough to converge faster.

From initial conditions to convergence, there are two modes of state trajectories in SMC. In reaching mode, the states are not on the sliding surface and they try to reach this surface. In sliding mode, they are on the sliding surface and they try to converge to zero. IBVS and SMC uses fixed gain-sliding slope but alternatively, in the literature, there are many different sliding surface designs which are important from the practical point of view and for high performance. Two main approaches are mentioned in the literature of sliding surface design: linear and nonlinear [10]. Although there are numerous designs for linear surfaces, it is very hard to obtain a nonlinear surface using linear surfaces for high performance, and it is hard to define the parameters of these designs. There are not too many options and the parameters are easily defined for nonlinear designs, but the magnitude of control signals should be observed to avoid saturation [10, 11]. The titles of the most common linear designs are linear constant surface [9], integral sliding surface [12], linear varying (rotating and shifting) sliding surface

http://dx.doi.org/10.5772/63046

[13], and linear time-varying sliding surface [14] designs. Nonlinear designs are more popular and titled as constant nonlinear sliding surface [15], higher order sliding surface [16], fractional sliding surface [17], terminal sliding surface [18], nonlinear sliding surface with nonlinear functions [19], and nonlinear moving sliding and terminal sliding surface designs [14]. Furthermore, intelligent methods like fuzzy logic (FL) and genetic algorithms (GA) are also deployed for parameter assignment of linear and nonlinear surface designs [20]. Detailed reviews on sliding surface designs can be found in [11, 14, 20].

Most studies on VS focus on image processing-feature extraction part of vision, but control part is still open to old and new approaches. In this study, five different sliding surface designs with analytical and intelligent methods are modified and applied to an IBVS system to expand these designs to visually guided robot manipulators. The design methods are selected according to their relevance and applicability to these manipulator systems. In the first design, linear varying sliding surface with FL is assumed. Error and error derivative are used as inputs of FL and to define linguistic rules of FL, the effects of gain on IBVS and experience on IBVS are used. In the second design, integral sliding mode is assumed and the sliding parameter of integral term is tuned using FL. In the third design, time-optimal varying sliding surface design with constant acceleration is assumed. A time interval is defined for this design and linear sliding mode is modified according to this time interval. In the fourth design, a nonlinear tangent hyperbolic function with a width parameter function is used to define a sliding surface. In the fifth design, nonlinear time-varying sliding surface is assumed. The surface is obtained by the product of initial error-error derivatives and an exponential time-varying term. To show the performance of these designs, an error cost function is defined as in [19]. An IBVS system with six-DOF manipulator is simulated and the designs are tested on this system. A comparison of these design methods according to convergence time, error cost function, defined parameters, and motion characteristics is given.

The paper is organized as follows. In the following section, IBVS and used sliding surface designs with modifications and adaptations to IBVS are explained briefly. In Section 3, simulation results for classical IBVS and IBVS with five sliding surface designs are shown. In the last section, an overall comparison of these designs is given and conclusions of the study and future goals are discussed.

2. A review on IBVS and sliding surface designs

In this section, a review on IBVS and sliding surface designs used in the study is given. The main objective of IBVS, as all VS approaches, is to minimize errors derived from k feature point vector s (1)

$$e(t) = s - s^{*} \tag{1}$$

where $e(t) \in \mathbb{R}^{k}$ is the error vector and s^{*} is the desired features for fixed-motionless feature points with zero derivatives. Changes in s depend only on camera motion. Furthermore, IBVS assumes that the camera is attached to the end effector of a six DOF arm as eye-in-hand configuration and $k \geq 6$.

In the classical IBVS, a point $P = (X, Y, Z)$ in 3D camera frame is defined in image plane with a point p using perspective projection and the velocity of P relative to camera frame is given in terms of linear velocity V and angular velocity Ω

$$\dot{P} = -\Omega \times P - V \tag{2}$$

This velocity is used to obtain transformation between the velocity of the coordinates of perspective projection point (u, v) with a focal length λ_f and the linear and angular velocities of point P. This transformation is defined as below:

$$\begin{bmatrix} \dot{u} \\ \dot{v} \end{bmatrix} = \begin{bmatrix} -\frac{\lambda_f}{Z} & 0 & \frac{u}{Z} & \frac{uv}{\lambda_f} & -\frac{\lambda_f^2 + u^2}{\lambda_f} & v \\ 0 & -\frac{\lambda_f}{Z} & \frac{v}{Z} & \frac{\lambda_f^2 + v^2}{\lambda_f} & -\frac{uv}{\lambda_f} & -u \end{bmatrix} \begin{bmatrix} v_x \\ v_y \\ v_z \\ w_x \\ w_y \\ w_z \end{bmatrix} \tag{3}$$
$$= \dot{s} = L_s.\upsilon_c$$

where υ_c (v_c, w_c) is the vector of camera's linear and angular velocities in reference coordinate frame. The transformation matrix, $L_s \in \mathbf{R}^{k\times 6}$ is known as the interaction matrix or commonly called image or feature Jacobian matrix. Z is the depth of P and it is hard to obtain the actual value of this term in practice. In most approaches, the estimation value for Z is used and the interaction matrix becomes an estimated interaction matrix $\hat{L}_s$.

By using (1) and (3), relation between error and velocity is obtained as $\dot{s}^*$ is zero

$$\dot{e} = L_s.\upsilon_c \tag{4}$$

IBVS tries to decrease the error exponentially by using the differential equation

$$\dot{e} + \lambda.e = 0 \tag{5}$$

From another aspect, this differential equation is the main equation used by classical SMC to define a sliding surface. Classical SMC defines a surface in terms of error and error derivatives according to the system degree and tries to hold the system states in this surface by equalizing this surface to zero. This definition strongly connects SMC and IBVS. IBVS proposes a kinematic velocity controller and the velocity signals are the control signals. Again, by using (4) and (5), velocity signals is defined as

$$\begin{aligned} &\dot{e}+\lambda.e=0\rightarrow\dot{e}=-\lambda.e\rightarrow\hat{L}_s.\upsilon_c \\ &=-\lambda.e\rightarrow\upsilon_c=-\lambda.\hat{L}_s^{+}.e \end{aligned} \tag{6}$$

where, $\hat{L}_s^{+}$ is the pseudo-inverse matrix of estimated interaction matrix in cases of non-square matrix and λ is the gain value. Here, it must be noted that this gain value can be in matrix form to define different gain values for each velocity term. This velocity controller is a proportional controller and detailed stability analysis of this controller for IBVS can be found in [1].

2.1. Linear varying sliding surface with fuzzy logic

Varying sliding slope is a common approach in sliding surface designs to achieve desired performance without exceeding velocity limits. The only design parameter in (5) and (6) is the sliding slope, and an on-line parameter tuning algorithm can be proposed by using varying sliding slope approach. Instead of an analytical approach which proposes different parameters to tune a parameter, and which has to be tuned carefully to allow soft parameter variation, FL can be a good candidate not only to avoid tuning twice but also to include linguistic definitions and user experience in the design [21]. IBVS velocity controller in (6) can be modified as in (7) and the block diagram of IBVS with linear varying sliding surface design using fuzzy logic is shown in **Figure 1**.

$$\upsilon_c=-\lambda_{FL}(e,\dot{e}).\hat{L}_s^{+}.e \tag{7}$$

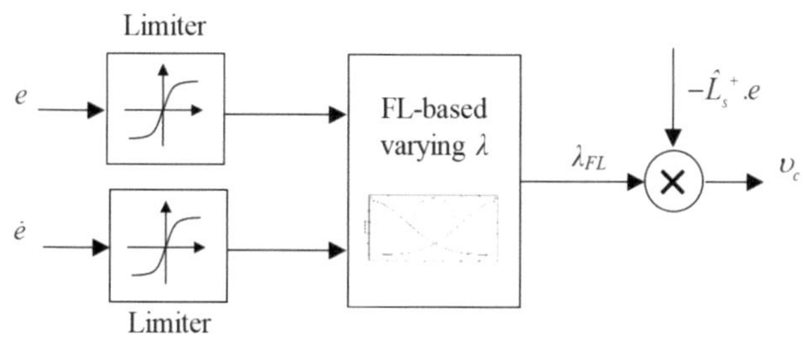

Figure 1. IBVS with linear varying sliding surface design using fuzzy logic.

In **Figure 1**, it must be noted that limiters should be placed before FL block to restrict λ_{FL}. Membership functions and FL type should be chosen wisely according to desired varying λ_{FL} surface, which is a function of error and error derivative. Furthermore, the rulebase should represent the behavior of classical IBVS under varying gain. An example rule from FL rulebase is defined as follows:

$$\text{IF } e \text{ is HIGH and } \dot{e} \text{ is HIGH, THEN } \lambda_{FL} \text{ is LOW} \tag{8}$$

2.2. Integral sliding surface with fuzzy logic

The classical linear sliding surface design in (5) is a PD-type sliding surface and an integral term can be added to this design to increase tracking performance [12, 22]. This term can be active for all error trajectories or only when the errors are in predefined bounds. Integral sliding surface is given below:

$$\lambda_p.e + \lambda_I.\int e.dt + \lambda_D.\dot{e} = 0 \tag{9}$$

Finding appropriate gain values (λ_P, λ_I, λ_D) for this surface design is the main problem. Again, FL can be applied to this design as in [23]. In this study, only gain value for integral term (λ_I) is assigned using FL as a function of$e$. (9) is reformulated for IBVS in (10) and the block diagram of IBVS with integral surface design using fuzzy logic is shown in **Figure 2**.

$$\upsilon_c = -\hat{L}_s^{\,+}.\left(\lambda_p.e + \lambda_{I(FL)}(e).\int e.dt\right) \tag{10}$$

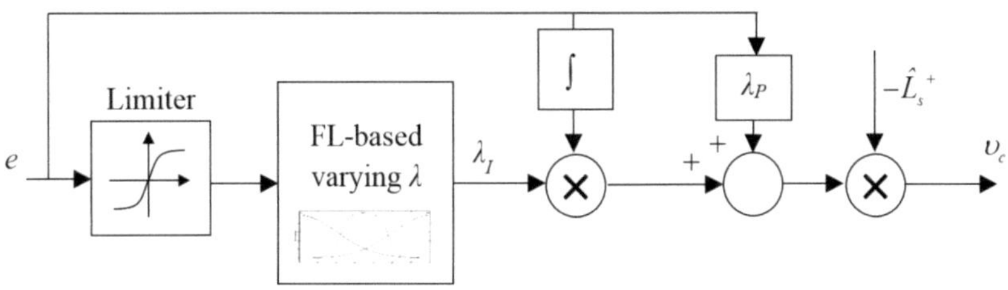

Figure 2. IBVS with integral surface design using fuzzy logic.

2.3. Time-varying sliding surface design with constant acceleration

As mentioned in [14], trade-off between short sliding slope reaching phase and slower responses in sliding surfaces can be bested by time-varying sliding slopes. A time-varying sliding slope term, which is defined as a function of time is added to classical sliding surface design and this term is only active until a predefined time instant. In his study, Bartoszewicz designed two different time-varying sliding surfaces, constant-acceleration, and constant-velocity, according to time dependence [14]. Constant-acceleration time-varying sliding surface offers a faster convergence speed to classical sliding surface and this design is chosen in this study. Constant-acceleration time-varying sliding surface design is given in (11) and definitions for the design parameters are given in (12), respectively

http://dx.doi.org/10.5772/63046

$$\dot{e} + \lambda.e + \begin{Bmatrix} A.t^2 + B.t + C & \text{for}\, t \leq T \\ 0 & \text{for}\, t > T \end{Bmatrix} = 0 \tag{11}$$

$$\begin{aligned} A &= -\frac{\dot{e}(0) + \beta.e(0)}{T^2} \\ B &= 2.\frac{\dot{e}(0) + \beta.e(0)}{T} \\ C &= -\dot{e}(0) - \beta.e(0) \end{aligned} \tag{12}$$

where β is fixed initial error constant and T is time instant for constant acceleration.

The velocity controller and the block diagram of IBVS with time-varying sliding surface design is shown in (13) and **Figure 3** with sample/hold (S/H) units, respectively

$$\upsilon_c = -\hat{L}_s^{+}.\left(\lambda.e + \begin{Bmatrix} A.t^2 + B.t + C & \text{for } t \leq T \\ 0 & \text{for } t > T \end{Bmatrix} \right) \tag{13}$$

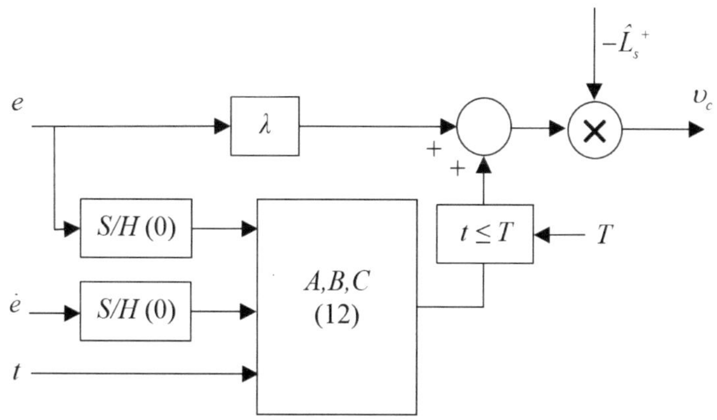

Figure 3. IBVS with time-varying sliding surface design with constant acceleration.

2.4. Nonlinear sliding surface design with tangent hyperbolic function

Sliding surfaces in the first three designs are linear, which means that error and error derivative will pursue a constant sliding slope. In fact, linear varying or time-varying sliding surfaces reveals piecewise linear surfaces. Instead of using these linear methods, a nonlinear function can be assigned as a sliding surface function [15]. Tangent hyperbolic function can be a good candidate as a nonlinear function [11] and it is preferred in this study. The definition of nonlinear sliding surface design with tangent hyperbolic function is given in (14)

$$\dot{e}+w_p.tanh(c_1.e)=0 \tag{14}$$

where w_p is the sliding magnitude parameter which represents convergence speed and c_1 is the sliding slope of the nonlinear surface. These parameters can be assigned constant but to reach sliding surface faster, w_p is chosen as a function of error. The velocity output and block diagram of IBVS with nonlinear sliding surface design using tangent hyperbolic function are shown in (15) and **Figure 4**, respectively.

$$\upsilon_c = -\hat{L}_s^+.w_p(e).tanh(c_1.e) \tag{15}$$

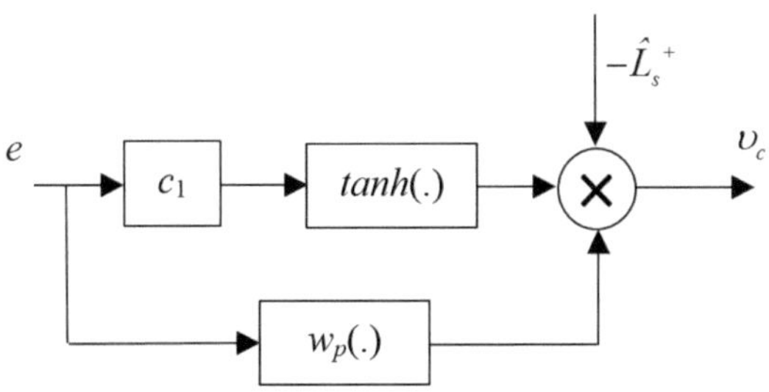

Figure 4. IBVS with nonlinear sliding surface design using tangent hyperbolic function.

2.5. Nonlinear time-varying sliding surface

As an alternative to nonlinear constant functions, nonlinear time-varying surfaces can be designed to shorten reaching phase. Exponential time-varying functions [14, 19, 24, 25] are proposed in the literature as nonlinear time-varying sliding surface functions. In this study, exponential nonlinear time-varying sliding surface design in (19) is chosen and it is given in (16)

$$\dot{e}+\lambda.e-\left[\dot{e}(0)+\lambda.e(0)\right].e^{-k.t}=0 \tag{16}$$

where λ and k are design parameters of sliding slope and time constant of convergence. This function also includes initial values of error and error derivative and this provides zero initial velocity signals for IBVS. The velocity output and block diagram of IBVS with nonlinear time-varying sliding surface are shown in (17) and **Figure 5**, respectively.

$$\upsilon_c=-\hat{L}_s^+\left(\lambda.e-\left[\dot{e}(0)+\lambda.e(0)\right].e^{-k.t}\right) \tag{17}$$

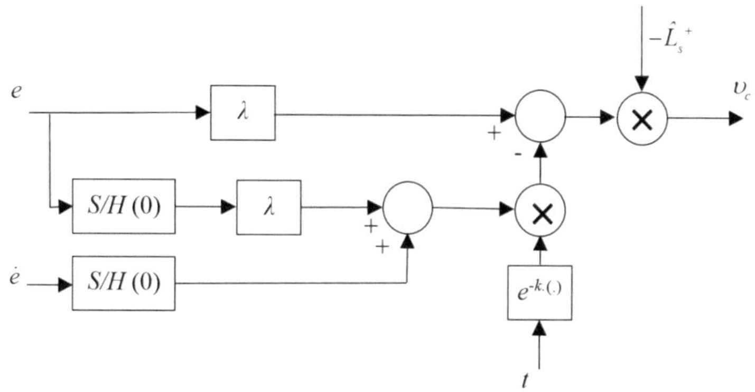

Figure 5. IBVS with nonlinear time-varying sliding surface design.

3. Simulation results

In this study, an IBVS system with intelligent sliding surfaces is simulated using MATLAB *Simulink, Robotics Toolbox, Machine Vision Toolbox* and *Fuzzy Logic Toolbox* [26]. As the robot manipulator platform, a six DOF Puma560 arm kinematic model is used in the simulations [27]. Here, it must be noted that inner loop robot manipulator dynamics and control can be fused with IBVS control as in [28], but this study neglects dynamics of the manipulator systems and assumes the IBVS controller as a kinematic velocity controller.

Some assumptions in the study should be given before simulation results:

Assumption 1: It is assumed that there is no transformation between the end effector and the camera mounted on the end effector with eye-in-hand configuration.

Assumption 2: All feature points are collinear.

The camera parameters are defined as follows: the resolution of the camera is 1024×1024, the principal point is (512, 512), and the focal length is 8 mm. The feature points in Cartesian coordinates are defined as P^* using four fixed corner points of a square with 0.5 m side length and $s^* \in \mathbb{R}^{2\times4}$. The center of these points should collide with the principal point as s^*. P^* and s^* in matrix form for feature points are given below:

$$P^*(X,Y,Z) = \begin{bmatrix} 0.25 & 0.25 & -0.25 & -2.5 \\ -0.25 & 0.25 & 0.25 & -0.25 \\ 2.5 & 2.5 & 2.5 & 2.5 \end{bmatrix}$$
$$s^*(u,v) = \begin{bmatrix} 612 & 412 & 412 & 612 \\ 412 & 412 & 612 & 612 \end{bmatrix} \quad (18)$$

The estimated depth value for $\hat{L}_s$ is assumed as 2 m and this value can be considered as a good depth estimation. In the following subsections, details and parameters of classical IBVS and five IBVS sliding surface designs are given and the results are illustrated. To show the performance and the robustness of the designs, random w disturbance with -1< w <1 and zero mean is added to each feature point. As an illustration of the simulated IBVS systems, the block diagram of the closed loop IBVS system with sliding surface design and its *Simulink* model is shown in **Figure 6** and **Figure 7**, respectively. For all these simulations, initial joint angle vector q_0 is given below and the desired pose of Puma 560 with P^* in 3D is shown in **Figure 8**.

$$q_0 = \begin{bmatrix} 0 & \pi/4 & \pi & \pi/10 & \pi/4 & -\pi/4 \end{bmatrix} \text{ rad.} \tag{19}$$

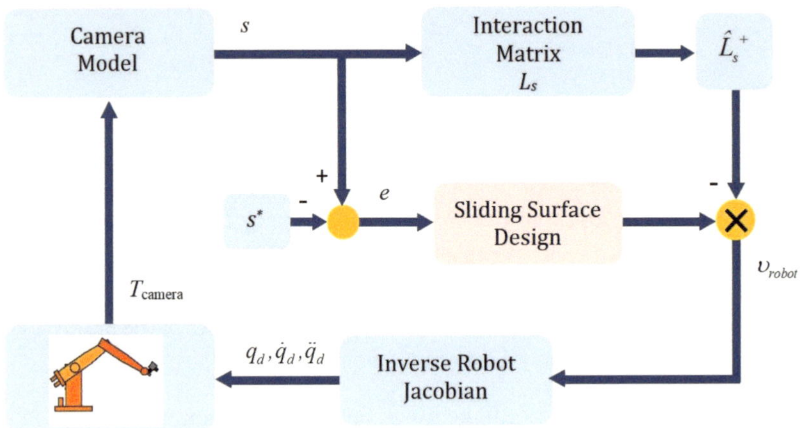

Figure 6. The block diagram of the simulated IBVS systems with sliding surface design.

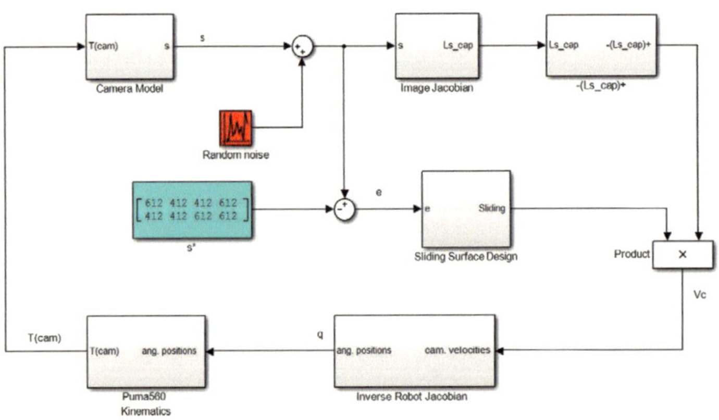

Figure 7. The *Simulink* model of the simulated IBVS systems with sliding surface design.

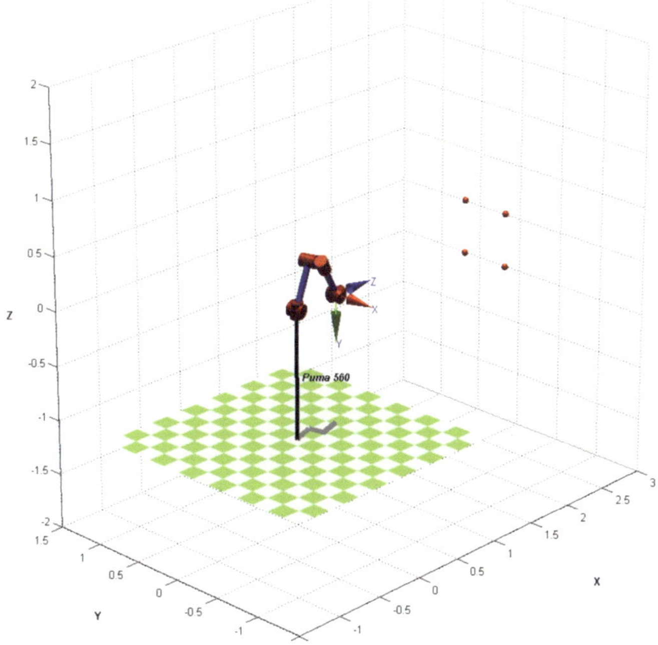

Figure 8. The desired pose of Puma 560 with P^* as red balls.

The main performance criterions for an IBVS system are convergence time (t_{conv}) and velocity limits. In this study, an error cost function is also added to these criterions to show the performance of each design and it is given in (20)

$$J(e) = \sum_{i=1}^{2\times k} \int_{0}^{t_{conv}} \left| e_i(t) \right| .dt \tag{20}$$

where e_i is the error of each feature and i is the index of feature error. Besides these performance numbers, the parameters which have to be assigned for each design are another metric for a closed loop system. These parameters are also discussed in each design. Furthermore, feature motions in image plane are examined to discuss FOV keeping capability for future studies. The inside of the sliding surface block for each design is also given.

3.1. Case 1: Classical IBVS with fixed sliding slope

To make a comparison between each design, a classical IBVS system with fixed sliding slope is assumed as in (5) and (6). The fixed value for λ is chosen as 0.5. Inside the *Simulink* block of the sliding surface design for this case is shown in **Figure 9**.

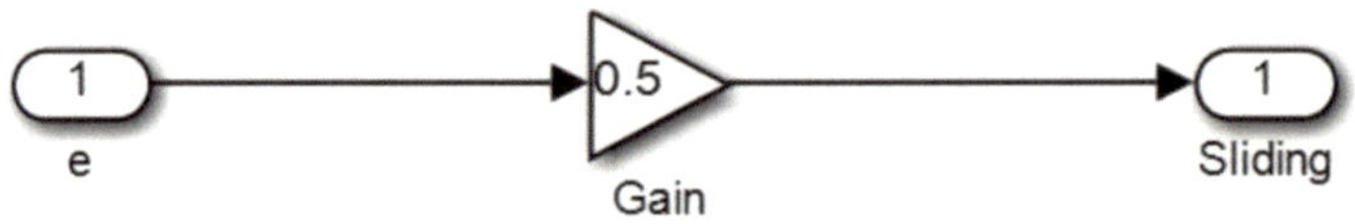

Figure 9. The *Simulink* block of sliding surface for Case 1.

The feature motions in image plane are shown in **Figure 10.a** with initial feature points in red circles and target feature points in blue circles. The velocity signals of the end effector are shown in **Figure 10.b**, and the error signals are shown in Figure 10.c, respectively.

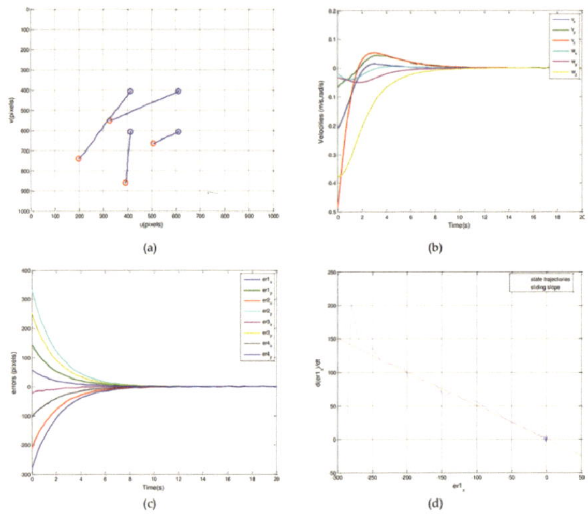

Figure 10. The results for Case 1. (a) Feature motions in image plane (b) Velocities of the end effector (c) Feature errors (d) Error vs. error derivative trajectory.

As shown in **Figure 10.a-b**, the paths of the feature points are linear and the errors are exponentially decreasing as expected from classical IBVS [1]. As the convergence time, the time instant when all absolute errors decreases under 1 pixel is assumed and it is 12.89 s as shown in **Figure 10.c**. The error cost for Case 1 is 2482. As an example of fixed sliding slope, error and error derivative trajectory $(er1_x \text{vs. } er1'_x)$ for the first feature in u coordinate is shown in **Figure 10.d**.

3.2. Case 2: IBVS with linear varying sliding surface using fuzzy logic

The choice of an appropriate λ plays a critical role in the performance of the proportional velocity controller in (6). As the second design, linear sliding slope design with varying λ for fast convergence and low velocity profile is aimed, and assigning the slope by using fuzzy logic that is an approach in fuzzy sliding mode is proposed.

IBVS derives different error signals for each feature. FL needs error and error derivative for an appropriate λ but it is very hard to decouple the error signals of each feature to associate

http://dx.doi.org/10.5772/63046

with velocity signals. To avoid this problem, Euclidian norm values of the error and error derivative vectors are used as the inputs of FL in the design of the sliding surface. Inside the *Simulink* block of the sliding surface design for this case is shown in **Figure 11**. Fuzzy Logic Controller block in **Figure 11** is implemented MATLAB *Fuzzy Logic Toolbox*.

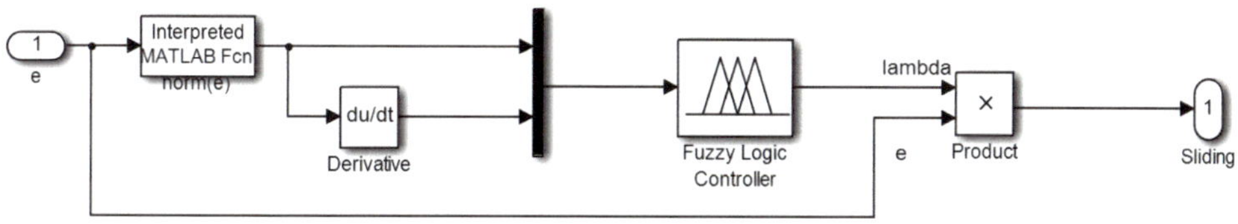

Figure 11. The *Simulink* block of sliding surface for Case 2.

The type of FL unit is Mamdani and the membership functions of the error, the error derivative norm inputs and output λ_{FL} are shown in **Figure 12**. For a better softened varying λ_{FL}, the membership functions are chosen as gaussian and gaussian-bell curve. For each input and output, three membership functions are defined. The rulebase for FL is defined using nine rules and this rulebase is given in **Table 1**. The rules are defined according to the approach as in (8). The FL surface for nonlinear mapping between the inputs and the output is demonstrated in **Figure 13**. Here, it must be noted that λ_{FL} varies between 0.51 and 1.85 as shown in **Figure 13**.

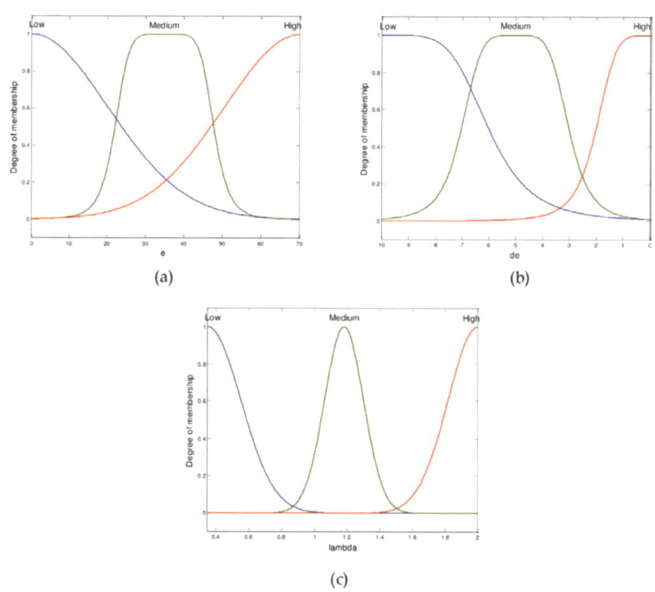

Figure 12. FL membership functions for λ_{FL} (a) Input *e* (b) Input d*e*/d*t* (c) Output λ_{FL} .

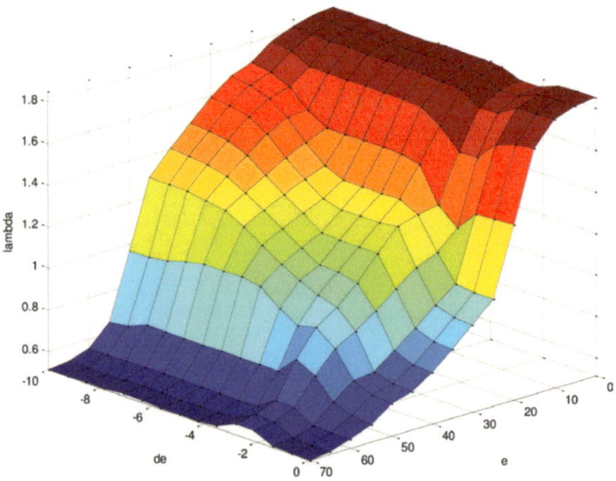

Figure 13. FL surface for λ_{FL} .

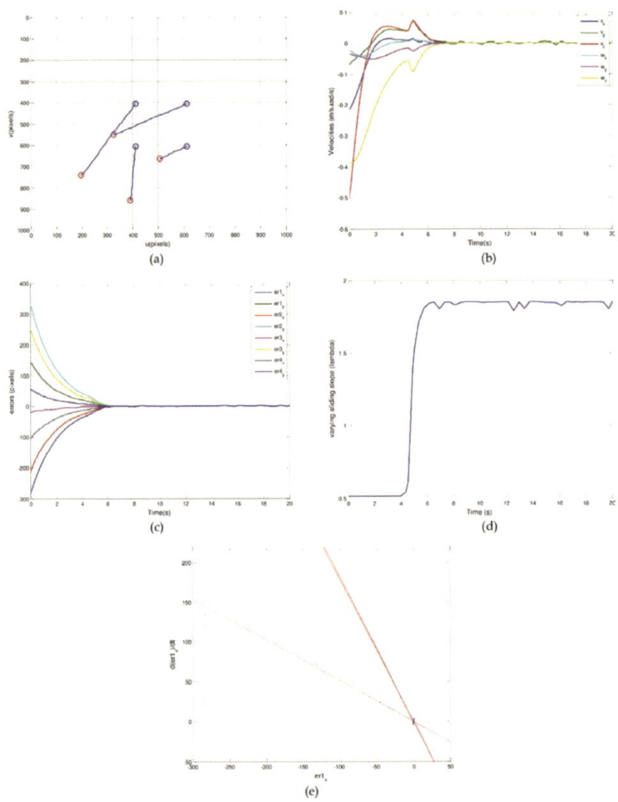

Figure 14. The results for Case 2. (a) Feature motions (b) Velocities of the end effector (c) Feature errors (d) λ_{FL} (e) Error vs. error derivative trajectory.

$e / \dot{e}$	**Low**	**Medium**	**High**
Low	High	High	High
Medium	High	Medium	Low
High	Low	Low	Low

Table 1. FL rulebase for linear varying sliding surface.

The feature motions in image plane are shown in **Figure 14.a**, the velocity signals of the end effector are shown in **Figure 14.b**, and the error signals are shown in **Figure 14.c**, respectively.

The varying sliding slope λ_{FL} is shown in **Figure 14.d** and it remains constant and low since error and error derivative norms are high. Time interval for this steady condition is between 0 and 3.98 s. Within this time interval, the slope is fixed and error and error derivative follows this slope as shown in **Figure 14.e**. Then, FL unit is activated by these norms and varying sliding slope shows a nonlinear characteristic without discontinuity. Again, it remains constant and high after norms are small with small fluctuations after 6.15 s. These fluctuations are a consequence of noise added to the features.

The velocity profiles dwell in velocity limits and increases after 3.98 s as shown in **Figure 14.b**. The errors decreases rapidly after varying sliding slope as shown in **Figure 14.c** and error and error derivative try to follow varying sliding slope after 3.98 s. The convergence time is 7.35 s and the error cost is 2591 for Case 2. In **Figure 14.a**, it can be seen that the feature motions are linear, which means that this sliding approach doesn't affect motion characteristics of IBVS.

3.3. Case 3: IBVS with integral sliding surface using fuzzy logic

IBVS with integral sliding surface in (10) is assumed as Case 3 and λ_P is chosen as 0.5. FL is used for λ_I assignment. Inside the *Simulink* block of the sliding surface design for this case is shown in **Figure 15**.

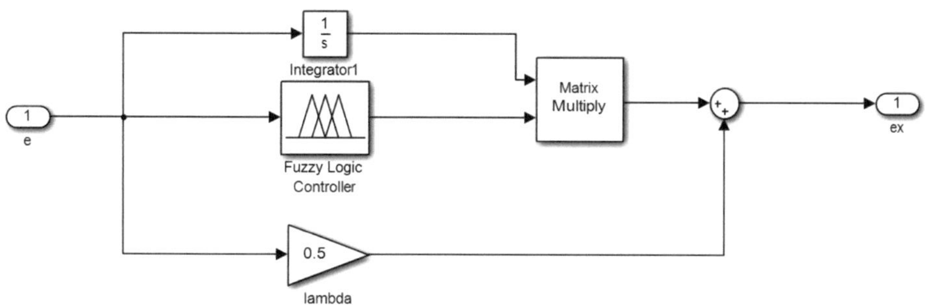

Figure 15. The *Simulink* block of sliding surface for Case 3.

FL unit uses error as input, two membership functions are defined for this input and the FL surface curve is shown in **Figure 16**. Here, it must be noted that limits of this curve, thus λ_I, can be changed but this affect velocity limits.

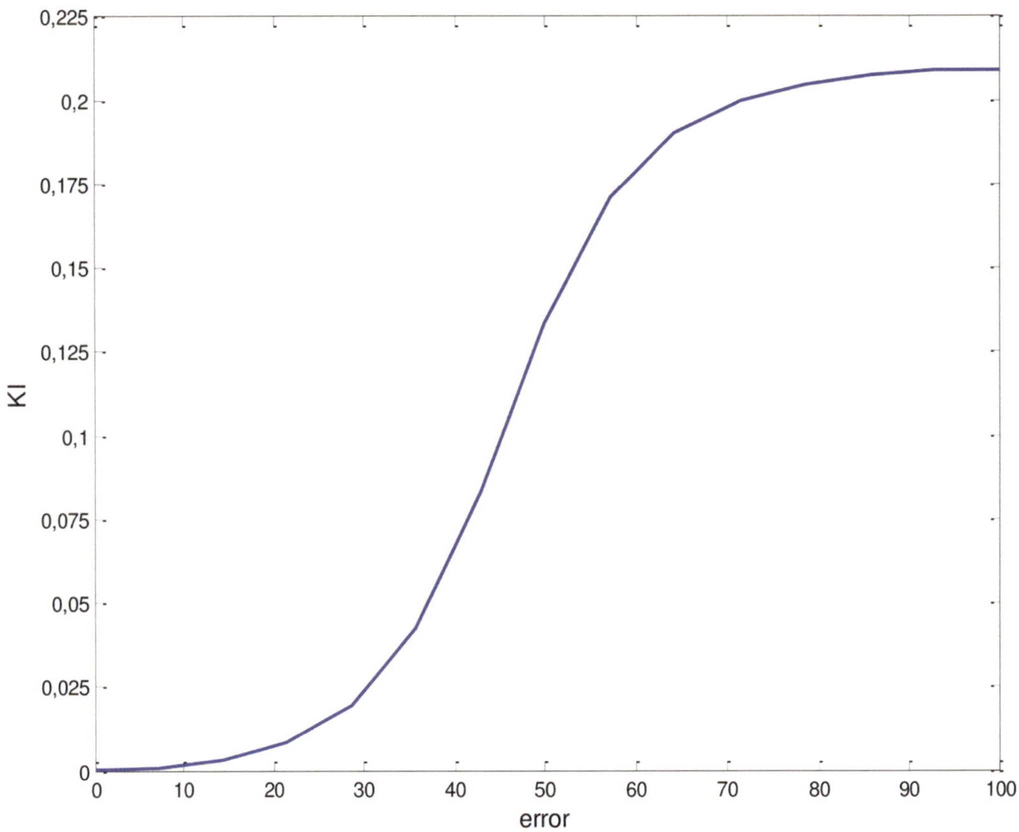

Figure 16. FL surface curve for λ_I.

The feature motions in image plane are shown in **Figure 17.a**, and the velocity signals of the end effector are shown in **Figure 17.b**, respectively. The error signals and the error integral term signals after λ_I product are shown in **Figure 17.c** and **17.d**, respectively. In **Figure 17.b-d**, it is clear that integral term forces fast convergence with high velocities, but this effort is not enough by itself for fast convergence. In (12), it is mentioned that an integral term can be active only when the errors are in predefined bounds if desired. It must be noted that this approach will cause discontinuities and sudden changes in velocity signals of IBVS. The feature motions in **Figure 17.a** show linear characteristics as classical IBVS. The convergence time is 9.41 s and the error cost is 1852 for Case 3.

http://dx.doi.org/10.5772/63046

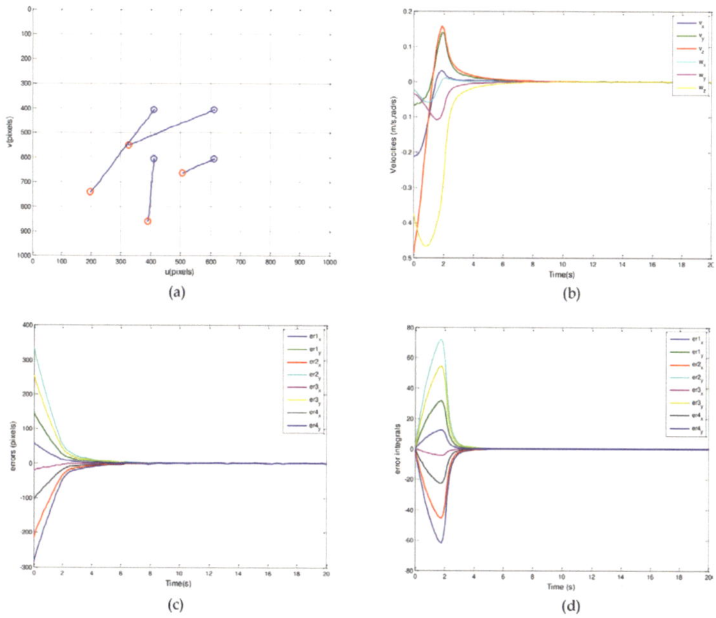

Figure 17. The results for Case 3. (a) Feature motions (b) Velocities of the end effector (c) Feature errors (d) Error integral term.

3.4. Case 4: IBVS with time-varying sliding surface design and constant acceleration

In his study, Bartoszewicz proposed a time-optimal sliding mode approach for robust control of second-order uncertain systems [14]. Time-optimality needs time-varying sliding slopes to adapt the system to initial conditions. These initial conditions for an IBVS system are dominant if they are far from zero. β is chosen as 0.5 for this case and A, B, and C are defined as in (12) and (13), respectively. Time dependent terms in (13) affect velocity limits and by some trials, T in (13) is assigned as 5 s. Inside the *Simulink* block of the sliding surface design for this case is shown in **Figure 18**.

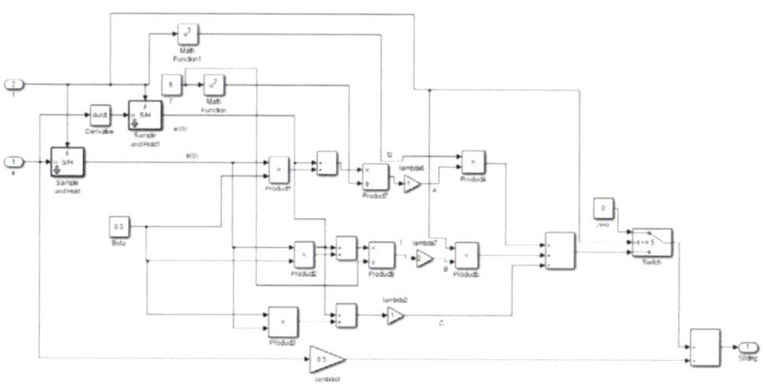

Figure 18. The *Simulink* block of sliding surface for Case 4.

The feature motions in image plane are shown in **Figure 19.a**, the velocity signals of the end effector are shown in **Figure 19.b**, the error signals are shown in **Figure 19.c**, and time dependent terms in (13) are shown in 19.d, respectively.

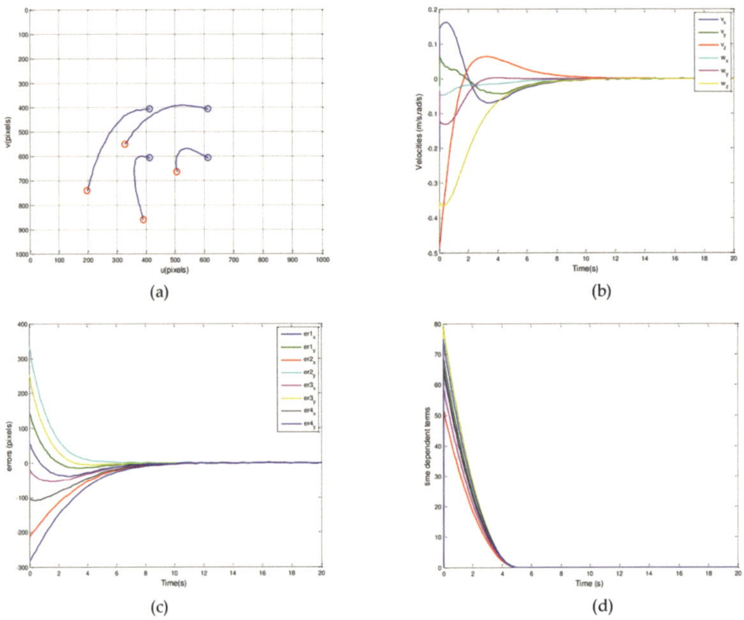

Figure 19. The results for Case 4. (a) Feature motions (b) Velocities of the end effector (c) Feature errors (d) Time dependent terms in (13).

The feature motion trajectories in the previous cases are quite similar but in this case, the motions are curvilinear as shown in **Figure 19.a**. This is the consequence of time dependent terms shown in **Figure 19.d**. They are the sum of the terms in (13) and they drag the motions throughout target features until the end of time dependence. β adjusts magnitude and signs of these terms in (12) and it has to be chosen wisely. Besides being curvilinear, VS may lose the feature points and stop processing when the features are close to FOV. The convergence time is 11.82 s and the error cost is 2891 for Case 4.

3.5. Case 5: IBVS with nonlinear sliding surface design using tangent hyperbolic function

Tangent hyperbolic function is chosen as nonlinear sliding surface function and the magnitude and slope of this function is also dependent on error and constant c_1 as given in (15). Parameter assignments of (15) are given below:

$$\begin{aligned} w_p(e) &= -0.07|e| + 80 \\ c_1 &= 0.01 \end{aligned} \tag{21}$$

Here, w_p can be defined as a function of time as in (11) but it is chosen as a function of error in this study. Inside the *Simulink* block of the sliding surface design for this case is shown in **Figure 20**.

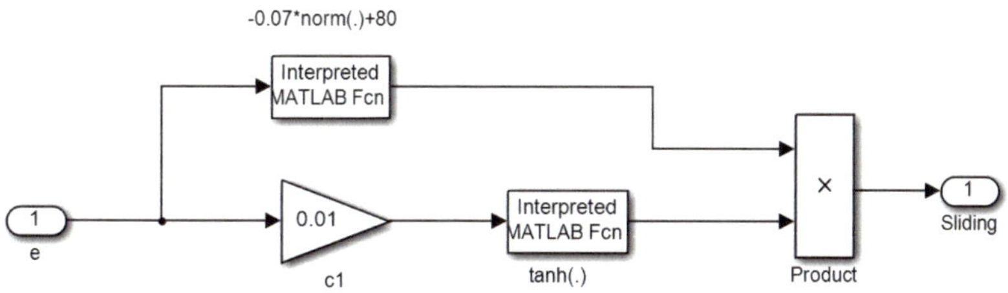

Figure 20. The *Simulink* block of sliding surface for Case 5.

The feature motions in image plane are shown in **Figure 21.a**, the velocity signals of the end effector are shown in **Figure 21.b**, and the error signals are shown in **Figure 21.c**, respectively. To show the nonlinear sliding surface, error and error derivative trajectories for the first feature in *u* coordinate is shown in **Figure 21.d**.

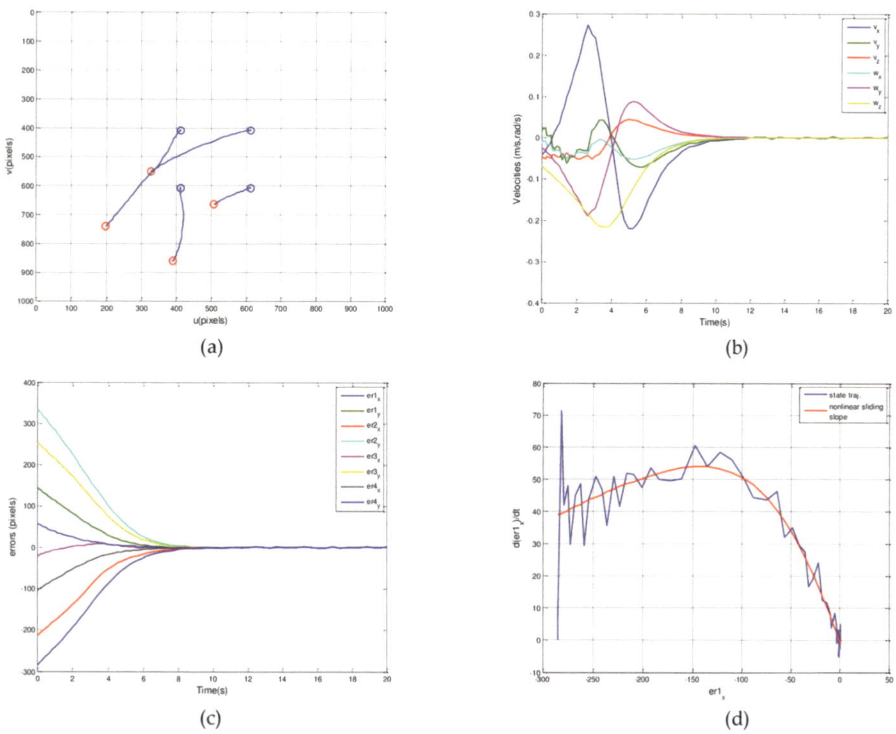

Figure 21. The results for Case 5. (a) Feature motions (b) Velocities of the end effector (c) Feature errors (d) Error vs. error derivative trajectory.

Unlike the first four cases, the initial velocity values are quite small as shown in **Figure 21.b** and that can be a big positive in the realization of an IBVS system as mentioned in [29]. The feature motions are slightly curvilinear as shown in **Figure 21.a**. The convergence time is 10.85 s and the error cost is 4094 for Case 5. Error vs. error derivative trajectory follows tangent hyperbolic function as shown in **Figure 21.d**.

3.6. Case 6: IBVS with nonlinear time-varying sliding surface

Exponential nonlinear time-varying sliding surface in (17) also utilizes initial error and error derivative values. λ is chosen as 0.5 and k exponential time constant is chosen as 1 for a fast transient response. Inside the *Simulink* block of the sliding surface design for this case is shown in **Figure 22**.

The feature motions in image plane are shown in **Figure 23.a**, the velocity signals of the end effector are shown in **Figure 23.b**, and the error signals are shown in **Figure 23.c**, respectively.

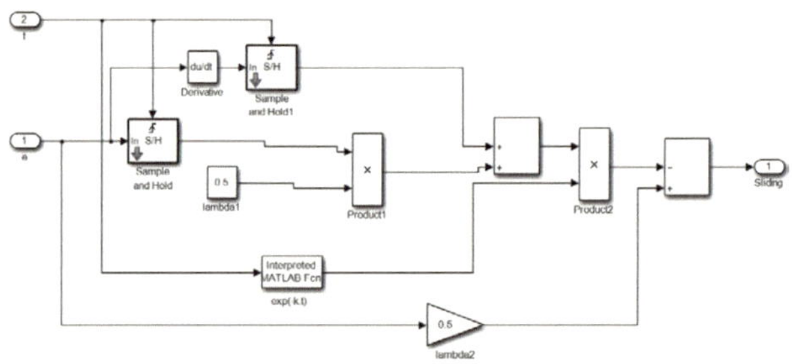

Figure 22. The *Simulink* block of sliding surface for Case 6.

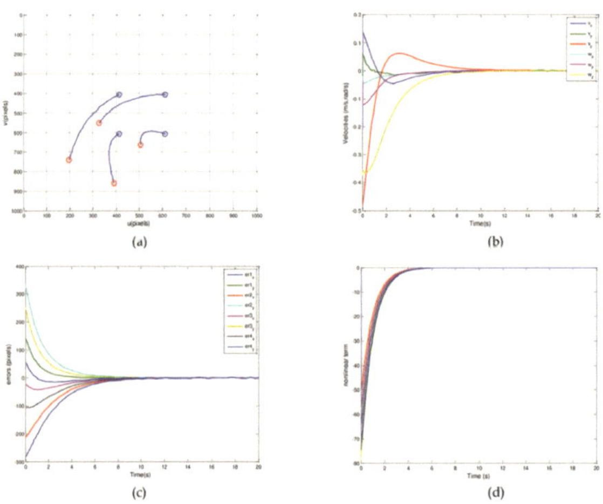

Figure 23. The results for Case 6. (a) Feature motions (b) Velocities of the end effector (c) Feature errors (d) Nonlinear term of each velocity.

Nonlinear term of each velocity in (17) with 5 s transient is shown in Figure 23.d. After this transient, the system behaves like classical IBVS system. The motions are curvilinear as shown in Figure 23.a. The convergence time is 12.12 s and the error cost is 2795 for Case 6.

4. Conclusion and future works

As a new field of control systems, most studies on VS focus on image processing or pattern recognition parts of the applications. The controller part has still gaps. On the other hand, SMC is a convenient control method for linear and nonlinear systems, and it is based on the design of sliding surfaces. In this study, five different sliding surface designs including analytical and intelligent methods are modified and applied to an IBVS manipulator system to adapt the designs and to compare the performance of these designs. The design methods are selected according to their relevance and applicability to this type of visually guided manipulator systems.

Sliding surface design is the first step of SMC and the designer has to consider robustness and transient behaviour of the system. When these designs are considered for an IBVS system, the designer has to deal not only with these issues but also the velocity limits, the convergence time, and motion characteristics. Furthermore, the designer must have experience on sliding surface design to tune the design parameters appropriately. In this study, these hotspots are considered. In the simulations, a random noise is added to each feature point to show the robustness of the designs. According to IBVS metrics mentioned above, a comparison of design methods used in the study is given in **Table 2**.

Design	Convergence time (s)	Error cost	Parameters	Motion characteristic
Classical IBVS with fixed sliding slope	12.89	2842	λ	**Linear**
IBVS with linear varying sliding surface using fuzzy logic	**7.35**	2591	λ_{FL}	**Linear**
IBVS with integral sliding surface using fuzzy logic	9.41	**1852**	λ_P, $\lambda_{I\text{-}FL}$	**Linear**
IBVS with time-varying sliding surface design and constant acceleration	11.82	2891	β, T	Curvilinear
IBVS with nonlinear sliding surface design using tangent hyperbolic function	10.85	4094	w_p (function), c_1	Curvilinear
IBVS with nonlinear time-varying sliding surface	12.12	2795	λ, k	Curvilinear

Table 2. Comparison of sliding surface designs in the study.

All designs in the study considered angular and linear velocity limits which are the most restrictive quantity of a manipulator system, and these limits also form a homogenous basis for comparison. In **Table 2**, it can be seen that IBVS with linear varying sliding surface using fuzzy logic is the fastest design according to convergence time. It can be concluded that changing sliding slope using FL with error and error derivative inputs results fast response with low velocity profiles. Nonetheless, the only parameter which has to be tuned in this design is not a parameter but an FL unit. As an intelligent method, FL utilizes user or designer experience and the designer has to be careful when using FL in order not to miss a rule. Compared to classical IBVS with fixed sliding slope, all design methods in the study decreases convergence time.

IBVS with integral sliding surface using fuzzy logic has the lowest error cost, but it must be noted that the integral term should be used wisely against wind-up conditions.

Three designs have linear motion characteristics and as mentioned in [1], it is important for keeping FOV. When the other designs with curvilinear characteristics are needed for a VS realization, additional methods should be used to avoid this drawback.

Parameter tuning of each design is another issue binding the theory with user experience. FL units in these designs directly need user experience. In the future studies, intelligent hybrid units which doesn't need user experience like ANFIS will be used.

In the future studies, the main goal will be the realization of these designs in real IBVS manipulator system. Furthermore, not only kinematics of the manipulator, but also the dynamics and inner loop control of the manipulator will be added to the realization.

Author details

Tolga Yüksel

Address all correspondence to: tolga.yuksel@bilecik.edu.tr

Department of Electrical and Electronics Engineering, Bilecik Seyh Edebali University, Bilecik, Turkey

References

[1] Chaumette F, Hutchinson S. Visual servo control. I. Basic approaches. IEEE Robot Autom Mag. 2006;13(4):82–90.

[2] Collewet C, Marchand E, Chaumette F. Visual servoing set free from image processing. Proc - IEEE Int Conf Robot Autom. 2008;81–6.

[3] Kallem V, Swensen JP, Hager GD, Cowan NJ. Kernel-based visual servoing. In: IEEE/RSJ International Conference on Intelligent Robots and Systems. 2007. pp. 1975–80.

[4] Tahri O, Chaumette F. Point-based and region-based image moments for visual servoing of planar objects. IEEE Trans Robot. 2005;21(6):1116–27.

[5] Bourquardez O, Mahony R, Hamel T, Chaumette F. Stability and performance of image based visual servo control using first order spherical image moments. 2006 IEEE/RSJ Int Conf Intell Robot Syst [Internet]. 2006;4304–9. Available from: http://ieeexplore.ieee.org/lpdocs/epic03/wrapper.htm?arnumber=4059090

[6] Chaumette F, Hutchinson S. Visual servo control. II. Advanced approaches. IEEE Robot Autom Mag [Internet]. 2007;14(1):109–18. Available from: http://ieeexplore.ieee.org/lpdocs/epic03/wrapper.htm?arnumber=4141039

[7] Chesi G, Hashimoto K, Prattichizzo D, Vicino A. Keeping features in the field of view in eye-in-hand visual servoing: A switching approach. IEEE Trans Robot. 2004;20(5): 908–13.

[8] Allibert G, Courtial E, Chaumette F. Predictive control for constrained image-based visual servoing. IEEE Trans Robot. 2010;26(5):933–9.

[9] Slotine J-J, Li W. Applied Nonlinear Control. Prentice Hall,USA; 1991.

[10] Bandyopadhyay B, Deepak F, Kim K–S. Sliding Mode Control Using Novel Sliding Surfaces. Springer, Berlin Heidelberg; 2009.

[11] Tokat S, Fadali MS, Eray O. A classification and overview of sliding mode controller sliding surface design methods. In: Recent Advances in Sliding Modes: From Control to Intelligent Mechatronics. Springer, Switzerland; 2015.

[12] Stepanenko Y, Cao Y, Su C. Variable Structure Control of Robotic Manipulator With PID Sliding Surfaces. Int J Robust Nonlinear Control. 1998;8:79–90.

[13] Park D-W, Choi S-B. Moving sliding surfaces for high-order variable structure systems. Int J Control. 1999;72(12):960–70.

[14] Bartoszewicz A. Time-varying sliding modes for second-order systems. In: IEE Proceedings - Control Theory and Applications. 1996.

[15] Cerruto E, Consoli A, Kucer P, Testa A. A Fuzzy Logic Quasi-Sliding-Mode Controlled Motor Drive. In: Proceedings of the IEEE International Symposium on Industrial Electronics. 1993. pp. 652–8.

[16] Fridman L, Levant A. Higher Order Sliding Modes. In: Sliding Mode Control in Engineering. 2002. pp. 1–52.

[17] Efe MÖ. Fractional order sliding mode control with reaching law. Turkish J Electr Eng Comput Sci. 2010;18(5):731–47.

[18] Yu S, Yu X, Shirinzadeh B, Man Z. Continuous finite-time control for robotic manipulators with terminal sliding mode. Automatica. 2005;41(11):1957–64.

[19] Kim J-J, Lee J-J, Park K-B, Youn M-J. Design of new time-varying sliding surface for robot manipulator using variable structure controller. Electron Lett. 1993;29(2).

[20] Kaynak O, Erbatur K, Ertugrul M. The fusion of computationally intelligent methodologies and sliding-mode control - A survey. IEEE Trans Ind Electron. 2001;48(1):4–17.

[21] Lee H, Kim E, Kang H-J, Park M. Design of a sliding mode controller with fuzzy sliding surfaces. In: IEE Proceedings - Control Theory and Applications. 1998. pp. 411–8.

[22] Eker I. Sliding mode control with PID sliding surface and experimental application to an electromechanical plant. ISA Trans. 2006;45(1):109–18.

[23] Kowalska O, Kamiński M, Szabat K. Implementation of a sliding-mode controller with an integral function and fuzzy gain value for the electrical drive with an elastic joint. IEEE Trans Ind Electron. 2010;57(4):1309–17.

[24] Mondal S, Mahanta C. Nonlinear sliding surface based second order sliding mode controller for uncertain linear systems. Commun Nonlinear Sci Numer Simul. 2011;16(9):3760–9.

[25] Raman R, Chalanga A, Kamal S, Bandyopadhyay B. Nonlinear sliding surface based adaptive sliding mode control for industrial emulator. In: IEEE International Conference on Industrial Technology (ICIT). 2013. pp. 124–9.

[26] Corke PI. Robotics, Vision & Control: Fundamental Algorithms in Matlab. Springer US; 2011.

[27] Armstrong B, Khatib O, Burdick J. The explicit dynamic model and inertial parameters of the PUMA 560 arm. In: Proceedings 1986 IEEE International Conference on Robotics and Automation. 1986. pp. 510–8.

[28] Sahin T, Zergeroglu E. Adaptive 3D Visual Servo Control of Robot Manipulators via Composite Camera Inputs. Turkish J Electr Eng Comput Sci. 2006;14(2).

[29] Mansard N, Chaumette F. Task sequencing for high-level sensor-based control. IEEE Trans Robot. 2007;23(1):60–72.

Chapter 11

Using NI-USB Data Acquisition Systems to Study the Switching Phenomena of Reactive Loads

Niculescu Titu, Marcu Marius, Niculescu Vlad and Popescu Florin Gabriel

Additional information is available at the end of the chapter

http://dx.doi.org/10.5772/62349

Abstract

The chapter presents a new and modern method to study the transient phenomena that occur when connecting the reactive charges to an AC power source using the MATLAB-Simulink software package. It is known that NI-USB data acquisition systems manufactured by National Instruments are not recognized by the Simulink software package in 64-bit systems. That is why a 32-bit system is obligatory. From this point of view, the article presents a method by which this disadvantage is eliminated, making the data acquisition process possible in the Simulink software package.

Keywords: capacitive circuit, data acquisition, diagrams, electrical diagram, MATLAB-Simulink, NI-USB

1. Introduction

Data acquisition systems of the NI-USB type, manufactured by National Instruments, allow real-time evaluation of analog measurements in various practical situations. These quantities can be read by the MATLAB software but cannot be processed in Simulink because MathWorks Incorporated does not offer support for this software in 64-bit systems. The chapter presents a method that makes this possible and studies the case when an inductive-capacitive load is connected to a voltage power source, with a data acquisition system in Simulink on 64-bit systems. In this scope, we will consider an RLC series circuit with concentrated parameters, which are connected to an AC power source.

INTECH
open science | open minds

© 2016 The Author(s). Licensee InTech. This chapter is distributed under the terms of the Creative Commons Attribution License (http://creativecommons.org/licenses/by/3.0), which permits unrestricted use, distribution, and reproduction in any medium, provided the original work is properly cited.

This scenario occurs in practice in case one wants to connect an electrical equipment that includes capacitors to an AC power source. In this case, over voltages or over currents can occur during transient regime, which can cause problems in systems sizing.

2. Theoretical considerations

The differential equation for transitory phenomena is presented below:

$$iR + L\frac{di}{dt} + \frac{1}{C}\int idt = U_m \sin(\omega t + \psi) \tag{1}$$

where R is the circuit resistance, L is the circuit inductance, C is the capacity of circuit, and Ψ is the initial phase of voltage when was connected the circuit. The current is denoted by i and the angular frequency by ω.

The most important and common regime is when the circuit resistance is very small, practically the resistance of the junction wires. This event is known in the scientific literature as an oscillating regime. If we consider the R resistance of circuit very small, the Laplace transform applied to this circuit conducts to the following solution [1], [7]:

$$i = I_m \cos(\omega t + \psi - \varphi_1) + \frac{DU_m e^{-\delta t}}{2\omega_e L} \cdot \left[\cos(\omega_e t - \gamma) - \frac{\delta}{\omega_e}\sin(\omega_e t - \gamma) \right] \tag{2}$$

$$u_C(t) = \frac{U_m \sin(\omega t + \psi - \varphi_1)}{C\omega\sqrt{R^2 + (\frac{1}{\omega C} - L\omega)^2}} + \frac{DU_m e^{-\delta t}}{2LC\omega_e^2}\sin(\omega_e t - \gamma) \tag{3}$$

where Equation (3) represents the voltage on the capacitor.

$$u_L(t) = L\frac{di}{dt} = -\omega L I_m \sin(\omega t + \Psi - \varphi_1) + \frac{DU_m}{2\omega_e} e^{-\delta t} \left[\frac{\delta^2 - \omega_e^2}{\omega_e}\sin(\omega_e t - \gamma) - 2\delta\cos(\omega_e t - \gamma) \right] \tag{4}$$

where Equation (4) represents the voltage on the coil, and δ is a dumping factor:

$$\delta = \frac{R}{2L} \tag{5}$$

and ω_0 is the resonance angular frequency of the circuit:

http://dx.doi.org/10.5772/62349

$$\omega_0 = \frac{1}{\sqrt{LC}} \tag{6}$$

The following notations are also used:

$$\omega_e = \sqrt{\omega_0^2 - \delta^2} \quad D = \sqrt{A^2 + B^2 - 2AB\ \cos(\beta - \alpha)} \quad tg\gamma = \frac{A\sin\alpha - B\sin\beta}{A\cos\alpha - B\cos\beta} \tag{7}$$

$$\alpha = \varphi_3 + \psi; \qquad \beta = \varphi_2 - \psi \tag{8}$$

$$\varphi_1 = arctg\frac{2\omega\delta}{\omega_0^2 - \omega^2} \quad \varphi_2 = arctg\frac{\delta}{\omega_e - \omega} \quad \varphi_3 = arctg\frac{\delta}{\omega_e + \omega} \tag{9}$$

$$A = \frac{1}{\sqrt{(1 + \frac{\omega}{\omega_e})^2 + (\frac{\delta}{\omega_e})^2}} \qquad B = \frac{1}{\sqrt{(1 - \frac{\omega}{\omega_e})^2 + (\frac{\delta}{\omega_e})^2}} \tag{10}$$

$$I_m = \frac{U_m}{\sqrt{R^2 + (\frac{1}{\omega C} - \omega L)^2}} \tag{11}$$

Due to the low value of the conductors' resistance, the regime is oscillating. Therefore, a high-frequency oscillation can be observed in the following charts, which overlaps the current and voltage curve at a 50 Hz frequency.

3. Interface circuits necessary for study of inductive loads

For the experimental evaluation of these parameters, a data acquisition system manufactured by National Instruments was used, namely, the NI USB-6003 type. The graphics and the electrical diagram presented in **Figures 1** and **2** were created using the MATLAB 2014b software. The inductive circuit is connected to the AC voltage through a capacitor C, and the DAQ input voltage levels are obtained using resistive dividers. A differential measurement was chosen to perform calculations.

To eliminate the risk of connecting directly the AC phase voltage to the input of the data acquisition system, symmetrical voltage dividers were used and the analog inputs of the measuring system were connected in parallel with the median divider resistors Ri0 and Ri1. To protect the analog inputs of data acquisition system to any voltage surge, the DZ Zener diodes were used (**Figure 3**) [8].

The measuring mode is a differential one, because it allows accurate measurements for low-voltage amplitudes (below 1 V).

The used system for data acquisition has the following important parameters:

- 8 analog inputs (16-bit resolution, 100 kS/s);
- 2 analog outputs (16-bit, 5 kS/s/ch); 13 digital I/O lines; one 32-bit counter;
- Lightweight and BUS powered for easy portability;
- Easy to install sensors and signals with screw-terminal connectivity.

The system is compatible with MATLAB software but not with the Simulink package, because the Data Acquisition Toolbox package does not appear in its graphical interface on 64-bit operating systems.

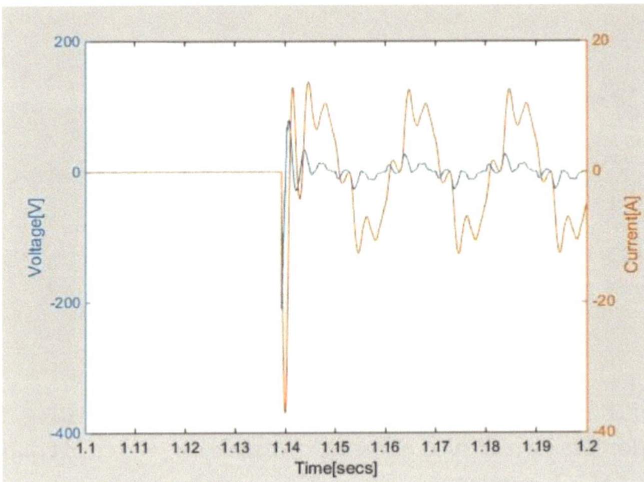

Figure 1. Connecting an inductive capacitive load.

To study switching transient inductive-capacitive loads, two situations were considered to be representative:

- **Connecting** an inductive-capacitive load to an alternating power supply made with the following values of electrical parameters:

U=220 V; *R*=1.2 Ω; *L*=2 mH; *C*=100 μF.

In this case the diagram from **Figure 1** is obtained.

- **Disconnecting** an inductive capacitive load from an alternating power supply made with the following values of electrical parameters:

U=220 V; *R*=1.2 Ω; *L*=90 mH; *C*=100 μF.

In this case, the diagram from **Figure 2** is obtained.

```
s=daq.createSession('ni');

addAnalogInputChannel(s,'Dev1', 0, 'Voltage');

addAnalogInputChannel(s,'Dev1', 1, 'Voltage');

s.Rate=45,000;

s.DurationInSeconds=1.5;

[data,time]=s.startForeground;

figure;

data(:,1)=data(:,1)*163;

data(:,2)=data(:,2)*27;

[ax,p1,p2]=plotyy(time,data(:,1),time,data(:,2),'plot');

ylabel(ax(1),'Voltage[V]'); % label left y-axis

ylabel(ax(2),'Current[A]'); % label right y-axis

xlabel('Time[secs]'); % label x-axis

grid;
```

Data acquisition is made with the Ni-USB 6003 system, which has a sampling frequency of 100 ks/s. The sequence of MATLAB program that reads current and voltage inputs and make data acquisition is shown as follows:

where 163 and 27 are values dependent on resistor values of interface from **Figure 3**. These values are dependent on the input resistive divider values of the measurement system (163 is the value of $2R_1/R_{i1}$ and 27 represents the value of $2R_0/R_{i0}$).

To run this code, it needs a system NI USB-6000 series connected to the PC and installing the driver from the National Instruments website. The first part of this code represent data acquisition with a rate of the 45 kS/s, and the acquisition time is 1.5 s. The second part of the code represents the plotting mode of voltage and current [6].

Because the acquisition time is relatively high (1.5 s), after the completion of the acquisition process, one can decrease this time to 0.1 s by focusing on the event (click **Edit figure>Axes properties…>xLimits**).

The sampling frequency is divided by two because there are two inputs to read. Therefore, it was used a sampling rate of 45 kS/s for each channel.

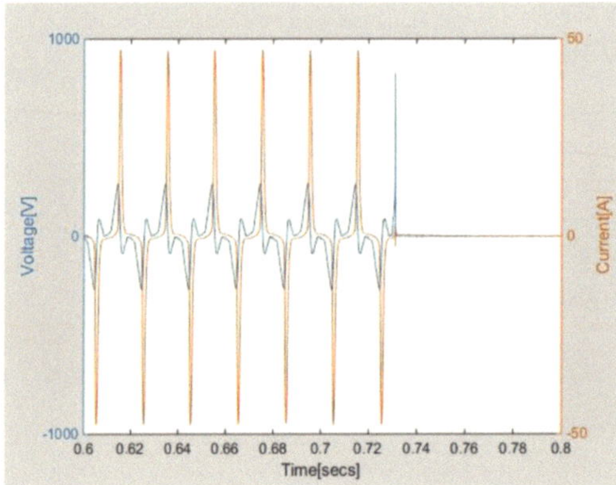

Figure 2. Disconnecting an inductive-capacitive load.

Connecting regime from **Figure 1** primarily highlights an oscillating process for current and coil voltage. In the first moment of connection, an over current appears, with a peak of over 30 A. The overvoltage peak is almost 200 V in the first moment, after which these values are stabilized to the oscillating values.

The disconnecting regime from **Figure 2** highlights a peak voltage that can be almost 1000 V. This value can be dangerous for consumers, connected to the alternating supply voltage. These overvoltages can cause the semiconductor destruction or insulation electric penetrations.

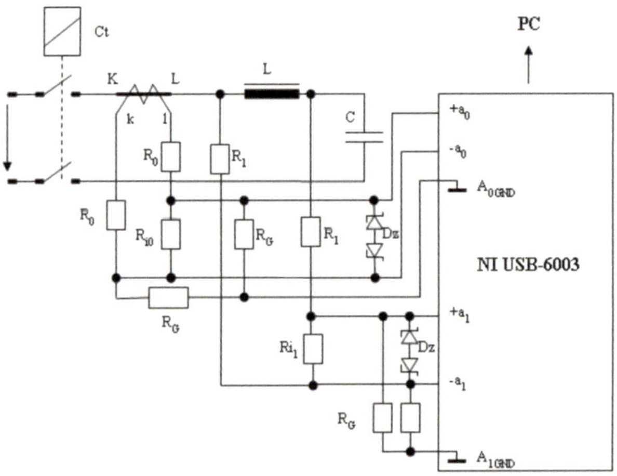

Figure 3. Electrical diagram of the measurement system for inductive loads.

http://dx.doi.org/10.5772/62349

4. Measurement processing in Simulink software package

Experimental measurements were made with a data acquisition system type NI USB-6003 with a rate of 100 kS/s, and the measurements were processed by the 2014b MATLAB version, which recognizes only data acquisition system in MATLAB, not in Simulink. Data processing in Simulink involves the following steps:

- It makes the appropriate data acquisition in MATLAB (using specific program lines for data acquisition system type);
- It saves the ***Workspace*** generated by the measurement (for further processing);
- The ***Data*** file from the ***Workspace*** opens;
- The ***Time*** file from the ***Workspace*** opens;
- Undock command is given to these files (**Figure 4**);
- The ***Time*** column is copied in the ***Data*** file and is placed at the beginning of the columns (**Figure 5**).
- It executes the **Dock *Variables*** command and saves the new ***Workspace***.

At this moment, the ***Data*** folder from the ***Workspace*** can be read from a Simulink simulation model (**Figure 6**).

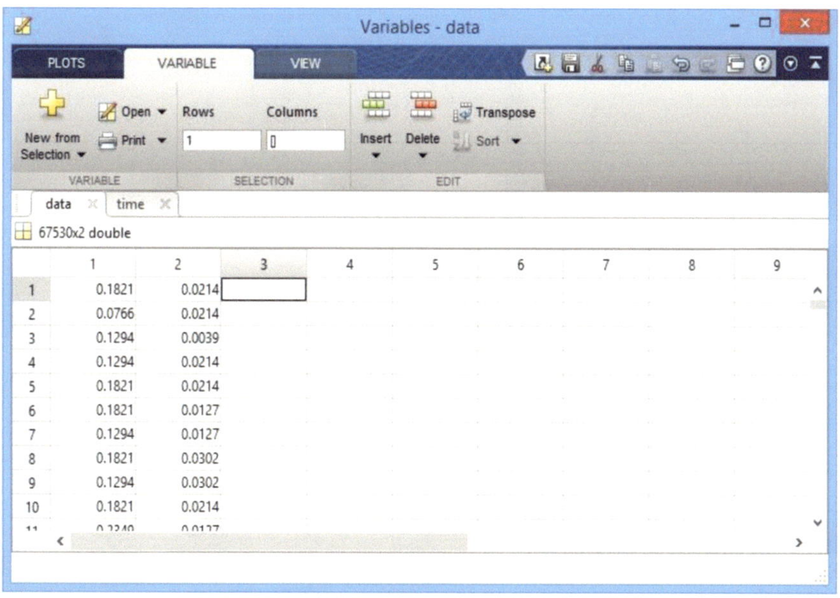

Figure 4. Original content of the ***Data*** folder from the ***Workspace***.

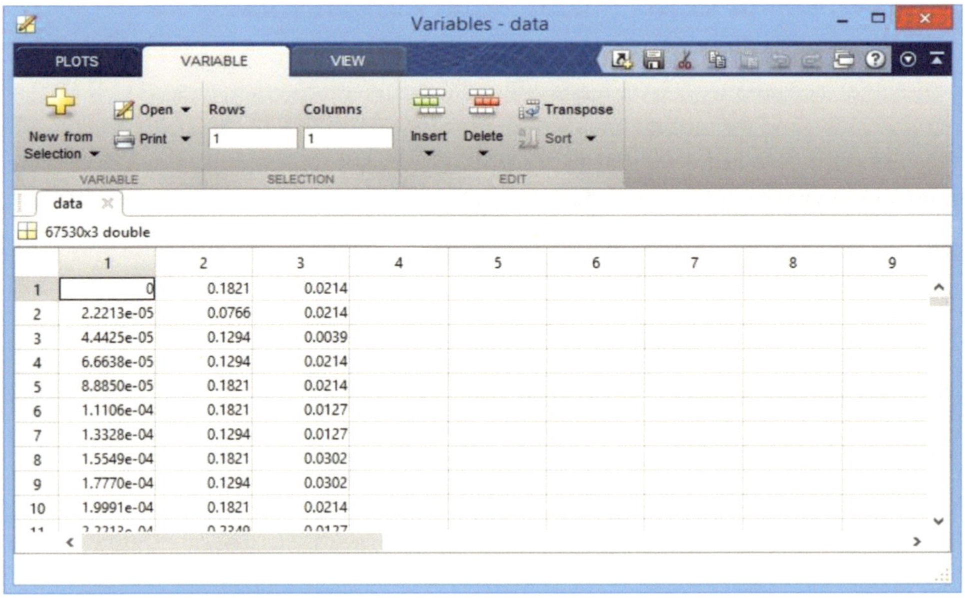

Figure 5. Modified content of the ***Data*** folder from the ***Workspace***.

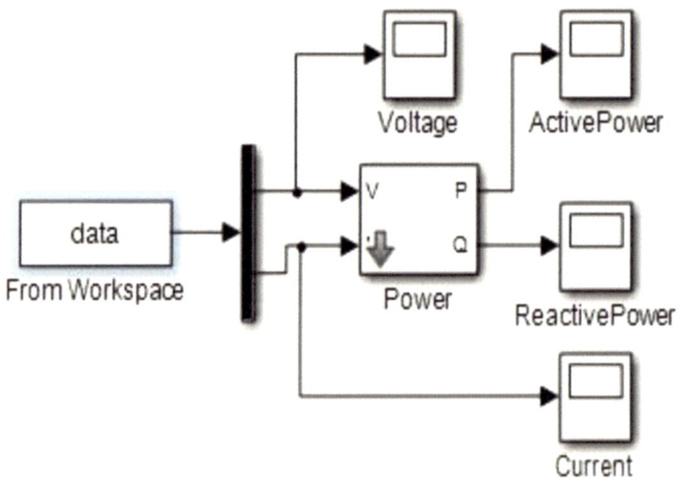

Figure 6. Simulink model for reactive load connecting.

5. Study of inductive loads

The first representative case for connecting the inductive-capacitive load leads to the following charts for the inductor voltage, circuit current, and the powers dissipated in the coil.

http://dx.doi.org/10.5772/62349

As one can observe, the coil voltage and current diagrams (**Figures 7** and **8**) show the identical dependences with **Figure 1** where the forms were obtained by data acquisition directly in MATLAB, by programming. The MATLAB program is presented in paragraph 3.

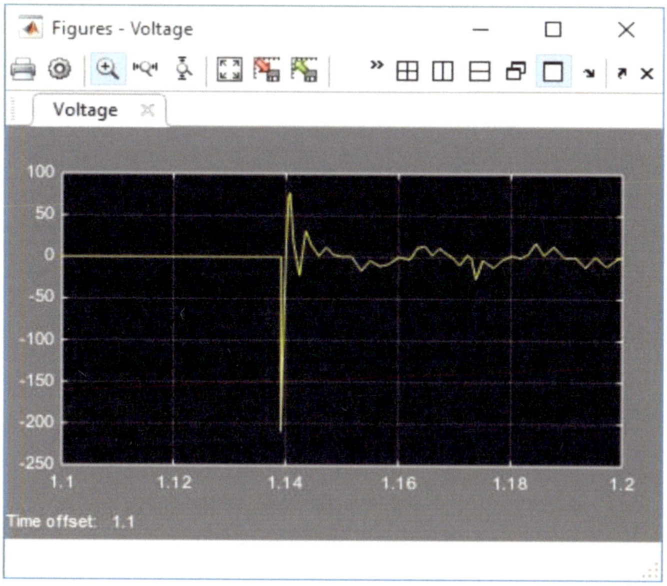

Figure 7. Voltage variation on coil when connection is initiated.

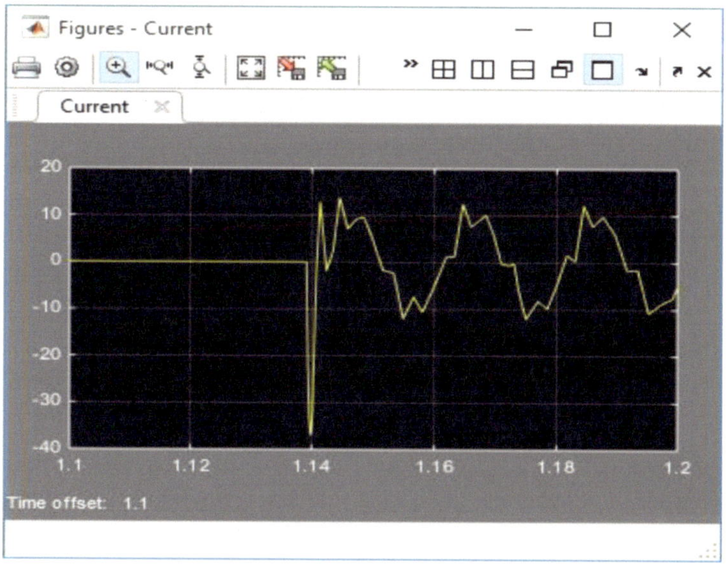

Figure 8. Current variation on coil at connecting.

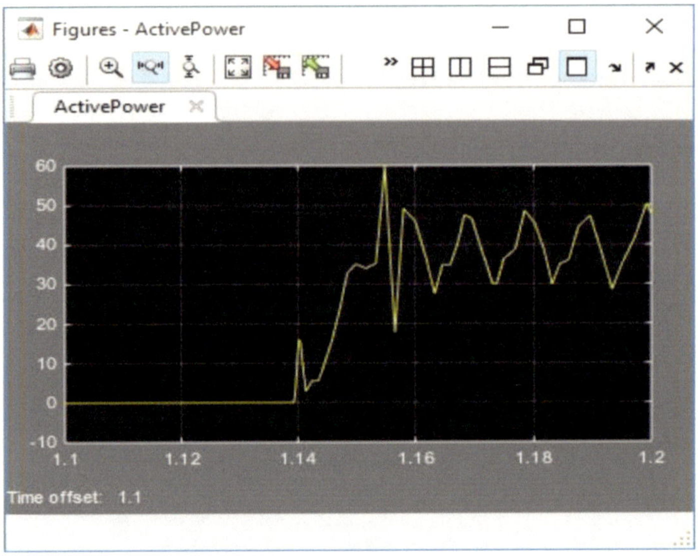

Figure 9. Active power variation on intern coil resistance at connecting.

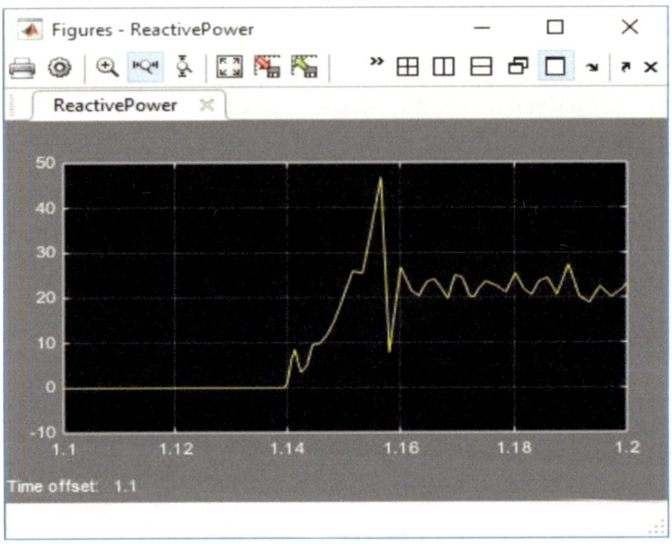

Figure 10. Reactive power variation on coil at connecting.

Figures 9 and **10** represent the diagrams of the active and reactive power variation during the commutation process. An inductive load of 2 mH was connected to an alternating power source.

Because of the capacitor, the oscillating process occurs in both the current curve and the coil voltage. The value of capacitance that made the connection process was of 100 μF. The voltage

http://dx.doi.org/10.5772/62349

oscillations and current circuit right after the connection was initiated are accompanied by the oscillations of active and reactive power. The measurement was done in the time interval of 1.1 to 1.2 s.

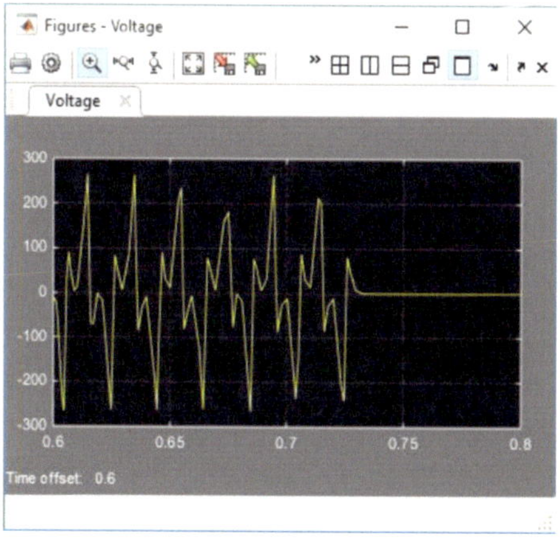

Figure 11. Voltage variation on coil upon disconnection.

If one considers the second case, the disconnection of inductive-capacitive load, Simulink model from **Figure 6** leads to the following diagrams for electrical quantities considered: the voltage variation on the coil at circuit disconnecting (**Figure 11**), the current variation in circuit at disconnecting (**Figure 12**), and active and reactive powers in this regime (**Figures 13** and **14**). As can be seen, coil voltage and current diagrams (**Figures 11** and **12**) show the identical dependences with **Figure 2** where the forms were obtained by data acquisition directly in MATLAB, by programming.

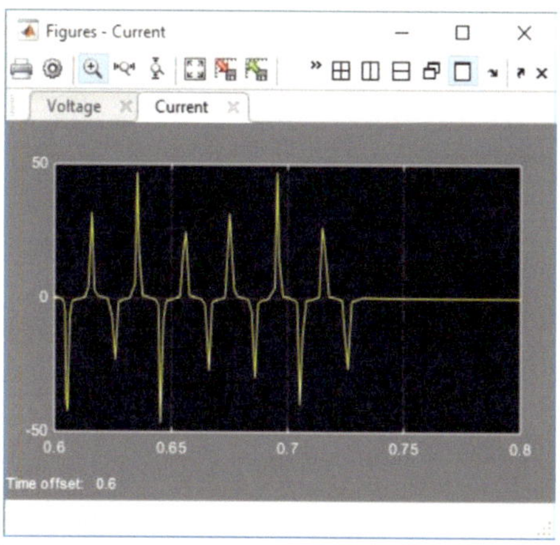

Figure 12. Current variation on coil upon disconnection.

The high-frequency oscillations of the voltage and current curves generate oscillations also in the two powers variation curves. The active and reactive powers dissipated on the coil upon disconnection are shown in **Figures 13** and **14**.

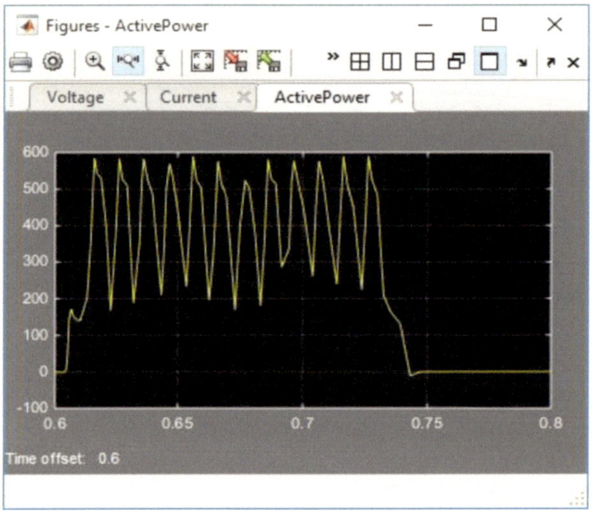

Figure 13. Active power variation on internal resistance of coil upon disconnection.

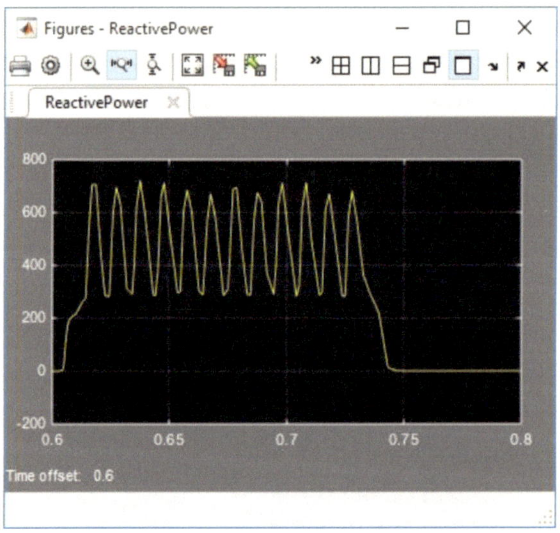

Figure 14. Reactive power variation on coil upon disconnection.

If we take into consideration the two regimes, connecting and disconnecting, from the first measurements, one can notice a reactive and active power peak in the powers chart. Then, these stabilize at oscillating constant values.

6. Interface circuits necessary for study of capacitive loads

For the study of transitory phenomena regarding capacitive loads, the interface circuits from **Figure 15** were used.

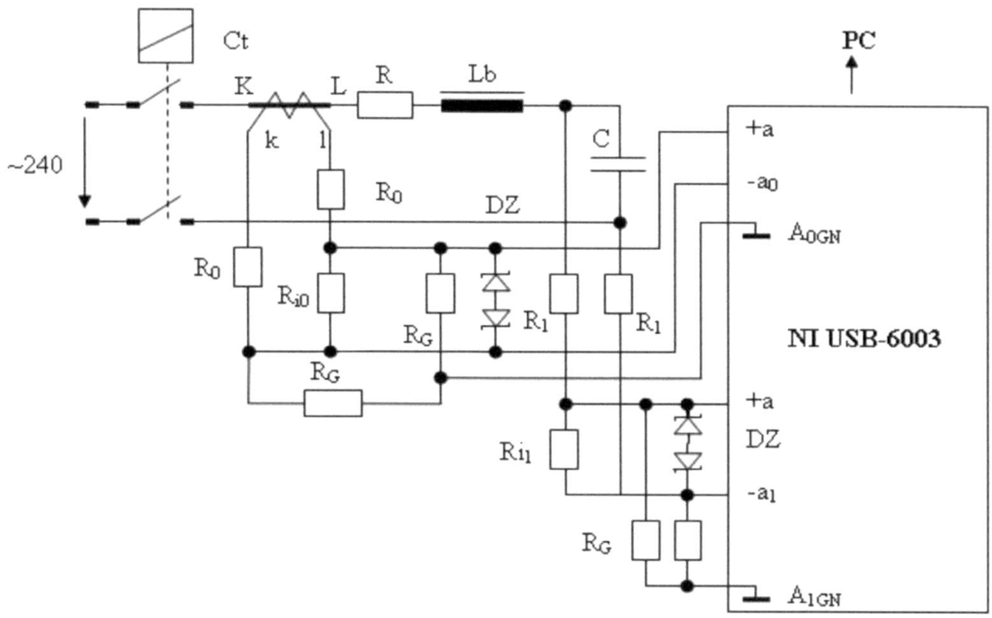

Figure 15. Electrical diagram of measurement system for capacitive loads.

The study of capacitive loads considered the case of connecting a capacitive load to an AC voltage power source through an inductivity.

The measuring circuit is similar to the one in **Figure 3**, differing by the fact that, on the input of acquisition system (−a1, +a1), the voltage on the C capacitor terminals is measured.

7. Study of capacitive loads

For the study of capacitive loads, take into consideration the case of connecting a capacitor to an AC voltage power source through an inductivity of 2 mH. The electrical parameters have the values:

- U=220 V;
- R=2 Ω;
- L=2 mH;
- C=100 μF;

The MATLAB code for the data acquisition is the same with the one used in paragraph 3, and as a result of its run, it was obtained from the diagram in **Figure 16**. This displays the current and voltage variation on capacitor in the same axis system.

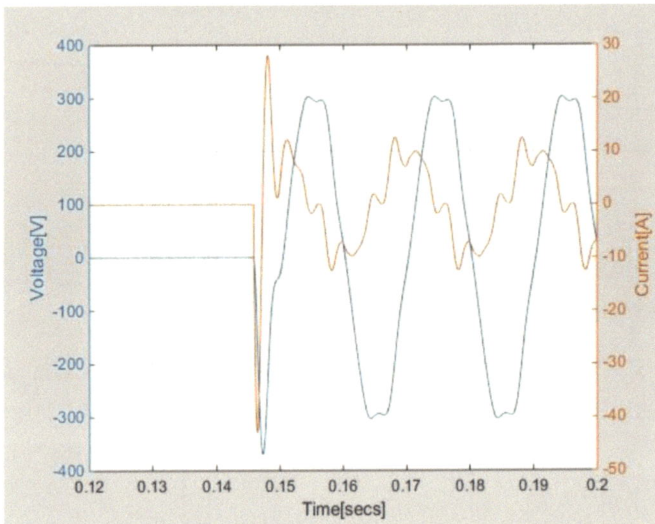

Figure 16. Variation of electrical parameters.

After Workspace processing, as described in paragraph 4, the Simulink model from **Figure 6** was used for the reading of this data, and the following charts were obtained. The capacitor voltage variation and current variation in the circuit are plotted in **Figures 17** and **18**.

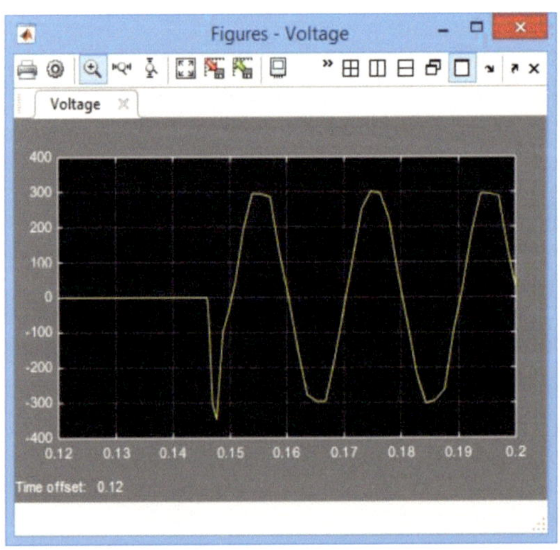

Figure 17. Capacitor voltage variation.

http://dx.doi.org/10.5772/62349

As seen in the voltage and current variation charts, a current peak appears in circuit, immediately after connection is initiated, and it can become dangerous for the other electrical equipment. This is accompanied by a small voltage peak, which disappears quite fast. In the current curve, a high-frequency oscillation can be noticed, which overlaps the current curve and disappears after a time.

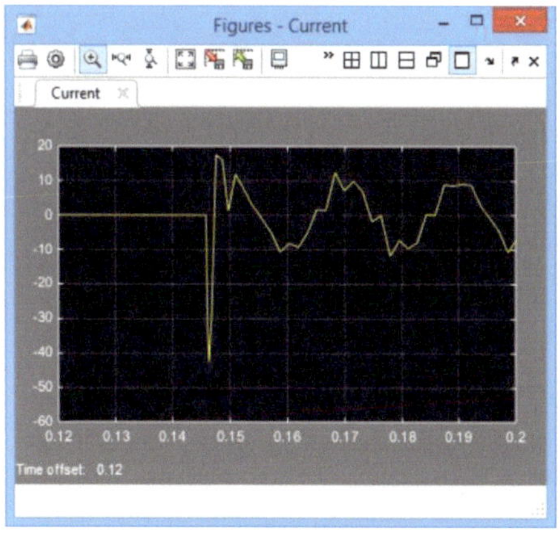

Figure 18. Capacitor current variation.

It must be noticed that these variation forms are dependent on the connecting moment, so they are dependent on the ψ angle from Equations (2) and (3).

Diagrams from **Figures 19** and **20** show the variation of the two dissipated powers. In **Figure 19**, the active power variation on the circuit resistance is plotted, and in **Figure 20**, the one of the reactive power dissipated on the capacitor.

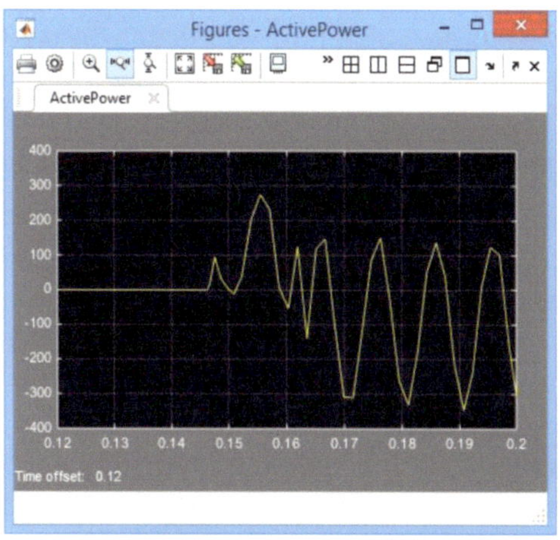

Figure 19. Active power variation.

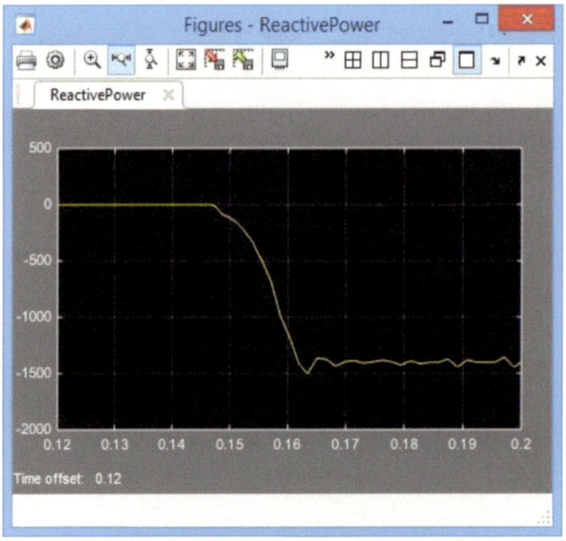

Figure 20. Reactive power variation.

Figure 19 highlights the active power oscillations, owing to current oscillations in the circuit. **Figure 20** highlights the fact that the reactive capacitor power is negative and its value can be read using the diagram. It is almost constant, with low oscillations around this value.

8. Conclusions

This analysis method allows the study of transient electrical phenomena on 64-bit operating systems. In this case, the Data Acquisition Toolbox package, which is specific to the 32-bit operating systems, does not appear in Simulink.

We have to mention that the transient regime for connecting the reactive loads to an AC power source depends on the moment of connecting, given by the Ψ angle from relations (2)–(4). In this paper, we considered a representative case of several measurements that emphasize the higher values of voltage and current occurring immediately after connecting.

The most dangerous regime is the oscillating regime and this is the most common regime that can be met in practice. In practice, this could be seen in the alternative power supply for electric motors, which includes the starting capacitor. In this case, oscillating overvoltage may occur and they need to be taken into account when sizing the systems. The value of these voltages depends on the connecting moment, which is the initial phase of the AC voltage. For the circuits designing and sizing phase, the overvoltage peaks occurring immediately after connection must be taken into account, which can endanger the internal isolation of the equipment. Overcurrent peaks in oscillatory regime can lead to the possible switching of protective relays.

It is important that the electric charge on the connected capacitor to be initially zero, otherwise a high value of over current may occur after the connecting moment.

http://dx.doi.org/10.5772/62349

In conclusion, it must be stressed that the proposed method can be applied to other Simulink models of greater complexity.

Author details

Niculescu Titu[1*], Marcu Marius[1*], Niculescu Vlad[2*] and Popescu Florin Gabriel[1*]

*Address all correspondence to: TituNiculescu@upet.ro, mariusmarcu@upet.ro, vlad.niculescu@cetti.ro, and floringpopescu@upet.ro

1 University of Petrosani, Petrosani, Romania

2 Politehnica University of Bucharest, Bucharest, Romania

References

[1] Ghe H. Electrical Devices. Ed.D.P. Bucharest, 1980.

[2] Ghinea M, Firteanu V. MATLAB, Numerical Calculus-Graphics-Applications. Ed. Teora, Bucharest 2000 2000.

[3] Nicolae Golovanov s.a. Electrical Energy Consumers. Materials, Measurements, Devices, Installations. Ed. AGIR, Bucharest, 2009.

[4] Titu N. Analysis of Electrical Circuits by Simulating in MATLAB Space. Ed. TehnoArt, Petrosani 2006.

[5] Titu N. Study of Inductive-Capacitive Series Circuits Using the Simulink Software Package. Publisher InTech, Technology and Engineering Applications of Simulink, Ed. InTech 2012, Chapter 2.

[6] Titu N. Study of Transient Phenomena Using NI-USB Data Acquisition Systems in MATLAB-Simulink Medium on 64bit Operating Systems. Journal of Advanced Computer Science & Technology. 2015, vol.4, pp.212-219, ID:4518.

[7] Titu N. Transitory phenomena in capacitive circuits connected to an AC source. In: Proceedings of the 4th International Conference on Circuits, Systems, Control, Signals —CSCS'13; Valencia, Spain; 2013. p. 162–166.

[8] Titu N, Marius M, Gabriel PF. Study of transitory phenomena at connecting the capacitive loads to an AC power source. Journal of Advanced Computer Science & Technology. 2015, vol.4, pp.198-203, ID:4518.

[9] Halunga-Fratu S, Fratu O. Simulation of Analog and Digital System Transmissions, Using MATLAB/SIMULINK Medium. Ed. MatrixRom, Bucharest 2004.

[10] Marinov A, Valchev V. Improved methodology for power loss measurements in power electronic switches using digital oscilloscope and MATLAB. 14th International Power Electronics and Motion Control Conference (EPE/PEMC), 6–8 September, Ohrid 2010.

[11] Czarnecki LS, Swietlicki T. Powers in nonsinusoidal networks: their interpretation, analysis, and measurement. IEEE Transactions on instrumentation and measurement, 39, 2, 1990.

[12] Willems JL. Mathematical foundations of the instantaneous power concepts: a geometrical approach. ETEP European Transactions on Electrical Power, 6, 5, 1996.

Chapter 12

Simulation of Discrete-Event Systems in MATLAB

Raul Campos-Rodriguez,
Mildreth Alcaraz-Mejia and Uriel Sanchez-Ramirez

Additional information is available at the end of the chapter

http://dx.doi.org/10.5772/63230

Abstract

The discrete-event systems (DES) are systems guided by asynchronous events rather than by the passage of the time as in traditional systems. There exists a wide set of systems that could be considered within this class, such as communication protocols, computer and microcontroller operating systems, flexible manufacturing systems, communication drivers for embedded applications and logistic systems, among others. Their proper study is a requirement for a suitable implementation of embedded hardware and software, for example. The aim of this chapter is to approach the simulation of this class of systems within the MATLAB/SIMULINK framework. A suitable simulation process, allowing the injection of input signals to the system and observing its output response, is a first step in the analysis of this class of systems, which may lead to more elaborated analysis such as reachability and deadlock avoidance. The advantage of the approach and techniques proposed in this chapter is the application of the set of tools, algorithms and visualization instruments present in the MATLAB/SIMULINK to the simulation of Discrete-Event Systems, which allows a simple integration of various DES by utilizing the matrices that define them. The concluding section of the chapter provides a link for downloading all the code for the examples developed here.

Keywords: discrete-event systems, analysis, modelling, simulation, MATLAB/SIMULINK

1. Introduction

The discrete-event systems (DES) are systems guided by asynchronous events rather than by the passage of time as in the traditional framework of Control Theory, for example [1]. There exists a wide set of systems that could be considered in the class of DES, such as operating systems

INTECH
open science | open minds

© 2016 The Author(s). Licensee InTech. This chapter is distributed under the terms of the Creative Commons Attribution License (http://creativecommons.org/licenses/by/3.0), which permits unrestricted use, distribution, and reproduction in any medium, provided the original work is properly cited. (cc) BY

of microprocessors and embedded microcontrollers, communication protocols such as IPv4/ IPv6, complex software architectures such as database management systems, production systems and flexible manufacturing systems (FMSs), delivering and logistic systems, among others. Their proper study is a requirement for the fulfillment of performance and safety requirements, for example. The traceability of requirements and its satisfaction is simplified by using a model that is suitable for a rigorous simulation process [2].

The aim of this chapter is to approach the simulation of DES within the MATLAB/SIMULINK framework. Analysis such as the application of random inputs to a DES and the visualization of system's output response are intended to be covered in this chapter. The overall goal is to enable the application of the set of tools, algorithms and visualization instruments present in the MATLAB/SIMULINK to the analysis of DES. There exist several approaches for the analysis of this class of systems. On the one hand, for example, empirical practices are used for addressing the problems that arise in the DES field. Most of these practices are based on experience and good knowledge among engineers in the daily execution of a system. On the other hand, in the formal point of view, scientists and engineers typically use mathematical tools based on automata theory, Petri nets (PN), Markov chains and Queue theory for addressing main aspects in the design and implementation of DES. The aspects most studied in the analysis of DES are the reachability and deadlock analysis, fault tolerance, control and observability schemes, to mention a few [3].

In recent years, the simulation methods have taken great relevance in the design and implementation of big systems. These methods allow engineers and scientists the study of complex behaviours by simulating in the lab different real-world scenarios. Intensive workload conditions, parametric variations, environmental changes and fault scenarios are possible to investigate by simulation methods. Statistical information, performance curves, and parameter optimization are some of the possible results obtained by a simulation process.

2. Discrete-event systems (DES)

As mentioned in the introduction, within a DES the state evolution depends on the occurrence of events that are asynchronous in time. An event is an instantaneous action occurred in the context of the DES that is relevant for the understanding of the system. An occurrence of an event may cause an immediate change in the system state. For example, an event could be a package arriving by the network connection, a button pressed by the user at a control panel, a timer's overflow within an embedded device driver, a change in a Boolean flag within an Interrupt Service Routine, etc. By convention, it is supposed that no time is elapsed between the event occurrence and the change of the state in a DES.

Some examples of DES's include communication protocols, supply chains, queue systems, task schedulers, logistic systems, device drivers, memory managers, landing and take-off systems of airplanes, urban rail systems and subway, and line of manufacturing and production systems, among others. For a wide list of examples of DES, see [4].

http://dx.doi.org/10.5772/63230

The study of a DES is important for several reasons, including safety and economic issues, for example. There exist several approaches in the study of this class of systems. For example, there exist empirical practices for addressing the problems that arise in the DES. Most of these are based on experience and good knowledge among engineers in the daily execution of the DES. In the formal point of view, scientists and engineers use automata theory, PN, Markov chains and Queue theory for addressing main aspects in the design and implementation of DES, such as the modelling, reachability and deadlock analysis, fault tolerance, and control schemes, among other interesting properties [5, 6].

In recent years, the simulation methods have taken great relevance in the design and implementation of big systems. These methods allow engineers and scientists the study of complex behaviours by simulating in the lab different real-world scenarios. Intensive workload conditions, parametric variations, environmental changes and fault scenarios are possible to investigate by simulation methods. Statistical information, performance curves, and parameter optimization are some of the possible results obtained by a simulation process.

2.1. Modelling DES with finite state machines

The finite state machines (FSM) are one of the first and most used mathematical models for the representation of the dynamics of a DES. A FSM is an extension of the concept of the automaton [7]. The states and events are basic concepts in the construction of a FSM. It is supposed that at every time, the FSM is in one of a finite number of states and that an incoming event causes an immediate change in the state of the FSM. Formally, a FSM is defined by $G=(Q, \Sigma, \delta, q_0)$ where [8]:

- Q is a finite set of states,
- Σ is a finite set of input symbols called events,
- $\delta : Q \times \Sigma \rightarrow Q$ is a partial relation called the state-transition function,
- q_0 is the initial state and is in Q.

As a graphical representation, the states are depicted as circles or ovals, while the events are represented as labelled arrows from one "source" state to other "destination" state. The initial state q_0 is designated by an incoming arrow, usually thicker than the other, with no source state.

Alternatively, the definition of a FSM may include a set of "marked states" designated as Q_m which represents the "acceptable" or "suitable" states of a DES. Moreover, an extension to the state-transition function may include subsets of Q as its range, allowing the representation of a non-deterministic FSM. For simplicity of the code implemented in this work, the deterministic definition of a FSM with no marked states is considered. The modification of the code here developed for the inclusion of those cases is not hard to achieve.

Figure 1 depicts a FSM model of the basic functionality of a typical microwave oven adapted from [9]. The initial state is Idle, as denoted by the thicker incoming arrow to s_1, where the oven performs no activity, and it is waiting for the buttons pressed by the user. The events that the user may execute in the system are denoted by the labels over the arrows. For example, at the "Idle" state the user may press the "Full Power" button (e_1) that causes a change to the state s_2 "Full Power on."

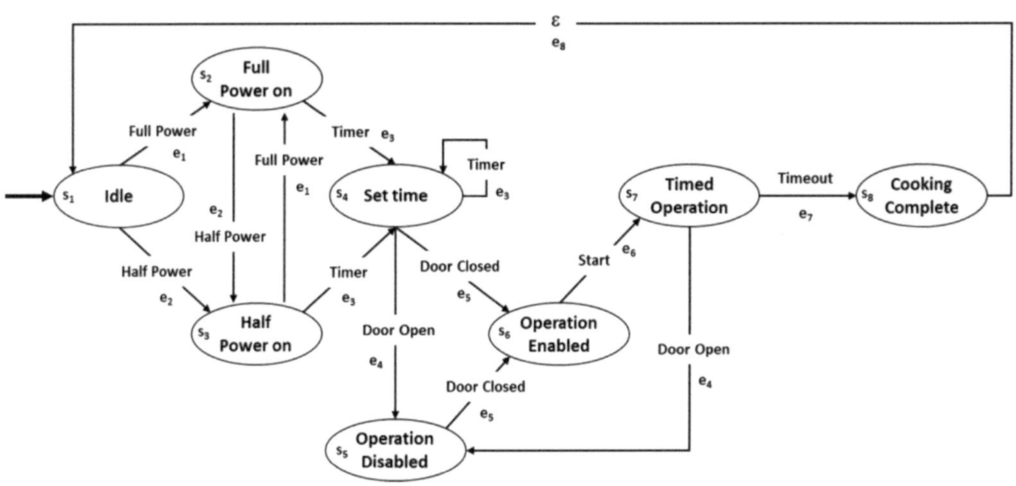

Figure 1. A FSM model of a microwave oven. The initial state is determined by the bold incoming arrow to s_1 which corresponds to Idle. The system events are labelled over the arrows and designated as e_i for $i=1\ldots8$ for an easy implementation. Similarly, the states are designated as s_j for $j=1\ldots8$.

Then the user may set the time for the cooking process at the "Set Time" state. For security reasons, if the door is opened, the operation of the oven is disabled, otherwise it is enabled. At the "Operation Enabled" state, i.e. s_6, if the user presses the "Start" button, the cooking process begins. Any opening of the oven's door immediately disables its operation. After a timeout event, the cooking process is completed and the FSM is restarted to its initial state ready for the next operations.

For simplicity in the construction of the state-event matrix, the labels s_i for i=1, ..., 8 and e_j for j=1, ..., 8, have been added to the FSM model representing the state and event, respectively. The initial state of the FSM in **Figure 1** is q_0=e_1 while the state-event matrix is the following:

http://dx.doi.org/10.5772/63230

$$\begin{array}{c} \\ s_1 \\ s_2 \\ s_3 \\ s_4 \\ s_5 \\ s_6 \\ s_7 \\ s_8 \end{array} \begin{array}{c} \begin{array}{cccccccc} e_1 & e_2 & e_3 & e_4 & e_5 & e_6 & e_7 & e_8 \end{array} \\ \begin{bmatrix} s_2 & s_3 & 0 & 0 & 0 & 0 & 0 & 0 \\ 0 & s_3 & s_4 & 0 & 0 & 0 & 0 & 0 \\ s_2 & 0 & s_4 & 0 & 0 & 0 & 0 & 0 \\ 0 & 0 & s_4 & s_5 & s_6 & 0 & 0 & 0 \\ 0 & 0 & 0 & 0 & s_6 & 0 & 0 & 0 \\ 0 & 0 & 0 & 0 & 0 & s_7 & 0 & 0 \\ 0 & 0 & 0 & s_5 & 0 & 0 & s_8 & 0 \\ 0 & 0 & 0 & 0 & 0 & 0 & 0 & s_1 \end{bmatrix} \end{array}$$

By using the information of the initial state and the state-event matrix, the next section provides a way of simulating an arbitrary FSM by the implementation of an S-Function in MATLAB. Before addressing the details of the implementation, the following subsection considers another useful method based on PN for the modelling of a DES.

2.2. Modelling DES with PN

A PN is another mathematical tool widely used for the design, the modelling, and the simulation of a DES [10]. The modelling process of a DES with a PN is quite natural and intuitive, due to its graphical representation as in the case of FSM. One advantage of the PN modelling technique is the compact representation of the systems. Moreover, the PN formalism resides in a strong mathematical basis from the linear algebra. Formally, a PN model is a pair (B, M_0), where B is a Petri net structure (PNS) $\{P, T, F\}$, such that:

- $P=\{p_1, p_2, \cdots, p_m\}$ is a finite set of places;
- $T=\{t_1, t_2, \cdots, t_n\}$ is a finite set of transitions;
- $F=I \cup O$ is a flow relation, where $I(p_i, t_j) \to \mathbb{N}^+$ and $O(t_i, p_i) \to \mathbb{N}^+$ are the input and output functions;
- $M_0 \in (\mathbb{N}^+)^m$ is a special vector known as the initial marking of the net, where $m = |P|$.

Pictorially, circles represent the places, while rectangles or bars, represent the transitions. The flow relation $F=I \cup O$, is represented as directed arcs or arrows. On the other hand, the matrices $B^-(i, j) := I(p_i, t_j)$ and $B^+(i, j) := O(t_i, p_i)$, capture the structure of the flow function, while $B := B^+ - B^-$, represents the incidence matrix of the PN. Thus, B is a matrix of size $[m \times n]$, where m is the number of places, and n the number of transitions. The net's state, or marking, is a vector $M(k) \in (\mathbb{N}^+)^m$, where m is the number of places in the PN. A marking represents the state of the net at time k, i.e., the number of tokens in each place at the time k.

In the classical definition of a PN, the number of tokens cannot be negative. Also, it is supposed that the index k is updated at every time that an event occurs. For simplicity, the marking $M(k)$ is represented by using subscripts as M_k, and $M_k(p_i)$, $p_i \in P$ for representing the number of tokens in place p_i at the time k. The *initial marking* M_0 represents an initial tokens distribution over the net's places. Thus, $M_0(p_i)$ for $p_i \in P$, represents the initial number of tokens in place p_i. The marking M_0 may enable one or more transitions to be fired. An *enabled* transition $t_i \in T$ at the marking M_0, denoted by $[M_0\rangle_t$, is one that fulfils $M_0(p_j) \geq B^-(p_j, t_i)$, $\forall\, p_j \in P$. Given any marking, say M_k, the set of all its enabled transitions is simply denoted as $[M_k\rangle$. The firing of enabled transitions leads to the dynamic behaviour of a PN, captured by the state equation:

$$M_{k+1} = M_k + B\vec{u}_k$$

The interpretation of the previous equation is as follows. The marking M_k, of size $[m \times 1]$, represents the system state at time k. The vector $\vec{u}_k$, of size $[n \times 1]$, represents the firing of one or more enabled transitions by the marking M_k. The matrix B, of size $[m \times n]$, is the incidence matrix of the net. The vector M_{k+1} represents the state reached by net's evolution. If $[M_k\rangle t_i$ and t_i is fired, then using (1), the net reaches a new marking computed as $M_{k+1} = M_k + B\vec{t}_i$. In this equation, $\vec{u}_k = \vec{t}_i$ is a vector with a one in the $i-th$ position and zero anywhere else. This marking's evolution is denoted as $M_k \xrightarrow{t_i} M_{k+1}$, in order to emphasize the fact that from marking M_k the net fires t_i and reaches M_{k+1}. The marking evolutions may consecutively enable other transitions to be fired, which leads to the concept of reachability set of a PN. The reachability set of the PN (B, M_0) is denoted by $R(B, M_0)$, for emphasizing the fact that it depends on initial condition M_0. Thus, $R(B, M_0)$ is the set of all markings M_k evaluated by (1), by only considering the firing of enabled transitions. A firing transition sequence of the PN (B, M_0) is a sequence of transitions $\sigma = t_i t_j t_k \cdots t_l$ such that $M_0 \xrightarrow{t_i} M_1 \xrightarrow{t_j} M_2 \xrightarrow{t_k} \cdots M_l \xrightarrow{t_l} M_s$, where the length of σ, denoted by $|\sigma|$, is the number of its transitions. If the number of transitions in σ is not finite, then $|\sigma| = \infty$. A short representation for this trajectory is $M_0 \xrightarrow{\sigma} M_s$, for highlighting the fact that from M_0, the net fires σ, and reaches M_s. If $M_k \xrightarrow{\sigma} M_s$ for some M_k and σ, then $[M_k\sigma$ means that the marking M_k, enables the firing of the entire sequence σ.

The Parikh Vector $\vec{\sigma} \in \mathbb{N}^m$ maps every transition in the set T to its number of occurrences in sequence σ. Thus, if $\sigma = t_i t_j t_i$ then, $\vec{\sigma}$ is a $n-vector$ with a two in the $i-th$ position, one on the $j-th$ position, and zero anywhere else. The firing language of an PN (B, M_0) is

$\mathcal{L}(B, M_0) := \{\sigma \in T^* \mid \sigma = t_i t_j t_k \ldots t_l\}$, such that $M_0 \xrightarrow{t_i} M_1 \xrightarrow{t_j} M_2 \xrightarrow{t_k} \cdots M_r \xrightarrow{t_l} M_s$, where T^* is the Kleen closure, as in automata theory [7], of the transition's set.

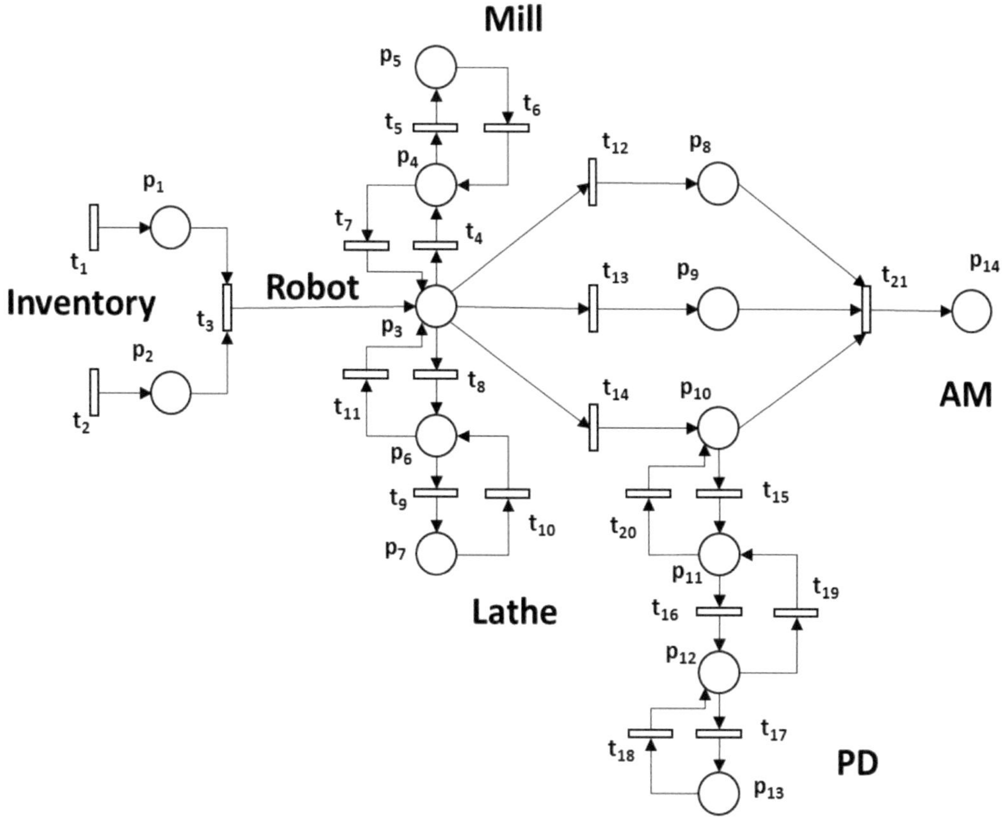

Figure 2. PN model representing a FMS. The system is composed of a mill machine, a lathe and a robot, connected through buffers. The incoming raw material arrives from the inventory to the robot's section. Then they are routed to the mill, lathe, painting or assembling stations.

Figure 2 represents a PN model of a FMS adapted from [11]. Be careful to not confuse the name of a FMS in this subsection with the name of a FSM of the previous one. It is composed of a robot arm (p_3), a mill machine (p_5), a lathe (p_7), a painting device (p_{13}) and an assembling machine (p_{14}). A set of buffers $\{p_1, p_2, p_4, p_6, p_8, p_9, p_{10}, p_{12}\}$ connects together the system. The FMS is able to process different components at the intermediate stages, which are lastly assembled at the AM stage (p_{14}). The firing of t_1 and t_2 represents the arriving of raw material from a non-depleting inventory, which is aleatory. It was interpreted and adapted from its original layout in [11]. The incidence matrix of the PN is of size $B[14\times21]$, while the initial marking $M_0[14]$ is a zero vector, meaning that the FSM is empty. The incidence matrix B of the FMS is the following:

$$
\begin{bmatrix}
1 & 0 & -1 & 0 & 0 & 0 & 0 & 0 & 0 & 0 & 0 & 0 & 0 & 0 & 0 & 0 & 0 & 0 & 0 & 0 & 0 \\
0 & 1 & -1 & 0 & 0 & 0 & 0 & 0 & 0 & 0 & 0 & 0 & 0 & 0 & 0 & 0 & 0 & 0 & 0 & 0 & 0 \\
0 & 0 & 1 & -1 & 0 & 0 & 1 & -1 & 0 & 0 & 1 & -1 & -1 & -1 & 0 & 0 & 0 & 0 & 0 & 0 & 0 \\
0 & 0 & 0 & 1 & -1 & 1 & -1 & 0 & 0 & 0 & 0 & 0 & 0 & 0 & 0 & 0 & 0 & 0 & 0 & 0 & 0 \\
0 & 0 & 0 & 0 & 0 & -1 & 0 & 0 & 0 & 0 & 0 & 0 & 0 & 0 & 0 & 0 & 0 & 0 & 0 & 0 & 0 \\
0 & 0 & 0 & 0 & 0 & 0 & 0 & 1 & -1 & 1 & -1 & 0 & 0 & 0 & 0 & 0 & 0 & 0 & 0 & 0 & 0 \\
0 & 0 & 0 & 0 & 0 & 0 & 0 & 0 & 1 & -1 & 0 & 0 & 0 & 0 & 0 & 0 & 0 & 0 & 0 & 0 & 0 \\
0 & 0 & 0 & 0 & 0 & 0 & 0 & 0 & 0 & 0 & 0 & 0 & 0 & 0 & 0 & 0 & 0 & 0 & 0 & 0 & -1 \\
0 & 0 & 0 & 0 & 0 & 0 & 0 & 0 & 0 & 0 & 0 & 0 & 0 & 0 & 0 & 0 & 0 & 0 & 0 & 0 & -1 \\
0 & 0 & 0 & 0 & 0 & 0 & 0 & 0 & 0 & 0 & 0 & 0 & 0 & 1 & -1 & 0 & 0 & 0 & 0 & 1 & -1 \\
0 & 0 & 0 & 0 & 0 & 0 & 0 & 0 & 0 & 0 & 0 & 0 & 0 & 0 & 1 & -1 & 0 & 0 & 1 & -1 & 0 \\
0 & 0 & 0 & 0 & 0 & 0 & 0 & 0 & 0 & 0 & 0 & 0 & 0 & 0 & 0 & 1 & -1 & 1 & -1 & 0 & 0 \\
0 & 0 & 0 & 0 & 0 & 0 & 0 & 0 & 0 & 0 & 0 & 0 & 0 & 0 & 0 & 0 & 1 & -1 & 0 & 0 & 0 \\
0 & 0 & 0 & 0 & 0 & 0 & 0 & 0 & 0 & 0 & 0 & 0 & 0 & 0 & 0 & 0 & 0 & 0 & 0 & 0 & 1
\end{bmatrix}
$$

The next section is devoted to the implementation of suitable functions for the integration of FSM models as well as PN models into a Simulink model.

3. Simulating DES in MATLAB

The S-functions are a mechanism in the MATLAB environment for extending the capabilities of SIMULINK. By writing an S-function, the user is able to implement complex behaviours of real systems that directly interact with other blocks in a SIMULINK model. The S-function API defines the structure of an S-function and accepts MATLAB, C, C++ or FORTRAN as coding languages. The S-function is compiled as MEX files, which are linked, loaded and executed dynamically. By using a special syntax, it is possible to write functions for continuous, discrete and hybrid systems. Moreover, with a proper solver and a suitable integration step, the modelling and simulation of a DES is possible with accuracy and great detail. The SIMULINK library provides a block called S-Function as a placeholder for the user defined S-functions. The block includes a dialog box where it is possible to specify the file containing the function and its parameters.

There are two different categories for the S-functions, called Level-1 and Level-2. Each of them has its advantages and disadvantages. A detailed comparison among them is out of the scope of this chapter. An interested reader may refer to the MATLAB documentation for more information. The Level-2 is the newest category and is the one used in the rest of this work. The functions are written in MATLAB as m-files.

The name of the m-file has to be that of the function it implements and has to include five standard sections. The *setup* section is executed in the initialization stage of the simulation process and allows specifying the number of inputs, outputs, states and parameters, among other characteristics of the function. The *DoPostPropSetup* is executed after the setup and allows defining the blocks of memory used by the function. It also allows the definition of discrete state variables. The *InitConditions* section specifies the initial conditions of the block, while the *output* section specifies the outputs it produces in the sense of the control theory. The *Update* is perhaps the most important section since it is the place where the system's dynamic is implemented. The Update and Output section are executed at every integration step in the simulation process.

3.1. Implementing the FSM dynamics

The state-event matrix of a FSM captures its behaviour and allows a straightforward implementation of its dynamics within a SIMULINK model. Following the structure of an S-function, the next code provides an overview of the main aspects of its implementation. The function is called my_fsm and corresponds with the file name.

```
function my_fsm(block)
% Level-2 M file S-Function for the implementation of a FSM
% dynamics. inherited sample time demo.
%   $Parameter:
%            -State-Event Matrix D
%            -Initial State d0
%   $Revision: 0.1 $

  setup(block);

%endfunction
```

The setup defines the number of input parameters and its characteristics, among others.

```
function my_fsm(block)
...
function setup(block)
%% Set the number of input parameters
block.NumDialogPrms   =       2;
%% Register the number of input and output ports
block.NumInputPorts   =       1;
block.NumOutputPorts  =       1;
        ...
%% Set the properties of the input port. The vector dimension is one
%% since it is equal to an input symbol in the FSM alphabet
block.InputPort(1).Dimensions        =       1;
block.InputPort(1).DirectFeedthrough = false;
%% Set the properties of the output port. The vector dimension is
%% one since it is equal to the current state of the FSM
block.OutputPort(1).Dimensions       =       1;
...
%endfunction setup
```

The DoPostPropSetup allows defining the state of the FSM that has to be preserved during the simulation process. Since this implementation is for a deterministic FSM, it is one dimensional and used as discrete state. The name is chosen conveniently to be "State."

The InitConditions allows defining which of the states of the FSM is selected as initial. The initial state is provided by the user as the second parameter of the block.

```
function InitConditions(block)
%% Initialize Dwork State to d0, which corresponds to the second
%% input parameter
block.Dwork(1).Data = block.DialogPrm(2).Data;

%endfunction
```

The Output function returns the current state of the FSM, which is stored in the 24 DWork vector previously defined in the DoPostPropSetup section.

```
function Output(block)
%% Outputs the PN marking Mk
block.OutputPort(1).Data = block.Dwork(1).Data;

%endfunction
```

Finally, the Update section implements the change of state experiments by a FSM due to the input signals it receives. For this purpose, the state-event matrix is represented with the rows labelled as the states of the FSM while the columns are labelled as its events. To simplify the codification within a MATLAB function, only integers are used for representing both the state as well as the events. In this way $D(1, 2)=3$ means that when the FSM is in the state one, i.e. s_1, and the input is the event two, i.e. e_2, then the FSM reaches the state three, i.e. s_3. When $D(i, j)=0$ means that at the $i-th$ state, the $j-th$ event is not defined, and accordingly, the state of the FSM is not changed. By assuming this convention in the codification of the FSM, the next code is straightforward and implements the change of state in a FSM due to the incoming events.

http://dx.doi.org/10.5772/63230

```
function Update(block)
%% Get the dimensions of the state-event matrix D[m,n] of the FSM
m = size(block.DialogPrm(1).Data,1);          %% states
n = size(block.DialogPrm(1).Data,2);          %% events
%% Get the current state of the FSM
currentState = block.Dwork(1).Data;
%% Get the incoming event of the FSM
currentEvent = block.InputPort(1).Data;
%% Compute the next state based on the current state and event
nextState = block.DialogPrm(1).Data(currentState,currentEvent);
%% Verify that there is a state update
if         (nextState >        0)
    block.Dwork(1).Data = nextState;
end

          %endfunction
```

3.2. FSM simulation example

The function my_fsm detailed in the previous subsection is used for the simulation of the FSM of **Figure 1**. The state-event matrix is coded as a matrix $D[8\times8]$ of integer where every entry represents a state, as discussed in the previous subsection. Thus, for example, $D(1, 1)=2$, as expected according to the FSM in **Figure 1**. The ε event from "Cooking Complete" to "Idle", i.e. from s_8 to s_1, is coded as e_8. That is, the event e_8 corresponds to the last column in the state-event matrix. The entire matrix coded in the MATLAB workspace is:

$$D=\begin{bmatrix} 2 & 3 & 0 & 0 & 0 & 0 & 0 & 0 \\ 0 & 3 & 4 & 0 & 0 & 0 & 0 & 0 \\ 2 & 0 & 4 & 0 & 0 & 0 & 0 & 0 \\ 0 & 0 & 4 & 5 & 6 & 0 & 0 & 0 \\ 0 & 0 & 0 & 0 & 6 & 0 & 0 & 0 \\ 0 & 0 & 0 & 0 & 0 & 7 & 0 & 0 \\ 0 & 0 & 0 & 5 & 0 & 0 & 8 & 0 \\ 0 & 0 & 0 & 0 & 0 & 0 & 0 & 1 \end{bmatrix}$$

By using the above matrix D, **Figure 3** shows a SIMULINK model that integrates the my_fsm for simulating the FSM model of the microwave oven in the **Figure 1**. The FSM block encapsulates a Level-2 S-function block with the my_fsm S-function inside. The parameters are the matrix D and the initial state $d0=1$ defined in the MATLAB workspace in the same directory of the SIMULINK model. A random number generator, together with constant of one, represents the aleatory generation of events for the FSM block.

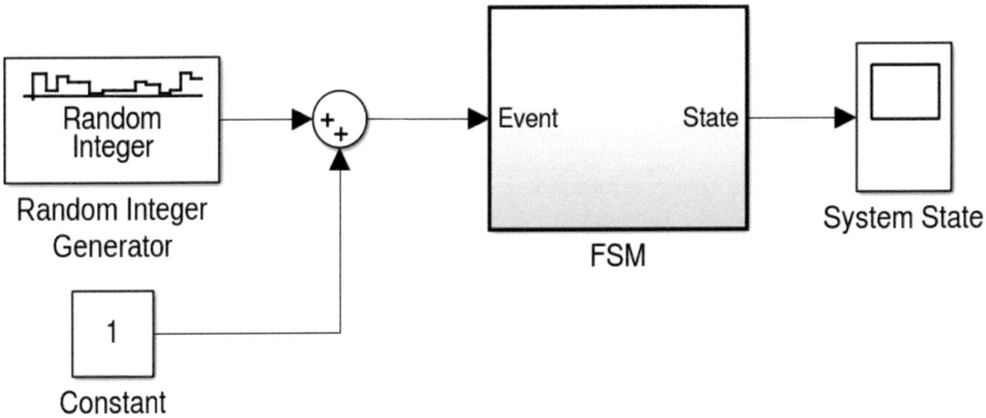

Figure 3. A SIMULINK model that uses the my_fsm function representing the microwave oven. The random integer generator produces a number in the range $[0, k-1]$ which represents the incoming events to the FSM model. The constant is added to avoid the generation of the zero event.

The constant is added to avoid the generation of the zero event which is meaningless in the context of the simulation process of the microwave oven. The FSM block clearly defines the input and output ports for the incoming events and system state, respectively. The scope allows the visualization of the events reached by the FSM as the process simulation evolves.

Figure 4 shows a simulation of 200 events of the microwave oven model in **Figure 3**. At the time zero, the FSM is in the state s_1, as defined by $d0=1$. Then, the system changes to the state s_3, which means that the incoming event was e_2, i.e. the user pressed the "Half Power" button in the oven panel. At that time, the simulation process shows that the user pressed the "Full Power" since the system state has down changed to s_2. Then, the system remains at the same state s_2 for some time. After that, the system state changes to s_3 again and it immediately moves to the state s_5 by briefly passing to the state s_4 before.

The system state remains at s_5 for a while and then it moves to the state s_6, then to s_7 and then back to s_5 again (the user opened the oven's door!).

Then, it seems that the user closed the door (e_5) and pressed the "Start" button (e_6). Thus, the cooking process ended above the event fifteen and the system state returns to its initial idle condition at s_1. Other interesting behaviours of the systems could be analysed from the chart. For example, it could be noticed that in a second execution, over the event 18, the oven was completing a more direct cooking process where the oven's door has not opened once the cooking process started. Above the event nineteen, the system returns to the idle state s_1. This could be considered a typical cooking process for a microwave oven.

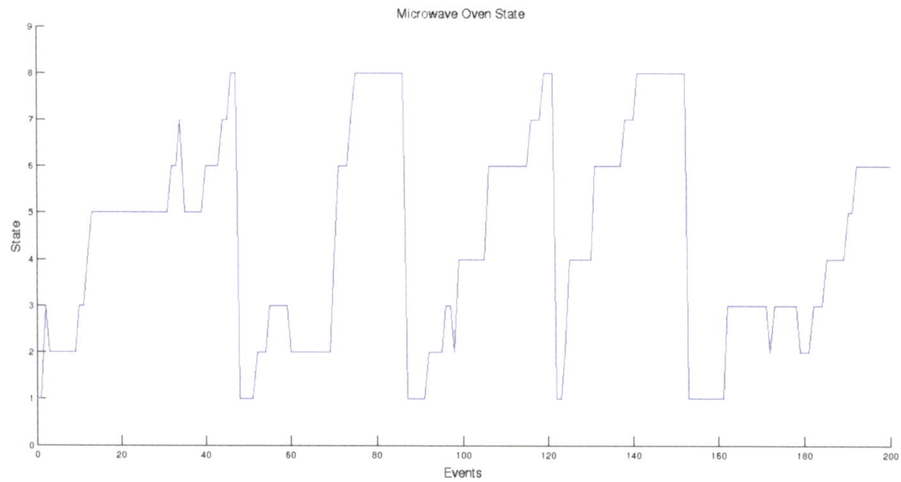

Figure 4. The different states of the FSM representing the microwave oven for a simulation process of 200 events. The chart shows four complete cocking process, represented by those reaching the state eight. The difference in those completed processes represents different action carried out by the user.

In a similar way, the chart in the **Figure 4** and others that may be obtained from different simulation processes of the model in **Figure 3** could be interpreted, allowing optimizations of the FSM behaviour to meet security and performance requirements.

3.3. Implementing the PN dynamics

The dynamic behaviour of a PN is governed by its state equation. The enabling condition for the transitions in a PN is an additional requirement for the trajectory evolutions in a model. The setup stage allows defining the size of the net model.

```
function my_ptn(block)
% Level-2 M file S-Function for the implementation of the PN
% dynamics. inherited sample time demo.
%   $Parameter:
%           -Incidence Matrix B
%           -Initial Marking M0
%   $Revision: 0.1 $

  setup(block);

%endfunction
```

The implementation considers two parameters. The first one is the incidence matrix B and the second one is the initial marking M_0. These parameters are used for defining the sizes of the input and output ports of the block.

```
function setup(block)
    ...
%% Set the properties of the input port. The vector dimension is
%% equal to the number of transitions in the PN, i.e., the size of
%% the second dimension of the first input parameter.
block.InputPort(1).Dimensions = size(block.DialogPrm(1).Data,2);
block.InputPort(1).DirectFeedthrough = false;
%% Set the properties of the output port. The vector dimension is
%% equal to the number of places in the PN, i.e., the size of the
%% first dimension of the first input parameter.
block.OutputPort(1).Dimensions = size(block.DialogPrm(1).Data,1);
...
%endfunction setup
```

The DoPostPropSetup stage allows the definition of the state of the PN. The PN marking has to be preserved between simulation steps and also is the output of the block.

```
function DoPostPropSetup(block)
%% Setup Dwork vectors
block.NumDworks                 =        1;
%% The vector required to be stored corresponds to the PN marking Mk
block.Dwork(1).Name             =        'Mk';
        %% The size corresponds to the number of places of the PN
block.Dwork(1).Dimensions        = size(block.DialogPrm(1).Data,1);
...
%endfunction
```

The InitConditions stage initializes the marking M_k, defined in the previous stage, to the second input parameter, which corresponds to the initial marking M_0.

```
function InitConditions(block)
%% Initialize Dwork Mk to M0, which corresponds to the second input
%% parameter
block.Dwork(1).Data = block.DialogPrm(2).Data;
```

The Output stage is used to provide to external blocks the current marking of the PN, which corresponds to the DWork vector defined in the DoPostPropSetup stage.

```
function Output(block)
%% Outputs the PN marking Mk
block.OutputPort(1).Data = block.Dwork(1).Data;

%endfunction
```

The Update stage is where the PN dynamics is implemented. This stage verifies the transitions that are allowed to fire by the input provided by an external agent, or controller, in the sense of the Control Theory. Likewise, it verifies that those allowed transitions are also enabled by the current marking M_k of the PN. A random number generator allows an aleatory firing among the transitions that are ready to fire. Finally, the current marking M_k is updated in accordance to the PN state equation.

```
function Output(block)
%% Outputs the PN marking Mk
block.OutputPort(1).Data = block.Dwork(1).Data;

%endfunction
function Update(block)
%% Obtain the dimensions of the incidence matrix B[m,n]
m = size(block.DialogPrm(1).Data,1);
n = size(block.DialogPrm(1).Data,2);
j=0;
%% Compute the enabled transitions that are allowed to fire
t_en=[];
for i=1:n
%% Check whether the i-th transition has been allowed to fire
   if        (block.InputPort(1).Data(i,1))
   %% This is the test of the enabling condition
   if        ( block.Dwork(1).Data>=(-block.DialogPrm(1).Data(:,i)))
      %% This transition is enabled. Add it to t_en
      t_en=[t_en;i];
        end
end

end
%% Fire an arbitrary transition among those that are enabled at the
%% current marking Mk and that have been allowed to fire. As well,
&& compute the marking change dMk.
        if        (size(t_en))
              rand('twister', sum(100*clock));
      r = size(t_en,1);
      j = fix(r*rand +         1);
              i = t_en(j,1);
      dMk = block.DialogPrm(1).Data(:,i);
        else
      dMk =         0;
        end
%% Update the current marking Mk
block.Dwork(1).Data = block.Dwork(1).Data + dMk;

%endfunction
```

3.4. PN simulation example

The S-function my_ptn is used for the simulation of the PN model in **Figure 2**. The SIMULINK model is depicted in **Figure 5a**. The only elements required for the simulation process are the incidence matrix $B[14\times 21]$ and the initial marking $M_0[14]$.

The model includes a block of 21 elements to represent that all of the transition of the model are allowed to fire. In this way, the dynamics of the PN model entirely depends on the marking of the net. The scope allows the visualization of the marking of all the places of the PN.

With a discrete solver and a fixed step of one, this model allows the simulation of the FMS. As shown in **Figure 5b**, the subsystem for the PN model includes blocks for inputs and outputs. These blocks could be used in the modelling of several controllability and observability problems by using matrices of proper size. For example, a matrix for the input function block may be arranged with columns representing the transitions of the PN and the rows representing the input commands to the system.

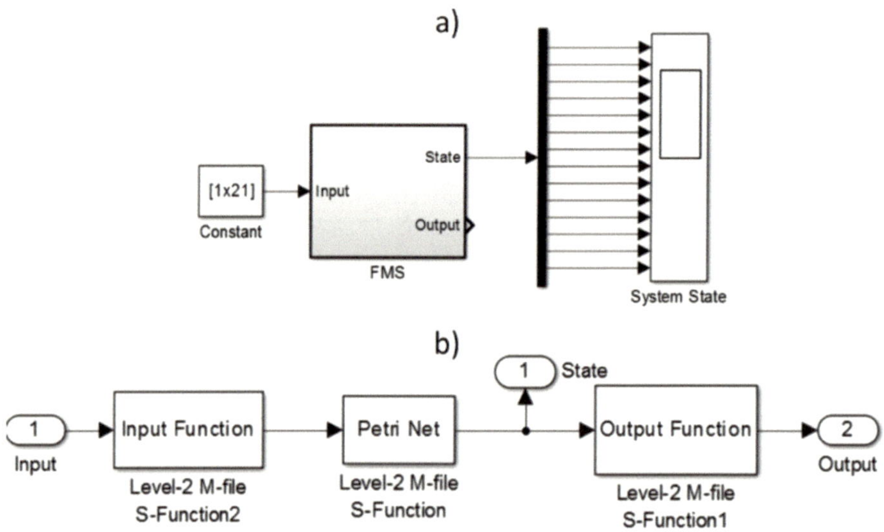

Figure 5. The integration of the S-Function implementing a PN model into the SIMULINK environment. In (a) a model for the FMS is depicted, with a constant input allowing all the 21 transitions to fire and a scope for signal visualization. In (b) an insight of the FSM block is shown, which includes blocks for inputs and outputs.

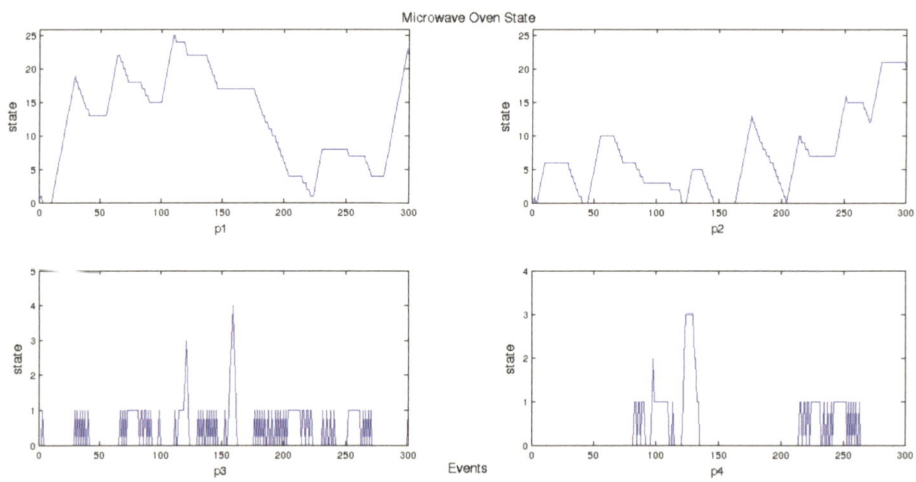

Figure 6. First part of the state of the PN representing the Flexible Manufacturing System. The chart shows the marking evolution of the places from p_1 to p_4 for a simulation process of 300 events. The first two places shows the pattern of the arriving material from the inventory to the system.

Similarly, a matrix for the output function block may be arranged with columns representing the places of the PN and the rows representing the output signals from the system. However, a deep study of these topics are out of the scope of this work, and are here mentioned for providing a more complete simulation model that could be used for more purposes. Thus, for both cases in this simulation, the core function for the input and output blocks are identity matrices.

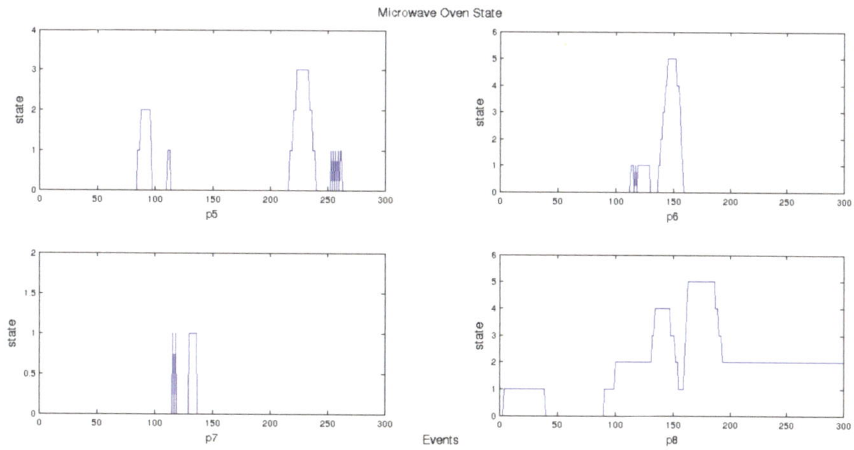

Figure 7. Second part of the state of the PN representing the FMS. The chart shows the marking evolution of the places p_5 to p_8. The place p_5 corresponds to the mill machine, while the places p_6 and p_7 correspond to the lather. The place p_8 shows the pieces waiting the AM machine.

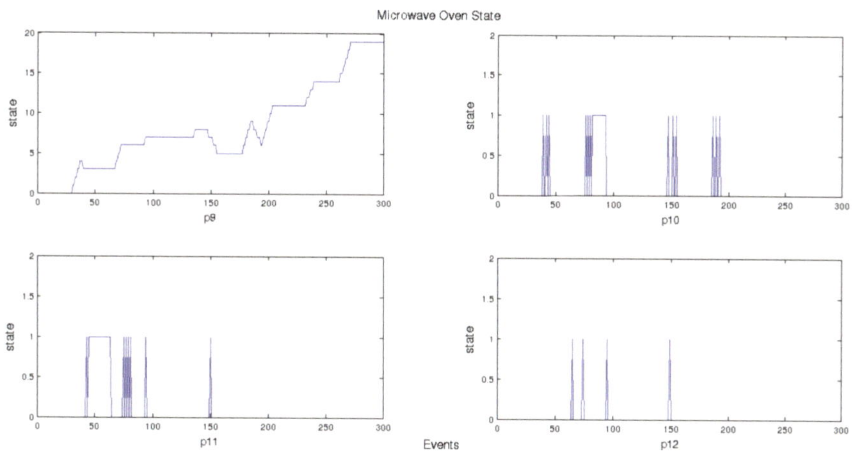

Figure 8. Third part of the state of the PN representing the FMS. The chart shows the marking evolution of the places from p_9 to p_{12}. The place p_9 corresponds to a waiting stage for the pieces prior to its assembling in AM. The places p_{10}, p_{11} and p_{12} correspond to the painting stage.

Figure 6 shows the marking of all the places in the PN model for a simulation process of 1000 events (seconds). Since the integration step was fixed to one, then every second in the scope could be interpreted as an event in the DES. The aleatory behaviour of the signal in the scope is due to the random selection of the transition firings in the Update section of the S-function, as detailed in the last subsection. It is easy noting an accumulation of tokens, or parts, in the place p_9 as well as in the place p_{14}. On the one hand, the accumulation of tokens in place p_9 means that the event associated to transition t_{13} is firing at a rate greater that of t_{12} and t_{14}. On the other hand, the accumulation of tokens in the place p_{14} is normal since there is where the finished products are stored (**Figures 7–9**).

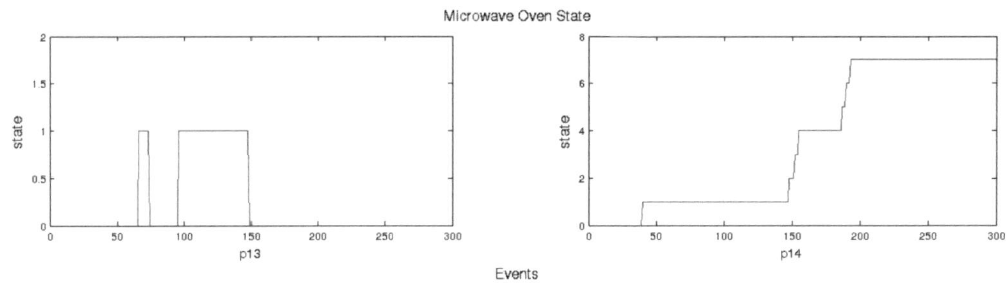

Figure 9. Last part of the state of the PN representing the FMS. The chart shows the marking evolution of the places p_{13} and p_{14}. The place p_{13} corresponds to the last section of the painting stage while the place p_{14} represents a buffer of pieces finished in the FMS.

Indeed, it is to be expected that the number of tokens in the place p_{14} increases over time. A good exercise is to modify the PN model including an extra transition with p_{14} as its unique input place, run the simulation and analyze the effects in the marking of this place. Such an extra transition may represent the interconnection of this system to another section in a more complex assembling line.

The markings of the places p_1 and p_2 represents an increase in the number of raw parts arriving to the FSM. The behaviour of the marking in the other places follows an aleatory pattern due to the random number generator used in the selection of the firing transition inside the Update section in the S-function.

4. Conclusions

This chapter showed a suitable way of simulating Discrete-Event Systems within a SIMULINK model in the MATLAB framework. The dynamics of a FSM as well as a PN has been implemented by using Level-2 MATLAB S-function. One of the advantages of the technique developed in this work is that for simulating a system, only the matrices that define a DES are required.

By using a discrete solver with a fixed step of one, accurate simulation processes in a SIMULINK model are possible. Two application examples illustrate the developed techniques. On the one hand, a FSM model representing a microwave oven has been simulated. On the other hand, a PN model representing a FMS has been simulated, as well.

Extension for FSM including marked states and non-determinism are simple to implement based in the code here provided. Similarly, extension for PN models including observability and controllability problems are as well simple to implement.

The link for free downloading the code for the examples developed in this chapter is: http://www.mathworks.com/matlabcentral/fileexchange/54959-simulation-of-discrete-event-systems-in-matlab

Author details

Raul Campos-Rodriguez*, Mildreth Alcaraz-Mejia* and Uriel Sanchez-Ramirez

*Address all correspondence to: rcampos@iteso.mx and mildreth@iteso.mx

Electronics, Systems and Informatics Department, ITESO University, Tlaquepaque, Jalisco, Mexico

References

[1] E. D. Sontag. *Mathematical Control Theory: Deterministic Finite Dimensional Systems.* Springer, 2nd Ed., New York, USA, 1998.

[2] C. Cassandras and S. Lafortune. *Introduction to Discrete Event Systems.* Springer, 2nd Ed., New York, USA, 2009.

[3] R. Boel and G. Stremersch (Editors). *Discrete Event Systems: Analysis and Control.* Springer, 1st Ed., New York, USA, 2000.

[4] G. A. Wainer and P. J. Mosterman (Editors). *Discrete-Event Modeling and Simulation: Theory and Applications.* CRC Press, 1st Ed., Florida, USA, 2010.

[5] R. Campos-Rodriguez and M. Alcaraz-Mejia. *A Matlab/Simulink Framework for the design of controllers and observers for discrete-event systems*, Electronics and Electrical Engineering, 2010, 3(99), pp. 63–68.

[6] R. Campos-Rodriguez, M. Alcaraz-Mejia and J. Mireles-Garcia. *Supervisory control of discrete event systems by using observers.* Proceedings of IEEE 15th Mediterranean Conference on Control & Automation, 2007, pp. 1–7, Athens, Greece, DOI 10.1109/MED.2007.4433816.

[7] J. E. Hopcroft and J. D. Ullman. Introduction to automata theory, languages, and computation, vol. 1. Addison-Wesley, 1979.

[8] P. J. Ramadge and W. M. Wonham. *Supervisory control of a class of discrete event processes*. SIAM J. Control and Optimization 25 (1), pp. 206–230. 1987.

[9] F. Wagner, R. Schmuki and T. Wagner. *Modeling Software with Finite State Machines: A Practical Approach*. Auerbach Publications, 2006.

[10] T. Murata. *Petri nets: Properties, analysis and applications*, Proceedings of the IEEE, 77 (4), pp. 541, 580. 1989.

[11] M. H. de Queiroz, J. E. R. Cury and W. M. Wonham. *Multitasking Supervisory Control of Discrete-Event Systems*. Discrete Event Dynamic Systems: Theory and Applications, 15, pp. 390–393, Dordrecht, The Netherlands, 2005. Example also available online at http://wwweb.eecs.umich.edu/umdes/manufact2.html